THE ART AND SCIENCE *of* UX DESIGN

A step-by-step guide to designing amazing user experiences

ANTHONY CONTA

The Art and Science of UX Design
A step-by-step guide to designing amazing user experiences

Anthony Conta

New Riders
www.peachpit.com
Copyright © 2024 by Pearson Education, Inc. or its affiliates. All Rights Reserved.

New Riders is an imprint of Pearson Education, Inc.
To report errors, please send a note to errata@peachpit.com

Executive Editor: Laura Norman
Development Editor: Robyn G. Thomas
Associate/Sponsoring Editor: Anshul Sharma
Senior Production Editor: Tracey Croom
Copy Editor: Scout Festa
Compositor: Kim Scott, Bumpy Design
Tech Editor: John Ray
Proofreader: Lisa Fridsma
Indexer: James Minkin
Cover Design: Chuti Prasertsith
Cover Illustration: cybermagician/Shutterstock, Rroselavy/Shutterstock
Interior Design: Kim Scott, Bumpy Design

ISBN-13:   978-0-13-806026-8
ISBN-10:   0-13-806026-6

ScoutAutomatedPrintCode

Written in loving memory of Christina Conta,
who taught with passion, acceptance, and joy.

TABLE OF CONTENTS

ABOUT THE AUTHOR

Anthony Conta's career in design began when he was four years old, thanks to the carelessness of another student at his school. His mother, Christina, was the school nurse for a K-12 school in New York City. One day, a student forgot their Game Gear in his mother's office. After a month of asking every student who came in if it was theirs and no one claiming it, she gave it to her son and opened his world.

From that day, Anthony knew he wanted to design experiences like the ones he played on that video game system (and many others). But at college, he found that coding those experiences was a lot more difficult than he expected, and he instead focused on understanding behaviors rather than understanding code.

Anthony graduated from Binghamton University with a master's degree in financial economics, a bachelor's in quantitative economics, and a bachelor's in mathematics. His first job was at a law firm, helping uncover illegal anti-competitive behavior by analyzing the economics of market sectors. Two years later, he moved to a consulting firm, where he did similar work.

Bored out of his mind suing people, Anthony pivoted back to what he loved—games. He started his own game company, producing tabletop games with his then girlfriend (and now wife), Carrie. From concept to completion, they came up with game ideas, prototyped them, crowdfunded them via Kickstarter, and eventually published them with large game publishers such as Mattel.

Eventually, Anthony moved on to digital education and entertainment at Nickelodeon, creating interactive television episodes of *Blues Clues*, *Bubble Guppies*, and *Team Umizoomi*. It was there that he gained prolonged exposure to (and interest in) the concepts of user experience (UX) design.

He attended General Assembly's UX certificate program, a three-month intensive learning bootcamp, where he met fellow aspiring practitioners and grew with them as he deepened his knowledge and love for UX.

From there, Anthony worked at several companies—Kaplan, Food Network, Vimeo, and Amazon—where he further developed his skillset. As of this writing, Anthony works for Amazon Music, designing digital experiences for millions of customers.

In his spare time, Anthony still educates those who come after him. He writes on Medium, he teaches at several colleges, and he mentors through various services. You can find him in a lot of places—feel free to reach out and say hi!

ACKNOWLEDGMENTS

To have the space to credit everyone who helped me on this journey to the level and extent that they deserve, I'd have to author a whole other book. Since I don't have the page count to double the size of this book, I'd like to call out a few people[1] who were instrumental in the creation of *The Art and Science of UX Design*.

My wife, Carrie Conta, for seeing the good in me, loving me unconditionally, and believing in me enough to be my partner for the rest of our days.

Our dog, Rosie, for keeping me going by providing the most emotional support a living animal could provide.

My mother and father, Christina Conta and Edward Conta, for not only instilling the values of hard work and perseverance within me but giving me the space and permission to apply those values to wherever I chose to focus.

My sister and her husband, Jennifer Conta and Tim Lam, for supporting me in all my endeavors and patiently listening to my ramblings whenever I discussed a topic in depth that I loved.

The editorial team at Pearson, for taking my raw words and ideas and forming them into a coherent, comprehensive book for you to read—Anshul Sharma, Laura Norman, Lisa Fridsma, Robyn Thomas, Rosa Wan, Scout Festa, and Tracey Croom.

My peer editors, who provided excellent, constructive feedback on the theories and structure of this book to ensure it represents a wide range of industry opinions and perspectives—Al Deliallisi, Derek Frisicchio, and John Ray.

My peers during my time at General Assembly, of whom there are too many to list fully, but a few in particular I'd like to mention for helping me grow into the designer I am today—Erin Hill, Ian Berger, James Fichera, Katherine Apelian, Mike Sanchez, Richard Park, and Tracy Michael (go Polar Bears!).

My peers in the industry, again, of whom there are too many to list fully, but several I'd like to call out for their constant unwavering faith in me and my efforts over the years—Andrew Gatto, Arushi Jaiswal, Caroline O'Toole, Celeste Rose, Haroon Ghafoori, Mark Sherrill, Max Majonis, and Sam Shapiro.

---

1 In alphabetical order within each section

My design mentor, Jayse Lee, for helping me get my start in UX and believing in me enough to devote countless hours to my education and development.

My career mentor, Bryant Alexander, for also helping me get my start in UX and giving me the confidence to keep reaching for what I want from my career (and for his kind words in this book!).

My mentees and students, for giving me the permission to help them with their problems and the opportunity to develop the principles and exercises in this book.

All my friends who have helped me along the way and for keeping me humble and honest as we grew alongside each other, but in particular those who helped me on this journey—Kyle Gallagher, Matt Ferrando, Mike Stanton, Miles Rodriguez, and Nieves.

And finally, the Nielsen Norman Group and every other designer and institution that came before me, who have laid out the amazing frameworks this book is built from.

FOREWORD

Have you noticed that almost everything we know today is in a constant state of evolution? It could be argued that almost every organism we see today has adapted into a better version of its original self. I believe that we as humans are constantly evolving, changing, and elevating to become a better version of ourselves.

I realized how true this concept was when I first met Anthony in 2018. I was living in Brooklyn, New York, as a career coach at a well-known technical training bootcamp, and Anthony signed up for one of my coaching sessions. During our first meeting, I asked him, as I routinely do in my sessions, about his background. To my surprise, Anthony explained how he'd made a successful transition from finance to entrepreneurship to working at Nickelodeon as an interactive media producer. I sat back in my chair, impressed but also slightly confused. He was so poised, reassured, and confident in his current life position. "Why is this guy here?" I thought. "He has already made such impressive career changes. What more could this bootcamp experience offer him?" It was then that I realized: Anthony wasn't my typical client.

As our conversation continued, it became apparent how introspective Anthony had been about the power of change and growth. Not only had he taken time to understand fundamentally how a career coaching experience tactically fit within his career plans, but he also eloquently explained how he was intentionally plunging into the deep end of discomfort. It then hit me that while most people I coached were interested in switching careers for professional reasons such as status, location, or finances, Anthony's reason was different—more personal. He simply wanted the space ... to grow. It was clear from this first conversation that he was ready to embark on a journey of self-discovery and was using career coaching as a vehicle to do so. Not only was he ready to accept the challenges of self-improvement head-on, but he was also open to accepting whatever job resulted on the other end—even if it was different from the outcome he had in mind. On that day, Anthony's approach to growth set a standard for my future clients, and even for me.

Anthony's profound approach to explore, experience, and excel in what I see to be the critical four components of growth[2] was deeply admirable and a fitting example for anyone looking to grow. For nearly a year, I watched as

---

2 The four critical components of growth are empathy, active listening, problem-solving, and remaining solution oriented.

Anthony put himself in the shoes of other people in order to actively listen, critically ask questions, synthesize the problem, and suggest a solution for a better experience. Some days he helped me think critically about big hairy problems and consider questions around career trajectory that I never considered. I believe Anthony's intentional effort and incredible ability to actively strengthen the four components of growth are what contributed to him being the powerful designer he is today. As an entrepreneur in real estate and learning development, I see every day how growth is the impetus to reaching self-improvement and ultimately purpose.

Whether you're looking to become a practicing UX professional or just a more critical thinker, *The Art and Science of UX Design* will help you understand the nuances of the design thinking process and potentially even offer a new perspective on an old problem. Most importantly, much as Anthony does, it will challenge you to expand your thinking and therefore grow in ways that you might never have considered. *The Art and Science of UX Design* is a thoughtful peek into Anthony's brain—guiding you along with critical questions to help reframe and rethink potential outcomes. As such, this book is for the individual who dares to not to stay stagnant, for the person who is trying to challenge traditional ways of thinking, and for anyone who aspires to evolve into their best self.

From Day 1, Anthony has been on a journey to become the best version of himself. This book is his way of giving you an opportunity to start yours.

Welcome to your Day 1.

—Bryant Alexander
Tech Career Development Consultant
www.linkedin.com/in/bryantalexander-jr

INTRODUCTION

Art is

> *The use of creativity, imagination, and skill to draw, paint, or sculpt works that evoke emotion or are meant to be appreciated for their beauty.*

And science is

> *The pursuit of knowledge of the physical world based on systems and structure to examine, test, and prove theories.*

Art relies on creativity and imagination to produce a work to be appreciated by others. Science leverages systems, structure, and experimentation to test theories and validate opinions based on evidence. Is there a relationship between the two?

It appears these two disciplines couldn't be more disconnected. One takes creativity and makes emotional works of art, while the other takes processes and procedures to produce a scientific conclusion. How could they possibly intersect?

The truth is, they don't fully meld into a singular experience. Rather, they play off one another, using their unique attributes to power various industries that require both the creativity of art and the structure of science.

User experience (UX) is one of those disciplines. UX requires our imaginations to create experiences that captivate us, that move us, that help solve the problems we encounter daily. UX also requires us to propose theories, run experiments to test those theories, and validate a solution using evidence and data.

If we rely solely on art to make a user experience, we may end up with something beautiful, but will it work? Would we be able to define what success looks like? How will we know if what we create helps the people we designed it for?

Conversely, if we use only science to create a user experience, we might produce something functional, but will it be desirable? Would it have any emotional power? Would it capture someone's imagination? We could make an experience, but would people want to use it?

We need both. We need art to think of new possibilities and make them appealing enough for people to want to use. We need science to validate our ideas and measure how usable and successful they are. By leveraging both art and science, we can not only create emotionally compelling user experiences but also validate that those experiences solve the problems of the people we design them for.

The UX Design of This Book

This book dives deep into the concepts of both art and science to explore ways to make amazing user experiences.

In Chapter 1, I discuss some theories and definitions surrounding user experience. I talk about UX, user interface (UI), design thinking, product development, and cognitive overload. These definitions help structure the rest of the book.

In Chapters 2 through 7, I go in depth with the design thinking process over six steps: empathize, define, ideate, prototype, test, and implement. Each step builds on the preceding one as we understand who we want to design for, explore possible ideas for our designs, and finally materialize our design solution and bring it to life. In these chapters, I invite you to work on the exercises I provide to practice the techniques I cover and create your own end-to-end design thinking project.

In Chapter 8, I cover what comes after design thinking. I talk about taking the work you have done in this book and forming a case study and portfolio. I discuss feedback, and how to give and receive it. Finally, I cover what it's like to work with others and work in the design industry.

In the appendix, I take the exercises I propose in the book and explore a possible version of what a good answer could look like, working through the same problem across the design thinking process. I provide examples of what you may have thought of yourself so that you can see a reference and compare it to your own.

Many of the exercises in this book require the use of digital tools. While the exercises aren't required to learn from this book, they do help reinforce topics and give you the opportunity to practice and hone your skills. I highly recommend completing them if you can.

Fortunately, each exercise can be completed with the assistance of free online software. As of this writing, the tools I used to go through each exercise for myself were all free (with registration):

- **Figma**—a wireframing and prototyping tool used to create digital designs of all types. www.figma.com/

- **Whimsical**—a diagramming and whiteboarding tool that is excellent for visualizing ideas quickly and iteratively. https://whimsical.com/

- **Google Workspace**—a collection of tools that allow people to write, share, and connect around the work they accomplish. https://workspace.google.com/

- **Otter.ai**—A transcription software that records a conversation and produces a written transcript for your records and analysis. https://otter.ai/

I invite you to join me in exploring how to create compelling user experiences. I encourage you to complete the exercises in this book so you can get hands-on experience going through the design thinking process—learning is more fun and successful when it's active and engaging.

I look forward to you joining me on this journey and hope you enjoy the user experience of reading this book!

~Anthony

UNDERSTANDING HUMAN-CENTERED DESIGN

To practice design, it is crucial that we maintain our perspective. When thinking about a user's experience with a product, we need to keep that user front and center in our minds. Our solution should benefit the user—it should consider their wants, their needs, their goals, and their frustrations.

The single biggest reason that products fail is misalignment with the people who use them. All too often designers meticulously craft a *round peg* only to be baffled when users with *square holes* are uninterested. But how could this happen? How can we, as designers, avoid making products that frustrate users? Most importantly, how can we create products that delight users and speak to their needs?

The answer is perspective. Not our individual perspective; rather, we must consider the many perspectives of the people who will use our product. We need to understand their wants, needs, goals, and frustrations. These tenets should be our North Star, our guiding light when we aren't sure how to proceed.

It's too easy to think of ourselves as the user, to think about what we want to see in a product, to incorporate our wants and needs into a solution, to use our tastes and aesthetics over the preferences of the people who will be using our product. These patterns lead us to incorporate our biases into our designs, and we end up creating a product we want rather than a product others need.

This is exactly what human-centered design tries to avoid. The goal is to design for others, not ourselves. We need to remove our wants and needs from the creative process and instead focus on the end users—the people we are designing for. By using a strong, well-thought-out process, we can maintain this perspective.

In this chapter, we'll cover the basics of human-centered design—what it is, where it comes from, and how to adopt a design practice that will keep us centered on the people we design for. We'll dive into the definitions of user experience (UX) and user interface (UI) and the differences between these commonly confused terms. We'll talk about how to build products, following processes used by large organizations to get work done. Finally, we'll dip into some cognitive theory and show that an understanding of how people process information can help us build human-centered products.

WHAT IS HUMAN-CENTERED DESIGN?

Have you ever come across a door that you couldn't figure out how to open? Sometimes you'll push a door and realize it won't move. Is it locked? Are you not allowed to use this door? Is it broken somehow? Usually, no—you missed that you must pull, rather than push, to open it. But for whatever reason, you didn't understand that, and you may feel silly or foolish for not noticing.

Realistically, it's probably not your fault.

AUTHOR'S NOTE
A signifier is something in a design that indicates how to use the design. The term comes from Don Norman's book *The Design of Everyday Things*.

It's most likely that the door was missing a clue, or a *signifier*[1], to let you know how it works. Doors sometimes have handles that indicate how they operate. It's common for a door with a big metal rod along the side of it to operate as a "pull." That rod is a signifier telling you to pull it to open the door. Other doors have nameplates (**FIGURE 1.1**) that tell you to push or to pull.

But sometimes, doors aren't intuitive to use. You'll see something that makes you think it's a push, but in fact it's a pull.

---

1 https://en.wikipedia.org/wiki/The_Design_of_Everyday_Things

FIGURE 1.1 A door with multiple signifiers that indicate how it operates. Large lettering indicates you should pull toward yourself to open the door. Additionally, there is a large metal handle you can fit your hands inside to pull the door toward you. (Chalit Silpsakulsuk/Shutterstock)

Nonintuitive doors are common. It's the classic example cited by Don Norman, the "grandfather of UX," as he discusses the concept of signifiers and affordances in his book *The Design of Everyday Things*. His name is even used to label nonintuitive doors, called Norman doors. Check out this video: https://tinyurl.com/asuxd1-1.

Essentially, every interaction a human has with an object (whether that be a door, a chair, a digital product, or anything else) can be broken down into what the object *communicates* that you can do and what you are actually *allowed* to do. A signifier sends a signal informing you what you can do—such as a handle on a door implying you can pull, or a plate on a door implying you can push. An *affordance* is the action you can take—in the case of a door, push or pull.

When a signifier and an affordance are aligned, an experience is easy, or intuitive—we've designed a situation where the signal sets an expectation, and the affordance is that expectation. When there is no signifier, or the signifier is ambiguous, then we've designed a situation where nothing sets that expectation—or worse, sets the opposite expectation. This is referred to as *mapping*—good mapping is when there's a clear relationship between controls (signifiers) and the effect they have on the environment (affordances).

If you have a door with a handle, that's a signifier to pull. However, if it opens only with a push (its affordance), then that's a bad user experience.

This is the practice of user experience design. It's the concept of thinking through how something works, then communicating that functionality to someone who has no idea how that thing was made or operates. When making an experience for someone else, including something as simple as how a door opens, think about who will use that experience. This consideration that we apply to our designs is called *human-centered design*.

Human-centered design is the practice of designing a product for the people who will actually use it and is grounded in empathy for those who will use it. It is performed by defining a problem to solve, ideating possible solutions to that problem, and prototyping and testing those solutions with the people who will use it. Eventually, the results of that testing will be implemented so that the people who encounter the problem will have a solution that works, works well, and works for them.

The need for human-centered design can be something complicated, like how doctors operate sophisticated surgical equipment or how an electrician fixes a power issue. Or it could be something quite simple, such as turning on a faucet or using a stove.

The concept of human-centered design has many definitions and takes many forms. Many people have written about it, and each has their own take on how to define it.

> *Human-centered design is an approach to creating a program, policy, service, or product that is tailored to the needs of the person who will use it or be impacted by it.*[2]
>
> —Bloomberg Cities

> *It is based on a philosophy that empowers an individual or team to design products, services, systems, and experiences that address the core needs of those who experience a problem.*[3]
>
> —DC Design

> *Human-centered design is an approach to problem-solving commonly used in design, management, and engineering frameworks that develops solutions to problems by involving the human perspective in all steps of the problem-solving process.*[4]
>
> —Wikipedia

AUTHOR'S NOTE In this book, I switch between the term *user experience design* and *product design*. There's a difference between them, but the nuance is so small that the terms are used interchangeably. The industry uses both terms; in fact, I have had multiple jobs where it was called both, depending on who I was speaking with.

---

2 https://bloombergcities.medium.com/explainer-what-is-human-centered-design-4d7883d406ce

3 https://medium.com/dc-design/what-is-human-centered-design-6711c09e2779

4 https://en.wikipedia.org/wiki/Human-centered_design

A common theme among these definitions is that they have the same structure:

- It is a process.

- It solves problems.

- It is based on the needs of others.

So when you follow the principles of human-centered design, you are using a process that enables you to solve the problems of other people.

This definition helps us understand what we should be doing. But how do we follow a process? How do we understand the needs of others? And how do we solve their problems?

Luckily, we can rely on design thinking to help. At its core, design thinking is a series of processes that allow us to better understand the problems of others so that we can design impactful solutions. Design thinking encourages us to research, empathize with others, think of possible solutions to their problems, and then test simulations of those ideas so that we can see if our solutions could actually work if we build them.

But where can we start? Before we decide on a specific model or framework to do our work, we should be aware of several design thinking models.

Design Thinking Models

A design thinking model is a framework for us to apply design thinking to the problems we want to solve. A model serves as a roadmap, a guide, or a series of steps or phases that we can follow or reference as we work. Sometimes a model can be used like a map—we travel to an endpoint and use a model along that journey. Other times, a model can be something we reference, comparing the experience we design to a series of principles that exemplify a good user experience.

Let's look at a few models that exist and then dive into the model we'll be using for the rest of this book.

AUTHOR'S NOTE The terms *human-centered design* and *design thinking* are often interchangeably used in the industry. There is a slight difference between the two—the former is used more often when wanting to put a human perspective in every step of the product creation process, while the latter is used more often when focusing on problem-solving. In this book, I don't draw a distinction and go back and forth between them.

Don Norman's Design of Everyday Things

Don Norman is famous in the design industry. In his book *The Design of Everyday Things*, he proposes a four-step process for creating a good user experience:

1. Observe

2. Ideate

3. Prototype

4. Test

First, we must *observe*. We have to understand the people we want to design for. We need to see how they act, what their problems are, and how they move around their environment. Throughout this process of observation, we take notes and record our findings to allow us to form an opinion on what the problems to solve are so that we can move on to the next step in the process.

Next, we *ideate*. From our observations, we think of ways to solve the users' problems. We brainstorm, sketch, and create ideas that could work. We spend time thinking of wild and crazy ideas, and eventually pare down to a couple that we think will work best.

After we ideate, we *prototype*. From our best ideas, we start to develop a functional representation of those ideas to show to users. We create digital mockups or even use pieces of paper to represent our ideas in a fast, iterative way with the purpose of getting feedback early, often, and quickly.

After we prototype, we *test*. Testing is a valuable way to gain feedback to see how others actually use our ideas. We use the prototypes and share them with people to see how they would use the designs. We test to see how intuitive our product is, how desirable it would be, and above all, if our ideas actually would solve the problem users experience.

Don Norman's original design thinking process is the core of modern design thinking. We observe, we ideate, we prototype, and then we test. This model has gone through several revisions and interpretations to create various design thinking frameworks that help improve the human-centered design practice.

Aarron Walter's Hierarchy of User Needs

Aarron Walter is an award-winning writer known best for his book *Designing for Emotion*.[5] In it, he defines a framework called the *hierarchy of user needs* (**FIGURE 1.2**).

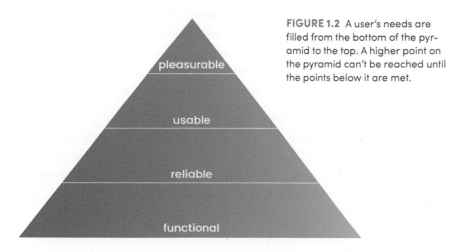

FIGURE 1.2 A user's needs are filled from the bottom of the pyramid to the top. A higher point on the pyramid can't be reached until the points below it are met.

Aarron Walter takes the psychologist Abraham Maslow's hierarchy of human needs[6] and adapts it to design. Essentially, when interacting with an experience, that experience needs to have the following elements, in order of importance:

1. Functional
2. Reliable
3. Usable
4. Pleasurable

Think of these as a pyramid. Each aspect builds on itself, satisfying the user more and more deeply. Beginning with *functional*, each element lays a foundation for the element that follows.

Start by imagining an experience with none of these things. Perhaps something is beautiful. If it's not functional, it won't satisfy the basic needs of the user and its aesthetic will become unappreciated. Perhaps you've experienced this yourself, when interacting with a design that looks good but doesn't make sense or can't be used.

---

5 https://abookapart.com/products/designing-for-emotion
6 https://en.wikipedia.org/wiki/Maslow%27s_hierarchy_of_needs

The lowest level of a user's needs is for an experience to be *functional*. It needs to perform the basic task it promises to do by existing. If it doesn't function, it will not meet the core needs of its users. By definition, it will be nonfunctional, or unusable.

Next, a product needs to be *reliable*. If it is functional, but only some of the time, then it can technically be used, but not on a consistent basis. For example, think of an unreliable internet connection. It functions, sure, but you can't count on it to function all the time, and as a result, you won't be able to use it as well as you could a functional and reliable connection.

After being functional and reliable, it must be *usable*. Usable may sound like *functional*, but there are core differences that make this category higher on the hierarchy of user needs. Usable means that a product is easy to learn, discover, and utilize. A user shouldn't have to search for functionality; it should not require much effort to operate. A usable product is one that not only works but works well.

Lastly, a product must be *pleasurable*. It is not enough for products to work well to reach this level of satisfaction in the hierarchy of user needs. They must be delightful to use and produce joy. Perhaps they solve a user's problem well, or they are aesthetically enjoyable to use. They have such a deeply satisfying user experience that users are not only able to use the product well, but they also have a good time doing so.

Let's work with an example. Imagine a mug. If that mug is not functional, then you won't be able to use the mug to solve your problem, like drinking out of it. The mug fails to satisfy the most basic tenet of the hierarchy of user needs.

Now, imagine the mug is functional—it holds liquid, it can be picked up, it can be drunk out of, and it operates like a normal mug. However, if it is not reliable—say, it leaks half the time—then we wouldn't want to keep using that mug. It works, but it doesn't work well enough and consistently enough that we'd want to keep coming back to it.

So let's say our mug is functional and reliable—it works, and it always works. Now let's imagine the mug's handle can fit only one finger—like your pinky. The mug wouldn't be usable—at least, not as usable as it could be. If there were a lot of liquid in the mug, it'd be hard to lift from the handle, so we'd have to grab it by the sides. If the mug were full of a hot liquid, like coffee, then we would need to use the handle, which would be too challenging.

Let's replace the handle to fit the size of your hand and make the mug more usable. Now, our mug is functional, reliable, and usable. It solves the problem of drinking liquid. But is it pleasurable? Is it "fun" to use the mug? Does it produce joy? Are there things that we can design into the mug to achieve this need? We could give the mug an aesthetic design that evokes joy, such as a pleasing graphic design or curvature to it that looks nice. Or perhaps there are additional functionalities that make it more pleasing, as with self-heating mugs that warm liquid that's gone cold. Or perhaps warm liquid changes the visual design of the mug, revealing a new pattern based on the temperature inside.

Using this model in our design thinking practice would enable us to ensure the experiences we create work, work often, work easily, and work in a way that people want to return more often.

IDEO's Human-Centered Design Process

IDEO, a world-renowned design agency, offers a variation on Don Norman's design thinking model. They think of human-centered design as comprising three steps (**FIGURE 1.3**).[7]

1. Inspiration

2. Ideation

3. Implementation

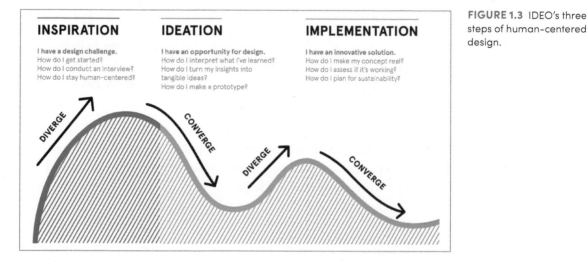

FIGURE 1.3 IDEO's three steps of human-centered design.

INSPIRATION

I have a design challenge.
How do I get started?
How do I conduct an interview?
How do I stay human-centered?

IDEATION

I have an opportunity for design.
How do I interpret what I've learned?
How do I turn my insights into tangible ideas?
How do I make a prototype?

IMPLEMENTATION

I have an innovative solution.
How do I make my concept real?
How do I assess if it's working?
How do I plan for sustainability?

DIVERGE   CONVERGE   DIVERGE   CONVERGE

---

7 ideo.org

Similar to Don Norman's method, this method involves observation, ideation, prototyping, and testing. However, it builds on his model by showing how we can diverge and converge during that process.

We start with *inspiration*. We know we have a problem to solve for our users, but we might not know the details. How can we become inspired? Here, we diverge and explore the problem space—we look at various resources and obtain different sources of information to gain the most inspiration. Think of yourself as an explorer—you are seeking the most information possible to know as much as you can about the problem.

Then, we move on to *ideation*. We have an opportunity to design. How do we make sense of it all? How do we interpret what we have learned and turn it into an idea? This is where we converge—we need to take our information from the inspiration step and make it make sense. We need to form opinions and create hypotheses as we think of ideas to solve our users' problems. During this step, we diverge again—once we form opinions and make sense of our observations, we diverge to think of solutions. We brainstorm, we sketch, and we create various ideas that eventually become prototypes for testing.

Lastly, we move on to *implementation*. Now that we have a solution, we need to see if that solution works. We find users, test with them, and observe how our solution functions in the hands of others. We converge again—as we test, we narrow down our ideas and see what works and what doesn't. We begin to build our solution, implementing our ideas into functional products.

The Double Diamond

The process of diverging and converging repeatedly is common in design thinking models. The British Design Council[8] has created a method that relies on diverging and converging as we conduct the design process called the Double Diamond (FIGURE 1.4).

The Double Diamond is a great way to think about the design process, as it relates to a specific problem in search of a singular solution. It lends itself well to design engagements that have a single, clear-cut set of deliverables and timeline. It is broken up into four steps:

1. Discover
2. Define
3. Develop
4. Deliver

8 www.designcouncil.org.uk/our-resources/framework-for-innovation

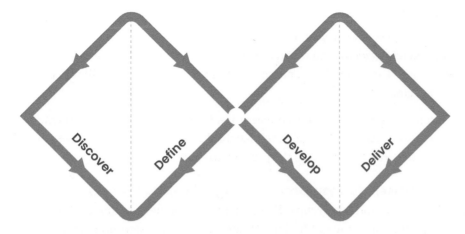

FIGURE 1.4 The Double Diamond design process.

The Double Diamond process begins with a problem that will flow through the entire project. Everything in this model hinges on the problem, and each design step incorporates it.

First, we *discover* more about the problem. What is the problem? How does it relate to users? How do users move around the problem? Are there others who have solved the problem before? What do they do, and how do they do it? This step is all about research—researching users, competitors, and technological solutions that have the problem. In this step, we are explorers, diverging from the problem and researching everything we can think of related to it.

Next, we *define*. This is where we start to converge—after learning everything we can about the problem, we synthesize that research and come to understand our findings more clearly. We work toward defining what the real problem is, or the "problem to solve." This definition is crucial to the success of the project—it is what we will ideate against, and what we will try to deliver a solution for. All the research during this step converges on a single point: the problem definition, which is our problem to solve.

The problem to solve is the turning point in the project. Once we understand it, we are prepared to diverge again, except this time with a better understanding of what we are trying to accomplish.

Next, we *develop*. We diverge again—now that we understand the problem, we must develop solutions to it. We ideate, brainstorming solutions and sketching ideas until we hit a critical mass of different options. Then, we begin to evaluate those options and prepare prototypes that allow us to test them.

Finally, we *deliver*. We take our ideas from the develop step and test them. We show users our ideas, gain their feedback, and make revisions as we converge toward our solution to the problem to solve.

The Nielsen Norman Group's Design Thinking Process

The Nielsen Norman Group (NN/g) offers a comprehensive model for the design thinking process.[9] It's broken into six steps of design, across three phases (FIGURE 1.5).

1. Empathize

2. Define

3. Ideate

4. Prototype

5. Test

6. Implement

Under the NN/g design thinking model, we *empathize* to understand our users, the problem, and the context. We must imagine what it is like to encounter the problem and learn how people interact with it.

Then, we *define*. After we learn of the problems our users face, we define those problems and determine the problem to solve. What will we try to solve on behalf of our users?

Afterward, we *ideate*. Once we have a clear understanding of the problem to solve, we think of solutions that could work for them. We brainstorm, sketch, and create ideas.

After we ideate, we *prototype*. This is when we create representations of our ideas, with the intent to test them. Our representations should allow others to see our ideas and interact with them so that we can learn more about how they would be received.

---

9 www.nngroup.com/articles/design-thinking/

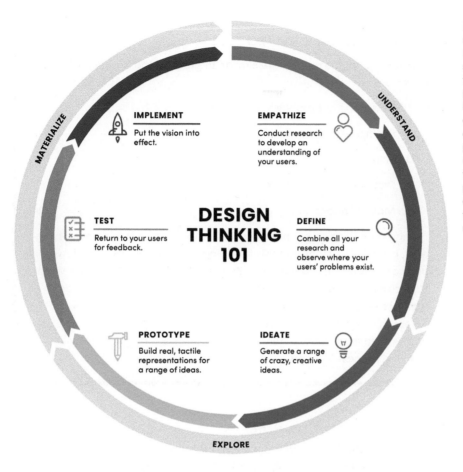

FIGURE 1.5 The NN/g model of design thinking. Each circle represents a step in the design process; the arrows represent the phases. Each circle has a line that leads back to an earlier step in the process, emphasizing that at any point a designer can reevaluate a step given what they've learned during the process. Each step is a loop, allowing for and promoting the idea that a step can be repeated as needed.

Next, we *test*. Once we have our prototypes, we find users and share our ideas with them. We test the ideas, not the users, and see how well our ideas hold up. We challenge our hypotheses and see if our ideas are usable and can solve users' problems.

Finally, we *implement*. Once we know how our ideas work, we build and deliver them to users. We turn our prototypes into functional products and release them to the world.

THE DESIGN THINKING PROCESS

In truth, a lot of the models are similar. In general, the design thinking process is:

1. Research your problem.

2. Synthesize your findings.

3. Think of solutions.

4. Prototype and test them.

5. Make revisions and ship.

Having a formalized, nuanced, well-described process to point to, however, provides us many benefits for doing right by our users. It allows us to communicate in detail with other teams around the work we want to accomplish. It allows us to advocate for time and resources to do the necessary steps to design a great user experience (for example, research is commonly excluded when designing in the industry). It also allows us to train the next generation of designers, by giving them a detailed process to follow.

Our Design Thinking Process

All the design thinking models discussed are appropriate ways to practice human-centered design. In your practice, you may prefer one model to another, and that's totally acceptable. Design practitioners around the world use other models not covered here.

For our purposes, we are going to adopt NN/g's process for several reasons:

- It is iterative.

  The NN/g design thinking model allows for iteration during each step of the process. In practice, design is rarely a linear process. Commonly, you learn things in each step that incentivizes you to return to an earlier stage. You may learn during testing that you didn't think of a possible use case and want to return to the ideation step. Or you might implement your solution and see that you solved part of the problem but not all of it. So you want to restart the empathize step. This model leaves us the room to do so.

- It is detailed.

  This design thinking model is broken into six steps that focus on a lot of detail and clarity. For example, the implement step explicitly focuses on delivering a solution, such as working with developers to create your idea. This level of specificity allows us to deeply explore the full extent of the design thinking process.

- It has phases that oversee its steps.

  In addition to the six comprehensive steps, it also has three phases that oversee those steps: understand, explore, and materialize. Each phase helps us understand how the steps play into the overall design thinking process. First, we must *understand* our users and the problem to solve, and we do so by empathizing and defining. Then, we must *explore* what we can do for our users by ideating and prototyping. Then, we must *materialize* our solution by testing and implementing. In this way, we have a clear process with actionable steps that offer a concrete approach to human-centered design.

Let's explore each of those steps in greater detail.

Step 1: Empathize

In the first step of the design thinking process, it is our goal to get a better understanding of the problem we want to solve. We have several ways to do this.

OBSERVE OTHERS

To better empathize, we can start by observing others as they experience the problem. We watch them complete tasks, try to use a product, or go through a day in their lives to see how they encounter the problem and how they currently try to solve it. We can leverage user interviews, diary studies, contextual inquiries, or other methods that allow us to be observers and see the problem in action.

EXPERIENCE THE PROBLEM

Alternatively, we can experience the problem ourselves. We can directly gain experience with the pain points of what we are trying to solve by completing tasks related to the problem. If it's a product, we can try using it to see the problems with it. If it's a process, we can go through the process to see how we experience it and how we feel during it.

TALK WITH EXPERTS

Another technique is to find experts related to the problem and speak with them about it. Experts could be industry leaders who have studied the problem or who have solved similar problems. Or experts could be users who frequently encounter the problem and have a lot of experience with it. We can interview these experts to learn more about the problem and how they deal with it.

SEARCH FOR SOLUTIONS

Finally, we can search for solutions that already exist. If it's a common or well-known problem, it's possible others have already solved it (or tried to solve it). Perhaps a solution exists that we can interact with and take inspiration from so that we can better solve the problem ourselves. We could perform a competitive analysis and look at other offerings in the problem space. We could analyze these companies from a strengths and weaknesses perspective, looking for ways to innovate around the problem.

However we decide to empathize, we do so with the intent to better understand the current state of things so that we can form opinions and better define what we want to accomplish for our target audience.

Step 2: Define

In the second step of the design thinking process, we begin to form opinions. We take the research from the first empathize step, synthesize it, then analyze the results. Here, we must answer several questions.

WHAT COMMONALITIES EXIST?

In our observations, we must categorize and sort our research. What trends or common points are present? Does everyone experience the problem in the same way? Does everyone have the same solution to the problem? Are there common issues that most people experience? We must draw parallels and, from those parallels, be better informed to think of ideas later in the process.

HOW ARE PEOPLE SERVED?

From our observations, did we notice any solutions? Did we notice a lack of solutions in a certain aspect of the problem? Are people underserved in any capacity? By identifying where people are satisfied and dissatisfied, we can better focus on a solution.

WHAT IS THE PROBLEM TO SOLVE?

In this step, we attempt to clearly define the problem to solve. We take our research and observations and form opinions on how people are struggling. We don't think of a solution just yet; rather, we try to well define what problems people have and what problem we specifically want to focus on for the remainder of the design thinking process. We may observe multiple problems, and that's OK—it is in this step that we want to focus our attention so we can think of solutions that are specific to what we want to solve.

With a clear understanding of the problem to solve, we will be well set up to ideate possible solutions.

Step 3: Ideate

In the third step of the design thinking process, we want to create solutions. Here, we take our research and our problem to solve and both diverge and converge around possible solutions.

DIVERGE AROUND POSSIBILITIES

First, we diverge. We go wide, thinking of all sorts of possible solutions that could solve the core problem users face. We brainstorm without restriction— no idea is "too crazy" during this step. We want to think of as many ideas as possible and then, from those ideas, converge. We do this with brainstorming, mind mapping, and other techniques that allow us to generate ideas for us to converge around.

CONVERGE AROUND PROBABILITIES

After truly exploring possible ideas through brainstorming, sketching, and other ideation techniques, we converge. We compare ideas against each other, evaluating through the lenses of the ones we think could best solve our users' problems, or the ones that are most feasible. We prioritize ideas so we can test them with users.

Once we have a few possible solutions, we prototype those solutions with the intent of testing our ideas with our audience.

Step 4: Prototype

In the fourth step of the design thinking process, we create representations of our ideas to see how they perform. We take our ideas and give them shape so we can see how they function in the hands of others.

LEAN AND IMPERFECT

In this step, it's not about perfection—it's about gaining information. We need to validate our ideas, not create a fully functional product. It's a waste of time to create a perfect, fully coded, or fully functional idea to test. We want something quick, yet accurate enough to give people an idea of how our solution could work—so we can spend the least amount of time validating our design direction and getting feedback. Create the smallest viable idea that will let you test your solution.

TACTILE

Our ideas need to be tested with others. Whatever you prototype, it has to be able to be used by others. This could be something as complex as a high-fidelity, pixel-perfect mockup of every screen in your product or as simple as a few pieces of paper you could show someone to give them a rough sense of your idea. As long as it conveys your idea, it can work.

With a functioning MVPr (minimum viable prototype, not to be confused with MVP for minimum viable product), we can move on and test our ideas with our target audience so we can learn whether our design solutions make sense in the context of their lives.

Step 5: Test

In this step of the design thinking process, we test our ideas. After creating representations of those ideas, we can see how users interact with them so we can test our assumptions and learn if our solution actually solves users' problems.

IS IT USABLE?

When people interact with your prototype, is the solution usable? Do people know how to navigate it? Have you clearly communicated the design in a way that satisfies their hierarchy of needs? Do your signifiers accurately communicate your affordances? Is it functional, reliable, usable, and delightful? It's OK if all these aspects aren't there for your prototype, as long as your testing suggests that they will be.

DOES IT ACTUALLY SOLVE THE PROBLEM?

Most importantly, does your idea satisfy the problem to solve? Have you created something that actually could solve your users' problems? This is the time to learn whether or not that's true, and if it's not, how you can adjust the design so it's more likely to solve the problems.

Assuming the prototype yields great testing results and we are convinced the design solution will work, we can move on to building the solution.

Step 6: Implement

In the last step, you implement your solution. In this step, you are certain your ideas work—now, you get them into the hands of your users in real life.

WHAT NEEDS TO BE BUILT?

How will someone create your solution? Will it need to be coded? Will you need a back-end architecture to keep it running? As you design your solution, you have to think of all the supporting structures needed for your solution to exist in the real world.

HOW WILL USERS USE IT?

How will users interact with your solution? For a functioning product, you will need to think of all the use cases of your design. What if there is an error? What if a user starts using your product and then comes back to it at a later point? You have to consider more than just the "happy path" of your designs—you must deliver a fully thought-out product experience that covers all edge cases a user could run into.

Design Thinking Is the First Step

There are many ways to approach human-centered design. We have many models available to us, tons of frameworks that help us keep the most important things in perspective: the problem we are trying to solve, and the people we are trying to solve it for. In this book, we will be applying the design thinking process so that we can approach our problem to solve in a human-centered way.

Human-centered design is just one piece of the puzzle. Design needs to operate with other job functions in order to implement the design solution in the real world. To do this, we need to be aware of how products are built so that we can integrate our processes with everyone else who is working on the problem to solve.

HOW ARE PRODUCTS BUILT?

Our goal as designers is to make something that solves the problems of the people we design for. We follow design thinking to accomplish this goal; however, our design thinking process doesn't live on its own. Rather, we have to balance the demands of design thinking with the needs of the businesses that produce the products we work on. Design thinking is one element of creating a solution to the problem to solve. In order for that solution to actually reach the hands of customers, we need the business to be able to produce, distribute, and maintain that solution.

To take the benefits of design thinking and bring them into the world, we need to build the solutions we come up with. To do so, we rely on product development processes to make sure we're on track, within budget, and able to deliver our ideas to the people that will benefit from them.

AUTHOR'S NOTE Like the terms *user experience design* and *product design*, the terms *user* and *customer* are also interchangeable. It comes down to the company culture. At Nickelodeon, I felt "user" was too cold to refer to our customers and tried to shift the culture to "child" over "user." However, this failed to catch on. Similarly, at Amazon, our end users are always referred to as "customers."

How Do We Implement Our Products?

We've talked about how having a good design thinking process helps us create usable, delightful user experiences. Another element of successful product design is having a good development process that helps us implement those user experiences.

In the UX industry, several different product development processes allow us to build products. While some are more common than others, it all depends on where you work, the problems you are tasked to solve, and the philosophies of the organizations that you belong to that influence which methods you may use in your day-to-day work.

Some organizations work in a linear fashion, where work is handed off from one group to the next as a project moves through phases. Different disciplines become involved at different stages in the project as their skill sets become more or less important depending on the phase of the work. If a project is at the beginning of the design thinking process, then it needs a lot of research and user researchers would be very involved helping to uncover the needs of the people the team is designing for. Alternatively, if we are at the end of a project and need to implement a solution, then developers would primarily be responsible for writing the code that ensures the product functions correctly.

Other organizations prefer to work in an iterative fashion, constantly evolving and improving the products they work on. Projects in these organizations also move in phases, though the time between these phases is a lot shorter—in some cases days or even weeks long. In these projects, we are constantly working on each part of the design thinking process to continually solve problems for the users of our solutions.

What's better—a linear, longform series of steps that lead to a final solution, or an iterative, shortform constant set of work that builds on a "never complete" solution over time? Is it better to have a relay race, where different disciplines pass a baton from one department to the next? Or is it preferable to capture the flag, where multiple disciplines simultaneously operate toward a common goal?

In reality, both approaches can work. It all depends on the problem to solve.

Waterfall: A Linear, Phased Work Stream

The Waterfall methodology, or more commonly, *Waterfall*, is a project management process in which each phase of the project flows like water going down a waterfall (**FIGURE 1.6**).

FIGURE 1.6 Waterfall project management. (Gail Johnson/Shutterstock)

In Waterfall, each phase of the project must be completed before the next one can begin. You start at the top of the waterfall and work your way down the project until you get to the next step in the waterfall, constantly flowing downward until your project is complete.

In **FIGURE 1.7**, you can see how each step of the project flows into the next one, with a clear roadmap for what work will be completed and what work comes next. The schedule does not include room for going to a previous step in the process—the project marches on, just as water falls from a cliff to its next destination.

FIGURE 1.7 Waterfall development steps. Each step of the waterfall design process occurs one at a time, with no time or ability to go back a step with new learnings or information.

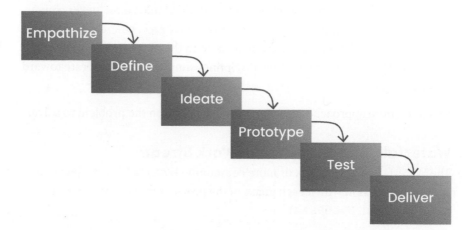

Under this methodology, it is common to have a really good sense of the problem you want to solve and all the requirements for a project up front before doing any work. For the model to function, it requires a deep planning process where people scope the project and perform the research required for the rest of the project to be successful. This can include the design of the problem to solve, the timelines for each phase of the project, and the eventual deliverable that's expected.

This method is common in industries with a lot of dependencies during each phase of a project. It's common in construction industries, for example, where a project needs to be scoped out and planned before the work begins. It's costly and challenging to change a building plan as you are creating the building, and having a really clear scope of your project prior to building it helps avoid the need to change requirements during the project.

This aspect of Waterfall is also one of its major criticisms. As you move through a project, you will learn new pieces of information that could directly influence what you want to build. As a result, this method is less flexible than other methods because each step must be completed before moving to the next step, and it's difficult to go to a previous step once it is complete.

Waterfall is a common method for building products, but most often those products have clear deliverables or require all the information to be known prior to starting the work.

For software development, this process may be preferred to others. Software engineers have a really good sense of what needs to be built and how long it will take because requirement-gathering and design work are done upfront. In an agency setting, for example, a client may come to the business with a clear problem and a clear task, and you may use a Waterfall methodology to deliver that product.

Here are some of the major benefits of Waterfall:

- Predetermined scope

  Because each step is dependent on the next, it's a lot more common to have a clear, predetermined set of deliverables for a project.

- Linear progression

  When one phase begins, it is informed by the previous phase, which leads to a good sense of what needs to be done and who's working on what. Development, for example, will be well informed by the design specs, and as a result the project will run more smoothly because of that clarity.

- Strong documentation

  Since each phase has dependency on the prior phase, projects end up well documented. Design preparing a handoff to development, for example, ends up creating a well-thought-out series of specification documents that inform how the design should function. As a result, the organization gains clear documentation for future works.

Waterfall, however, is not without its criticisms:

- The initial problem to solve might not be the right one.

  Usually, people don't exactly know what they need up front; nor do they know what's possible with technology. As a result, the initial task isn't usually what's best for the user, or there's an idea that ends up being better. This leads to tension between the nature of Waterfall as a process and the possibility of a better product.

- We learn things during the process.

  In reality, the problem is not very easy to define. Usually, a lot of exploration and understanding is required to fully define the problem to solve (let alone solve it), and as a result, things are missed. In a Waterfall process, time and resources aren't allocated to pivoting, which can hurt the eventual shipped product.

- Changing requirements affects everything.

  Waterfall isn't an adaptable process. If something changes (like business goals, user needs, or market conditions), it is harder to adapt and shift the project (and stakeholder expectations).

I'll give you an example of a time I worked in a waterfall environment. Media companies usually have tight content timelines. As a result, we had to lock in the product schedule so that we could release each piece of content when the business needed it. If we shipped a piece of holiday content late, then that content wouldn't be as relevant (a Christmas episode should release before Christmas, not after). Since we were working back from a fixed date, we didn't have the opportunity to launch the product iteratively—it was more of a one-time launch strategy. These project parameters are why we operated in a waterfall fashion—create the script, collect the assets, produce the content, test it, allow for minor revisions, then release and work on the next piece of content. We didn't go back to earlier steps to revise, and we never addressed content after it was released—we were already moving on to the next project.

Overall, Waterfall provides the most structure and expectations for a project, at the expense of flexibility as the project goes on.

Agile: An Iterative, Continual Process

Agile product development, or *Agile*, is the opposite of Waterfall. Instead of a rigid structure of predefined phases with scoped-out deliverables and timelines, Agile emphasizes lean, iterative product development. Under the Agile methodology, we focus on incremental product gains rather than making large, substantive changes or product releases (FIGURE 1.8).

Agile is focused on incremental product gains via product iterations. Perhaps your first product launch is an MVP (minimum viable product). Then your next launch enhances the work of that release, adding a new feature or fixing problems you've encountered now that your product is out in the wild with real, daily users.

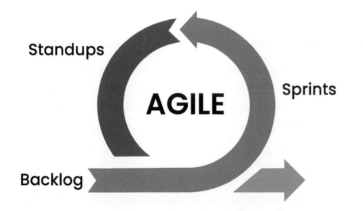

FIGURE 1.8 Agile creates small incremental changes instead of major product releases.

In **FIGURE 1.9**, we focus on a smaller release during the first *sprint*, or deliverable, then move on to the next sprint and focus on the next release. In this way, we solve smaller problems and iterate more frequently on the product, taking the learnings from each sprint and applying them to the next one. This allows us to incorporate feedback into the product because the room for iteration is built into the process.

Using Agile, the work isn't as planned out in advance. We have a general sense of what we want to accomplish, but the roadmap might be shorter because we don't have a great sense of what we're going to work on—we're going to release a version of our product, then measure as we go. This can lead to less certainty and predictability for stakeholders, which may give them concern.

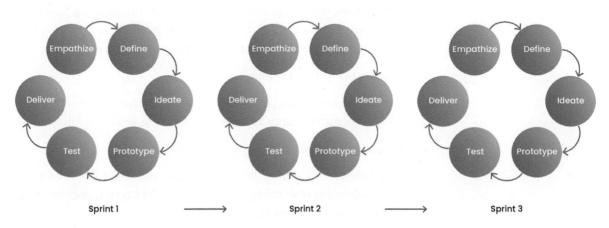

FIGURE 1.9 Sprints deliver small incremental changes.

Some of the major benefits of Agile include:

- Frequent software releases

  The focus is on shipping minimum viable features and iterating on an existing product, so the product receives constant updates and enhancements. Instead of shipping a singular product and being done with it, the product continues to receive support and improvements.

- Product change at any moment

  The product development life cycle is so short and lean that a change in requirements, market conditions, or business priorities can be much more easily accommodated.

- Better cross-functional collaboration

  Teams are handing off smaller increments of work more frequently, so those teams have better communication because they talk constantly. Designers, developers, and product managers usually speak with each other daily, discussing product enhancements, requirements, and feedback.

Some criticisms of Agile include:

- Potential lack of human-centered design

  In Agile, it's more difficult to be humancentric because there isn't a lot of time to go deep into the problem and its definition. We're so focused on the current release/sprint that we fail to look into future sprints and releases because we evaluate as we go. In Waterfall, there's time built into the schedule to research and understand a problem adequately.

- Harder to estimate deliverables

  You're measuring as you go, so it's harder to estimate how long the work will take because you aren't completely sure what you're building.

- Less documentation

  You're focused on shipping the work today, so you're not focused on good notekeeping or handing off deliverables. As a result, documenting processes usually falls short.

I've operated in an Agile fashion while working at tech companies. With an already released product, we focused on adding features and functionalities in order to remain competitive and continually deliver enhancements for our customers. Sometimes these would be new features, while other times it would be updates to improve quality of life. We would gather feedback from our users, analyze which feedback was most impactful and actionable, and then prioritize product improvements that we felt would deliver the most value to the highest percentage of users. The roadmap would change constantly as we gathered information from the market, our customers, and the business. As a result, we would continually make improvements and iterate on the product in month long increments, constantly pushing the product forward.

Hybrid: A Combination of the Two

Hybrid product development combines aspects of Waterfall and Agile to form a blend of both methods (**FIGURE 1.10**).

FIGURE 1.10 Waterfall and Agile methods working together. (RomanticSunday/ Shutterstock)

Under a hybrid model, a project would start as Waterfall, gathering requirements and defining the problem to solve. The user need would be well defined at the beginning of the process, and we would have a clear understanding of what we were trying to accomplish. However, once we begin to ideate, we would shift to an Agile approach, using sprints for the ideate, prototype, and test steps of the design thinking process to better understand if the solution solves users' needs well. We could even use the implement step of the design thinking process in this model, shipping small parts of the product incrementally as we continue to iterate via sprints (**FIGURE 1.11**).

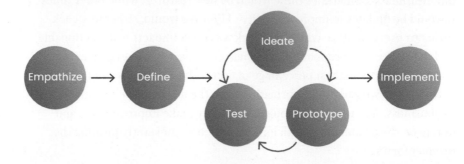

FIGURE 1.11 A hybrid method blends Waterfall and Agile to use the best of both.

I have worked in a hybrid environment in several companies, usually when first releasing a product. We would conduct a lot of upfront research to empathize with customers and define the problem to solve, being really clear about what people wanted and what we were trying to accomplish for them and the business. Then, we would do several design sprints to ideate, prototype, and test possible solutions to those problems. After finding a solution we felt confident in, we would move forward and release a minimum viable product that solved our customers' problems. After release, we would do several "fast follows" to enhance the product further, iterating even more. If we felt the product was doing well, we'd ideate, prototype, and test more features, adding to the product over time. Sometimes the product would stay alive for years, while other times we'd see that the cost of operating the product didn't justify the benefits it provided, and we'd "sunset" or otherwise stop working on it.

Which Process Is Good for Your Projects?

The process that's best for your projects depends on where your project is in its lifecycle.

If you are early in your product development, you need a lot of research to define the problem you want to solve in addition to phasing out the work. In that case, Waterfall would be your best place to start.

If you have already released a product and are trying to enhance or improve it, you would do so on an incremental, steady, iterative basis. In this case, Agile would be a better methodology.

If you are working on a new feature for a product that already exists, then you may prefer a blend of the two, a hybrid approach. Perhaps you want to spend a lot of time doing research, and then a smaller amount of time ideating and iterating on what you've already created in order to incorporate that feature into an existing product.

The process you choose will also depend on the type of company you work for.

If you work at an agency, you may end up in a Waterfall environment. A client will come to you and ask you to solve a problem of theirs, and over the course of many months, you'll meet timelines and deliverables in a linear fashion until you deliver a singular product or a design for the client to use in the way they see fit.

If you work in-house, you may be in an Agile environment. Embedded software teams will be in constant communication to enhance and improve the product they work on, making small changes over time as the business evolves and market changes.

The process you choose will also depend on the industry you work in.

In the entertainment industry, for example, it's common for businesses to move slowly and plan out content releases over a calendar year. In some cases, a product is released, the hype around that product fades, and the product doesn't get iterated on. The business moves on to the next product, or the next release, and doesn't go back to enhance or modify last year's releases. As a result, entertainment companies like large TV networks will work on a Waterfall basis.

If you work at a technology company, your industry will move at a faster pace, constantly iterating on your product and releasing new features. Perhaps your product is seen as a service, one that needs to evolve with the ever-shifting needs of its customers and the competition. As a result, you will probably work in an Agile environment, taking on smaller initiatives that, over time, significantly enhance your product.

For our purposes, design thinking can fit into any of these processes. I recommend adopting the process that best fits the type of work you wish to do in the industry. If you wish to work at an agency or create brand new products, Waterfall will be more common. If you wish to work in-house on existing products, Agile will be more common. Target the process that best fits the type of work you wish to do in your career.

WHAT IS USER EXPERIENCE, OR "UX"?

Have you ever walked in a park and seen a path like the one in **FIGURE 1.12**?

FIGURE 1.12 Users sometimes make their own path. (Miguel Dominguez Muñoz/ Pearson Education Ltd)

Someone spent the time and money to make these beautiful, aesthetic-looking paths for people to use. They are paved, neat and clean, and well laid out. But not everyone uses them, because they don't fit their needs. If someone wants to head to a location not along the existing paths, they make their own. The shortest distance to their destination is diagonal—through the grass rather than on the brick path laid out for them.

The path in **FIGURE 1.13** avoids the well-designed, laid out path; people use the new path to reach their location as fast as possible.

FIGURE 1.13 Sometimes what we design doesn't match the experience users want. (Miguel Dominguez Muñoz/ Pearson Education Ltd)

DESIGN

USER EXPERIENCE

These types of paths created in parks are called *desire paths*. Pedestrians desire to walk along certain pathways in parks—ones that are natural to them. It's natural to take a diagonal path through an open space to get to a location faster. While the artificially designed path is easier to walk along, it goes against the desires of getting to a location with less effort—in this case, by spending less time and energy walking an indirect route. The artificial path is more aesthetic, is more pleasurable to walk, gets less dirt on one's shoes, is paved so it's easier to walk, and may even be designed to accommodate foot traffic. Despite all these advantages, enough pedestrians have found it easier to make their own path—and as a result, have walked through the grass so much—that a natural path has emerged through the park.

Even though someone designed a way for people to navigate this experience, it doesn't match these users' wants and needs, and people made their own way through the "product." We can design an experience, but we have to consider our users and the user experience of our product. How will people use it? What do they want from it? How frictionless is it?

The UX, or the user experience, here is the experience of a person walking down the paths—they want to use the product in a manner that meets their needs, not necessarily the paths laid out by the designers.

Let's take a closer look at a few examples that can give us a better idea of what UX truly is.

UX Is Usercentric

UX Design is a commitment to building products with the customer in mind.
—Marieke McCloskey, UX researcher and product strategist

When considering the user experience of a product, the goal is to remain usercentric throughout the design of that product. We have to consider all users—not just the primary users we would expect, but the secondary, tertiary, and additional users of the experiences we design. Are we considering all the demographics? All possible use cases? How does the experience we're designing fit into the lives of the people we are making them for?

When we think of making an experience, we may have a customer in mind. When making a camera, for example, we may think of a photographer who is very familiar with composition, lighting, and aligning the perfect shot. We may design a camera with features and functionalities for this savvy photographer, implementing features that allow for multiple conditions and subjects.

However, during this process, we may forget other users of the products. We may ignore the non-savant, the user who uses their camera only for special occasions like birthdays or family gatherings. We may forget the first-time user, who wants a high-end camera but doesn't know how to operate it (**FIGURE 1.14**). We need to build our camera with all customers in mind and what they hope to accomplish with the experience we design. We may design multiple experiences, one for the entry-level or newer user and one for the expert. Keeping the customer in mind is crucial, as they're the one using the end experience.

FIGURE 1.14 Cameras have a lot of options available to adjust for lighting, distance, and subject, among other variables. Creating an "optimal lighting" function for less experienced users can help educate them on how to use the camera and can develop their confidence for future uses. (Witthaya Prasongsin/123RF)

UX Is More Than a Screen

UX Design is so much more than just designing for a screen.

—Paul Boag, author of *User Experience Revolution*

So often people think of UX as digital design. They equate UX design to a set of wireframes, screens, or mockups that a user moves through. But UX is so much more than a set of images on a digital screen. It's the experience that exists around those images.

How does someone use the product that the images sit in? Is it used by touch gestures, a keyboard, a screen reader, or something else? Is it even digital? UX exists outside of the platforms and features we design for—it's the full experience someone has when using your product (**FIGURE 1.15**).

Even for digital-only experiences, the act of designing an experience extends far beyond the visual representation of that experience. To communicate a vision, it requires more than just the screens that represent that vision. We must research how people will use an experience so that we are well informed around the problem we want to solve. We must design the information architecture, structuring how the experience is organized. We must execute that experience by forming product tenets that let us deliver the best experience we can for users.

To accomplish these things, we prepare research results. We create user journeys and flows throughout the product experience. We organize our information into site maps and taxonomies that allow users better navigation. We create common design patterns so users can better understand our signifiers and affordances. While an experience may predominately occur on a screen, designing for that experience happens just as much off the screen as it does on it.

FIGURE 1.15 Notice the large font, green success screen, and giant check mark, all designed bigger than normal so the customer can quickly verify the purchase was successful and continue moving through the physical space they are in. (asiandelight/Shutterstock)

UX Is All Around Us

UX doesn't live inside our phones or our websites.

—Matt Hryhorsky, UX manager at Shopify

UX, at its core, is about a user's experience with a product. That product doesn't have to be digital. It could be a physical product (**FIGURE 1.16**), like a pair of scissors or a tea kettle. It could be a set of instructions, like those for building a new set of IKEA furniture. It could even be a door. When we diminish UX down to a series of screens, we end up losing sight of the entire customer journey.

FIGURE 1.16 IKEA continually innovates in the flat-pack furniture space by spending a lot of its resources on instruction manuals. Engineers team with designers to create the user experience behind the step-by-step instructions that allow customers to put together complicated pieces of furniture in their own homes, without the assistance of screens. (Vadim Guzhva/123RF)

We can think of UX as a system—a user has experiences across the entire system, from when they shop for furniture in a store to buying that furniture, bringing it home, assembling it, and incorporating it into their lives.

The Basic Elements of UX

UX Design is all about the process of creating experiences for the users of those experiences. At its core, UX Design covers several key elements that make up an experience.

Usability

Usability is the ease with which people use products. It is also referred to as *ease of use*. Usability is a measure of the difficulty someone has when trying to use a product, often used in the context of completing a task. We measure a product's usability and try to create the most intuitive, frictionless products possible by using the design thinking process. This is commonly thought of as how we communicate things to our users, or how easy or difficult it is to find information.

For example, we can apply the concept of usability to all mobile products by considering how people hold the devices and use their thumbs to navigate on the screen. Because we hold a phone at the bottom to support it against the pull of gravity and maintain balance, our thumbs can reach different parts of the screen with different degrees of ease. Closer to the bottom, as shown in the green zones in **FIGURE 1.17**, is easier, while it is difficult to reach the upper corners of the screen. This is why we have navigation controls at the bottom of the screen on our mobile apps, for example, instead of at the top.

FIGURE 1.17 Users commonly cradle the bottom of their phones in one hand and use their thumb to navigate around the device. This image ranks tap zones based on level of comfort. (octdesign/Shutterstock)

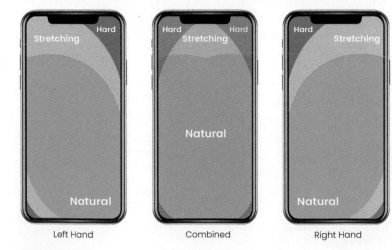

Left Hand   Combined   Right Hand

Let's take a closer look at two of the most popular browsers on phones: Chrome and Safari. The placement of the UI controls for typing in a website—which are, arguably, the most important controls when opening a new tab—exist in different places in these browsers. For Chrome, the focus is on consistency with web patterns. On a desktop, the input for a domain name is at the top of the page, which is where Chrome keeps it for its phone app. For Safari, however, they put the domain name input on the bottom of the screen so that users have an easier time tapping that field to open it. Safari prioritizes mobile usability, since the user's thumb is at the bottom of the phone. These differing design philosophies—consistency versus usability—are apparent across similar experiences (FIGURE 1.18).

We can measure usability by observing our users interact with a product and hearing their feedback. Additionally, we can measure usability through objective metrics like the time it takes to complete a task or how often a task is completed successfully.

FIGURE 1.18 Chrome (left) has the search bar near the top of the screen, which is harder to reach when a user holds the phone at the bottom; Safari (right) has it at the bottom of the screen.

Usefulness

For something to be useful, it has to allow users to get closer to, or meet, their goals. If something is useful, then it can be used to achieve a goal. This is different than usable—if something is usable, then it can be used, but it is not necessarily useful.

Consider a product designed for no purpose. This product could be usable, in that it could function, could be reliable, and could be used by someone. But if that product has no purpose and has no usefulness, then that product won't have a meaningful user experience for its users.

Consider a product that is a feather, intended to be a paperweight for loose pieces of paper (**FIGURE 1.19**). This product is usable—to use it, you place it on top of a stack of papers and it keeps the papers in place. But it's not very useful—in fact, the feather will blow away and not keep the papers in place. Thus, the user experience is not useful and is, as a result, poor.

FIGURE 1.19 A feather is too light to act as a paper-weight. It's usable (you can put it on a stack of papers), but it isn't useful (it won't hold that stack in place). (Cheuk-king Lo/Pearson Education Asia Ltd)

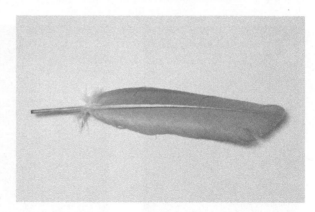

Desirability

Desirability is the measure of how much a product is wanted by a user. It's more subjective than other elements of UX, as it relates to tastes and aesthetics. It also lives higher in the hierarchy of user needs in that it becomes more important after usability and usefulness are established.

Imagine a mature marketplace—all the products in that marketplace are probably usable and useful. What ends up differentiating those products, then? Why buy an Apple computer when plenty of PC counterparts exist, at cheaper prices? Are AirPods really better than all other wireless headphones on the market?

To some, they are. Apple products provide a better user experience than other products in the eyes of these users, because they desire them. They may have similar usability and usefulness, but the desirability factor that Apple puts in its products, as well as its brand perception, allows it to surge ahead of its competitors.

Brand Perception

The desirability of a single product from an organization leads to a good user experience. Over time, if that organization continues to deliver good user experiences across different products, they become known for their excellent UX. People see brand names and automatically associate their past user experiences with that company's products to future user experiences with new products. The brand name adds legitimacy and expectation to new product releases, and users assume that those releases have or will have a good UX, even if those new products fail to provide that.

This can go both ways—if a company continues to deliver bad UX, it will be known for doing so. The perception of that brand filters down to the perception of the experience. Apple has created a perception that their brand is synonymous with high quality. Other companies, however, have had mixed reception of their product releases—some have been very good, and others have not. As a result, their brand perception is mixed, and the perception of the user experience of their products is mixed as well.

UX Touches Many Disciplines

In reality, user experience is made up of many different disciplines (**FIGURE 1.20**).[10]

As designers, when we consider someone's experience with our product, we must think of all sorts of elements related to that experience. We must consider how it looks (visual design), its structure (information architecture), how it operates (interaction design), how it's built (computer science), and how it communicates with our users (content design), among other factors. When considering these elements, the idea of creating a "good" user experience can feel daunting. Thankfully, we start at a much simpler place when considering our design process.

AUTHOR'S NOTE Like other terms in the design industry, the term *content design* has shifted over the years, from communication design to UX writing to content design. Sometimes, we change the names of terms to convey alternative meaning, to be more specific, or to capture more use cases as our understanding improves and technology evolves.

---

10 https://visual.ly/community/Infographics/computers/disciplines-user-experience-design

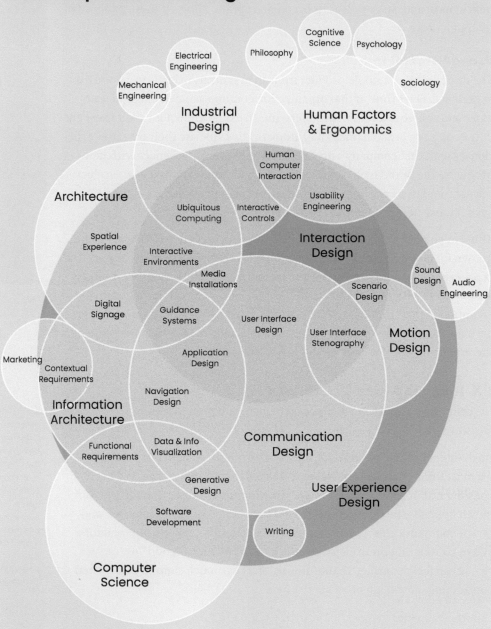

FIGURE 1.20 The disciplines of user experience, by Dan Saffer.

The UX Triad

For our purposes, broadly speaking, when pursuing product design, we can think of user experience as the intersection between a user's needs, a business's goals, and the technology that connects them (FIGURE 1.21).[11]

As designers, we can create great user experiences as long as we balance the following three elements of UX.

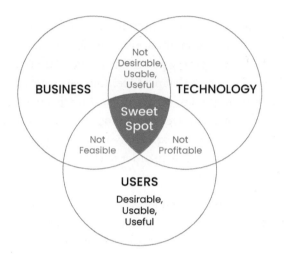

FIGURE 1.21 UX combines the needs of the user that uses it, the goals of the business that pays for it, and the constraints of the technology that powers it.

User Needs

You can't have user experience without "user," so this element is straightforward. We need to think about all the needs of our users—it's why they will come to us for help solving their problems. As a result, we need to understand everything we can about them. What is their problem to solve, and how does our experience help them? What are their goals? Their wants? Their needs? Their frustrations? Understanding these and delivering a solution that incorporates them creates a strong user experience that satisfies the basic components of UX.

Business Goals

In reality, it is not enough to think about users—we must think about businesses as well. Businesses will be the entities creating these experiences at scale. To allow the maximum number of users the opportunity to access the experience we design, we must convince and rely on the business to deliver

---

11 https://voices.berkeley.edu/art-and-design/user-experience-design

the experience. Why would a business invest in a strong user experience? What goals does the business have by releasing this product? How will they measure success and know what it looks like? How do they make money? You can create the best experience considering your users' needs, but if you ignore the business's concerns and goals, then that experience won't be able to sustain itself or scale.

Technology Constraints

If we understand what the business and the users gain from a potential experience, that puts us in a great spot to create something amazing. However, we have to be mindful of what's even technologically possible to create. If users want a robot that cleans the floor every day, is that possible? Can we create a delivery service that drops off our medication to our front door? Is what we want to create possible from a feasible perspective? From a logistical one? We are bound by the technology that can power our experiences, and when we design, we have to know what is and isn't possible in order to craft the best experience.

If we aren't aware that our phones can use their cameras to scan information, we'll miss a potential opportunity to create a digital menu at restaurants. If we don't know that computers can recognize the text in sentences, we'll miss the opportunity to design a product that helps with our grammar as we write. We need to be mindful of what's possible today, and what could be possible tomorrow, as we design.

The UX triad needs to incorporate all three of these elements—the users, the business, and the technology. Not only must these elements be considered, they must be balanced—there may be a technology that exists that would satisfy the problem to solve, for example, but if it's too expensive for the business to buy, or too complicated for users to understand, then we cannot create a good user experience.

UX Incorporates All Elements of an Experience for All People

UX is the holistic, complete experience all users have with a product. It extends beyond a singular individual and must incorporate all users. It extends beyond the solution itself, incorporating all the research, architecture, and implementation of that solution. It even extends beyond screens, making its way into the physical surfaces and locations where the experience takes place.

By balancing the UX triad—the users who interact with the experience, the business that produces and maintains it, and the technology that empowers it, we can create a balanced, well-designed user experience for our audience.

WHAT IS UI?

A UI, or user interface, is the surfaces that allow a user to interact with a product. A user interface can be a series of digital text fields, a set of physical buttons, or any other collection of signifiers and affordances that allow a user to operate a product. It is the means that allow users to use the things we create for them.

Our industry suffers from an identity crisis. Internally, as designers, we have a good sense of the difference between UX and UI. Externally, however, things become a little bit blurry. The perception is that design is a deliverable. Design involves visuals, and it involves artifacts that are given to other teams to build. Design is something that we can see, that can be given to others, so that they can use it. It's a series of wireframes or mockups that a developer can build, and whatever interface a designer creates is the full extent of the UX that goes into it.

Outside the industry, a lot of confusion exists around the difference between UX and UI for those trying to understand it, work with it, or enter it. But this confusion also exists within the industry, among organizations that deliver products for users to experience, and even on the teams that make these experiences. Many think UX = UI = the design.

Compare the definition of UI with the definition of UX. A user interface allows users to operate a product, whereas a user experience is the entire holistic experience with a product.

Ken Norton has a very good definition for the difference between UX and UI:

> *UX is focused on the user's journey to solve a problem; UI is focused on how a product's surfaces look and function.*
>
> —Ken Norton, partner at Google Ventures

UX is involved with solving problems for users. We must identify the problem to solve, and then by following good UX practices we solve that problem.

UI is involved with how the solution works. How does it look? How does it operate? How does the solution communicate with users?

More simply, UX is the entire experience a user has with a product, while the UI is how that experience is represented. It is a part of the UX (FIGURE 1.22):

At the same time, the UI defines the UX. The UI is a part of the UX, so slight variations in UI for similar products can result in drastically different user experiences. The two are interconnected, which is why the industry at large sometimes struggles with defining the two.

Different UI, Same Problem to Solve

Let's take a look at this problem a little more deeply and try to understand how UI is related to UX by seeing the UIs of products that solve similar problems.

Food Delivery Apps

Uber Eats, DoorDash, and Grubhub allow people to order food from restaurants. All three solve the same problem: "I'm hungry, and I don't want to spend time or money on preparing my food." But each has its own way of showing the solution to that problem (FIGURE 1.23).

FIGURE 1.23 The home screens for three food delivery apps.

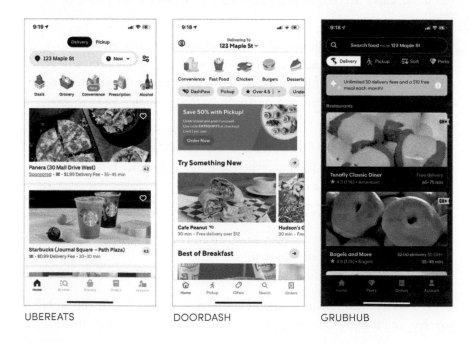

UBEREATS   DOORDASH   GRUBHUB

All three products have a filter at the top that lets users choose either delivery or pickup, but each has a different way of showing that filter. Uber Eats and Grubhub have a text input, while DoorDash uses a drop-down arrow to change your location. DoorDash is assuming users won't need to change their location often, thus deprioritizing that option visually and saving space for the main aspect of this experience—connecting users to their food.

Continuing down the page, we see filters at the top for Uber Eats and Door-Dash that let users search by cuisine. Grubhub chooses not to include this option, instead focusing on the content—places for people to eat. As for content, Uber Eats and Grubhub offer single vertical scrolls, while DoorDash offers sections based on topics. This allows users to preselect an area of interest, such as "something new" or "best of breakfast."

Each app attempts to solve the same problem but approaches it in slightly different ways—this is obvious in their UIs, but a little more subtle in their UXs. The changes in the UI affect the user experience. This is because the UI is a part of the UX.

Search Apps

Let's take a look at another problem and how different companies approach it. Let's imagine that you are browsing the internet and want to search for something. As a user, you have something you are trying to find and want to use a search engine to help you look for it. Several different businesses try to solve this core user problem, but because they value different things as a business, their UX varies.

Microsoft Bing presents the user with the UX and UI in **FIGURE 1.24**.

FIGURE 1.24 Microsoft Bing's homepage for search. Besides the ability to search, it includes a background image, trending articles, and various account settings.

This page's primary function is to search the internet for information using Bing's search engine. However, the search bar is not the primary element on the page. It's the user's primary goal, but it's not the primary goal of the business. The business distracts from the search functionality by showing beautiful imagery and even pushing content for the user to engage with on the bottom bar. If the user scrolls the page, they can find more information that Microsoft wants them to engage with.

This is an example of a user experience that combines user and business goals. Users want to search, while Microsoft wants users to click on specific information. As a result, we end up with a mixed experience.

Let's take a look at another example, Yahoo (**FIGURE 1.25**).

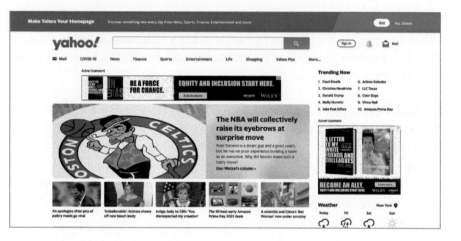

FIGURE 1.25 Yahoo's homepage for search. Like Bing, it includes multiple features beyond search, including advertisements, trending searches, trending articles, weather information, and account settings.

Yahoo provides a different way for users to search. Like Microsoft, they want users to be able to search, but also want to nudge users into engaging with content that benefits them. Advertisements, trending content, featured content, sponsored content, and more are displayed. This is a search page for a search engine, but Yahoo wants to create a home that users go to—you may come to this page to search for something specific, but you might also come to check the weather or read up on the news without having a specific goal in mind. Yahoo prioritizes creating a home for users and uses its search engine as one ingress point for people to come to this page.

Let's look at a third example, Google (**FIGURE 1.26**).

FIGURE 1.26 Google's homepage for search. It has fewer features than Bing or Yahoo, focusing on the ability to search or adjust the user's account settings.

Google's approach is completely usercentric. As a business, Google cares about its search engine logic (and the massive amount of revenue generated by advertisements and sponsored content after searching). As a business, they want a critical mass of users using their platforms and infrastructures to improve their data analytics and push their products. Google cares about an ecosystem of products that users adopt, in addition to their brand perception.

This UI is an easy-to-use, usercentric direct solution to the user's need of "I want to search the internet." It's not a surprise that Google is one of the most widely adopted search engines in the world, and one of the most beloved user experiences related to search. It's fast, it's easy, and it gets out of the way of the user. It speeds up their workflow and makes search easy.

The problem to solve hasn't changed among these examples—users want to search the internet. The business goals, however, vary greatly, which impacts the UI and the UX.

The Basic Elements of UI

With a better understanding of the philosophy behind UI, we can start to understand the components that define a UI. There are several high-level elements that make up a user interface.

Color

In UI design, color can be used as either an aesthetic or a signifier (**FIGURE 1.27**). Color creates moods in an interface. A bright UI can create a vibrant atmosphere of constant activity or movement; a dark UI can create a nighttime atmosphere that suggests secrecy or sleep. A UI can be monochromatic and stick to a single color scheme, or multichromatic and pull from a wide set of hues. Color is used to establish a setting for users.

FIGURE 1.27 Color is a foundational UI element that sets mood, communicates interactivity, and expresses brand values. (Lotus_studio/Shutterstock)

Color can also tell us what's actionable in an interface, for example, by creating a visual language that communicates certain colors meaning interactivity. A paragraph of black text with a few blue words in it can communicate a hyperlink to a different part of the product. A rectangle with text in it that's a different color than the rest of the UI can indicate a button to be pressed. Through the visual design principle of contrast, we can use color to teach our users how to use our product (**FIGURE 1.28**).

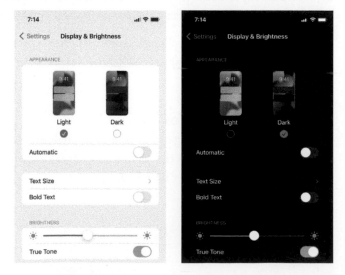

FIGURE 1.28 Apple's light and dark mode options. The light mode feels brighter and more active, as if it's day and time to move around, while the dark mode feels less bright and active, as if it's night and time to sleep.

Typography

In UI design, typography is the arrangement of text in a way that makes the copy legible, clear, and visually appealing to the user (**FIGURE 1.29**).[12] Typography communicates crucial information to the user, such as how to navigate the interface, the status of the user, and how to solve the problem they came to the product for.

FIGURE 1.29 An arrangement of typography on a magazine cover to draw interest from the reader, grab their attention, and communicate what's inside the magazine. (Artisticco LLC/123RF)

Typography also does a very important job of communicating the brand values to the user. Depending on the font style and typeface you choose, you can end up setting completely different moods (**FIGURE 1.30**).[13]

FIGURE 1.30 Despite having the same words, different fonts can lead to different messages. (Kaspri/Shutterstock)

---

12 https://unsplash.com/photos/2X6bkiL0GDo
13 https://www.reddit.com/r/funny/comments/977s8h/font_matters/

In UI design, typography must be more than legible—it must be readable as well. A typeface may be legible—that is, its letters are easy to distinguish from one another—but how we apply that typeface in our designs is how we impact and improve how readable it is.

In **FIGURE 1.31**, both sentences are legible. Each letter in the sentence can be identified. However, the first sentence is much harder to read than the second. This is because each letter is spaced very far away from the next, thus adding extra effort for the reader to identify what is being said. Our typography decisions should be made so that our designs are a lot more usable—in this case, more readable than legible.

Images

In UI design, images are used to communicate brand ideals or content to users.

If we are a luxury brand that values a clean, minimalistic look, then the images we select for our UI would try to create that aesthetic. Perhaps we're a photography studio and we choose single-subject, high-focus objects to portray in our imagery. Or maybe we're a children's brand and we choose imagery filled with lots of colors, shapes, and movement to suggest fun and energy for our users. The style of the images we use in our UI help impart our brand values.

If we are a streaming service, we will use our images to convey the content available for users to engage with. Our UI will use scenes from the streaming content we provide to partition content and suggest different things to watch. We may use specific scenes from those movies to imply the type of content it is, like a ghost walking down a hall to suggest horror, or a woman laughing to suggest comedy. If we are a food company, we may use pictures of recipes to incentivize people to interact with our content, implying the types of meals they could cook.

The images we choose provide context and establish setting and, through our UI, play into the user's experience.

Icons

Like images, icons are visual representations that provide context and establish setting. However, they are a specific type of image in that they have symbolic value that is used to communicate to the user.

Icons symbolize actions a user can take in a UI (**FIGURE 1.32**). A magnifying glass represents the ability to search. A house represents the ability to go to the home of the product. A speaker represents the ability to change the volume. Icons allow us to use fewer words and rely on common images to represent concepts in our UI.

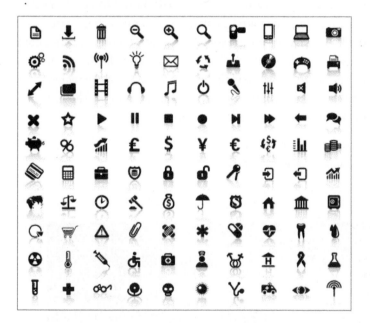

FIGURE 1.32 A set of icons that includes common actions like search, play, pause, email, and volume. Icons pull from real-world representations to communicate common actions to users. (Vector Fave/Shutterstock)

Icons are also influenced by other UIs outside of themselves. Since icons are a representation of a concept, users find UI to be more intuitive if similar concepts are represented in similar ways across different experiences. The icons for "play" and "pause" are fairly universal—a triangle can represent the ability to play content, and two vertical lines next to each other can represent the ability to pause content. This is such a common pattern in UI design that it would be strange to create a UI with the same functionality but different icons.

AUTHOR'S NOTE The meaning of icons changes over time. For example, a Rolodex icon used to represent the contacts in your phone. Now, they're represented by an avatar. As the real world evolves into new meanings, the digital representations of those meanings evolve as well. Since few people use a Rolodex anymore, the design industry has evolved the concept of a Rolodex icon into something that more closely represents the real-world representation of that concept.

What about the icon for "favorite," though? Is there a common icon to represent that action? Perhaps a star? Or a heart? Or a bookmark? These icons have fewer universal patterns across products and tend to represent the content that can be favorited. As a result, these icons vary visually across different interfaces.

Layout

When we take all our UI elements into consideration, we need a system for putting them into our product and having the user move between the various available affordances. To do this, we must establish the layout of our UI. A layout is a set of rules for how you measure, size, and space your UI elements.

Layouts help us establish rhythm and balance for a design. We can use layouts to assign common groupings to related elements, such as creating a card component in the UI that has an image, some text, and an icon of various colors to communicate a singular element. Perhaps this is an episode of a show, and by laying out the elements in a way that makes them look connected (**FIGURE 1.33**),[14] we can communicate the title, an image from the show, a description of it, and an icon that indicates we can play it.

Layouts have a history in print design, but the principles of that history greatly influence digital design to this day.

FIGURE 1.33 Food Network's homepage. There is a main piece of content (the large image in the middle), three additional pieces of content below it, and a TV schedule. The layout of images and text, combined with the rectangles they are bounded by, helps you understand which elements are related and which are separate.

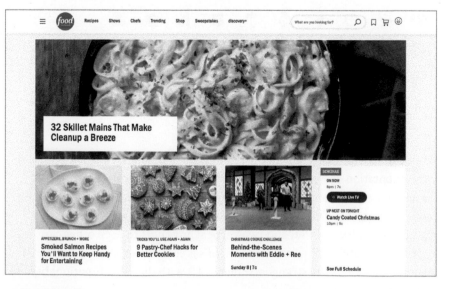

14 www.foodnetwork.com

UI Is a Part of UX

UI exists within UX (**FIGURE 1.34**).[15] It is a part of the user's experience and helps to define how strong that user experience is.

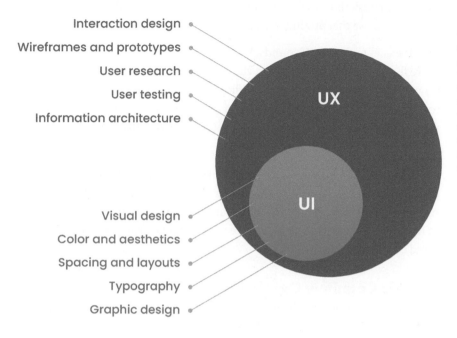

FIGURE 1.34 Kustard's description of the relationship between UX and UI. Although UI is responsible for the visual elements of an experience, visual elements do not compose the entire "design" of that experience—there are additional design elements that make up the user's experience with a product.

At the same time, it is not the complete user experience. The visual elements of a user experience do not fully represent that experience. Although it's an integral part of how a user interacts with a product, the UI of that product makes up but one part of its UX.

Similarly, UX does not exist without UI. A user cannot experience a product without the surfaces that allow that user to operate that product. The UI is a deeply important part of the experience a user has with a product.

---

15 https://medium.com/kustard-design/ui-and-ux-a-simple-explanation-622c4009add3

COGNITIVE OVERLOAD

It is a designer's job to craft and curate experiences. We design products so that users can enjoy them as easily and effortlessly as possible and so that they may accomplish their goals. The design of a product should get out of the way so users can use that product for their own wants and needs.

AUTHOR'S NOTE The next section shows several products that suffer from cognitive overload. While the design of these products does create more for its users to process, the truth is that all these businesses are successful and have been in business for quite some time. The observations made here are not to disparage these companies; rather, they are to illustrate that even successful products have room for improvement.

This is easier to do than it sounds. With the pressures of the business to add more features and functionalities, the constraints of the technologies that power those experiences, and the difficulty to know how to best set up users to succeed at their goals, we can end up creating experiences that overwhelm users and prevent them from getting the job done that they came to us for in the first place.

But there's hope. We can rely on some general heuristics to reduce how much information our users need to absorb. By removing steps in the process, remaining consistent in our visual language, and making information easy to find, we can avoid a situation where users struggle using our products and avoid cognitive overload.

What Is Cognitive Overload?

Imagine you're browsing the web, looking for a new car to purchase. You search using Google for auto dealerships, hoping to find a website where you can browse for different models of cars to compare. While searching, you come across the website shown in **FIGURE 1.35**.[16]

FIGURE 1.35 LingsCars. com has a lot of competing visual elements, from color to motion to typography to sound. Combined, they may lead to overstimulation—a component of cognitive overload.

16 www.lingscars.com

This company is most likely intentionally making the choice, as a brand, to include all these elements in an over-the-top, cheesy, personality-driven way. As a user, however, you might feel overwhelmed. Scanning the website, we see tons of colors, shapes, sections, videos, GIFs, and other visual elements. Where are you supposed to look on the page? Why are there so many moving elements? What does any of this have to do with cars?

You may feel overstimulated when looking at this site. This is a side effect of various design elements of the page affecting your cognitive load. You are trying to understand color, typography, shape, layout, and motion, not to mention the content itself.

In essence, as you try to understand each of these elements and make sense of them all, you are experiencing *cognitive overload*. Your brain literally cannot process all the information it has absorbed until you discard some of it and make sense of the rest. As designers, we don't want our users to experience this. It is our goal, using the design thinking process, to create solutions to our users' problems—not to make their lives more difficult.

To understand cognitive overload and how to avoid it as designers, we must understand what cognitive load is, followed by what affects it.

Cognitive Load Theory

People perceive information, understand it, and hold onto it to use later. We draw from our experiences and make sense of not only the current experience but past experiences as well. Our ability to perceive, understand, and retain information can be broken into three stages: sensory memory, working memory, and long-term memory.

Sensory Memory

First, we must receive information. To do so, we have our senses—our eyes, ears, nose, and everything else that receives sensory information. When experiencing a product, we can use our eyes to read words on a page, to look at shapes and images, or to scan a product for the element we want to interact with.

If we are looking at a page to buy a car, we can use our eyes to scan for something that represents that car, like an image of a car or the word *car*.

Working Memory

Once we perceive information via sensory memory, we move on to working memory. We take the information we received from our senses and start to analyze it. In this stage, we review, or "rehearse," the information. As we do this, we either add this information to our long-term memory or forget it.

When experiencing a product, we might look at a webpage for cars and start to translate information into our working memory. We see images on the page that aren't the image we are looking for, and we forget them. Some of those images might be memorable, however, and we put them into long-term memory for a later date.

Long-Term Memory

Our long-term memory allows us to pull and use information we've perceived and retained. We've experienced information in the past that left an impression, that we took the time to sense, work on, and eventually encode into our long-term memory.

When experiencing a product, we may pull from long-term memory to find what we are looking for. Perhaps we're on that webpage for cars looking for car information—we can pull from our long-term memory to remember what a car looks like and look for a similar image. Or we can remember the previous webpages we've experienced and try to look for that car information in a similar place.

How They Work Together

These three memory banks—sensory, working, and long-term—allow us to navigate an experience, as they all influence our cognitive load.

Cognitive load is the total amount of information your working memory can handle. If your working memory is empty, you can process information. If it's full, then you can't.

Your working memory is influenced by both your sensory memory and your long-term memory. If you have too many pieces of information overloading your sensory memory, then you can't process them all in your working memory. Similarly, if you can't access your long-term memory for information, or spend too much brain power trying to access your long-term memory, you can't process the information in your working memory (**FIGURE 1.36**).[17]

---

17 www.mindtools.com/pages/article/cognitive-load-theory.htm

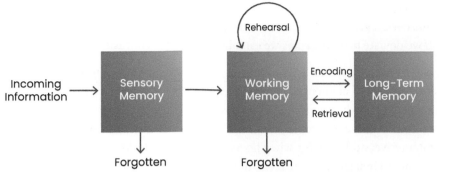

FIGURE 1.36 The model for cognitive load theory. Information enters our senses (such as what we read on a website or hear in a song) and moves through our memory until it is forgotten entirely or encoded in our long-term memory.

Having an understanding of how people process information greatly influences how we design experiences. Ideally, we create experiences that have a low impact on sensory memory and help users avoid needing to access their long-term memory. As designers, we want to enable our users to solve their problems in usable, useful, and delightful ways. Producing cognitive load in our users is something we should strive to avoid.

The issue with the car website is that there are too many design elements that overload sensory memory—we simply have too many things to process into our working memory. As a result, we slow down, we struggle to make sense of the experience, and worst of all, we fail to easily accomplish our goal with the product—to find a car to buy.

Examples of Cognitive Overload

As designers, we have two ways to mitigate cognitive overload:

- Reduce the impact on sensory memory. Less information to process upfront means we can process the information that is present more easily.

- Reduce the need to draw from long-term memory. More information immediately available to us allows us to avoid pulling from our past experiences to make sense of our current one.

Both sensory and long-term memory directly affect working memory, and by balancing these, we can avoid cognitive overload. Let's look at some examples of cognitive overload and how we might be able to address them.

Internal Inconsistency

The design patterns we create in our experiences establish rules for our users. If we deviate from the rules we establish, we create confusion.

A coffee company that sells coffee, tea, food, and other products uses a lot of different visual elements to engage users (FIGURE 1.37). Unfortunately, those elements have different interaction design rules for how they operate. Some of the links have different colors, so it is unclear immediately what is or isn't interactive. Additionally, when hovering over those links, there is no change in state to indicate that the element is interactive.

FIGURE 1.37 A coffee company's homepage. Their design is internally inconsistent—while no one design decision is "better" than another, when used together, they mislead the user.

From a layout perspective, the sections are misaligned. The typography changes as you move through the experience, using different kerning, font weights, sizes, and capitalizations without a consistent set of rules.

In essence, this product is inconsistent with how it displays its visuals and its rules of interactivity.

How could we fix this? Well, as designers, we can create a set of rules for our visual design. We can come up with typography styles and use cases for each of those styles. We can choose a common color for our interactive elements and indicate at a glance which elements are meant to be interactive (FIGURE 1.38).

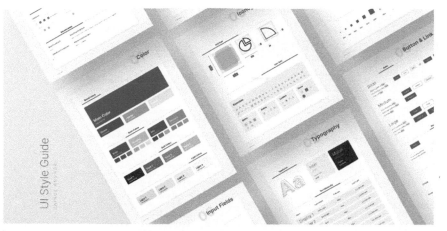

FIGURE 1.38 A UI style guide published via Figma's community. It outlines rules for the visual elements in a product so that the product can be internally consistent across screens.

Establishing these rules for our product, via a design system or a style guide,[18] would greatly reduce the cognitive load of the users who use it.

Unnecessary Actions

A user's sensory memory is dependent on the information that they process, so the more information we present to users, the more they have to process. Therefore, if we can remove information from our products but still allow users to accomplish their goals, then we are reducing their cognitive load in a positive, helpful way.

Consider the e-commerce process of buying an item from a website. If you could eliminate a step in that process, you would reduce the cognitive load of users trying to purchase things from that site. Traditionally, users add an item to a virtual shopping cart, navigate to that shopping cart to view all their items, and then purchase those items on a separate series of pages (FIGURE 1.39).

For e-commerce design, it is becoming more common to reduce steps in the checkout process. Amazon introduced a way to "buy now" instead of adding an item to a cart. This takes the process from multiple steps (add to cart, go to cart, check out from cart) to a single step (buy now). Reducing steps in the process helps users avoid processing unnecessary steps when trying to solve their problems.

---

18 www.figma.com/community/file/905337008546827994

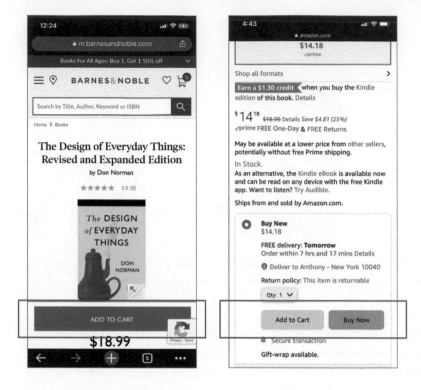

FIGURE 1.39 The product detail pages for Barnes & Noble (left) and Amazon (right). Barnes & Noble has two steps to checkout, while Amazon has one, which removes the cognitive load of an extra action.

Difficult-to-Discover Information

Another way we can inadvertently overload working memory is by making information difficult to discover. This can occur when we bury information in a website or make our website too distracting to notice information—overloading sensory memory. If users rely on their long-term memory to recall common places to look for that information and don't find it in those places, then we tax long-term memory as users continue to access it.

One example of a UI that has hard-to-discover information is Teaa Cafe's website,[19] shown in **FIGURE 1.40**.

On their menu page, we can see all the tea options they sell online. However, there is no additional information here—no nutritional information, product details (size of drink? taste?), or price. At the least, some indication of price or quantity would greatly assist users in evaluating their choices. Unfortunately, that information isn't available in their menu, as none of these cards are interactive—it is just a list with pictures.

---

19 www.teaacafe.com/teas-menu

A fix for this would be to follow the common conventions that other products in the same space have. If many other products offer the same type of information in the same spots on the screen or in the product, then we should probably do the same for our product. There is an expectation that prices are associated with an item in an e-commerce setting, for example, and we should closely link those pieces of information to avoid hiding it from our users unintentionally. For example, Starbucks[20] (**FIGURE 1.41**) is one of the largest beverage companies in the world, and they have a similar UI to Teaa Cafe. However, each of these cards is interactive and provides more details if you click it, such as price, nutritional info, and the ability to add it to your cart.

FIGURE 1.41 Starbucks' online menu. Clicking an image provides information like size, price, availability, and more.

20 www.starbucks.com/menu

Too Many Choices

AUTHOR'S NOTE Hick's law describes this phenomenon. It states that the time it takes to make a decision increases with the number of and complexity of choices. A large library of content will increase the amount of time it takes for a user to find content they want to consume—which has helped lead to a trend around personalization and recommendations.

Another way to overload working memory is by presenting a user with too many choices in the UI. This may not overload sensory memory—it may be easy to understand each option in a streaming service, for example. But the challenge is that working memory must evaluate each option and decide. To hold all those items in working memory is a challenge and will eventually become an overload. This may have happened to you as you scrolled Netflix (**FIGURE 1.42**) looking for something to watch.

One way to address this issue would be to provide other ways for users to navigate the choices you provide them. Netflix provides recommendations, the ability to search for any content item, and, if you scroll far enough, a randomizer that picks a show for you. Netflix realizes that finding something to watch is a problem for their users, even when they provide thousands of options for users to choose from.

FIGURE 1.42 Netflix's UI for browsing content to watch. Netflix has hundreds of options to choose from, which can lead to *choice paralysis* for users.

Overstimulation

If we present too many options to sensory memory, then it may feel like too many things are "talking" to our users at the same time. A combination of color, images, animation, and audio all trying to communicate simultaneously can result in too much stimulation (**FIGURE 1.43**).

We've already discussed the homepage of the Ling's Cars site, but the issues of overstimulation find their way into other parts of the website as well. Text extends out of textboxes, breaking the layout. Various gradients communicate different sections of the website. Each card has different visual treatment, using color as either a signifier or a decorative element—do the blue, yellow, and red behind each card have a meaning in this UI or is it for aesthetics? It's unclear.

The only way to address overstimulation is to reduce. Cut functionality, visual elements, or content in a way that allows users to easily navigate the product.

Reduce Cognitive Overload for Your Users

Every time the user must think while using a product, their working memory is weighed down. The more things a user must process while interacting with a product, the harder it is to complete their goals with that product.

As designers, it's our job to manage the cognitive load of our users. If we have too many design elements or put those elements in the "wrong" places, the cognitive load of our users will increase until they overload and are unable to use our product.

Every design decision we make has the chance of affecting cognitive load. As you make decisions in your work, ask yourself whether your design choices help people reduce their working memory, avoid cognitive overload, and accomplish their goals.

LET'S WORK TOGETHER!

Up to this point, we've covered general definitions and theories for design thinking. Now that we're getting into more practical, hands-on work, we're going to change things up a bit. Together we are going to apply the design thinking process, from start to finish, on a specific problem using the Nielsen Norman Group's model.

I'll start by introducing a problem, then we'll walk through each step of the design thinking process, exploring the problem. I'll introduce a concept or component of the design thinking process, provide examples, then encourage you to do work on that part of the process.

AUTHOR'S NOTE
People really do learn better when they actively apply what they learn. To get the most out of this book, I highly recommend applying the techniques covered here on a problem. If you're transitioning into design, you can even use it as a case study.

If you have a problem in mind that you'd rather work on, go for it! Otherwise, I recommend working on the problem I present so you can practice the concepts we talk about as they come up. This will lead to better retention of these concepts over time.

The problem we'll be working on is the idea of solo travel—how we encourage it, what issues do people experience when traveling alone, and what motivates them to do so in the first place.

For the exercises I propose, Appendix at the end of this book will include example "What Good Looks Like" solutions. I encourage you to follow along!

$$\hat{\mathbf{p}}\Psi = -i\hbar\nabla\Psi = \mathbf{p}\Psi$$

CHAPTER 2

USING EMPATHY AS A DESIGN TOOL

The first step in the design thinking process is to empathize—to imagine ourselves standing in the users' shoes, look through their eyes, and feel what they feel. This allows us to better know their like and dislikes, what motivates them, and what gets in their way.

To accomplish this, we need to conduct research with our users. We can conduct lots of types of research, but one of the most common types (which we will go into depth about) is to talk with our users and hear from them directly. Through conversations, we learn more about their experiences and begin to develop the empathy we need.

Empathizing through design thinking is artistic—to have a conversation with someone else is an art form. Navigating the complexity of a conversation—the content, the context, the emotions—all within seconds of a response time requires you to be nimble, attentive, and present. Conversations are unique, and everyone's style is just a little different.

Empathizing through design thinking is also scientific. There is a methodology in choosing what questions to ask, in what order, and in what ways, so we can avoid bias, allow the participant to feel comfortable, and seek out answers.

By applying both art and science to the empathize phase of design thinking, we can have the conversations that allow us to understand our users' wants and needs, better understand how to solve their problems, and start to develop a solution that changes their experiences for the better.

TYPES OF RESEARCH

You've arrived! You're ready to begin the design thinking process. Looking at the model (FIGURE 2.1),[1] you are at the first step: empathize.

FIGURE 2.1 The NN/g design thinking model. The first step of the model is *empathize*. It is part of the understand phase of design thinking, where you seek to understand more about your users and the problem you are trying to solve.

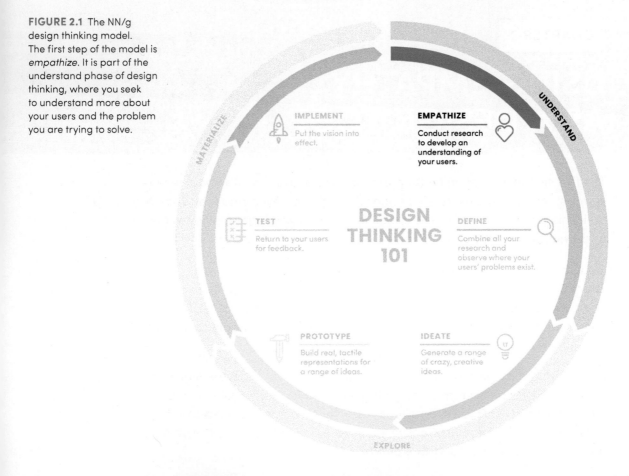

1 Adapted from www.nngroup.com/articles/design-thinking/

You are ready to begin the phase of the project where you try to understand. Who are the users? What are their wants, needs, and goals? What problem are you trying to solve? You will hopefully come to these answers as you move through this phase.

To empathize with users and their problems, you must perform research. You need to talk with the users, or observe them, or learn more about them in some way that lets you empathize with them. Thankfully, there are plenty of research methods that will allow you to do this.

Research, as it applies to design thinking, can be broken into four categories, which are discussed in the following subsections along with ideas from NN/g, the Nielsen Norman Group.[2] Christian Rohrer (an NN/g researcher)[3] has developed matrices for these categories, which are also included in the following subsections.

Behavioral vs. Attitudinal

You can approach research from a usercentric perspective and think about the users' actions, such as what they do in a situation. Perhaps you could create a prototype, give it to people, and watch where they click around the interface. This would be *behavioral research* in that you would observe behaviors as people took actions in an experience.

Alternatively, you could think about the opinions of the users, such as what they think or feel about a situation. Perhaps you use that same prototype, but instead of watching people click around the interface, you ask for their opinions of that interface. Is it intuitive? Does it solve their problems? Would it help them with their goals? This would be *attitudinal research* in that you would record what people say as they were asked questions about an experience.

If you map these two characteristics of research in a chart, you'd get something like FIGURE 2.2. On the top of this axis are behavioral types of research, based on what people *do*. On the bottom of this axis are attitudinal types of research, based on what people *say*.

---

2 www.nngroup.com/articles/which-ux-research-methods
3 www.linkedin.com/in/crohrer/details/experience/

FIGURE 2.2 Christian
Rohrer's research methods
landscape matrix. This portion of the matrix maps out
behavioral research versus
attitudinal research.

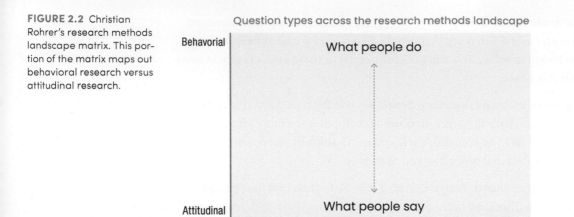

An example of behavioral research would be something like eye tracking, where a user's eye movements are monitored as they look at an interface. This type of research has produced, for example, the F-pattern and Z-pattern[4] for the web.

An example of attitudinal research would be something like a user interview, where a researcher talks with users to understand more about their goals, wants, and needs. This type of research has produced design artifacts like personas (representations of our target user), where you attain a better under-standing of the people you design for.

F-PATTERN AND Z-PATTERN READING BEHAVIOR

In digital products, there are common layouts that help users read text on a page. Two of the most popular are the F-pattern and Z-pattern, which get their names from the shapes of their letters. An F-pattern causes users to scan for information on the page in the shape of a letter *F*, reading the top first, then a little bit of the next section, then finally looking down the left side of the page for information. The Z-pattern does something similar, except in the shape of the letter *Z*.

4 https://99designs.com/blog/tips/visual-hierarchy-landing-page-designs/

Qualitative vs. Quantitative

You can also approach research strategy from a feedback perspective. Are you obtaining information directly, by having a conversation with users? Or are you obtaining it indirectly, by having them fill out a survey?

If you map those characteristics to a chart, you'd get something like FIGURE 2.3.

Question types across the research methods landscape

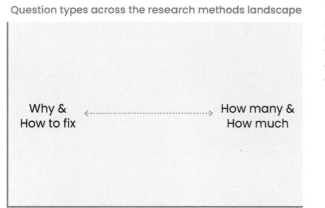

Qualitative (Direct) Quantitative (Indirect)

FIGURE 2.3 Christian Rohrer's research methods landscape matrix. This portion of the matrix maps out qualitative research versus quantitative research.

On one side of the x-axis are direct research methods, which are qualitative and based on a *why*. On the other side of the x-axis are indirect research methods, which are quantitative and based on a *quantity*.

An example of qualitative research would be a focus group, where you bring in several users to discuss a problem and work with them to understand why that problem exists and how to fix it. Focus groups are less common in product design, but could still occur in the context of branding, for example.

An example of quantitative research would be an unmoderated UX study, where participants try to complete tasks in a UI without any direction or guidance. You gain quantitative data, learning how many users can complete a task or how much time it takes to complete the task without guidance.

The Research Landscape Chart

If you combine these two axes, you get the chart in **FIGURE 2.4**. Using this matrix, you can map out all the different types of user research to consider (**FIGURE 2.5**).

FIGURE 2.4 Christian Rohrer's research methods landscape matrix, fully put together.

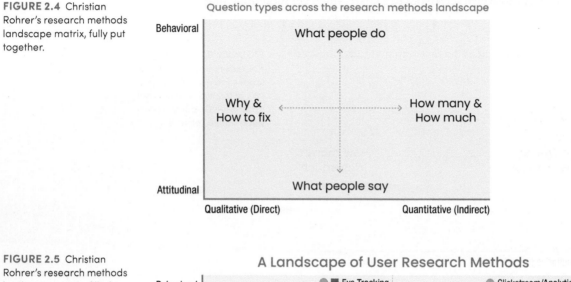

Question types across the research methods landscape

FIGURE 2.5 Christian Rohrer's research methods landscape matrix, filled in with example types of research. An interview, for example, is a form of attitudinal, qualitative research, as you record the opinions people have and form qualitative data. A/B testing is a form of behavioral, quantitative research, as you record the actions people take in an experience and form quantitative data.

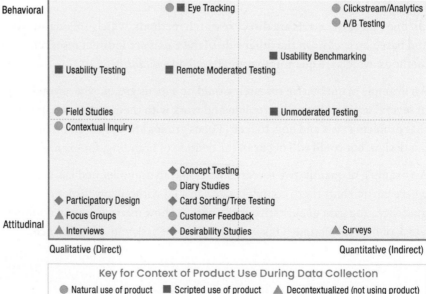

A Landscape of User Research Methods

Figure 2.5 includes a comprehensive list of the different types of research available to you as a designer. Based on this matrix, you can start to think about how to conduct research.

Do you need to talk with users via an interview? If so, you need direct contact with those users and attitudinal questions to ask them. What are their goals when they come to the product? What are some of the pain points when using our product? How do they currently solve their problems? You can start to structure the research approach depending on the type of research you choose to conduct.

Conversely, you can use this matrix to think about the type of data you want to know. Are you curious about click-through rates in our product? Well, you need to know how many people can complete a task on our website, and how much time it takes for them to do so. Referencing the matrix, you see that you want quantitative, behavioral information, and from there choose a method like clickstream analysis.

Now that you have a sense of the types of research you can conduct and what categories they fall under, let's look at the instances in which you'll want to use these methods.

Stages of Design Research

Depending on where you are in your projects (and your research budget), you will want to conduct different types of research. You can think of research occurring in three points in time:

- Before you begin to design (before the *ideate* step of the design thinking process)

- After you have created some designs (after *ideate*, but before *implement*)

- After your designs have been released (after *implement*)

Formative Research

The purpose of formative research is to align what you want to make with what users want to use. The goal is to build a picture of users while also understanding any solutions that currently exist to their problems. You have several methods you can use to get a better understanding of these things.

SURVEYS

Surveys are a great way to get a lot of information about users with a small amount of time invested. You can create a form with a few questions you want answers to and send it to a lot of participants to generate qualitative and quantitative information. Additionally, you can create screener surveys, which function as a filter for finding users you really want to talk with (**FIGURE 2.6**).

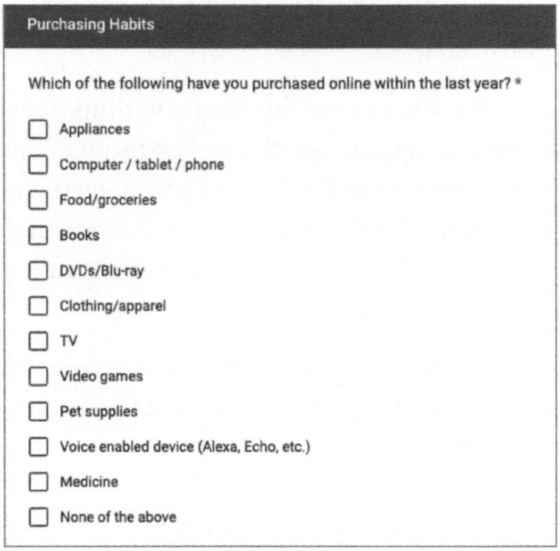

FIGURE 2.6 A survey question about online purchasing habits

Purchasing Habits

Which of the following have you purchased online within the last year? *

☐ Appliances
☐ Computer / tablet / phone
☐ Food/groceries
☐ Books
☐ DVDs/Blu-ray
☐ Clothing/apparel
☐ TV
☐ Video games
☐ Pet supplies
☐ Voice enabled device (Alexa, Echo, etc.)
☐ Medicine
☐ None of the above

INTERVIEWS

Once you've identified a few users you want to talk with, you can schedule conversations with them. User interviews (**FIGURE 2.7**) are excellent opportunities to directly ask questions and better understand people's motivations. You can go into detailed conversations to understand what they need, and dive deeper into those needs by asking "why?" directly.

FIGURE 2.7 In a user interview, a researcher asks questions about a person's opinions and experiences to gain data about their wants and needs. (Edvard Nalbantjan/Shutterstock)

COMPETITIVE ANALYSIS

In addition to understanding your users, it's crucial to understand the products that exist in the marketplace. Are there other businesses that have solved this problem already? What can you do to solve the problem differently? Are there common conventions in your industry that you need to be aware of as a designer, such as the way users are used to seeing content? By understanding the competition, you can get a sense of what works, what doesn't, and how you can improve it.

You can do competitive research in many ways. You can create a comparison table (like the one in FIGURE 2.8) to identify which features are most prominent across different products, which would let you know market expectations. You can conduct usability tests of your competitors' products to better understand the usability of those products and see what does or doesn't work for users. You can do user-perception tests of other products to learn how people experience those products and what they think of the competition. You can do a lot related to competitive analysis. Chapter 3, "Defining the User's Problem," will go into more detail.

Figure 2.8 is an example of some formative research I did for a project at Kaplan. I was working on a dashboard redesign for educators that informed them of their students' progress throughout a course. The product manager for that project talked to teachers daily and asked a few of them to participate in user interviews. We spoke to those teachers to understand how they used the platform in its current form, and we learned of some places we could improve. This research was formative—it allowed us to form opinions about the problems we wanted to solve.

Features by Platform	Atom	Moodle	Blackboard	Canvas	ACT	Edementum	Edulastic
View Scores for All Students	✔	✔	✔	✔	✔	✔	✔
View Scores for Single Student	✔	✔		✔	✔	✔	✔
View Assessment Area Breakdowns		✔			✔	✔	✔
Self-Service Table Customization	✔	✔	✔			✔	
Score / Status Categorization	✔	✔	✔	✔	✔		✔
Manual Grading	✔	✔	✔	✔			
Set Grading Rubrics		✔	✔	✔		✔	
Add Notes		✔	✔	✔			
Message Student		✔	✔	✔			
Predict Final Score					✔		
Compare to National					✔		
Sync with SIS			✔				
Import Scores		✔	✔	✔			
Export Scores	✔	✔	✔	✔		✔	
IMS Score Integration	✔						

FIGURE 2.8 A table comparing the features of a new platform to those of its competitors.

Additionally, we looked at competing educational platforms that had dashboards for teachers to learn about student progress. We made a comparison table (Figure 2.8) that allowed us to understand which features were more common across all our competitors. This was also formative research. Based on the table, we formed opinions on what features to focus on for the relaunch of our platform.

Once you have a good understanding of your users and competitors, you would move on in the design thinking process. You'd define the problem to solve, ideate possibilities, and eventually design solutions. When those solutions are ready to be shown to users, you'd conduct usability research.

Evaluative Research

The purpose of evaluative research (**FIGURE 2.9**) is to validate assumptions and make sure designs work. Can users use what you made? Does it make sense, and is it intuitive? Or does it fail? That's OK too—you haven't launched it yet. You need to know what works and what doesn't so you can improve your designs and release them.

FIGURE 2.9 A usability study in which a researcher asks someone to use an experience and provide feedback about it. (GaudiLab/Shutterstock)

This works with anything you've made: sketches, wireframes, prototypes, live apps, or even websites. You can conduct usability research in the earlier steps of the design thinking process with, for example, competitor products to expose the usability issues in those products. Or you can conduct usability research on your existing product, to learn how you can enhance it.

You can also revisit conversations with users you spoke with during the background research. A user you interviewed at the start of your project could come back to test the designs, and you could ask them how well you succeeded.

Going back to the Kaplan example, we also performed evaluative research on our redesign of the dashboard. We conducted usability testing with the users we interviewed—the teachers who were going to use the platform—and asked them to complete a few tasks in a prototype. We observed their thoughts and feelings as we tracked task completion rates, places where the designs didn't make sense to them, and the elements of our design that really worked well. With this evaluative research, we were able to evaluate what worked about the design and what didn't so that we'd know what we needed to revise before we built the product.

Once your evaluative research is in a place where you feel ready to implement the designs, you can move on in the process. You would finish your designs, build them with developers, then watch as users start to adopt your product. After some product usage, you could conduct research to see how our product is doing.

Summative Research

The purpose of summative research (sometimes called *ROI*, or *return on investment*, research), is to see the product's performance. How is what you made doing? How is it performing in terms of its design, usability, sales, revenue, conversion, or engagement?

Several methods are very informative for this type of research.

ANALYTICS

Analytics allow you to gather a large amount of quantitative data (**FIGURE 2.10**) about how things are performing. For example, you could observe your SEO (search engine optimization) to understand how many people come to your website and how often. It's behavioral rather than attitudinal, however, so you won't necessarily understand why.

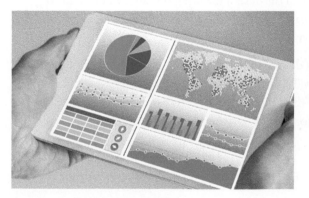

FIGURE 2.10 Analytics provide behavioral insight into how people move around a product and use it, such as what source they come from, how long they stay in the product, and what actions they take while they are in it. (a-image/ Shutterstock)

A/B TESTING

You could also conduct A/B testing in your product (**FIGURE 2.11**). What is it like to change a word or a color? To move an image from the left side of the screen to the right? This type of testing is quite granular and happens with more mature products looking to optimize their designs. Google is famous for an extreme example of this type of testing, where they tested 41 different shades of blue to determine the optimal color for incentivizing engagement.[5]

FIGURE 2.11 A/B testing allows you to test two versions of a design to understand which one performs better. Even simple changes, like changing a color, can result in improved results for the product. (MPFphotography/Shutterstock)

USER ENGAGEMENT SCORES

A more attitudinal research method for understanding the performance of your product is to ask users how they feel after using it. One way to do so is by using CSAT, or customer satisfaction, scores (**FIGURE 2.12**). This method asks users to rate whether their expectations have been met after using the product. You can take those ratings and average them to determine how satisfied users are after using a product.

Since this is the first stage of the design thinking process, you'll want to conduct background research. That means you'll need to understand who the users are, and what currently exists to help them.

For the student progress dashboard redesign project at Kaplan, we conducted summative research as well. After we launched the redesign, we spoke with teachers to hear more of their thoughts about the product. We tracked the performance of the platform, such as which features were being used more

---

5 www.theguardian.com/technology/2014/feb/05/why-google-engineers-designers

than others. We also collected user-engagement scores in a process like the survey in Figure 2.12.

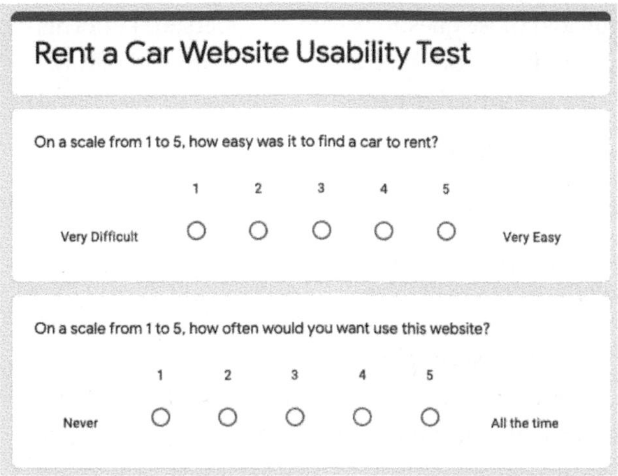

FIGURE 2.12 A survey that asks for user engagement scores.

Research Is an Ongoing Process

User research can happen at any stage in your product's lifecycle. You may need to understand more about the problem you're trying to solve—if so, conduct background research. If you're wondering whether people can use your solution, conduct usability research. If you're more curious about how your product is performing, conduct ROI research.

Truthfully, you should be doing all three types of research for your products. Learning more about our users and how you can help them with their goals is an ongoing process that allows you to make the best solutions you can for the people you design for.

SURVEYS

One primary way you can understand more about users and empathize with them is to hear their stories, their thoughts, their wants and needs by asking them questions about their opinions and experiences. Surveys are a perfect tool for us to do so. In this section, we'll cover surveys—what they are, how to write them, and how to use them in the empathize step of the design thinking process.

What Is a Survey?

In the context of design, a UX research survey is a set of questions sent to a targeted group of users that probes their attitudes and preferences. Users are asked questions in a form, and those questions help us understand information about our product, an industry, or users' attitudes toward something (remember that surveys are attitudinal in nature, as opposed to behavioral).

You use research surveys for two purposes:

- To gain information about users (qualitative or quantitative)
- To recruit potential users for research (user interviews, usability studies, and so on)

For both purposes, surveys can be very valuable as a scalable form of research. It's difficult to invest time talking to each user and asking them questions; with surveys, you can send a link to a large number of people and get a lot of data quickly with low effort. There's an initial investment, but it pays dividends once you do the work to create the survey.

To make a survey, and to make it well, you need to consider the steps to conducting survey-based research.

Start with an Objective

Surveys begin with a research objective. What is the purpose of the survey? Why do you need to use this research method to obtain the information (or users) you're looking for? What do you hope to gain by opening a survey? And how will you analyze your responses? You need a research plan so you're well prepared for recruiting participants and analyzing your results.

Ask Questions Around the Objective

Once you know the point of your study, you can ask questions around it. Your questions should be focused on that objective—don't ask questions that do not directly support your objective.

For example, if you are trying to learn about ride-share app habits, do you need to know the average annual income of your users? Do you need to know their age? Or their ethnicity? You may be tempted to ask questions you think would help you build a profile of your users, but each question you ask makes it harder for your users to complete your survey. Stick to the crucial questions that support your objective.

Recruit Participants

Once your survey has a good structure, you can research people for your study. How will you find participants? Do you have an email list you can send a link through? Do you have a product with the ability to survey your users within it? Do you have any company (or personal) social media accounts that you could post to? Any of these methods could be appropriate for your research—the purpose is to get participants, ideally ones who are your target users, though sometimes you can be a little more relaxed about who you send surveys to (such as for a usability study).

AUTHOR'S NOTE I send surveys for my personal projects via social media. I use LinkedIn, Slack, and Discord design groups that I belong to, and I ask my friends if they'd like to be involved.

Analyze Responses

Once you've sent your survey and received enough responses, you can use those responses as a data set. Some survey providers, like Google Forms, provide data visualizations for each question you ask, which you can use to form opinions about your users and better empathize. These responses can inform your opinion of who you want to design for, influence your ideation, and even help you determine certain people to interview.

Reach Out to Key Participants

As you look at your responses, you may find certain participants who would be great candidates to follow up with for an interview. You can contact these respondents and ask if they would be open to speaking with you about some additional questions. In fact, there is a subset of surveys, called *screener surveys*, that are designed to filter for appropriate candidates to do individual research with (like a user interview).

AUTHOR'S NOTE I like to include a question at the end of all my surveys asking if the respondent is open to participating in a 10-to-15-minute call. That way, I can more easily follow up with respondents I want to interview.

With a good understanding of how to structure a survey, let's look at how you can structure questions.

Survey Question Types

Broadly speaking, a survey can have two types of questions:

- Closed-response questions

- Open-response questions

Closed-Response Questions

Closed-response questions are those that offer users a limited number of possible answers. The set of possible answers is "closed" and is defined by you, the researcher.

The example questions in **FIGURE 2.13** are closed. The two questions have a set number of response possibilities, all of which were written and decided by the researcher. In this example, the researcher is seeking a specific information point about participants and is using these questions to filter users into categories around that point. For example, this researcher may want to see the patterns of people who shop online "often." In that case, they may want to look only at responses from those who shop online once a month. If that's the case, the researcher would filter out responses from users who select the responses that are longer than one month.

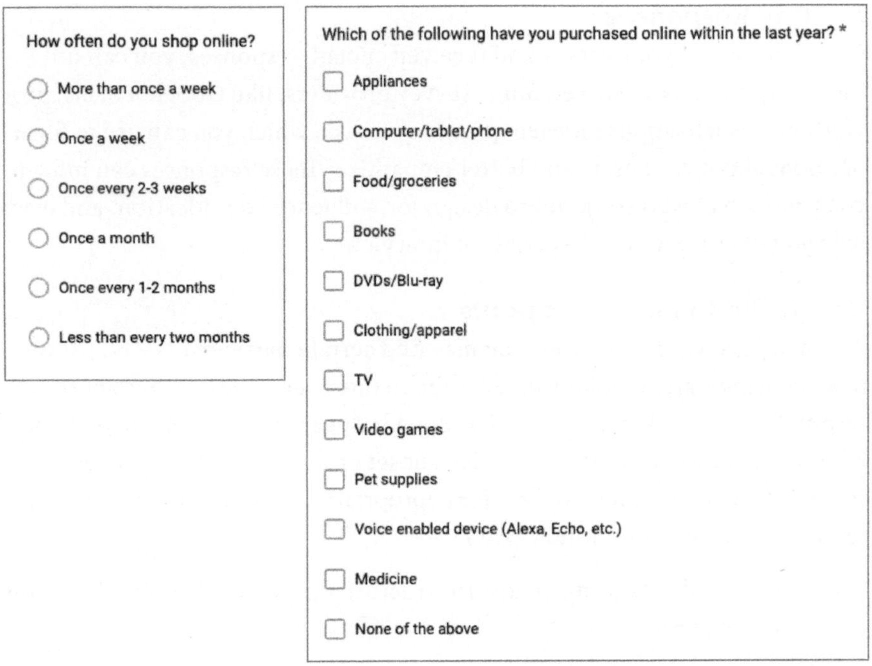

FIGURE 2.13 Two examples of closed questions. Closed questions can be single response (radio buttons) or multiple response (check boxes).

How often do you shop online?

◯ More than once a week

◯ Once a week

◯ Once every 2-3 weeks

◯ Once a month

◯ Once every 1-2 months

◯ Less than every two months

Which of the following have you purchased online within the last year? *

☐ Appliances

☐ Computer/tablet/phone

☐ Food/groceries

☐ Books

☐ DVDs/Blu-ray

☐ Clothing/apparel

☐ TV

☐ Video games

☐ Pet supplies

☐ Voice enabled device (Alexa, Echo, etc.)

☐ Medicine

☐ None of the above

Closed-response questions are quantitative in nature. They lack context, motivation, or cause, but they are easy to visualize and simple for participants to answer (they click a button rather than write a response).

Closed-response questions are usually easy to identify—they have check boxes or radio buttons and are usually multiple choice.

Open-Response Questions

The opposite of the closed-response question is the *open-response* question, for which users can provide whatever answer they feel is appropriate. The set of possible answers is **open** and is defined by your users, who provide answers in the words they think are best.

The example questions in FIGURE 2.14 are "open," as they allow users to provide whatever answer they feel is appropriate. Here, the researcher is a teacher looking to learn what the class understood from the lesson. The teacher has no way of knowing what students specifically learned and, as a result, needs them to say what they understood. Here, the teacher is seeking feedback from students, and it's up to the students to provide that feedback. The teacher would use the results of the survey to better adjust educational materials, or revisit concepts in class that a lot of students say they didn't understand.

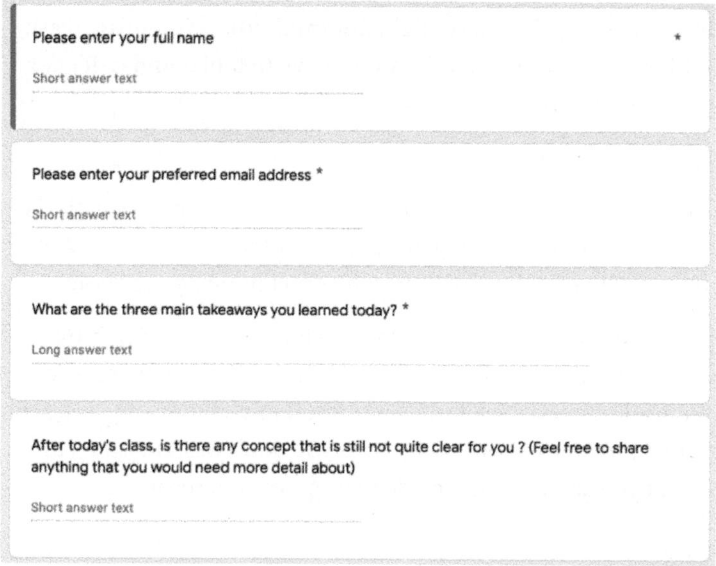

FIGURE 2.14 Several open-response questions that ask the user to input information rather than select from a set of prede-termined answers.

Open-response questions are qualitative in nature. Answer responses contain behavior around an action, or how a user thinks about a problem. They're excellent at getting users to describe the situation in their own words, which flows nicely into persona work or advocating for users when building your product. But because the answers aren't organized into a system (like they are with closed questions), they take a lot longer to analyze and are harder to sort.

You can recognize an open-response question in a survey by looking for text boxes. These input fields are the primary way researchers structure open-response questions.

Survey Best Practices

When writing your own surveys, you should keep in mind some best practices to ensure you get quality and quantity responses.

Ask "Easy" Questions

Users will need to navigate your entire survey. If you ask complicated questions, or ones that are long or have a lot of responses to choose from, you are at risk of overwhelming your users. Questions should be easy to understand and easy to answer.

Ask "Neutral" Questions

Questions should be asked in a neutral way, to avoid assuming an answer or introducing bias. If you ask, "What is great about our product?" you are assuming your product is great (users might not think so). If you instead ask, "What do you think about our product?" you remove that bias and will get a different quality to the responses.

Cover All Conditions

When structuring closed-response questions, you need to think through the logic of those questions. Make sure you have every answer choice in your set of responses, or else you may alienate users who don't fit into your choices.

Let's revisit the closed-response question from before (**FIGURE 2.15**). Think about our question with the last answer choice removed. If you did so, the survey question would be comprehensive but would miss out on any user who doesn't shop online every two months. Perhaps you don't want to know more about that user, but you should still include that option as a response.

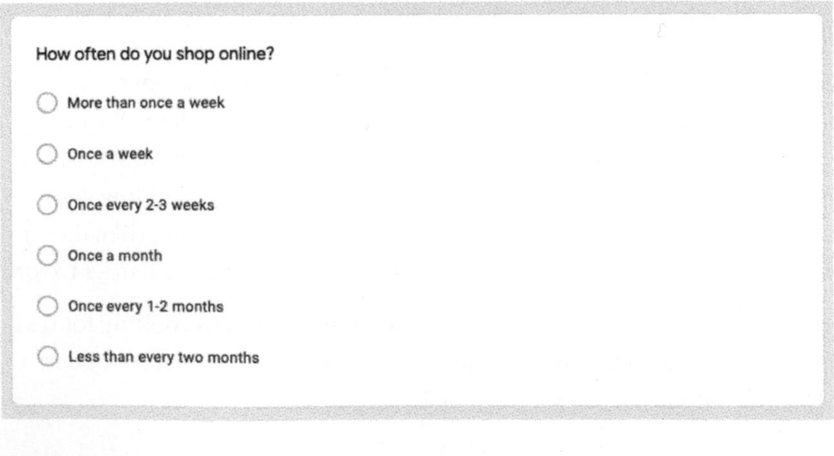

AUTHOR'S NOTE Although you should be neutral in your questions to avoid intentionally directing your user's feedback, you can still ask the questions "What do you like?" and "What do you dislike?" as they give good general feedback about the user's sentiment.

FIGURE 2.15 When using closed-response questions, make sure every logical possibility is covered. What if a respondent shops online every day? What if they never shop online? We've covered all logical possibilities by structuring the question in this way.

How often do you shop online?

- More than once a week
- Once a week
- Once every 2-3 weeks
- Once a month
- Once every 1-2 months
- Less than every two months

Keep It Short

Be mindful of how long your survey is. The longer your survey, the lower your completion rates will be. Write shorter surveys to have better completion rates. This is why it's crucial to ask the most important, most relevant questions for what you're trying to learn. Even a single wasted question will affect how many people complete your survey.

Show Progress

If you can, use a tool that allows users to view their progress when taking the survey. Knowing how long a survey will take will improve your completion rates for users who begin your survey, as users will have an understanding of how much time they must spend on it. Tools like Google Forms, Qualtrics, and Typeform are good at displaying completion rates for respondents as they fill out the survey.

Test It

As with all your designs, you should test your survey before inviting users to complete it. As you should for a prototype, test your survey internally or with a small segment of people before sharing it widely with the public. Does the survey behave as you expect it to? Did you leave out crucial questions? Do some questions feel incorrectly written? This is the perfect time to make sure what you wrote works.

AUTHOR'S NOTE I like sharing my survey with a team member and asking them to fill it out to get some good feedback on how other people will interpret it.

Survey Bias

When you're creating and distributing surveys, be mindful of introducing bias. Bias can adjust the quality of responses and result in you drawing conclusions from research that are incorrect or don't accurately represent the users. There are various forms of bias—how you write your questions, how you distribute your surveys, and how you interpret your results.

LEADING QUESTIONS

Priming occurs when you write questions in a way that leads users to an answer choice. Imagine you list all your website's service options in a question and ask users which ones they use. Then in the next question, you ask users if your website is robust and has a lot of options. You're introducing bias in this test—you just showed users all your options and then asked if you have a lot of options. Instead, flip the order of these questions—first ask if users think you have a lot of options, then ask which options they use. It may look like a small change, but it's important to avoid that type of bias in your study.

DOUBLE-BARRELED QUESTIONS

Double-barreled questions ask two things at the same time. Each question should elicit a single response to make it clearer and easier for your users and to avoid bundling answers together. For example, if you ask, "Do you want to buy jeans and a T-shirt?" you exclude users who want to buy one of those items but not both.

UNDERCOVERAGE

Undercoverage occurs when you send out a survey and miss a percentage of the population in the results. For example, think of telephone surveys. It's common to survey people's opinions of political candidates by calling landlines and questioning the people who respond. This technique, however, misses any person who doesn't have a landline or who screens their phone calls.

To avoid undercoverage, try to send surveys to multiple locations.

NONRESPONSE

Nonresponse bias occurs when you send out a survey and the people who choose to complete it are meaningfully different from the people who don't. Perhaps the people who are inclined to complete the survey have a different personality type or set of opinions, which would affect the results meaningfully. Consider census data, for example, where non-respondents may be in a different economic situation than respondents. Or perhaps they could be digital nomads, traveling from city to city without a permanent address or one that they check often.

It's hard to avoid all types of bias. But being aware of them will allow you to best structure your surveys and to best search for people to take them.

Recruiting Participants

Once the survey is ready to go and you are confident about its structure and content, you can begin to find people to talk with. There are many methods of recruitment—some more feasible than others, depending on your working situation.

AUTHOR'S NOTE Recruiting the right participants has a lot of nuances. It varies widely, depending on the product, audience, and questions you want answered. As a result, it's very challenging to have a one-size-fits-all survey. Try to find people that fit the parameters of who you are designing for and what you want to know.

Current Users

One of the best ways to get feedback about your product is to ask the people who currently use it. They have the most context and are the most invested in your product to provide quality feedback about it. You can find these users by putting links in your product to surveys or emailing your users through the product itself.

Social Media

Social media is the best way to get feedback for your personal projects or if you have a limited research budget. Posting your survey on LinkedIn, through Slack or Discord groups, or through other social media channels can get participants quite easily. The quality of these participants is uncertain, however, since you lack the context of their experience with your product (and you don't know if they even fit into your user demographics). This is a method that's valuable for fast and easy research, however, and one that is common among students especially.

Recruitment Services

If you have an extensive research budget, this option can help ensure quality participants. Services like Maze, UserTesting.com, and more can find users for you based on a set of parameters you provide. You can filter by age, income, product usage, or professional industry to target more specific users. This also allows you to avoid asking these types of questions in the survey itself, which gives you more time to ask the questions you really want to know the answers to.

Online Advertisements

As with the social media approach, you can take out ads asking for users to complete your surveys. Sometimes paired with compensation, this method is the widest-reaching one for finding users—which puts the quality of your survey at risk. Still, it's a possible method that research teams with the budget to do so employ.

AUTHOR'S NOTE If you
work for a large organi-
zation, you may be able
to pull some of this from
your company's databases
and avoid asking a few of
these preliminary demo-
graphic questions. It'll save
your users time filling out
the survey.

Survey Example

With all this in mind, let's look at an example survey created for a student
project to understand user opinions regarding electronics e-commerce.

The survey begins with some simple logistical information: name and email
(FIGURE 2.16). These pieces of information are relevant for us to reach out to
this individual should we want to conduct an interview.

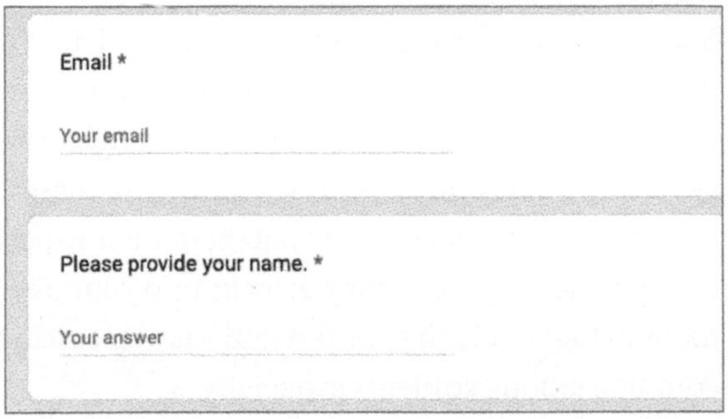

FIGURE 2.16 The first two
questions of our survey.
They're easy, not too commit-
tal, and logistically important.

Next, we ask about online shopping behavior—here (FIGURE 2.17), we want
to filter for people who shop online often, as they are the target audience and
more familiar with online shopping.

FIGURE 2.17 A closed,
single-response question.

Next, we ask about purchasing habits (FIGURE 2.18). We want to avoid priming users or leading them to a specific response, so even though we care only
about electronics purchases, we add other types of goods here as well to avoid
that type of bias. We are most interested in the electronics purchases, such as
a computer or TV.

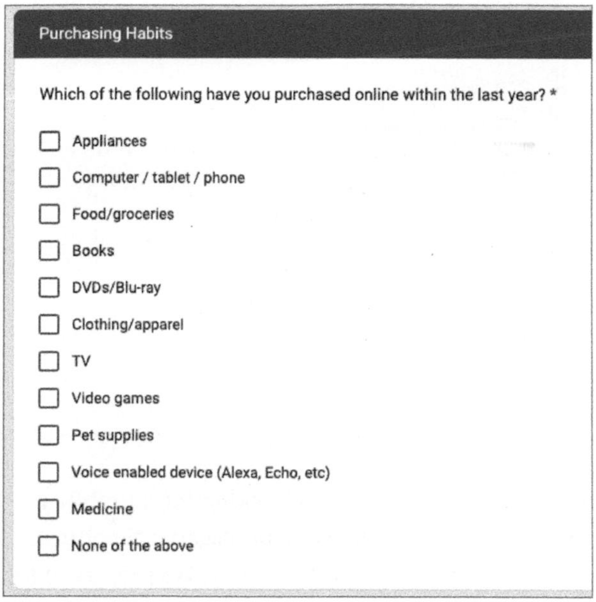

FIGURE 2.18 A closed, multiple-response question.

Next, we ask about the device used to make the purchase (**FIGURE 2.19**). We care mostly about desktop devices for the design problem, so we are trying to filter for that device.

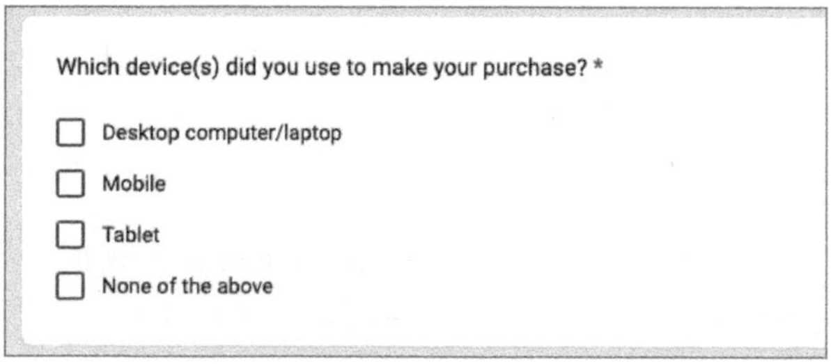

FIGURE 2.19 Another closed, multiple-response question.

Next, we ask about the stores (**FIGURE 2.20**) used to make the purchase. In this project, we are trying to redesign Best Buy's website, so we hope to speak to users who have used that site before. However, we're still open to talk with people who use other sites, so it all depends on how users respond to this question.

FIGURE 2.20 A closed,
multiple-response question
to determine the stores
where the respondent
makes purchases.

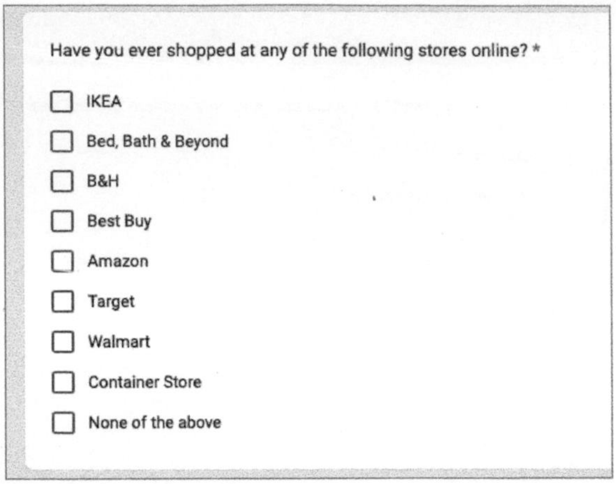

Have you ever shopped at any of the following stores online? *

☐ IKEA

☐ Bed, Bath & Beyond

☐ B&H

☐ Best Buy

☐ Amazon

☐ Target

☐ Walmart

☐ Container Store

☐ None of the above

Lastly, we want to know whether the user is open to conducting a usability test with us during a certain time range—we had a tight research timeline for this project and needed to talk with people immediately. We prescreen for users willing to speak to us (FIGURE 2.21) so we don't waste time asking them and waiting for a response from someone uninterested.

FIGURE 2.21 A closed, single-response question to determine the receptiveness to an interview.

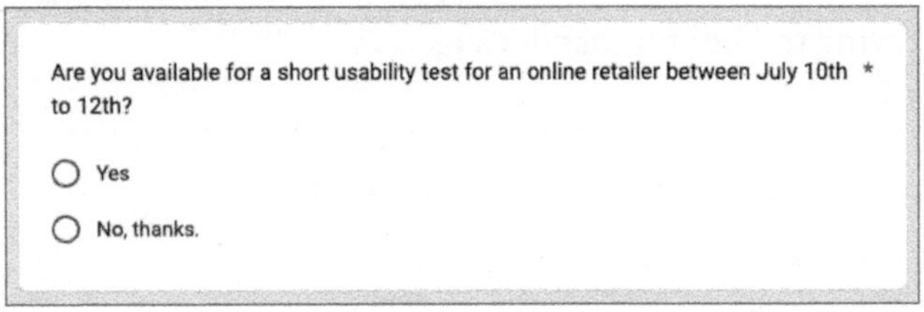

Are you available for a short usability test for an online retailer between July 10th * to 12th?

○ Yes

○ No, thanks.

This survey was sent out via social media, and after 30 participants took it, we found enough people for us to talk with directly for our research.

Using methods like these will enable you to conduct your own research, no matter the problem you are trying to solve.

Let's Do It!

Now that we've covered what makes a good survey, let's make one for ourselves! Remember that the problem space you want to apply design thinking to is solo travel—what can you do to encourage or otherwise support solo travel? You want to enrich and improve the lives of solo travelers.

To do so, you need to understand more about the solo traveler. Who are they? What do they want? What do they need? What are their goals?

To do this, you need to find solo travelers and talk with them.

To find solo travelers, one method to use is the survey. If you create a survey and distribute it to the public, you can find solo travelers to speak with and ask them about their experiences.

Your task? Create a screener survey for solo travelers. To do this, keep the tenets of good survey design in mind:

- **Be neutral.** Don't lead users toward one answer or another.

- **Be short.** Don't ask too many questions, or people won't fill out your survey.

- **Ask easy questions.** Survey respondents shouldn't have to think too hard when answering questions, and they shouldn't be writing essays. Save the harder questions for the actual interviews.

Remember, you are *screening* for participants. The survey should be designed to find *great* people to talk with, not to answer all your questions.

You can use whatever platform you like, but I recommend Google Forms for simplicity, cost, and the ability to share with others.

AUTHOR'S NOTE Refer to the "Surveys" section of Chapter 2 in the appendix for examples to compare your survey with.

PREPARING FOR USER INTERVIEWS

One of the primary ways you learn from others when designing is by talking with them about their opinions and experiences. You do this through user interviews—a technique that allows you to have a conversation with users, learn their goals and frustrations, and hear stories about their experiences. You then use the data generated this way to move forward in the design process, creating design artifacts that help you empathize with users as you start to think about solutions.

So much of design thinking involves designing for other people. Imagine yourself in a scenario and think about what you would do in that scenario, but you must remember that you aren't the user. Although you may have opinions about a situation, you can't assume that your wants and needs are the same as those of the people you are designing for. The best way to understand the target audience is to learn from them directly.

Let's take a closer look at what a user interview is and how to prepare for one.

What Is a User Interview?

A user interview is a research method in which a researcher asks a participant questions with the intent to uncover information regarding that participant's behavior and preferences. User interviews are a great way to collect insights directly from users, one on one. They can be done at multiple stages of the design process, depending on where your team is at and what you're trying to learn. Most commonly, they are done at the beginning of the design thinking process, when you are trying to empathize and understand the users.

Generally speaking, a user interview consists of the following elements:

- A facilitator to conduct the interview

- A participant to provide information during the interview

- A note-taker or note-taking device to capture information from the interview

- A script that the facilitator uses to conduct the interview

Each one of these elements helps ensure you are prepared for the conversation, able to pay full attention to the user, and can capture the data you need to move forward in the design thinking process.

How Do You Start Preparing?

To have an efficient, successful interview, it's important to do as much preparation as you can. One way to prepare is by coming up with a list of questions you have about your users' experiences. By knowing what questions you want to ask in advance of the interview, you can create a well thought-out, structured interview that gets the most information possible from the people you speak with. To do this, you can create something called a *user interview script*.

A user interview script is a list of questions you want to ask research participants, structured around the topic you wish to understand better. It's a roadmap, or a set of guidelines, to conduct research and navigate a conversation with real users to obtain the information you need to empathize with them and design for them.

To build one, align as a team around the questions you want to ask participants. Debate the pieces of information you need to learn during a conversation so that you are well-prepared to ask the right questions and not waste users' time or bias the test in any way. By taking the time to build a script, you can enter an interview with clear, unbiased, and non-leading questions.

Let's look at the anatomy of a user interview script.

Introduction

At the beginning of each user interview, take time to introduce yourself. Explain who you are, why you're here today, and the context around what you're working on. Set the expectations for how much time it will take and the types of questions you'll ask. Provide time for your participant to ask any questions as well.

Here's a sample introduction I've used before on projects:

> *Hi there! I'm a designer working at [company] on [product vertical]. I'm looking to learn more about your thoughts and opinions on the [industry I work in]. I'm going to ask you some questions today about how you interact with [product]. Overall, this should take around [number of minutes]. How does that sound? Do you have any questions before we begin?*

The goal at this stage is to make sure the user is comfortable, that expectations are clear, and that everything is ready to go for the interview.

I also like to add one extra part at the beginning that helps segue into the interview and allow the user to feel comfortable with recording the conversation:

> *Great. One last thing—before we begin, would you mind if I record this session? It'll be used only to share internally with my team later.*

This piece is important to ask so that the user is aware they are being recorded and gives you their permission to do so. You're capturing data about your users, and it's respectful to inform users you are doing so and to gain their permission before you start recording.

You might think users won't give you permission if you ask explicitly, but it's the right thing to do, to preserve their wishes and treat their information as sensitive. Additionally, in some states, it is illegal to record someone without their permission. Thankfully, just about every user I've asked this question has given me permission—out of all the user interviews I've done before, I've had someone request not to be recorded only once.

Opening Questions

These questions get the interview started. They should be easy to answer and easy to follow. They aren't typically demographic in nature, as that information comes from something like a screener survey. Rather, they're used to get the user comfortable and ready to think about the topics you want to discuss.

What do you do for a living?

Are you familiar with [product]?

How often do you use [product]?

The goal here is to get users warmed up for the interview. These questions are supposed to be simple, introductory questions that establish rapport with the user and get them comfortable with providing answers. A few simple questions that invite the user to participate and show that you're listening to their responses opens the interview for deeper questions (and responses) later.

These questions also frame the user interview, as they get the user to start thinking about the product and how they use it.

Specific Questions

After the users are comfortable and thinking about the main topic, ask questions that allow you to better empathize and design. These are the questions that help inform the features, the product you want to make, or how you can better solve the users' problems.

Imagine you were working on a payments product and trying to understand more about users' behaviors around making donations. You seek to understand how people find and donate to charitable causes. To do so, you need to learn more about the specifics around these topics—how do people find them? How often, in general, do they donate to them? What motivates them to donate, and why? You could ask several different questions, like so:

How do you usually discover causes to donate toward?

When was the last time you donated to a cause?

What motivates you to donate to a cause?

Additionally, you may have research goals around creating campaigns for causes, not just discovering and donating to them. You can probe into this behavior, with the goal of creating a marketplace for people to create causes and for others to find and donate to them:

Have you ever created a campaign for people to donate toward?

How did you promote your campaign?

What would encourage you to create a campaign?

Closing Remarks

At the end of the interview, it's important to provide a few minutes to wrap things up and give the space for any information you didn't plan to discover. To do so, you will want to invite the user to share anything they haven't yet. End the interview with the question:

Is there anything else you'd like to share with us?

This will allow you to learn about new pieces of information you may want to explore in your research. If a user responds with:

Yes, I'd love to tell you about this product I use all the time…

Then you have a new source of inspiration you can look at for your ideation, a step that occurs later in the design thinking process. Give users the space to tell you about unprompted information. Great questions to ask at the end of an interview include:

Is there anything else you'd like to share with us?

Is there anything we didn't talk about today?

What's one thing I didn't mention yet that I should know about?

Once the interview is over, thank your users for their time, and take some time on your end to review your notes or write down any observations that stood out in your mind during the interview. Ideally, you'll have another person taking notes, you'll record the session, or both so that you can review it later.

Question Quality

To help scripts be as effective as possible, you should consider the quality of questions and how you structure them, to achieve the best information possible from users so that you may help them.

Open-ended

Open-ended questions are crucial for getting the most information out of users. They require elaboration and can't be answered as easily as a binary question. Look at the following question:

Do you like our product?

What are the possible responses here? A user will answer the question—yes or no. Did that give you enough information? Do you know more about their preferences or attitudes? Unfortunately, these types of questions don't add enough to give you more context and need to be elaborated on. Usually, you'll have to follow up with "why" to get more information.

Let's improve it:

What do you like about our product?

Now, it's more open ended. It requires the user to think and say what they like. This question will give you more information.

Unbiased

Questions should avoid biasing users' responses. Instead of assuming a certain quality or attribute about a situation or attitude, remain neutral—and the questions should as well. Consider the previous question:

What do you like about our product?

Sounds pretty innocent—it is an open-ended question about the user's attitude toward the product. However, this question already assumes part of the answer—that our product is liked.

Let's improve it:

What do you think about our product?

Now, that bias is gone—the user may not like it. Maybe they don't like anything about the product. That's information you need to know! This gives the user the opportunity to share what's on the top of their mind, rather than stay in the confines of a liked aspect of the product.

Past Experiences

By nature, user interviews are attitudinal. You are asking questions about how users feel, what they perceive, and what they think about situations and experiences. You get data about their current state of thinking.

AUTHOR'S NOTE You don't have to already have a product to do user interviews. For example, you could ask about a user's situation instead of their use of a product. Write interview questions that help you get the answers you're looking for.

However, it can be advantageous to ask users to recall how they acted, to gain context around their use cases. Getting users to think about the last time they took an action will get them to think about the situation, and the context around that situation, which will improve the quality of the information you get from them.

Consider the question from before:

What do you think about our product?

This is a good interview question, and one you should ask, but let's toss another question in front of it:

Could you tell me about the last time you used our product?

Here, you are asking users to imagine a scenario in which they used the product—in this case, the last time they used it. They'll think deeply of that experience, trying to recall the goal they had, the steps they took, and the outcome. By asking this question first, then asking what they think about it, they'll be able to recall their most recent experiences with the product information you'll want to know.

AUTHOR'S NOTE If you didn't have a product to work on and instead were curious about behavior more generally, you could ask something like "Tell me about the last time you experienced _____."

How Can You Structure the Script?

People always want to know how many questions to ask in an interview. Too few and you waste a lot of opportunity to learn the answers you wish to know. Too many and you run out of time or fail to go deep enough into behaviors and desires to get great data.

I find it's good to work backward from the questions I have and how long the interview will be. I like to approach my interviewing flexibly, with enough content to make the interview worth it but not so much content that I fail to gain answers to my most critical questions.

Generally, I structure interviews like so:

1. Have a core set of your most important questions. These are your biggest, deepest unanswered curiosities, which will represent the bulk of your interview time.

2. Have a set of follow-up questions to your most important questions. These allow you to probe more deeply in case your core questions don't reveal enough data.

3. Have a set of backup questions. These are things you're curious about but are secondary to the most important unanswered areas for your research.

I then structure my interview script around my core questions, with follow-up questions for the core questions should I need them, and backup questions to help probe for ancillary wants and needs. It would look something like this:

1. Greetings

2. Permission to record

3. Icebreaker/easy-to-answer question

4. Core question 1
   Follow-up

5. Core question 2
   Follow-up

6. Core question 3
   Follow-up

7. Core question 4
   Follow-up

8. Core question 5
   Follow-up

9. Backup question 1

10. Backup question 2

11. Backup question 3

12. Final thoughts

If I make it through all my script, great! If not, that's OK too—I got most core questions answered because I put them first.

Structuring the script in this way allows for multiple interviewee participation styles:

- *If the participant talks too little*, I have enough content to fill the interview and follow-up questions to promote dialogue.

- *If the participant talks too much*, I prioritize the main content and if I don't hit the extra content, that's not a big deal.

I like having a short, simple warmup question to start most interviews. This helps ease the participant into the interview, breaks the ice so the participant feels more comfortable, and sets the tone for the conversation. Having an easy-to-answer question at the start gives the participant confidence in their answers and loosens them up to be more candid for later questions.

I also like to structure my scripts so the participant isn't jumping around mentally. I'll group related ideas and make sure the script flows between ideas naturally, rather than jump around between similar concepts. Asking a participant to recall an answer from two questions ago adds cognitive load and confuses them. I like to keep the script flowing between related concepts rather than ask about a thing, ask about a new thing, and then go back to the old thing.

It looks something like this:

1. Greetings

2. Permission to record

3. Concept 1

4. Concept 2 (builds off 1)

5. Concept 3 (builds off 2)

6. Concept 4 (unrelated to any previous concepts)

7. Concept 5 (builds off 4)

8. ...

This way, each question flows into the next (and sometimes builds off the previous) so that the participant logically proceeds from one step of the interview to the next—just like a product experience I would design for them.

As for the number of questions to ask, that depends on how much time you have and how complicated your questions are. I can't give a general answer that will cover all use cases, but a good rule of thumb for a 30-minute interview is six to eight core questions and as many backups as you'd like. Setup and final thoughts take a few minutes, and you don't want the interview to feel rushed, so expect to get good answers to six to eight of the questions you have.

Prepare Beforehand for a Smooth, Well-Structured Interview

By preparing and putting thought into your script—the way you ask questions, the language in those questions, and the order to those questions—you can construct a well thought-out, well-flowing script to interview users with.

Let's Do It!

Now that you've seen how to create a user interview script, let's make one for our project. Remember that the problem space you want to apply design thinking to is solo travel—what can you do to encourage or otherwise support solo travel? You want to enrich and improve the lives of solo travelers.

To do so, you need to understand more about the solo traveler. What are their wants, their needs, their frustrations? Why do they travel alone? What stops them from doing so?

To understand more about their experiences, you need to talk with solo travelers. With your screener survey, you were able to find good candidates to speak with. Now, you want to ask them all your questions.

Take some time to think about what questions you have for solo travelers. Do you want to know why they travel alone? Perhaps how they travel alone? What about the difference between traveling alone versus in a group? These are all valid questions to have in mind for conversations with solo travelers.

Your task is to create a user interview script that you will use to talk with the solo travelers you found via your screener survey.

AUTHOR'S NOTE Refer to the "Interview Script" section of Chapter 2 in the appendix for examples to compare your survey with. Remember to keep the tenets of good interview scripts in mind:

- Ask permission to record and remind participants that conversations are private.

- Keep questions open-ended and unbiased. Don't assume answers and put those assumptions into your questions.

- Make sure your questions have a flow to them—try to think of a logical progression to your questions, and make sure you group themes into similar sections in your script.

CONDUCTING USER INTERVIEWS

Once you've put together the user interview script, you're finally ready to start talking to users. Hopefully, you find users to speak with via the screener survey or another recruitment method that homes in on finding the ideal candidate, but you can also ask friends, family, or strangers, provided you think they will be representative of the target users.

After you schedule interviews, start having the conversations that will establish the backbone of research efforts and filter into future design thinking work.

Finding Participants

Finding the right users to interview is crucial. Since design thinking builds off itself as you move through each step in the process, the users you speak with become the foundation of the product you build. Thus, it's ideal if you find the "right" people to speak with.

Who are the right people, though? That's up to you and your team to decide. Who do you want to target? Are you building a mobile recipe app? Then you'll probably want to talk to people who cook a lot or are interested in cooking but are blocked in some way. Are you building a learning dashboard? Then you'll want to talk with students, or with teachers who would manage those dashboards. Try to think of the ideal types of people who would use and love the product you want to build.

What about the right number of people? For user interviews, this isn't clear. For complex persona work, for example, you need to talk with a lot of people to develop a robust, clear understanding of the market and your users. Unfortunately, most teams don't have the time or money to invest in this. For quicker projects, you can make proto-personas, or archetypes of your users, with just a handful of interviews. To start, I'd recommend at least six—that should give you enough data to work with when analyzing your results. If you're looking for more nuanced details for your personas, I'd recommend somewhere from 15 to 20 participants.

After you have an idea of who and how many people to interview, you need to find them. You can do that in a few ways.

AUTHOR'S NOTE Although they may not be the "ideal" users, friends and family can be a great resource when conducting the design thinking process for a personal project.

AUTHOR'S NOTE I've had teachers tell me they speak to no fewer than 100 people to develop personas for clients. This is deep, high-level research best handled by specific client engagements and dedicated research teams in multiyear projects. You don't need that many interviews to get a sense of how you can help people and where to start.

Surveys

Sending out screener surveys is an effective way to find users to interview. You can write a survey that is structured to home in on the ideal user. If you have an idea of your users—such as that they shop online often—then you can write a survey and include questions about shopping habits. You can reach out to the users who indicate that they shop a lot.

It's common to send out screener surveys that answer high-level questions you have about the market (perhaps how often people take a certain behavior) and gain some information about market trends. For the users who seem promising, bring them in to talk. It's a two-tiered approach to getting really good information.

It's common to receive surveys in emails, on websites, and even in specialized groups via Slack, Discord, or message forums. When researching your project, you can do the same. Try to find the communities that could have the users you want. If you want to interview writers, try looking at common blogging sites like Medium. To talk with gamers, you can hop onto popular Discord servers and drop a link to your survey to see who answers.

Social Media

You can find the popular communities for your users and post to social media asking for user interview participants. If you want to find people who like guitar, you could head to Facebook and post to guitar groups.

Alternatively, if you have a social media presence, you can ask your friends and family to participate in research to help you. This is a common method for students, for example, who may not have the budget or network to afford compensating individuals for their time.

Recruitment Services

To recruit users, you can also rely on companies like UserTesting.com, Mechanical Turk, or Maze. These companies find users for you, for a fee. Although potentially costly, they help filter for demographic information, which lets you home in on the best user possible. Additionally, the user population has already opted in to being involved in research, so you know that whoever passes your criteria will want to be involved in a research study. Since user interviews are so crucial to the entire design thinking process, it's common to make the investment upfront to get the best quality you can.

Guerilla Testing

On the opposite end of the spectrum of targeted service-driven user recruitment is guerilla testing. This is a do-it-yourself approach to recruitment—you go to a physical location where your target users congregate and talk with them yourself.

If you know you want to talk with avid book readers, go to a bookstore and find strangers willing to answer a few questions. Or perhaps you want to talk with nature lovers—go to a park.

This method has the highest variability, because you don't know if the willing people will be good interview candidates. However, it's a faster way to get results and a low-cost way to do so.

Each method of recruitment has its pros and cons and can be valid depending on your time, budget, and comfort level. Once you have your users, the next step is to conduct the interview.

Interviewing Your Participants

After all your preparation, it's time to interview! This is one of the most exciting parts of the process—when you speak directly to the people you want to help. It can be challenging to have these conversations because there are so many ways to navigate them, and it takes practice to become good at doing interviews.

Your users are probably nervous too! You're about to ask them a bunch of potentially personal questions about what they do and what they think, and they might not know what to expect.

Luckily, you can do some things to make this process easier.

Make Sure Users Are Comfortable

At the beginning of the conversation, ensure your users are comfortable. Asking if they want any water or need anything before the interview starts can go a long way toward making them more comfortable.

If your users aren't comfortable, the conversation will be awkward, and it will be difficult to learn from them. Start by asking them how they are doing today, then explain the interview process:

> *Hi there! I'm [name], and I'm working on a problem to better understand [issue]. How are you doing today?*

We're meeting today to discuss your experiences with [issue]. We're going to spend around [amount of time] talking. Do you have any questions for me before we begin?

Capture Audio/Video

To make sure you capture all the information revealed during the interview, record the conversation. If you can, you can avoid taking notes. This has a powerful, subtle effect—you can focus completely on the conversation and the user, fully engaging them in the interview, rather than focus on taking notes or writing down a quote. Ideally, there is both a notetaker and a facilitator present, but you can get by with just yourself and rely on technology to record the conversation.

When recording a conversation, make sure you have your user's permission:

Would you mind if I record our conversation? It will be helpful to have a record to refer to. I promise that I'll use it only for internal purposes, to share with my team and reflect on, and it won't be used publicly.

Ask Why/Clarifying a Response

When asking questions from your script, it's easy to stick to each question and move through it, like going down a shopping list. However, make sure you have received a satisfactory answer to your question before proceeding to the next one. If you don't fully understand a user's motivation behind an answer, you need to ask for clarification. Simply asking "why?" can get you that clarity.

Imagine the following conversation:

Do you like our app?

"*Yes!*

Perfect! Moving on...

The interviewer missed an opportunity to learn why the user likes the app. Knowing that reason helps you probe into motivation, attitudes, and feelings around the behaviors and opinions you seek to understand. Let's see what could happen if you follow up on that response.

Do you like our app?

Yes!

Interviewer pauses for a moment... why do you like our app?

Because it's easy to use!

...Why is it easy to use?

Because I understand where everything's placed, and it's just there, ready for me to use!

Ah, OK, great!

Another tactic you can use in place of asking why is silence. If you don't say anything, your participant may feel compelled to fill that silence with more information.

Do you like our app?

Yes!

....

...because it's easy to use!

....

...I understand where everything's placed and it's just there, ready for me to use!

Ah, OK, great!

User interviews are really challenging to do, and to do well. To see an example of a talented researcher (**FIGURE 2.22**) in action, check out this great video where a researcher speaks with a participant about her experiences (www. youtube.com/watch?v=eNMTJTnrTQQ).

FIGURE 2.22
A demonstration of a qualitative interview done well. (Studio 8/ Pearson Education Ltd)

After the Interview

Once the interview concludes, thank your participant for their time. If there's any follow-up, like payment, make sure you have a plan for that as well.

As for the content of the interview, you can do a few things to make it easier for you to analyze your results.

Take Notes Post Interview

Immediately after the interview, write down key observations. The conversation is still fresh in your mind, and you'll want to highlight things. Some shorthand notes of where to look back, or overall impressions, will help you later.

AUTHOR'S NOTE I like to schedule interviews with 10- to 15-minute breaks between them so I have time to reflect on a completed interview and write down my most important observations. This helps me highlight the important parts of the last interview while adjusting the script if needed as I prepare for the next one.

Transcribe Audio into Text

Once you have the recording from the interview, it can be difficult to transcribe that information into design thinking artifacts like transcripts and pull quotes (which are really valuable for highlighting key insights from the conversation). Using audio transcription services like Otter.ai[6] make this process a lot faster and will help you pull information once you're ready to synthesize all your interviews.

Let's Do It!

Let's start finding some users to talk with for our project! You have the screener survey and the script. Now, you can send out that screener survey (if you haven't already) to various forums and social media channels to start finding users to talk to.

AUTHOR'S NOTE Whatever number you target, I recommend adding one or two more users to that number in case an interview goes poorly, such as if you don't get enough data, the user cancels, or the user isn't a good fit for your project.

Alternatively, if you want to spend a bit of money to find users, feel free to use some of the other resources discussed in this chapter to recruit users, like UserTesting.com[7] or another recruitment service.

The goal of this activity is to speak to users for our project. Schedule six to eight interviews and start having conversations with your target users.

To make the interviews more successful and capture good data, try the following:

- Be polite and explain the purpose of the interview—that you are looking to learn more about solo travelers and their experiences.

---

6 www.otter.ai/
7 http://usertesting.com/

- Ask permission to record, and remind the participants that conversations are private.

- Ask follow-up questions if you don't understand the core reason behind a participant's answer. The question "why?" or silence after a response are perfect ways to get users to elaborate further.

- Schedule breaks between your interviews to take notes and prepare for the next conversation. Even a few minutes of down time helps you reset and focus for the following interview.

AFFINITY MAPPING

Once interviews are complete, you'll have a lot of data from users. You'll have heard a lot of stories about their experiences and have a good understanding of what they want and what they need. But what are you supposed to do with all this information? How do you sort it in a way that helps focus and move forward in the design thinking process?

Luckily, there is a technique that allows you to take the data from all your user interviews and organize that data in a way that helps you understand users better. This process is known as *affinity mapping*, and it's the final step to paint a clear picture of the types of people you are trying to design for.

What Is Affinity Mapping?

The purpose of the first step of the design thinking process is to empathize. You must find users, learn more about them, and discover their wants, needs, and frustrations. The goal is to understand them so you can create something that helps them.

As a final part of the empathize step, you have a good understanding of who you are designing for. Here, you take all the user research and combine it into something called a persona—a type of person to design for. To do so, you need to take insights from the user interviews and search for any themes that emerge (**FIGURE 2.23**). This process is called affinity mapping.

AUTHOR'S NOTE This can also be done with digital tools if you prefer, such as Miro or FigJam. The purpose of the exercise is to organize similarities across different users to produce themes.

Affinity mapping is a way to turn interview notes into insights about users. The process begins by writing observations on sticky notes. You comb through user interview transcripts for insights that stood out during the interview, like a quote, a behavior, a like, or a dislike. You write each single observation on its own sticky note and put that on a wall or whiteboard.

FIGURE 2.23 An affinity map, which groups user interview data into themes that inform our design thinking goals.

FIGURE 2.23 An affinity map, which groups user interview data into themes that inform our design thinking goals.

AUTHOR'S NOTE If you choose to do this with sticky notes, I recommend using a Sharpie and writing in all capital letters. This will allow you to see each note more clearly at a glance.

Once you have written all the observations from across all the interviews, you start the sorting process. Place similar notes into groups. Analyze those groups to form insights. Finally, refine and reframe the groups as needed until you come to a clearer picture of the users.

To watch this process in action, the Nielsen Norman Group has prepared an excellent video[8] of a real-world affinity mapping session (they call it affinity diagramming in this video, but it's the same concept).

Affinity Mapping Process

Affinity mapping is simple. First, write down all the key observations from your research.

FIGURE 2.24 shows three participants that were interviewed about a food app, for example. They answered questions about their pain points, goals, frustrations, and behaviors around cooking. Those observations became sticky notes in the affinity map.

---

8 www.youtube.com/watch?v=C4nYxZxteJY&ab_channel=NNgroup

Next, take similar concepts and create groupings.

For the food app, we took the individual observations and grouped similar ones. FIGURE 2.25 shows observed food preferences, how often people cook, and where they find recipes. This will help when trying to create someone to design for! Trends are developing in the data.

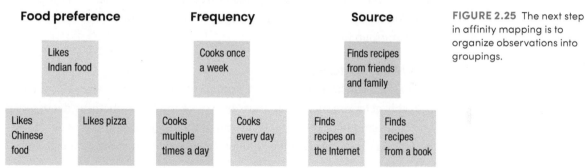

FIGURE 2.25 The next step in affinity mapping is to organize observations into groupings.

Finally, take those groupings and come up with *I statements* for each category.

In the food app example, we change less empathetic phrases like "frequency" or "source" into powerful, user-driven sentiments like "I cook regularly" or "I find from all over" (FIGURE 2.26). Imagine someone saying these things, which is where their power lies. It's a lot easier to feel for users and be empathetic with these statements. They are statements you can define the problem to solve with. Perhaps you want to create an app for someone who cooks regularly—that's an aspect you can ideate around. Maybe a food app with reminders, or rotating content? This puts you in an excellent place to eventually design.

FIGURE 2.26 The last step in affinity mapping is to create titles for each grouping. The titles become behaviors and attributes for the persona—the representation of the target user.

I like certain food

Likes Indian food

Likes Chinese food

Likes pizza

I cook regularly

Cooks once a week

Cooks multiple times a day

Cooks every day

I find from all over

Finds recipes from friends and family

Finds recipes on the Internet

Finds recipes from a book

As you make your clusters, be wary of the distribution of information in them. Let's look at a few potential pitfalls when making groupings.

Too Few Data Points

If you have too few data points, you can't call it an insight that applies to a lot of users. For example, if you interview six people and then create a group in the affinity map that has fewer than three sticky notes, then that observation doesn't show up frequently enough. Try putting those observations in another group instead.

Too Many Data Points

Similarly, if you have too many data points in a group (more than 10), you can probably get more specific. It's possible you're missing something deeper, or you could gain multiple insights instead of the single insight you're currently getting. Try breaking them up into multiple insights by splitting the group.

Too Few Perspectives

If you have a grouping with too many sticky notes from a single source, then that insight might not apply to the entire group. Be mindful of having a single user interview skew the results of your affinity map. If a grouping has too many of a single user, see if other users can fit into that theme as well, or consider not including that theme in your results (**FIGURE 2.27**).

Not Sure Where It Goes? Put It in the Parking Lot

If you can't immediately find a home for an observation, that's OK! Sometimes you'll see an observation, not be sure where to put it, and feel confused. That's a natural part of this process.

Too few

FIGURE 2.27 Examples of group-ings that could be better sorted in an affinity map. Too few observa-tions in an insight won't apply for everyone. Too many observations in an insight can be split out into multiple insights. Too many obser-vations from a single user will lead to bias for your persona.

Too similar

Too many

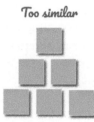

Luckily, there's a technique called the *parking lot* to store observations temporarily as you decide where they should go. As you sort your data, come back to the parking lot from time to time and see if any of those observations fit into a category. Over time, you'll add and remove items from the parking lot as you make more sense of your data.

Let's Do It!

Now that you have the user interview data, you can start to affinity map that data to better understand users.

To do so, take the observations, put them on sticky notes, and sort those sticky notes into themes.

Remember the following advice as you sort your data:

- One observation per sticky note.

- Groupings should have "enough" observations in them to be called themes (not too few, not too many, and not all from a single user).

- Write *I statements* for your insights once your observations have been grouped. These statements will be helpful for the next step in the process.

AUTHOR'S NOTE Refer to the "Data Set" section of Chapter 2 in the appendix for examples to compare your data set with.

AFTER YOU EMPATHIZE, YOU DEFINE

You've successfully completed the first step in the design thinking process—to empathize with your users. You've done research to understand who they are, what they want, what motivates them, and what gets in their way. You've put together surveys to find the right users to talk with, written a script to have conversations with them, and finally had interviews with them to uncover those behaviors and needs. You've then taken observations from those interviews and sorted them into groupings, to develop insights into the target users. With that information, you'll be able to move on to the next step in the design thinking process—to define the target user, explore their current state, and determine the problem to solve for them.

CHAPTER 3

DEFINING THE USER'S PROBLEMS

Design thinking is about solving other people's problems. It's a process that gets us out of our heads and helps us see things from another person's perspective so we can understand their wants and needs.

To do this, we need a baseline. We need to define the current state of things—to come up with a clear understanding of who we are designing for, what their experiences are like, and what problems we want to solve for them. Only when we have a well-structured foundation can we build on top of it in a meaningful way.

To define this baseline, we need to create a representation of users that we can refer to when talking about the current state. We need to portray how these users live today so we can create a better tomorrow. We also need to define the overarching problem to solve so we have clear alignment and understanding of where to look for that tomorrow.

Defining the problem is an art. We create design artifacts that tell stories based on the stories we've heard throughout the research. We look to other examples of comparable products to experience how users solve their problems today. We carefully craft the language of the problem to solve, choosing words carefully and artfully.

Defining the problem is also a science. We make statements based on thorough research and data. We gather additional data from comparable products. We rely on a formula to write the problem to solve, working systematically toward the structure of the problem statement.

The second step in design thinking is all about definitions, and it begins by defining the people we are designing for—our users.

WHERE ARE YOU IN THE DESIGN THINKING PROCESS?

As you wrap up the user research, you transition from the empathize step to the define step (FIGURE 3.1).[1]

During the define step, the goal is to take all research and understanding about the users and apply it to the initial problem you want to explore. At the end of this step, you should have an excellent understanding of the target users, a great sense of their experiences, and a more clearly defined problem to solve.

What are their motivations? Their frustrations? What do they want to accomplish, and what gets in the way for them? These are all things that you need to understand so you can design experiences that allow them to achieve their goals despite their blockers.

But who are the users, and what do they want? You can create a process artifact that allows you to represent the target user—a tool called a persona.

1 www.nngroup.com/articles/design-thinking/

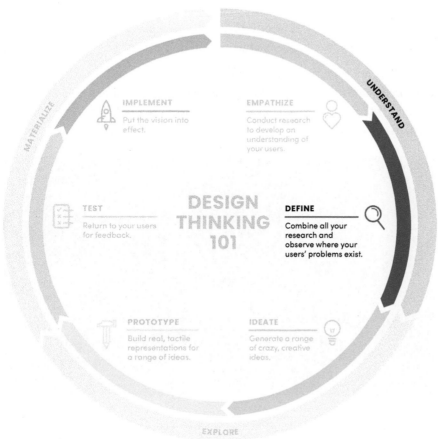

FIGURE 3.1 The NN/g design thinking model. The second step of the model is *define*. It is part of the understand phase of design thinking, where you take the information you've learned from users and put it together to form a better understanding of the problem to solve.

PERSONAS

Designing for someone else is challenging when you don't know who they are—what they like, what they struggle with, what they want to achieve. Realistically, you won't be able to fully understand every single person who uses your product—you can't be everywhere at once, so you probably won't be with them as they use your product. However, design thinking has a technique that allows you to approximate the characteristics of the people who will use your product—the persona.

What Is a Persona?

A persona is a functional yet realistic description of a typical or target user. It's not a living human, but rather an abstraction of one. You create them based on what you observe in the research with users. You call them personas but refer to them by a real name rather than call them "users." Empathizing with a *person* is easier than empathizing with a *user*.

FIGURE 3.2 is a persona I created while working on a project for a cryptocurrency platform that functioned similarly to an NFT marketplace. This persona, Matt, embodies all the research that went into the project before we created our designs.

FIGURE 3.2 A persona for a non-fungible tokens (NFT) marketplace.

BIO

Matt enjoys watching football, participating in fantasy sports leagues with friends, playing esports, and watching people stream his favorite games. When watching a stream, Matt enjoys that he can interact in real time, no only learning about the streamer's in-game strategy, but their personality as well.

Matt loves the social aspects of esports and feels at home in the community, whether chatting online during a stream, attending a live event, or watching from a bar. Because he spends so much time with the game, he forms opinions about the players. His opinions are backed by research, statistics, and his "gut", and he makes predictions on who will win based on information and intuition. He enjoys being right as much as he enjoys the trash talk that comes from discussing the game with his friends.

Matt Age: 25
Job: Developer

LEAGUE OF LEGENDS DOTA 2
OVERWATCH NFL

GOALS
- Stay up-to-date with players and community
- Connect with others online and in person
- Discuss individual games and the metagame
- Compete with others based on the player and Matt's game knowledge
- Feel invested in players long-term

FRUSTRATIONS
- Not receiving recognition for his knowledge/predictions
- Playing with the limited regular fantasy sports roster
- Waiting until the season begins to play fantasy sports
- Searching through scattered news and data
- Evaluating information can be challenging

AUTHOR'S NOTE There are a lot of ways to organize the information in a persona, with many templates and iterations available to use. We'll be working from an example persona, but feel free to visually lay out your persona in whatever way you like—provided it contains all the information in the following subsections.

When you create a persona, you take the observed goals, wants, needs, motivations, and frustrations of users from your research and map them into trends that the user population experiences. You take those trends and create a persona based on those trends so that you have something to point to while designing. Give the persona a name—"Jane" or "John"—and when you design, point to those personas to influence your thinking. Ask questions like "How does this feature help Jane?" or "Would John be able to use this product?" Personas help align teams around who the design is for.

What's the anatomy of a persona, and how can you create a persona for your projects? Generally, personas contain certain elements that you looked for during your research:

- Name/photo
- Overview
- Background/bio
- Likes/goals
- Dislikes/frustrations

Name/Photo

Every persona consists of identifying pieces of information that allow you to refer to that persona during conversations about your product. Your persona needs a name and photo, so everyone on the project can call it by its name and use its photo in other design deliverables.

Looking at the example persona in **FIGURE 3.3**, you see two immediately identifying pieces of information that help center and contextualize the target users—the name and the photo. A face and name help you empathize with the target user and make it easier to care more about them. You may even start to associate the name and photo with people you know.

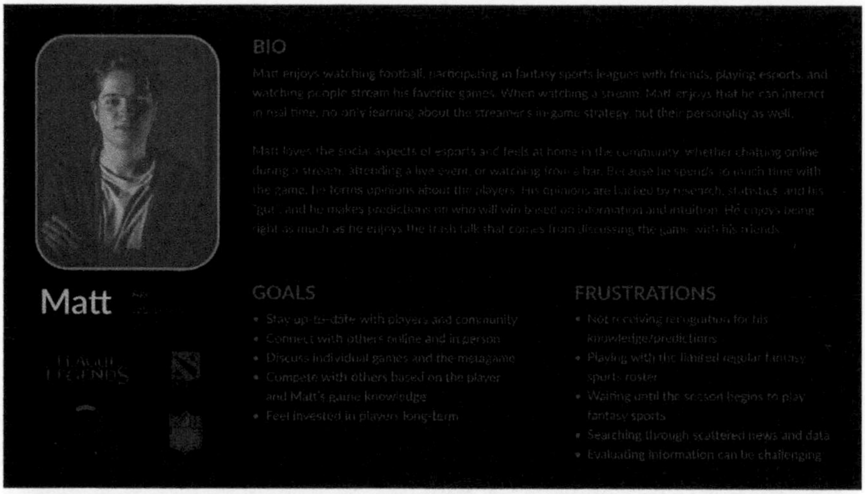

FIGURE 3.3 Several of the interviewees for this project were named Matt, which felt appropriate to use for the target persona for the project. The stock photo represents the target user—generally a younger, male audience, set with darker lighting to reflect the environment in which we thought they'd participate in the platform.

Later, when you design, you can make decisions from the perspective of "Matt" and even use his likeness in the design deliverables—such as, profile pictures in the product or in user journeys discussing how Matt experiences the product.

For the name and photo, you don't have to use a real name or a clear photo if you don't want to; you can be more abstract so as to avoid creating any identity bias in your design, such as gender bias. If you choose, you could come up with a name that isn't based on a real-world name and use an icon to represent the photo of your persona. Perhaps instead of "Matt," we could have gone with "the Techie Investor" for our cryptocurrency project and shown a picture of an NFT, to avoid implying a gender for our target user.

Overview

After choosing a name and photo, you need to start painting the high-level picture of your persona. What is their profession? How old are they? What brands do they like? Think of this information as the summary statistics of your persona.

FIGURE 3.4 shows that Matt is a software developer—this makes sense given that this persona applies to a technology project that predates the popularity of NFTs. Cryptocurrency is a complicated marketplace, and someone working in technology was more likely at the time to understand it. Also, several software developers participated in the user interview process.

FIGURE 3.4 Profession, age, and favorite games, which stood in for the brands he had the most affinity with, are included in the persona.

Matt is 25 years old, which also makes sense given the subject area—a gaming platform powered by cryptocurrency transactions. Additionally, that age also represented the median age of the interviewed people.

He has favorite games as well—this was a gaming marketplace designed to attract fans of video games and sports. Therefore, the high-level summary in Figure 3.4 includes some of the games that the interviewed users were passionate about, and the persona includes them as areas of interest to the target user.

AUTHOR'S NOTE
A common point to include in personas is the favorite brands of a target audience, which influences marketing strategy and design aesthetic. Instead of using brands for this project, games are used.

Background/Bio

After choosing your high-level overview, you need to tell the story of who your persona is. What are their hobbies? What do they do, as it relates to the problem you're working on? Think of this information as the elevator pitch for who your persona is and how they spend their time—the bio (FIGURE 3.5).

BIO

Matt enjoys watching football, participating in fantasy sports leagues with friends, playing esports, and watching people stream his favorite games. When watching a stream, Matt enjoys that he can interact in real time, no only learning about the streamer's in-game strategy, but their personality as well.

Matt loves the social aspects of esports and feels at home in the community, whether chatting online during a stream, attending a live event, or watching from a bar. Because he spends so much time with the game, he forms opinions about the players. His opinions are backed by research, statistics, and his "gut", and he makes predictions on who will win based on information and intuition. He enjoys being right as much as he enjoys the trash talk that comes from discussing the game with his friends.

Matt

GOALS
- Stay up-to-date with players and community
- Connect with others online and in person
- Discuss individual games and the metagame
- Compete with others based on the player and Matt's game knowledge
- Feel invested in players long-term

FRUSTRATIONS
- Not receiving recognition for his knowledge/predictions
- Playing with the limited regular fantasy sports roster
- Waiting until the season begins to play fantasy sports
- Searching through scattered news and data
- Evaluating information can be challenging

FIGURE 3.5 We cover the games he likes, how he spends his free time, and how he engages with others online. The platform was heavily focused on esports, so the persona highlights how our Matt participates in esports.

For this section, you should also include any behaviors or actions your persona takes. Are there things they do on a regular basis? Is there something they are particularly passionate about, something you heard in your research? Include it! This could be its own separate section in your persona as well.

The research in this NFT marketplace example project revealed that our target audience played all sorts of games—from digital ones to tabletop ones to sports. Our interview participants also mentioned they loved fantasy sports—they formed leagues with their friends and competed to win prizes and bragging rights as they compared the performance of the teams they put together as if they were coaches or managers of sports teams. We wanted our persona to do the same—be focused on gaming, competition, and socialization with others.

Matt spends his time engaging with games—digital ones online, but also real-world games like football. He loves esports, since they are the intersection of all his passions—competition, games, and teamwork. He also spends his spare time watching leagues and rooting for his favorite teams as he analyzes and predicts their performance, commonly in fantasy sports leagues.

Likes/Goals

To ensure your eventual design solution matches the needs of your users, you need to understand their goals. What do the users want to accomplish? What do they like? What are they looking for? This information can help you determine the features to focus on and think of any areas of delight you could add to the product.

AUTHOR'S NOTE To help build out goals, think about intrinsic versus extrinsic motivation. What things are internally motivating, such as personal satisfaction or enjoyment? What things are externally motivating, like an asset or reward?

In our research, we learned that our target users loved playing games, not only because they loved games, but because games connected them to their friends. They also loved competing in games to display dominance and show-case their capabilities—even more so with their friends. It was a mix between camaraderie and competition.

For Matt (**FIGURE 3.6**), he loves connecting with others, discussing games, and competing where he can. That means that for any features we want to design, we should focus on these elements—perhaps we make a message board, or a leaderboard, to allow Matt to express himself, connect, and compete.

FIGURE 3.6 Goals included connecting with others, talking about games, and competing.

Dislikes/Frustrations

As with their goals, you need to know what gets in the way of your users. You need to know what they struggle with, what's complicated for them, and where they currently fall short. This is where the design solution you create can really help users—by knowing their frustrations (**FIGURE 3.7**), you can design a solution that directly addresses those pain points.

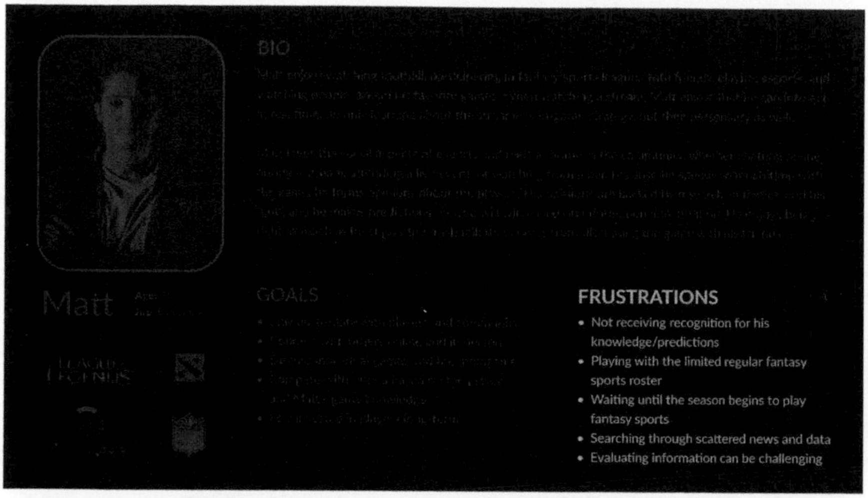

FIGURE 3.7 Our persona loved competing and playing games; their pain points were things that got in the way of that, like an off-season, or being limited to fantasy sports only. A design solution that solved for these would be more enjoyable for our users.

In our NFT marketplace research, we noticed that our users wanted more options. They wanted to play more frequently—fantasy sports lasted for only a part of the year, not all of it. Additionally, information was scattered and hard to evaluate—users needed to comb through statistics and news articles to understand how successful a player might be for their fantasy team.

Therefore, we designed our persona to reflect that. Matt really wants recognition and the means by which to compete. Since he loves competition (directly and indirectly), he's frustrated that his current products lack the ability that allows him to compete. He wants to engage on his terms with fantasy sports all year long, and he wants to be rewarded for that, ideally as it relates to his main interest—esports.

All Together

Putting all these things together—the goals, the frustrations, and the other elements of the persona—starts getting you closer to a possible solution. In the NFT marketplace example, perhaps Matt would benefit from an esports marketplace? Or one that allows him to bet on esports in addition to physical

AUTHOR'S NOTE For this project, we decided to create a single persona based on our research. However, it is very common to have multiple personas for a product, especially as that product's complexity grows and looks to serve different user interests. Additionally, you may end up with conflicting insights from your research, which will lead you to create multiple personas. To start, I recommend focusing on a single persona if you can.

sports? Perhaps it has social elements, like a leaderboard, or leagues he can play in with his friends. Maybe even a news aggregator that collects news articles and game statistics from the players Matt wants to add to his team.

These are just some of the features that could make it into a product experience for Matt. The ideas start flowing easily once we have a sense of who we are designing for, and why.

Note that for both goals and frustrations, we didn't include any of these feature ideas in the persona. This is because features aren't things that people feel—they are things that attempt to satisfy people's emotions. A leaderboard isn't one of Matt's goals—the ability to showcase his skills is. We avoided including features at this stage because we cared about the root behavior or desire of our audience, not something that could satisfy that desire. That comes later, when we start to think of solutions to the problem to solve.

How Do You Make Personas?

Hopefully this paints a clearer picture of how to put together a persona for your projects. Ideally, talk to users through user interviews. Affinity map the user interviews, then generate *I statements* from that research. With those I statements, you can fill in the persona's goals and frustrations more easily, to create a greater understanding of who you are designing for. Statements like "I am frustrated that I can't compete when I want" or "I enjoy competing with my friends" would directly map to the persona Matt and influence our design.

Personas Help You Define Who You're Designing For

A persona is a critical component of the design thinking process. It serves as an *ideal* user to design for—someone you can point to and ask questions about to inform product decisions. "What would Matt think?" "Would Carrie like that?" "Could Miles be able to use that?" Imagining things from the perspective of a persona allows you to make better design decisions.

Personas aren't based solely on opinions, either. They are backed by research, performed by talking with real users. By having these conversations and hearing real-world stories about what people experienced, you can understand an audience's goals and frustrations and form a general opinion about who the users are.

After all, if you don't know the users you're designing for, then how can you make a user experience for them?

Let's Do It!

Now that you've seen how to make a persona, let's make one for your project. Hopefully you have completed both your user interviews and your affinity map, which will allow you to make a persona based on that data.

If you haven't, that's OK—you could pause on the persona for now and work on those elements of your project, then make the persona afterward. Alternatively, you can use the I statements from a practice affinity map exercise I created, which is available here: https://tinyurl.com/asuxd-affinity.

If you need a place to start, I put together an example you can use to make a persona, which is available here: https://tinyurl.com/asuxd-persona-template

Remember, the persona is designed to help you understand the target user. What do they like? What blocks them? How do they spend their time? What are their favorite brands or experiences?

You don't have to include a name, age, gender, or photo if you feel that makes your project less inclusive. Instead, think of ways you can identify or refer to your persona without using those characteristics. A nickname or phrase that helps identify the type of person you are designing for can help.

Remember to keep the tenets of good personas in mind:

- **A persona is not a real person.** It is a representation of a real person, and one that you use to help you design the solution.

- **A persona should "feel" like a real person.** Things like quotes, descriptive biographies, and preferences based on real-user interview data help flesh out a persona.

- **A persona has goals to accomplish.** Just like a real person, a persona has goals, but things get in the way. The identification of what those goals are, and how blockers affect those goals, is key to developing a great persona and should influence the solution you design.

AUTHOR'S NOTE Refer to the "Persona" section Chapter 3 in the appendix for examples to compare your persona with.

- **Don't include solutions in a persona.** A feature is not a goal or frustration. For example, a person doesn't want a search bar; they want the ability to find information. It might seem subtle, but an important part of personas is not to include solutions in them. You're still exploring the problem; you're not ready for solutions yet.

USER JOURNEY MAPPING

Once you understand who the target users are—the persona—you need to understand their experiences as well. A clearer understanding of the users will help you design better. You need to know more than their wants and needs. How do they move through an experience? What is the current state that they go through? How do they prepare for an experience, and reflect on it? Knowing the before, during, and after of a user experience provides a holistic view that allows you to think of better solutions.

Is someone struggling with something in the middle of an experience? Maybe that's something you can solve beforehand. Do people want to be able to reflect on an experience more easily? Perhaps a way to record information during that experience will allow them to look back on it more easily.

It's not enough to know about the users. You need to imagine them in an experience so that you can empathize with their goals and frustrations, and you need to understand how they experience something so that you can create an even better experience for them.

To understand more about how a user experiences something, create a story that explains how they experience that thing—a user journey map.

What Is a User Journey Map?

During the define step of the design thinking process, the goal is to better understand the state of things. Who are our users? What do they like or dislike? And what do their experiences look like? Journey maps play a crucial part in this process.

A *journey map* is a visualization of the process a person goes through to accomplish a goal. Quite literally, it is a map of the user's journey through an experience, and it includes all the aspects of that journey—their motivations for starting the journey, their actions as they move through their journey, and their feelings as they experience elements of that journey.

FIGURE 3.8 is the real-life journey map I created for the persona named Matt in the cryptocurrency marketplace project example. I used an excellent template created by Geunbae Lee.[2] The project involved early-stage NFTs, and the onboarding process was confusing—users didn't understand what the

---

2 https://dribbble.com/shots/4232985--Free-Template-Journey-Map-Bundle

platform was, how long an order took to clear, and the actual value of their portfolio as they made trades.

To better understand where the confusion was, I interviewed users, synthesized those interviews via an affinity map, created a persona named Matt, and then mapped Matt's journey before, during, and after first using the product. I used the user journey map to advocate for revisions to the existing product experience and focus ideation around what we could do for Matt on his product journey.

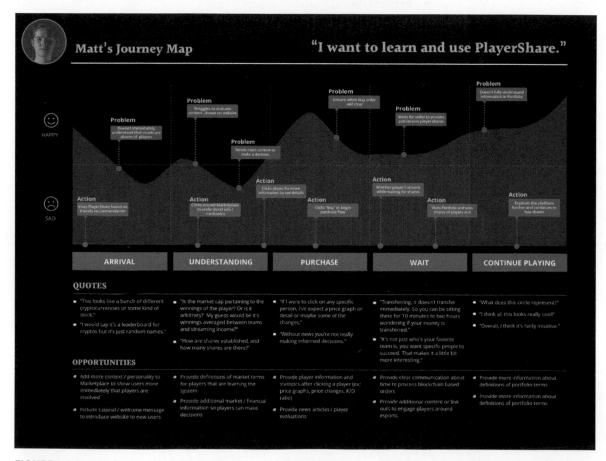

FIGURE 3.8 A journey map shows the highs and lows of a user experience so that you can understand and communicate the points that are working well and the areas that need improvement.

AUTHOR'S NOTE
Depending on how many personas you have and how many goals those personas have, your project may require multiple user journey maps. Make sure you represent all the key journeys of each of your personas.

A journey map's main function is as a storytelling tool used to align the team. It uses your persona and takes them on a journey through a scenario. The scenario is of your own design—you can choose what journey your user is taking. The content of that journey is ideally based on your research—what you've observed as you talked with users or looked at data that indicates their behaviors and opinions regarding an experience. Most commonly, user journeys are based on user interviews.

So what goes into a journey map? Usually, every journey map consists of several key elements that help communicate the user's experience:

- Persona/background
- Phases
- Actions
- Thoughts/feelings
- Insights

Persona/Background

To create a user journey map, you need a user! Commonly, this is your persona, since journey maps go hand in hand with persona work. Since the journey is told from the perspective of the user, it's good to have that user *own* the journey. To facilitate this idea of ownership further, nearly everything in this deliverable should come from the perspective of the persona, as if you were inside their mind, experiencing the things they experience on their journey.

To align the NFT project team further, it's helpful to have a background in the map as well (FIGURE 3.9). Who is this person? What is this journey? What is this person trying to accomplish on this journey? Setting the stage helps everyone get on the same page.

FIGURE 3.9 Instead of a long biography (stakeholders could review the persona itself), we included a quote that summed up why Matt was going on this journey. He's interested in the product and wants to learn how to use it so that he can start making trades and compete with his friends.

For the user journey with Matt, we kept the background simple—stakeholders were familiar with the problem, and we used this "background" space to communicate Matt's core user need: learn, then use the platform to play with his friends and try to beat them.

Phases

Since a user journey map is a *journey*, it can be broken down into parts or phases. These phases are the high-level steps taken in the user's journey and help organize the rest of the journey map. Think of them as the high-level flow for a persona's experience—what are each of the milestones in the user's journey? If you had to communicate the steps a user takes through a product, without going into too much detail, what would those steps be?

For Matt, I created five phases (**FIGURE 3.10**). First is Arrival. Matt comes to the platform, either by advertisements, word of mouth, or an invitation from his friends. Then comes Understanding. He begins to comprehend what the platform is and what it offers him. After that comes Purchase. To participate in the platform, he needs to make a trade and buy some assets for his portfolio by making his first purchase. Afterward, he needs to Wait. His trade needs to clear (which can take a long time via the blockchain), so he waits not only for confirmation, but also to see if the assets he bought change in value (think of it as an investment). Finally, he reaches the last step in his initial product journey, Continue Playing. After some time, he keeps "playing" the game via the platform, competing with his friends, and investing in more and more assets to grow his portfolio.

| ARRIVAL | UNDERSTANDING | PURCHASE | WAIT | CONTINUE PLAYING |

FIGURE 3.10 The phases of Matt's journey through the product. These phases help explain, at a high level, each step in the user's journey.

Actions

Now that you have phases that broadly discuss the user's journey, you can go deeper and talk about the specific actions the persona takes along the way. Phases are like chapter headings; actions are more like the subchapters within each of those chapters.

Actions are still somewhat high level—you don't need to get as granular as every step in a user flow from screen to screen, for example. This is more like what the persona is doing in the story. These actions aren't exclusive to the product, either—they can include the product itself but can also extend to devices (like turning on a phone or computer) or even physical places.

AUTHOR'S NOTE
A person's journey in a user experience exists outside the product itself. As a result, user journeys should include out-of-product experiences. For Matt, that can include conversations with friends to learn about the platform, or the time it takes for a trade confirmation.

For Matt, I mapped out all his steps through the five phases of getting used to the platform (**FIGURE 3.11**). I also split each step into two categories. *Actions* which represent choices Matt makes, and *problems* which represent issues Matt has along the journey. In this case, these problems usually come from the platform itself and are opportunities for improvement later in the design process.

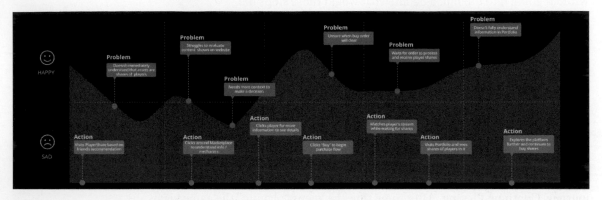

FIGURE 3.11 Actions lead to an emotional response, represented on the graph as things that make Matt happy or sad. As Matt progresses on the journey, he encounters problems, which lead to a change in his emotional response and additional actions he chooses to take.

But how did I know that Matt takes all these actions and encounters these problems? Well, the data comes from research. This story we've created is based on talking with users and hearing their experiences. The actions and problems users encountered in research directly translate to this map.

I also added an extra element—a general satisfaction score for Matt. As he takes more actions and encounters more problems, his happiness with the product changes. A visual representation of that satisfaction using this curve helps us empathize with Matt even more. For example, the understand phase of this journey map is Matt's saddest point in his journey—he just wants to start using the platform and understand it. Once he gets past that step and starts investing (which was his original reason for coming to the platform), he is a lot happier.

Thoughts/Feelings

Along your user's journey, the persona has thoughts that influence how they feel during the journey. Knowing how users feel as they go through a user experience is an excellent insight into their goals and frustrations, and this influences how you design a solution for their needs.

These thoughts could be abstractions of what you observed in user interviews, like user insights or I statements, or they could quote what users said during interviews.

For Matt, I chose to include specific quotes (FIGURE 3.12) over high-level observations. I find that in general, quotes are more powerful at communicating how a user experiences something—it's their words, after all—and these quotes help drive additional empathy for the team. Interpreting what a user says and extrapolating an insight is an extra step that dilutes how the user feels—why not just have them say it, in their words? If I say "Matt found the leaderboard confusing," it doesn't have the same weight as his words. One user told us how confused they were by the product: "I would say it's a leaderboard for cryptos, but it's just a bunch of random names." Hearing it in this way adds empathy and weight to the journey map, which is a main reason why we make them in the first place.

AUTHOR'S NOTE Quotes serve as "evidence." Your evidence could be photos, videos, anecdotes, or some other form of "proof" of people saying and doing the things that your journey map depicts.

QUOTES

- "This looks like a bunch of different cryptocurrencies or some kind of stock."
- "I would say it's a leaderboard for cryptos but it's just random names."

- "Is the market cap pertaining to the winnings of the player? Or is it arbitrary? My guess would be it's winnings averaged between teams and streaming income?"
- "How are shares established, and how many shares are there?"

- "If I were to click on any specific person, I've expect a price graph or detail or maybe some of the changes."
- "Without news you're not really making informed decisions."

- "Transferring, it doesn't transfer immediately. So you can be sitting there for 10 minutes to two hours wondering if your money is transferred."
- "It's not just who's your favorite team is, you want specific people to succeed. That makes it a little bit

FIGURE 3.12 The thoughts and feelings of the persona, sometimes represented as user insights and other times represented as actual quotes from user interviews.

Insights

As an optional step, you can include an analysis of the action items or areas of improvement in the user's journey during each phase (FIGURE 3.13). These action items are framed as insights from research, opportunities for design solutions, or even tasks for the team to complete later in the process.

OPPORTUNITIES

succeed. That makes it a little bit more interesting."

- Add more context / personality to Marketplace to show users more immediately that players are involved
- Include tutorial / welcome message to introduce website to new users

- Provide definitions of market terms for players that are learning the system
- Provide additional market / financial information so players can make decisions

- Provide player information and statistics after clicking a player (ex: price graphs, price changes, K/D ratio)
- Provide news articles / player evaluations

- Provide clear communication about time to process blockchain based orders
- Provide additional content or link outs to engage players around esports

FIGURE 3.13 Since the goal of this project was to improve a product, the opportunities in this user journey are platform enhancements that address the points at which Matt is less happy during his user experience.

For Matt, I included interpretations of the core problems that he had during the onboarding experience. This pairs well with quotes, for example—the quotes allow Matt to express his unfiltered thoughts, and the opportunities allow me to express my interpretation of those thoughts, which could turn into ideation topics. Since Matt said he didn't recognize the names on the platform, I suggested that we provide more context around those names as a product enhancement.

How Do You Make a User Journey Map?

Hopefully this helps paint a clearer picture of how to put together a persona for your projects. Ideally, you talk to users through user interviews. You affinity map the user interviews, then generate I statements from that research. With those I statements, you can fill in the goals and frustrations of the persona more easily to create a greater understanding of who you are designing for. Statements like "I am frustrated that I can't compete when I want" or "I enjoy competing with my friends" would directly map to the persona Matt and influence the design.

User Journeys Help You Understand

User journey maps help you better understand users. Once you have the research into the users' wants and needs, you can take that information and make a persona. With a persona and the stories from the user interviews you can go one step further and create a narrative for that persona.

Humans are driven by stories. Stories are memorable and help you relate to others. By creating a story for users, you can make it so much easier to empathize with them, define their problems, and understand the problems that you are trying to solve.

Let's Do It!

By now, you hopefully have a good understanding of where to start when making a user journey map. Let's practice that skill by making one for our solo traveler project, using the persona you've created from your research or the data that I've provided over the last few exercises.

To get started, search Figma's community resources, which have several templates for you to explore: https://tinyurl.com/asuxd-journeymaps

If you are stalled as you try to create a journey map, you might try to create a simple one for a familiar topic. I've had students map out simple user journey maps to get started, such as a trip to the grocery store or how to figure out what to eat for dinner.

Feel free to use a persona you may have from one of your projects, or alternatively, think of your own journey with either of the following scenarios:

- Imagine you just got home and are starving! You go to the fridge and find you have no food. What would be your journey?

- Imagine you are going to buy groceries for a week. What would be your journey?

To accomplish either of these scenarios, take the following steps:

1. Write down your goal.

2. Write down the actions you'll take.

3. Keep track of your thoughts and feelings as you take those actions.

4. Categorize your actions into phases.

The purpose of a user journey map is to communicate the user's current state. What is the persona's experience before, during, and after interacting with a product? What are their actions? How does the system respond? How does that make the user feel? Use quotes, insights, and other supporting evidence to explain this journey and each of the steps along the user's journey.

AUTHOR'S NOTE
Although you can make a journey map that communicates the future state, that won't be the purpose of this exercise (especially since we don't have a product in mind yet).

Here's some tips for making your user journey map. I recommend working on your journey map, in the following order, to create a strong narrative for how your users experience their current state.

1. Who is the persona going on this journey? Include a name, photo, and a high-level synopsis of your persona.

2. What are the high-level steps they take in their experience? These are the phases of the user journey.

3. What actions do they take along the way? These are the individual steps that make up each phase in the journey.

4. How do they feel after each action? How does the system respond? This is the emotions that your persona experiences in the user journey map.

5. What opportunities exist based on the user journey? These are the potential design solutions and areas of exploration for your project once the journey map is complete.

THE PROBLEM TO SOLVE

The purpose of the first few steps of design thinking is to understand. Understand an initial problem, our users, and the context around how that problem affects them. When all this research is complete, we reach a clearer picture of the true problem we wish to solve with our designs.

This is where problem statements come in. A problem statement, or *problem to solve*, is the focal point of the rest of our project. It's the goal we strive for when conducting the rest of our design thinking process—it's what we ideate around, what we design a solution toward, and what we reference as we deliver our product. Thus, problem statements are the pivotal point of our project. It's where we move from research to exploration.

How Do You Use a Problem Statement?

Looking at the Nielsen Norman Group's design thinking model (**FIGURE 3.14**), we can visually express the exact point where problem statements should be formed.

FIGURE 3.14 NN/g's design thinking model. Problem statements occur in between the define and ideate steps in the process.

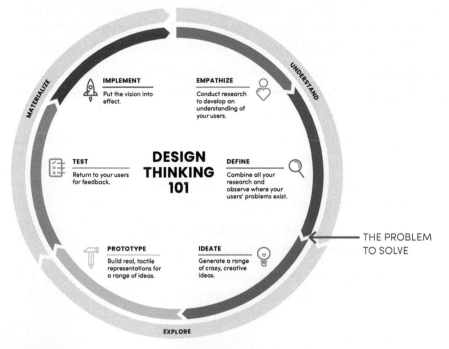

The problem statement is the last piece of the define step in design thinking. It is the result of research. It is essentially the definition of what we are trying to accomplish. From that definition, you finally fully understand what you are going to do with the project, and you are in a great position to start exploring solutions through ideation and the rest of the process.

Problem statements aren't exclusive to this specific design thinking model. Looking at other models, you can see that the problem statement is crucial to the process and that some models specifically include it as a part of their process.

Looking at FIGURE 3.15, the Double Diamond from the British Design Council,[3] you can see that the entire project converges on a single point: the problem definition, or problem statement, that powers the rest of the process. The problem definition is an integral component of design thinking—without it, you lack a compass to design with, a North Star to follow, a direction to head for ideation. The problem statement is effectively the prompt around which the rest of the project is framed.

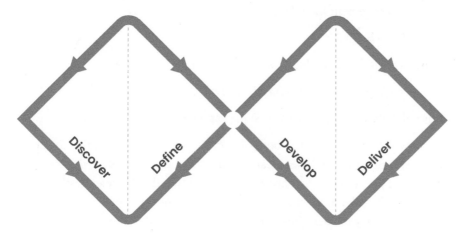

FIGURE 3.15 The problem definition is a key element of the Double Diamond design thinking process and occurs right in the middle of it, where all the research and the definition of that research converges on a single point.

It's clear that problem statements are an important part of the design thinking process. But how do they help you design? Well, the primary purpose of a problem statement is to align teams on where to focus their attention and bring consensus on what they're going to solve. It's a concise way to communicate the user, their need, and the impact of the problem so that everyone can agree on what solutions to pursue to address the need for those users.

3 www.designcouncil.org.uk/our-resources/framework-for-innovation/

The problem statement is so important that some of the world's most famous inventors would rather spend most of their time on defining the problem rather than thinking of a solution. Albert Einstein said it best:

> *If I had an hour to solve a problem, I'd spend 55 minutes thinking about the problem and 5 minutes thinking about solutions.*

Let's take some time to dive into a simple formula for problem statements and see how you can apply them to a project.

How Do You Make a Problem Statement?

Writing effective problem statements can be challenging. They can succeed or fail depending on the words chosen. Small changes to language can drastically alter the effectiveness.

Fortunately, keeping a few guidelines in mind will help you craft the best problem statements that you can.

Start with a Formula

A problem statement should follow a simple formula:

User + Need = Goal

If you express this formula as a written statement, it becomes:

> *As a [user], I need/want [need] so that [goal].*

This will help you structure the first pass at the problem statement.

Let's say you're working on a food delivery service project. For this project, let's assume that you did the research and interviewed a lot of customers who order food delivered to their homes. You found that the interview participants usually order food when they feel overwhelmed or don't have enough time in their day to cook. Ordering a prepared meal allows them to eat quickly without having to spend the time to shop for groceries, cook a meal, or do dishes afterward.

Seeing this problem, you want to write a problem statement that will help you design for these users. Let's give it a shot:

> *As a [person], I want [to be given food] so that [I have more time].*

This problem statement could help you design something for users. But it lacks substance. It doesn't have a lot of context around the user—a "person" lacks definition, empathy, and focus.

The user's needs are quite broad as well. What type of food does the user want? Is the food uncooked or prepared and ready to eat?

And the goal is too ambiguous. People want more time—to do what? Why do they need that time? This goal lacks empathy, which reduces the human-centered nature of designing for this cohort of people.

Let's focus on how you can make this problem statement better.

Be Specific

Your problem statement should be specific. The previous problem statement was too broad. You need some constraints to design a better, more impactful solution that is a little more targeted. Let's try again:

> As a [25-year-old single adult], I want [to call a restaurant] so that [I don't have to cook meals].

This problem statement is a lot more targeted. It focuses on 25-year-old single adults, and you can guess that they don't need to provide for anyone else because they are single. An ordering experience that caters to younger adults is a great place to start.

The need is also clear—let them call a restaurant. Something like a database of restaurants the user can contact would probably satisfy this need.

Finally, the goal is also clear—the users don't want to cook meals. You don't really know why, but by referencing the research, you can dig into that user goal and get a deeper understanding.

At the surface, this could look like an excellent problem statement—after all, everything is clear and the solution basically designs itself. But that's the problem—there's no room to apply design thinking, because this problem statement is so specific that it includes the solution within the problem.

Allow Room to Explore

The last problem statement included some information that would have constrained the design. Users were specifically single, 25-year-old adults— in reality, you would want to design for a wider range of users so that the product could scale to satisfy many different types of people.

Additionally, the need is very specific—it is a need to call a restaurant. What about people who don't want to talk over the phone? Perhaps people want to contact a restaurant via text or email instead. Maybe they don't even want to contact the restaurant at all; they just want the food. Or even more broadly, it's not that people want to get food from a restaurant, it's that they want to eat—a restaurant doesn't even need to be involved in the solution—but with the problem statement written this way, it's assumed that there needs to be one.

As for the goal, although it's clear, it lacks the true motivator behind that behavior. Users might not want to cook meals, sure, but why don't they want to cook? Do they lack the skills to cook and are insecure about the food they would make? Or do they like to cook but simply lack the time to do so or the access to the ingredients they want to use? With this problem statement, you are left wondering why.

Let's try again:

> As a [working adult], I want [to order prepared food] so [I have time for other things].

This is getting closer to a well-crafted problem statement. The user is broader, yet still someone you can design for: the working adult. There's room to allow for multiple types of users, such as an adult with a large family, an adult who works late hours, or an adult who is exhausted after a long day. Ideally, the persona fits into one of these categories.

As for the user need, it's broader than calling a restaurant. Now, it has expanded to ordering prepared food. The users need to eat and want to order food that's already been made for them so that they don't have to prepare it themselves.

Lastly, for the goal, the users want more time to do other activities. You don't assume that they lack the time or interest to cook; rather, the conversation shifts to say that the users want to spend their time in places other than the kitchen.

This problem statement is much better. It has specificity to provide focus during ideation, yet enough room to allow for multiple solutions to satisfy the users. This problem statement could be used to continue the design thinking process, but some modifications can make it even better.

Don't Assume a Solution

Let's take another look at the last problem statement:

> *As a [working adult], I want [to order prepared food] so [I have time for other things].*

AUTHOR'S NOTE One good way to tell whether your problem statement assumes a solution is if your user need is a noun or a verb. A noun is usually a solution, while a need is more commonly expressed as a verb.

This statement includes an assumption about the solution. We broaden our user and our goal, but in doing so we assumed a product solution as a user need. Prepared food isn't a need; it's an idea. We need to define the underlying need that's driving that possible solution. Our problem statements should be problem focused, not solution focused.

Let's try again:

> *As a [working adult], I want [to spend less time thinking about my food] so that [I have time for other things].*

This one is getting closer! It doesn't assume a solution in the users' needs. Rather, it focuses on the needs discovered in the research. User interviewees expressed that they didn't want to spend their time on cooking. Rather, they wanted to spend their time on other activities. You can craft the problem statement to reflect this need and this goal in a way that gives you even more room to design a solution that addresses the users' needs directly.

This is a pretty good problem statement. With just a few more adjustments, it will be a great one.

Write with Empathy

The goal of a problem statement is to align teams around what problem you are trying to solve. It's an alignment tool but also a tool to generate empathy. Being empathetic in the problem statement will help carry forward the users' needs through the project and gives them a higher chance of surfacing in your design solution. Let's try one more adjustment to the problem statement.

> *As a [busy, working adult], I want [to spend less time thinking about my food] so that [I can spend my time on other things instead].*

Here, the statement has a slightly adjusted user and goal. The last iteration had a good sense of the users' needs, but for this one, let's really amp up what good looks like for the user. This is the vision you have when making your product—this is how you can succeed, by delivering on this promise. If you can enable busy users to have more time to spend on the things they'd rather do instead of focusing on what they will eat, then you will have made a product that addresses their core need—more time to do things other than figure out what to eat.

Keep in mind that this problem statement hasn't assumed a solution. This statement allows for plenty of possible solutions to explore during ideation, such as a food delivery service that sends requests to restaurants and delivers complete meals, ready to go. Another solution could be a recipe app for a customer who likes to cook but doesn't have a great way to discover new meals to make. A solution to this problem statement might not even be a digital product, such as a meal kit service that delivers an entire week of meals for users to heat up when they are ready to eat.

This problem statement gives you a lot of room to ideate and could be enough for you to design. However, you can combine this with another technique to really form a powerful prompt to guide you during the ideation step of the design thinking process.

"How Might We?"

The problem statement is one piece of the prompt used when headed into ideation. Another element that's commonly used with it is a How Might We statement—a statement that frames ideation further and allows you to focus on areas of exploration more specifically. This How Might We statement helps uncover opportunities for design and adds more empathy to the ideation process. It's more actionable than having just the problem statement, and it helps push the process along.

Let's take the problem statement and try a How Might We statement to see the combination of the two in an ideation session:

As a [busy, working adult], I want [to spend less time thinking about my food] so that [I can spend my time on other things instead].

How might we provide a way for our users to spend less time figuring out what they want to eat?

Here, the problem statement is applied to a design prompt by asking How Might We. With these combined statements, the team will want the users to save time when thinking about their meals.

You could try again with a different area of focus of the ideation by switching up the How Might We statement, like so:

How might we allow our users to find something to eat more easily?

Now, you can focus the ideation on a different topic. You will generate new ideas, yet those ideas will still be linked to the original problem you are trying to solve.

A Great Problem Statement Is Challenging but Powerful

Writing stellar problem statements is extremely challenging. It requires a lot of research, clear synthesis of that research, and a great deal of wordsmithing to arrive at a clear enough problem to solve that is specific enough to be rooted in your research, yet broad enough to avoid assuming a solution.

With practice, however, having a great problem statement (and pairing it with a good How Might We statement) will make it a lot easier to create a solution that's rooted in your users' problems.

Let's Do It!

With a better understanding of how to make problem statements, let's make one for your project. You'll need your user-interview insights and your persona.

A great problem statement is crucial for the next step of design thinking. It helps frame ideation and guide the rest of the project to completion.

You can be iterative here—start with a sentence that combines the user, the need, and the goal into a single area of focus. Use the problem statement formula:

As a [user], I need/want [need] so that [goal].

Remember, keep the tenets of good problem statements in mind:

- **Be specific.** Include a clear understanding of the user, the need, and the goal in the problem statement.

- **Allow room to explore.** You should be specific, but not so specific that there is no room to ideate.

- **Don't include a solution.** Problem statements state problems, not solutions.

AUTHOR'S NOTE To add additional focus and empathy, you can replace "our users" in the second statement with any personas you have generated during this process. That will link it back to your research, develop more focus on your specific users, and help to generate additional empathy for your users.

AUTHOR'S NOTE Problem statement generation is iterative. You might not like your first, second, or tenth try at writing one for your project. That's OK. You can keep refining and iterating on the statement as you craft it to get it just right.

AUTHOR'S NOTE Refer to the "Problem Statements" section Chapter 3 in the appendix for examples to compare your work with.

- **Include empathy.** You're designing for people, in a human-centered way, so the problem should include the empathy that you want to include in a solution.
- **Combine with a How Might We statement.** These statements further guide ideation sessions and explore possible solutions.

COMPETITIVE RESEARCH

Up until this point, we have been focused on our users. Who are they? What are their needs? What problem are we trying to solve for them?

Now that we have a good understanding of those questions, we can shift our focus. We can ask ourselves questions about the current state of the market and the options our users can currently turn to.

What products exist in this space? What companies are working on this problem? How do users solve their problems today? These are the questions we seek to answer when conducting competitive research for our projects.

What Is Competitive Research?

As you prepare to design a solution for the users, it is beneficial to gain an understanding of what already exists for them. You should develop a sense of the marketplace, and what other products or services they have available to use. There are several things to learn from this.

AUTHOR'S NOTE I'd like to draw the distinction between two concepts: competitive research and competitive analysis. All the methods discussed here, including competitive analysis, fall under the umbrella of competitive research. The terms may be used interchangeably in your place of work, but for our purposes, I'm referring to competitive analysis as a specific method you can use when conducting competitive research.

What works? Is there a current solution that satisfies users' needs that you can draw inspiration from? Will you have to compete with that solution once you design your product? What works about those products? Can you borrow ideas from them for your users?

What doesn't work? Are there solutions available, but users don't know about them? Do they fail to truly satisfy their needs? How can you improve upon it to make something that does work?

This is where competitive research comes in. Competitive research is the process of drawing inspiration from other companies to inform the way you build your product.

FIGURE 3.16 is an example of competitive research I performed for an education platform—a competitive analysis of features across different products. I analyzed our product and each competitor to audit which platforms had what

Features by Platform	Atom	Moodle	Blackboard	Canvas	ACT	Edementum	Edulastic
View Scores for All Students	✔	✔	✔	✔	✔	✔	✔
View Scores for Single Student	✔	✔		✔	✔	✔	✔
View Assessment Area Breakdowns		✔			✔	✔	✔
Self-Service Table Customization	✔	✔	✔			✔	
Score / Status Categorization	✔	✔	✔	✔	✔		✔
Manual Grading	✔	✔	✔	✔			
Set Grading Rubrics		✔	✔	✔		✔	
Add Notes		✔	✔	✔			
Message Student		✔	✔	✔			
Predict Final Score					✔		
Compare to National					✔		
Sync with SIS			✔				
Import Scores		✔	✔	✔			
Export Scores	✔	✔	✔	✔		✔	
IMS Score Integration	✔						

FIGURE 3.16 A feature comparison across competing products.

features. This helped us analyze our product and determine what features we wanted to release and when.

We performed this competitive research right at the end of the define stage of the design thinking process—where we are now. In reality, you can perform competitive research at any point in the design thinking process. Some designers prefer to design first, then come back and look at the market to see what exists and how they may be influenced by it. Others prefer to do this analysis up front, to inform which features they want to work on or to use the research as inspiration for the ideation phase. It's up to you to decide where you want it in your process.

AUTHOR'S NOTE These situations happen when applying design thinking. While there is a general flow you will follow for a project, there will also be times you need to determine what techniques you want to use, when, and why. Applying the right technique at the right moment is an art.

To do competitive research, we follow several steps:

1. Develop a rubric based on what you want to know.

2. Gather solutions from existing companies.

3. Compare solutions and identify what user needs are met and what needs are underserved.

4. Explore opportunities for innovation.

Several different types of competitive research exist, but they all follow these steps: develop your comparison metrics, find your companies, and analyze their products.

Let's look at several forms of competitive research you could use in your process.

SWOT—Strengths, Weaknesses, Opportunities, Threats

A *SWOT analysis* is a popular technique for analyzing how a business performs across four categories:

- Strengths

- Weaknesses

- Opportunities

- Threats

SWOT analysis is a comparison tool that helps you analyze yourself, other businesses, and various opportunities you may want to pursue (FIGURE 3.17).

FIGURE 3.17 Each element of SWOT is mapped to a spot in the grid, where you write observations.

Strengths	Weaknesses
Opportunities	Threats

To perform a SWOT analysis, you must consider four different areas of a company, split into two categories: internal factors and external factors. You take the elements of each of these factors, put them in a matrix, and use that matrix to guide the product strategy.

Internal Factors

A company's *internal factors* are ones that they directly control. These are the things the company produces, has agency around, and can influence directly. They are broken down into two subsections.

Strengths

Strengths are the things that a company does well. What is a company's competitive advantage? What does it succeed at? What is that company known for?

Let's consider Netflix (**FIGURE 3.18**). What are some of its strengths? Well, it has a very large content library, which it can leverage for subscriptions. It has content you can get only there. It has a lot of different types of users all across the world. It also collects a lot of data about those users to influence future content and its own content recognition software. Finally, it has a very strong brand presence—millions of people are familiar with the company.

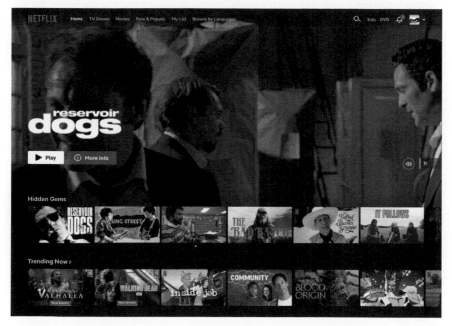

FIGURE 3.18 The landing page for Netflix.com.

Weaknesses

Weaknesses are the things that the company does not do well. What needs to be overcome? How could the company be even better? What internal elements can the company control to increase its position or strength in the market?

Let's keep analyzing Netflix. One weakness is how it determines what content to invest in. Content has a small window of opportunity to succeed— basically, in its first 30 days. With all the content that its customers can consume, this may not be a fair way to gauge quality shows. Sometimes, it takes a show a long time to develop a following. As a result, Netflix has gained a reputation for canceling shows shortly after they release—much to the annoyance of fans who liked the content.[4]

Additionally, finding something to watch on Netflix is a challenge. While a strength of Netflix is that it has so much content to appeal to a broad audience, a weakness is determining something to watch. Because it has so much content, sifting through it all is a chore.

Lastly, Netflix has no social engagement features. What if I want to watch with someone else? It's hard to use one or multiple accounts to engage through Netflix itself, like with a social watch feature or a friends list.

External Factors

A company's *external factors* are ones that they indirectly influence but that are market oriented and cannot be controlled directly. These often deal with market position, competitor influence, or other things related to the industry a company operates in. External factors are also broken down into two subsections.

Opportunities

Opportunities are the things a company can take advantage of in the market. What options exist? What could be capitalized on? What external market conditions are present that a company could leverage?

For Netflix, some of its weaknesses come into play here. For example, improving its social features could increase engagement and retention—streaming services don't have many social features at large, and as a result, Netflix could innovate and be a leader in this space.

Additionally, Netflix could take advantage of one of its strengths and release more exclusive content. Since the streaming wars are fueled by the content they offer, Netflix could continue to build out its robust content library. Perhaps even release more interactive content (FIGURE 3.19), which is something unique to Netflix.

---

4 https://collider.com/cancelled-netflix-shows-get-down-julie-and-the-phantoms/
#the-get-down-2016-2017

Finally, Netflix could explore different ways to monetize. It has monetization options based on the number of users in an account, but are there other ways to incentivize users to pay more? Some other streaming services do this, with things like premium day 1 exclusives timed to theatrical releases. Historically, Netflix avoided an ad-based subscription tier, but after pressure to deliver better financial results, it has since released an ad-supported version of its service at a lower price to capture more market share.

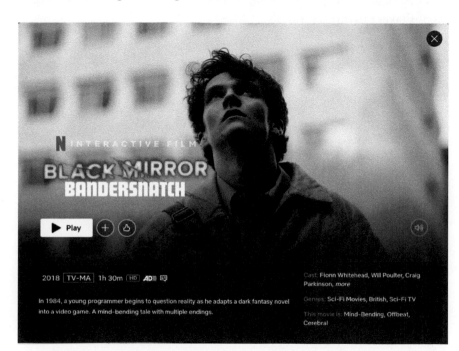

FIGURE 3.19 Netflix is known for interactive video content, where viewers take actions while the story unfolds.

Threats

Threats are the things in the market a company needs to avoid, or be aware of, that could negatively impact the company. What obstacles exist for a company? For Netflix, there is the threat of market consolidation. As cable channels both launch their own services and acquire each other, the streaming service market will become oversaturated and large streaming service hubs will develop. This could threaten Netflix's hold on the market. Already, some streaming services have consolidated, like Disney+ bundling with Hulu, or HBO Max and Discovery+ combining their services.

Additionally, Netflix is losing big licenses and exclusives for streaming content. They've lost Marvel movies, popular TV shows like *The Office*, and more. These shows moving to competing streaming services threatens Netflix's position in the market.

Lastly, Netflix must be aware of its prices. As it continues to raise prices, other streaming services start to become more appealing, especially those that cost significantly less. Releasing its ad-based subscription tier shows that Netflix takes this threat seriously.

Putting everything we've discussed together for Netflix, the SWOT analysis would look like FIGURE 3.20.

FIGURE 3.20 A SWOT analysis of Netflix.

NETFLIX

Strengths	Weaknesses
• Wide content library • Exclusives • International market • Large demographics • User data • Brand presence	• Ratings approach • Finding something to watch • Social experience (watching together)

Opportunities	Threats
• Social features • More exclusives • Interactives • Monetization options	• Market consolidation • Losing licenses • Pricing

We now have a good picture of where Netflix stands. To use this in your design thinking process, you could observe the opportunities Netflix has, for example, and ideate possibilities as it relates to your problem to solve. Here are a few ways this analysis could help you think of new product features for Netflix:

- Seeing that interactive specials, exclusives, and social features are all opportunities for Netflix, you could make an exclusive interactive video that users play together.

- Since finding something to watch is challenging, you could use Netflix's strong recommendations (based on its user data) to create much more personalized content recommendations for users.

- To promote watching specific content from Netflix, perhaps Netflix creates a "remix" feature allowing a user to take a short clip from a moment in a show and share it to social media with that user's reaction to that moment.

- As pricing and market consolidation threaten Netflix's market position, perhaps they introduce some form of micro-transactions or additional ways to monetize on their product library.

A SWOT analysis can lead to a lot of potential options for a product—it gives you more information on the companies in an industry and allows you to create ideas for opportunity by being aware of the current state of things.

Admittedly, SWOT analysis is more common to consider for business strategy rather than UX strategy, though like the previous analysis, it can be used to help influence the direction of your product and, thus, the user's experience.

Lightning Demo

Suppose you aren't as concerned with analyzing your competitors and instead want to focus on the best internal experience you can create. Instead of a SWOT analysis, you could conduct competitive research to specifically help drive your ideation. One of the best techniques you could use for that purpose would be the lightning demo.

A lightning demo is a show-and-tell group session geared toward inspiration. Lightning demos usually take place when you need rapid ideation and are working toward a design solution in a short amount of time, like for a design sprint.

To conduct a lightning demo, participants from your team gather examples from real products and create a "mood board" of ideas for your product. Examples can range from competing products to completely unrelated products—the point is to inspire and motivate a team toward finding a design direction.

FIGURE 3.21 is a sample output from a lightning demo about a car rental service. In this demo, I searched for various examples that inspired me when thinking about the problem of designing a car rental website. I wanted to find examples of how other companies talk about cars so that I could gain inspiration for how to position the user experience of the product I was working on.

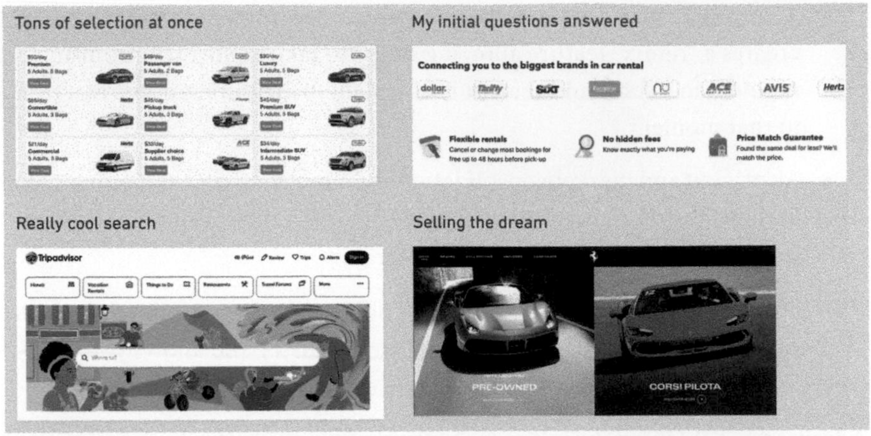

FIGURE 3.21 This lightning demo includes product screenshots related to the project, such as those from competing car rental services. It also includes screenshots from products that wouldn't compete with this one, like travel sites and car manufacturers.

You'll notice that not all of these are car rental related. Airbnb, for example, is not directly related to renting a car (though it is related to travel). That's OK—the purpose of a lightning demo is to gather what inspires us, and that inspiration can come from anything. Here, I choose to include Airbnb because I am inspired by how it sells the vision of travel, as that concept relates to a car rental.

How Do You Do It?

Lightning demos are meant to be short, fast exercises that gather a bunch of examples for you to draw inspiration from. You could approach a lightning demo in a lot of ways, but this is the way I most prefer to do it:

1. Open a whiteboarding tool like Miro, Whimsical, or FigJam.

2. Open an internet browser to look for product examples.

3. Search for products to draw inspiration from.

   - Products that your idea would compete against

   - Products that relate to your idea

   - Products that don't relate to your idea but that you find inspiring

4. If you find a product you like, take a screenshot.

5. Put the screenshot in your whiteboarding tool with a very short description of what it is and why you like it.

6. Repeat until you have 8 to 10 examples.

Let's go through an example where we do a lightning demo together. Let's say we are working on a streaming service and want to make our own streaming product. Let's see if we can find some examples for a lightning demo.

We'll open a whiteboarding tool and an internet browser and look for sources of inspiration—first, direct competitors like Netflix, Hulu, and Disney+. For Netflix, we're feeling inspired by their landing page—how they have a video front and center, already playing, as if we've already started watching without having to even press a button. If we like the content, we can keep watching easily with a single click (**FIGURE 3.22**).

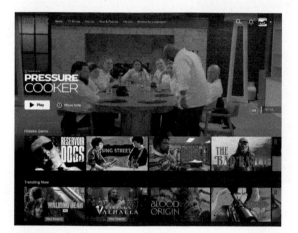

FIGURE 3.22 The home screen for Netflix.com.

We'll take a screenshot and add it to our list of inspiration (**FIGURE 3.23**).

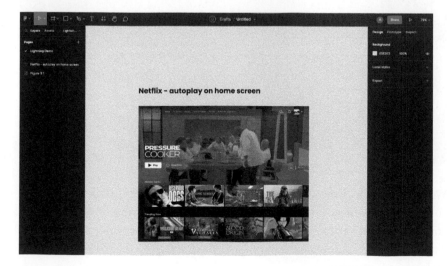

FIGURE 3.23 The first image for our lightning demo.

Next, we'll look at another competitor for inspiration. Looking at Apple TV (**FIGURE 3.24**), we'll play with the product for a minute or so and look to see what we like. Navigating to their show detail page, we see a really nice layout that clearly communicates what episode we're on, what's up next, and what to expect from the tone of the show.

FIGURE 3.24 Apple TV's UI for a show detail page.

Let's add it to the list with a note (**FIGURE 3.25**).

FIGURE 3.25 Updated lighting demo based on the second example.

We could keep looking at competing products, but let's branch out to some comparator products—ones that are like our product but that wouldn't be competing with us directly. Our product is a streaming provider that makes its own original content. We make money from subscriptions to our service and from ad revenue.

When I think about streaming movies and TV, I think about video. Let's look at video streaming products that don't monetize solely through consumer subscriptions.

A popular video streaming product, Vimeo, makes its money by selling subscriptions to businesses for its enterprise video tools. Perhaps Vimeo has some interesting designs we can leverage. Going to their site (**FIGURE 3.26**), it looks like they have a tool that lets people create their own video offerings, and that tool has interactive components.

FIGURE 3.26 The video player at Vimeo.com. They offer interactive options on streaming video, which could be interesting for our project.

I feel inspired by allowing viewers to interact with the content they are streaming. This is a great example of how it could be done for our product, so we'll add it to our list (**FIGURE 3.27**).

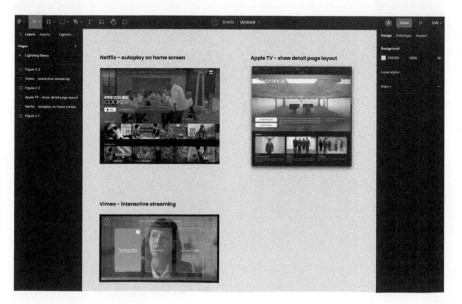

FIGURE 3.27 Updates to our lightning demo examples.

Lastly, let's see if we can find any other sources of inspiration from products that we like. I know we'll need a search function for our streaming product, so I'll look at a website (FIGURE 3.28) that has a really good search feature but is completely unrelated to video streaming.

FIGURE 3.28 The Awwwards website, a website dedicated to finding the most striking and compelling designs on the internet.

Awwwards.com has an excellent search feature that helps filter things easily without allowing those filters to get in the way of the content. I feel inspired just looking at their site's motion and interaction design, in addition to its layout, so I'll include them in our board (FIGURE 3.29).

FIGURE 3.29 Our mood board with several examples of what we find inspiring.

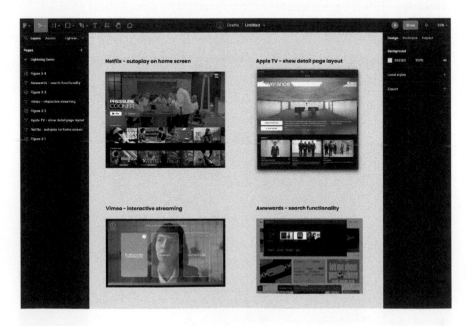

We would keep going to try to find a few more examples—somewhere around 8 to 10 is a good for a mood board like this and would kickstart the conversation for how we could design our product.

This process can be modified to your own liking. It can be done in groups for a group ideation session, or it can be done by yourself on your own project. As a technique for you to use in your own process, it's completely up to you.

If you do it with a team, have everyone spend some time researching examples on their own and finding their own inspiration (ideally 25 minutes). After everyone has had time to look, come back as a group to present your ideas. Give each person three to five minutes to present their findings. As people are presenting, have a facilitator organize the findings by sketching on a whiteboard what people are saying or by collecting screenshots from participants. A group brainstorming tool like Miro or FigJam can help facilitate this.

At the end of this process, you'll have a set of examples that inspire the team and generate ideas during ideation.

How Do You Do It Well?

Though lightning demos sound straightforward, there are some strategies you can use to ensure a successful experience.

- Inspiration can come from anywhere. Let it!

- Ideas can be visual or written. You don't have to visualize everything for your idea board.

- Sometimes lightning demos work better as *homework* than as a workshop. Experiment with what works for you.

- Always use a timer. This will keep everyone on track, since it's easy to lose focus and veer off track with this method.

- Keep your ideas concise. Shorter ideas are easier to scan and digest.

Competitive Analysis

Competitive analysis is an alternative to both SWOT and lightning demos. Where SWOT is a product strategy tool and lightning demos are an ideation technique, competitive analysis is more like an audit. It is a mix of qualitative and quantitative cross-comparisons of different products or businesses. It examines the qualitative aspects of those products, such as purpose, brand,

and competitive advantage. It also examines the quantitative aspects of those products, like revenue, subscribers, and ratings.

Competitive analysis can focus on the business aspects of various products, choosing to home in on financials, ratings, platforms, and upsell opportunities (FIGURE 3.30).

FIGURE 3.30 A competitive analysis of the pricing structure of different companies.

Competitors	Revenue Model	App Store Rating	App Store Reviews	Target Market	Content Types	Free Trial?
(1) Disney+	Subscription (yearly/monthly)	4.5	1M	All ages	Entertainment	Yes
(2) Discovery+	Monthly subscribtion	4.7	139k	18-29	Educational/lifetstyle	7 day free trial
(3) Hulu	Subscription	4.5	601k	18-49	Movies, TV Shows, live streaming	1 month free trial
(4) Apple TV	Monthly subscribtion	4.8	337.6K Ratings	18-34	Movies, tv shows, live streaming, entertainment	If you buy an apple device, you can get it for free for 3 months. Also a 7 day free trial
(5) HBO Max	Subscription	2.8	62.9k	25-44	Entertainment	7 day free trial
(6) Amazon Prime Video	Subscription	4.8	2.7M	18-34	Entertainment	Yes
(7) Peacock TV	Subscription	n/a	986K	12+	Entertainment (TV, Movies, Sports, News)	Free feature
(8) Paramount+	Subscription-based	4.5	327K	Family, all ages	Entertainment, live sports, CBS content	1 week

This example competitive analysis examines various companies and the difference between their free and premium offerings. This analysis was done in the context of launching a premium service and finding the ways to optimize the user experience of that service—in this case, that service's pricing structure.

Alternatively, competitive analysis could focus on the functionality of various products, choosing to highlight features, interaction patterns, or options a user can take in a product, as shown in FIGURE 3.31.

This competitive analysis was done in the context of enhancing a learning product, and we compared our service to other services to see where our roadmap stacked up. This analysis allowed us to advocate for which features to include at launch, which to include immediately after, and which to ignore altogether.

There is no *right* way to choose between these two styles of competitive analysis. Instead, consider what you need to know about the companies you look at as you build out your analysis.

Features by Platform	Atom	Moodle	Blackboard	Canvas	ACT	Edementum	Edulastic
View Scores for All Students	✔	✔	✔	✔	✔	✔	✔
View Scores for Single Student	✔	✔		✔	✔	✔	✔
View Assessment Area Breakdowns		✔			✔	✔	✔
Self-Service Table Customization	✔	✔	✔			✔	
Score / Status Categorization	✔	✔	✔	✔	✔		✔
Manual Grading	✔	✔	✔	✔			
Set Grading Rubrics		✔	✔	✔		✔	
Add Notes		✔	✔	✔			
Message Student		✔	✔	✔			
Predict Final Score					✔		
Compare to National					✔		
Sync with SIS			✔				
Import Scores		✔	✔	✔			
Export Scores	✔	✔	✔	✔		✔	
IMS Score Integration	✔						

FIGURE 3.31 A competitive analysis of different features across different products.

How do we get started? As with the other forms of competitive research, there's a process you can follow to conduct competitive analysis.

Define the Goal

First, define the goal of your analysis. Are you seeing who offers what features? Are you gathering company information for a marketing analysis? What are you assessing?

In the context of the streaming service example, let's say you were trying to figure out what to charge and what to call the service. That means you would turn to competitive analysis to analyze the pricing structure of other products so that you can determine a better one for yours. Let's define your goal as *understand the market landscape of how companies communicate a subscription to customers and what they charge for it.*

Set Your Criteria

Next, set the criteria for your competitive analysis. Establish each piece of data you want to capture from your competitors. Consider the types of things you want to look at relative to the analysis you want to perform.

Is your analysis about product market fit—as in, is your product something that people want and that could compete in the marketplace? If so, then your analysis should be more financial, showing the viability of the business.

Is your analysis more executional—as in, centered on succeeding in the market, since you know your product's idea will satisfy customers? Then your analysis should be more feature oriented, showing how other products solve the same problems and how you can innovate within that.

Choosing the key observation points helps focus your analysis. Let's assume you know people want your streaming service and that you need to execute on its user experience and quality rather than prove there's a market for it.

To do your analysis, you'll want to at least capture the name of the company, the name of the streaming service, the name of paid tiers, and their costs.

You might want more information than this, but this is a good start for you to work from.

Gather Your Companies

After your metrics are set, you need to gather a list of the companies you want to look at. Consider both *direct* and *indirect* competitors.

For example, for the streaming service, you could look at direct competitors like Disney+, Hulu, and Amazon Prime. The indirect competitors could include Twitch, movie theaters, and cable TV.

You could also consider *comparator* sources of inspiration you can draw parallels from.

Continuing with the streaming service, assuming you were trying to reach a younger audience, you could analyze Snapchat, TikTok, or video games. Comparator companies can be a great source of inspiration for your analysis.

For the streaming service project, let's look at direct competitors like Netflix, Disney+, and Hulu. For indirect competitors, you could look at YouTube to start.

Gather Logistics

Next, you will want to gather your logistical materials for conducting the analysis. What is the *location* of each product? Is it a website link, an app store link, or somewhere else?

What's required to access the product? Does someone need a login and password? If so, call that out so the team is aware they will need profiles and so that they can get the required credentials to individually access the product. Creating a repository of this information, in your spreadsheet, will help the project team significantly during the process.

If you were working on the streaming service and wanted to gather this information for the team, it could look something like **FIGURE 3.32**.

---

6 www.vanityfair.com/hollywood/2019/01/netflix-competition-disney-hulu-fortnite

Competitors	URL	Login
Netflix	www.netflix.com	Required
Disney+	www.hbomax.com	Required
Hulu	www.peacocktv.com	Required

FIGURE 3.32 The names and URLs for different companies in our competitive analysis, which helps the team access the products they need for the analysis.

This spreadsheet includes the name of the company, the location, and if a login is required so that anyone on the team can more easily navigate to the product.

Collect the Data

After your spreadsheet is all set up, you can finally begin to collect the data for your analysis. Start by going through your list one thing at a time. You could begin by analyzing either a single competitor across all categories or a single category across all competitors. There's no specific right way to approach this, and both methods have their own benefits.

No matter how you choose to fill out your spreadsheet, make sure you capture visual examples for your analysis. Take screenshots and record video of each product, as these will help you reference specifics and have examples to share when you summarize your insights.

You can save this information in a common place for everyone to access, such as Figma, Google Drive, Dropbox, or some other storage solution.

For our streaming product, we can collect information about the pricing tiers of each product—what tiers are there, what they are called, and how they are communicated to users. In **FIGURE 3.33** is a collection of company names and tier names for their products, which can help you determine what you want to call your tiers. Most companies call their most expensive, ad-free option "premium," so you may want to adopt that convention, so as not to confuse new users who want to sign up for your service.

Competitors	What is ad supported called?	What is premium called?
Netflix	Basic	Premium
Disney+	Basic	Premium
Hulu	Hulu (With Ads)	Hulu (No Ads)
Apple TV	n/a	Plus
HBO Max	With Ads	Ad-Free
Amazon Prime Video	n/a	Prime Video
Peacock	Premium	Premium Plus
Paramount	Essential	Premium
YouTube	n/a	Premium
Discovery+	discovery+	discovery+ (Ad-Free)

FIGURE 3.33 A comparison of pricing plan names for different products.

Summarize Your Results

After your analysis is complete, you will have to summarize your results. You can create a presentation or share-out summary that highlights the high-level takeaways of your analysis. Be sure to use visual examples to illustrate concrete examples of your takeaways—this will help align the team further and provide additional context around what you observed.

Visual examples for your streaming service project can help influence how you want to structure your design solution. In **FIGURE 3.34**, you can see that the pricing plans from your competitors are presented in a way that compares pricing options. You would probably want to do the same. However, you can have a debate about how you execute this plan—some of the services, like HBO Max and Disney+, show only the high-level prices and names of tiers. Others, like Netflix and Hulu, go into more detail, showing exactly what you get for each of those tiers.

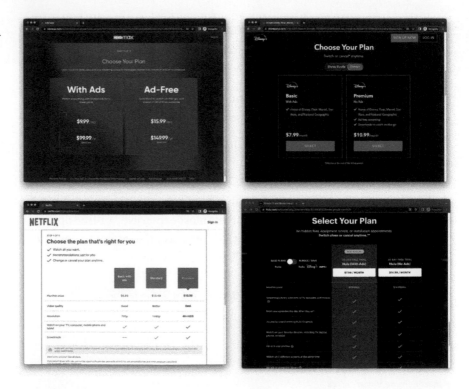

FIGURE 3.34 From left to right, top to bottom: screenshots of pricing plans from HBO Max, Disney+, Netflix, and Hulu.

Is it better for your streaming service to include more details or fewer? Do you want to be upfront with customers and communicate everything before the transaction, perhaps showing them the breadth of your service? Or do you want them to get through the sign-up process as fast as possible, and share the details later? That's a conversation you would have as a team to determine the user experience of your customers signing up for your service. You might not think to have that conversation if you don't do a competitive analysis comparing pricing features across different products.

Apply the Right Technique for the Right Question

There are many ways to conduct competitive research—including techniques we have not discussed. There's no single correct way to understand the market and analyze companies in the space you are targeting. Rather, you must define the purpose of your competitive research and then choose the appropriate technique for conducting that research.

Additionally, competitive research isn't something you do once in a project—rather, you may do it multiple times as you get further and further along in your process. You may learn of new competitors as you go and add them to your analysis. Or you may shift the focus of your research and explore a new question you have, using a different technique than you did previously.

As leaders applying design thinking to projects, we must know what techniques exist, when to use them, and to what end.

Let's Do It!

Any of the competitive analysis techniques covered in this section can be helpful for the solo traveler project.

Do you want to understand the strengths and weaknesses of travel competitors to develop a sense of our position in the market? You can do a SWOT of different companies.

Do you want some inspiration about travel products as you head into ideation? You can do a lightning demo to get started.

Do you want to audit different travel companies and experience them as a customer to understand their features or user experiences? You can do a competitive analysis and create a list of facts and features of your competitors.

Each of these is a valid option for you to move forward in this project. It helps to get a sense of what's out there before you head to the next step in the design thinking process: ideation.

No matter which competitive analysis technique you try, keep a few things in mind:

- **Define the goal of your research.** What do you want to learn? Choose the appropriate technique that will maximize that amount of knowledge for you.

- **Look at your competitors.** Who is a leader in the space you are exploring? Why are they so successful? Study them and learn from their successes while analyzing what they could be doing better.

- **Look at some comparators.** Who is related to the space you are exploring? You won't compete with these companies, but you can still draw inspiration from looking a step or two away from your target market.

AFTER YOU DEFINE, YOU IDEATE

This chapter started at the beginning of the define step of the design thinking process. You did a great deal of work defining the target audience via a persona, explaining how they experience their current state with a journey map, and exploring what already exists for them via competitive research. At this point in the process, you have converged on the research and now understand what it is you are trying to accomplish and for whom.

In the next step in the design thinking process, you will build off your understanding of the problem to solve and start thinking of ideas to help users. You will ideate, diverging around the possibilities for users and thinking of many solutions to address the problem to solve. From those, you'll narrow down your choices and pick a few ideas to carry through the rest of the process.

AUTHOR'S NOTE You could save this step in the design thinking process for after ideation. As you progress through design thinking, you'll learn which techniques to apply, when, and why. For our studies, let's stick with the things that I've laid out in this book.

AUTHOR'S NOTE Refer to the "Competitive Research" section for Chapter 3 in the appendix for examples to compare your research with.

CHAPTER 4

EXPLORING IDEATION TECHNIQUES AND TOOLS

The third step in the design thinking process is all about coming up with ideas. You must think of as many ideas as you can to explore the design space as thoroughly as possible. Once you have accomplished this, you must prioritize and choose several of these ideas to move forward with.

To explore the design space, you must ideate. The process of ideation allows you to be divergent, generative, and creative. It allows you to explore the relationships between concepts, patterns, or even existing solutions and see things in a new light.

Ideation requires you to be artistic. You rely on your creativity and imagination to come up with fantastical new product ideas. You think of features and functionalities that could enhance those ideas. You sketch out your ideas and visualize concepts to imagine the user's experience.

Ideation also requires you to leverage science. You work from a problem to solve based on research, observation, and evidence. You analyze products and remix their characteristics by adjusting variables. You organize ideas into prioritizations, systematically deciding which ideas to pursue further.

It is through this blend of art and science that you will navigate the ideation phase of design thinking and arrive at a solution that best fits users' wants and needs.

WHERE ARE YOU IN THE DESIGN THINKING PROCESS?

As you wrap up your understanding of the problem you want to solve, you begin to transition from the define step of the design thinking process to the next step—ideate (**FIGURE 4.1**).[1]

FIGURE 4.1 The NN/g design thinking model. The third step of the model is *ideate*. It is part of the explore phase of design thinking, where you work from the problem to solve and think of solutions that could help your users.

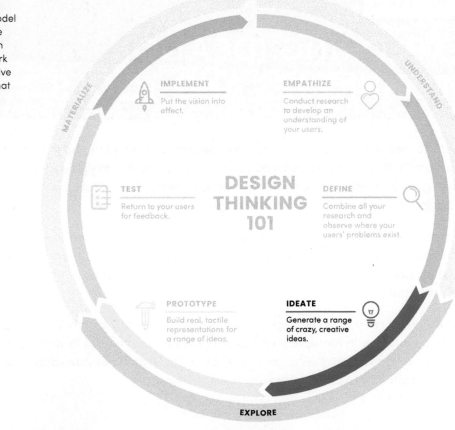

IMPLEMENT
Put the vision into effect.

EMPATHIZE
Conduct research to develop an understanding of your users.

TEST
Return to your users for feedback.

DESIGN THINKING 101

DEFINE
Combine all your research and observe where your users' problems exist.

PROTOTYPE
Build real, tactile representations for a range of ideas.

IDEATE
Generate a range of crazy, creative ideas.

MATERIALIZE

UNDERSTAND

EXPLORE

---

1 www.nngroup.com/articles/design-thinking/

During the ideate step of the design thinking process, the goal is to come up with ideas that will address the problem to solve. Now that you know the users and their struggles, what can you do about it? What ideas can you generate that might work? The goal is to explore the design space and create a solution for your users.

Coming out of this step, you should have looked at all the ideas that you generated by diverging around the possibility space, then converging around a few of those options to proceed with.

IDEATION

Now that we have a problem to solve, let's start solving that problem! We're at the point in the design process where we get to come up with all sorts of ideas that could work for our users.

This can feel like a daunting step. Where do we begin? How do we generate ideas that can change people's lives or, at the very least, actually solve the problems they are experiencing? Will our ideas even be any good? These are common and valid concerns. Fortunately, to get to this point, you've done a lot of research and definition around what you want to accomplish. Now, you get to move forward and start accomplishing your goals—through ideation.

What Is Ideation?

Ideation is a creative process where you generate ideas with the intent to build concepts that solve users' problems. It's rooted in problems—this is why it is so crucial to define a "problem to solve" in the earlier steps of the design thinking process, and why you shouldn't think about solutions until you have a clearly defined problem to work from.

Ideation is also divergent. The purpose of ideation is to come to a solution that works for users. To get there, you must generate many, many ideas and possibilities that could solve that problem. You'll pare down eventually, but to start, you need to allow yourself the room to explore. Who knows? An idea you think might be too crazy or outlandish could end up working well, or perhaps it could be modified to be a real, practical solution.

Finally, ideation is judgment free. Because you should focus on being divergent and create as many ideas as possible, your focus should be on quantity, not quality. At the end of the ideation process, you will evaluate your ideas and pursue a few you think would work best.

The d.school said it best:

> *[Ideation] is not about coming up with the right idea; it's about generating the broadest range of possibilities.*[2]

When Could You Ideate?

In the context of the process, you turn to ideation after you have a clear problem to solve. That problem to solve, however, could vary depending on the stage of the product, the goals of the company, or the needs of the user. You should turn to ideation for many reasons.

Create a New Approach

You may use ideation when you want to create a new approach to solving a specific problem for customers. This could be like Tinder, who wanted to create a new way to engage with the dating culture to make it faster to meet potential matches. Their app popularized an interaction pattern for speeding up the matchmaking process.

Improve the Current User Experience

You may ideate to improve the user's experience with the current product. This could be like Microsoft, who over the years, have invested a lot of time and energy iterating on Microsoft Teams, especially during the shift toward a more remote workforce.

Explore New Revenue Strategies

You may turn to ideation to think of new revenue streams or business strategies for a product. This could be like Uber leveraging its drivers to deliver food or packages to users, allowing Uber to expand their product offering, allowing drivers to make more money, and allowing customers to leverage multiple services from the same provider.

All of the Above

From my own experience, I've used ideation in all these use cases, sometimes on the same project. For example, I used ideation to accomplish all these goals when I worked at Food Network. We needed a new approach for our product to reach more customers, so I had to port a native mobile product to the web. I also had to improve those customers' current user experience, since we already had an existing website and the features I was bringing

---

2 www.alnap.org/help-library/an-introduction-to-design-thinking-process-guide

over were meant to enhance that experience. Finally, I had to consider how this user experience generated new revenue for the business, as it was a new monetization opportunity for Food Network to take their premium app to a new platform.

What Types of Ideation Exist?

Ideation comes in many forms. Not only does the purpose of ideation vary, but the processes to generate ideas vary as well.

Conceptual Ideation

What concepts can you come up with? Some ideation techniques focus on generating high-level concepts for you to debate and explore. The most common form of this is brainstorming (**FIGURE 4.2**), but other techniques exist as well.

FIGURE 4.2 Designers (me included) in the middle of a brainstorming session.

Conceptual ideation is a great place to start the ideate step of the design thinking process because it is a high level, broad strokes, what-can-you-do type of ideation. It generates a wide range of ideas, from which you can choose several of these ideas to explore further using another style of ideation—visual ideation.

Visual Ideation

What could a solution look like for users? Several ideation techniques rely on visual depictions of an experience to help guide idea generation. You could draw a flow by roughly sketching ideas on a piece of paper, create a short story about our users by storyboarding their journey, or even create a mood board of ideas and inspiration via a lightning demo (**FIGURE 4.3**).

FIGURE 4.3 The lightning demo from Chapter 3, which is not only a form of competitive research but also a form of visual ideation.

Visual ideation is a great technique to turn to when solutions already exist, or when you have a clearer idea of the solution you want to explore further. For example, once you've completed a brainstorming session and chosen a few ideas to explore more, you could use a visual ideation technique like sketching to expand on those ideas.

Relational Ideation

How do related concepts connect in the problem space? Several ideation techniques explore the links between elements to think of ideas. Starting from a root concept, these techniques allow you to branch off an initial idea and create relationships to new ones. These techniques include creating a "family tree" of ideas via mind mapping (**FIGURE 4.4**) or remixing existing products into new ideas via a technique called *SCAMPER (substitute, combine, adapt, modify, put to other use, eliminate, rearrange)*[3] (see the "SCAMPER" section for more information).

---

3 https://en.wikipedia.org/wiki/SCAMPER

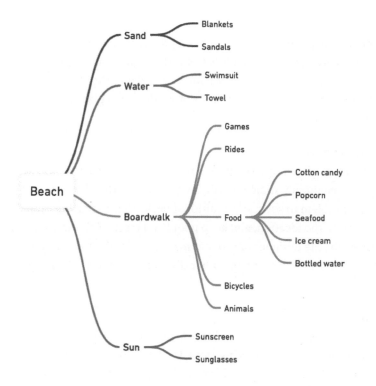

FIGURE 4.4 A relation-based idea generation technique called a mind map. This one explores the connections between elements related to a pier to generate new revenue ideas for the business owners of that pier.

Relational ideation is good to turn to if you are stuck at any point in the ideation process and are struggling to come up with ideas—conceptual or visual. By creating a mind map of related concepts, for example, you will start to generate areas of focus for your conceptual ideation or more details to explore for your visual ideation.

What Are Some Ideation Best Practices?

To ensure a successful ideation, it's critical to establish the right environment for idea generation. Thankfully, you can rely on a few best practices when creating that environment.

Assemble a Team, Not an Army

For most ideation techniques, it's best to have multiple people involved. By inviting different disciplines into the ideation process, you will be able to leverage various perspectives and thought processes. Multiple forms of representation will allow you to generate better ideas to choose from—and it will also let you represent the perspectives of different people in your design thinking process.

That being said, you don't have to invite everyone. In fact, you may want to invite some but not all of your team, since more people in the room means more perspectives to consider, more ideas to sift through, and more time spent prioritizing ideas. Amazon is known for popularizing the "two pizza rule" when conducting ideation: Don't invite more than two pizzas' worth of people (six to eight people).

Choose a Facilitator

For a successful ideation session, you need a person to drive the conversation. Regardless of the technique, someone will have to explain the ideation's context (such as the problem to solve and additional background information), establish the rules of the ideation, and keep people on track as the session proceeds. Generally, the designer or product manager of the initiative is the facilitator, though at times people from other disciplines can lead the session as well.

Set Time Limits

Ideation sessions are usually constrained to a specific length of time; this keeps the process flowing and limits how long the team has to spend in debate about ideas. A common phrase in the industry is to "time box" the session so that everyone focuses on the ideation and doesn't get caught in any specific step.

Establish the Context

Since ideation requires some sort of goal, it's important for the facilitator to establish what the goal of the session is. Usually, the goal revolves around the problem to solve, or has some background that needs to be understood to focus the session. If you're conducting a brainstorm, for example, you need to be able to explain what you are brainstorming against. Establishing the problem to solve, the users you want to solve it for, and any pertinent background information on the project is a good way to prime participants and guide the ideation session.

Quantity Over Quality

Ideation is all about generating ideas. It doesn't matter what the quality of your ideas is at this point—rather, it's more important to generate as many ideas as possible. This is because you want as large a list as possible to choose ideas from so you can explore the problem space fully. You evaluate ideas at the end of the ideation process—you diverge around as many ideas as possible, then converge on a few ideas that you want to explore further.

Weird Ideas

Because you diverge, it's encouraged that you diverge as far as you can. Come up with wild, crazy ideas that probably won't work—those ideas will influence other team members and cause you to think of ideas that could work. The sky's the limit in ideation!

Create a "Safe Space"

When coming up with ideas, it really is important to evaluate them at the end of the process. Postpone judgment or criticism of any idea. Let people know they will be heard, not judged—this will free them up to think of those wild and crazy ideas that could change your users' lives and produce amazing user experiences.

This applies not only to words but to body language as well. Try to avoid any types of negative body language that you can, like crossed arms, rolled eyes, or anything else that signals a disapproval of someone's idea. Think of ideation as an improv class—use the framework "yes, and" to build on the ideas of others.

Using Ideation in the Design Thinking Process

Now that you understand what ideation is, have a few types of ideation styles to choose from, and have a good set of heuristics to adhere to in your ideations, you can start to explore each one in more depth. This chapter looks at each type of ideation, how they work, and how to use them to generate ideas.

CONCEPTUAL IDEATION

At the start of the ideation process, all you have is the research you've done up to this point. You understand the problem you want to solve, who you want to solve it for, and how other companies are solving it today. Armed with this knowledge, what will you make? It can be a challenge to get started, even when you have a lot of information that guides your thinking.

Luckily, you have more than just information. You have the design thinking process as well—all its structure, techniques, and exercises that allow you to keep going. You can turn to this process to generate solutions using conceptual ideation techniques that let you get started on what a solution could be. Out of all the most common ideation techniques that exist, the most popular is brainstorming.

What Is Brainstorming?

Brainstorming is a conceptual ideation technique used by teams to solve clearly defined problems. As a group, you generate ideas that could help solve a design problem. To brainstorm effectively, you work from a clear problem to solve—you need a problem so that you can think of solutions to that problem.

It's a common misconception that brainstorming means ideation. However, it is not the only ideation technique—just the most common one. So, people tend to confuse the two. In the same way that UI is a part of the UX, brainstorming is just one of the techniques available to use when you want to ideate (**FIGURE 4.5**).

FIGURE 4.5 Just as UI exists as a part of UX, brainstorming exists as a part of ideation. Ideation is broader than brainstorming, just as UX is broader than UI.

How Do You Brainstorm?

At its core, brainstorming is a group activity in which participants try to think of ideas to solve a problem. It usually involves a whiteboard, some sticky notes, or some other notetaking method that allows participants to write down short, quick solutions to a possible problem.

To brainstorm, you gather a group of people (ideally with different perspectives on a problem) and ask them to think of as many ideas as possible that could solve a problem you are working on. Participants take time to individually write down their ideas (on sticky notes, for example), and after a few minutes of solo thinking, each participant shares their ideas with the group (**FIGURE 4.6**).[4] Afterward, the group discusses the possibilities, building off each other's ideas, and eventually votes on a few of those ideas to proceed forward.

---

4 www.youtube.com/watch?v=WIVlACbAWio&ab_channel=IDEOU

Let's go through a sample brainstorming session together to see how it could all play out.

First, you'll need a problem to solve. Let's assume that you own a banana stand at a pier and want to increase your revenue by attracting more customers. How can you achieve this result for your business?

To conduct this brainstorm, you'll need to gather supplies. You could do this in person with sticky notes and Sharpies, or you could do it digitally using a tool like Figma or Miro. I'm going to use Figma's whiteboarding tool, FigJam, to record all my ideas for the brainstorming session (FIGURE 4.7).

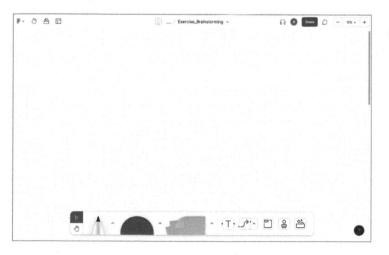

FIGURE 4.7 A blank canvas in Figma for the brainstorm.

Next, you'll want to set a time limit. This is easily achieved using Figma's timer function (**FIGURE 4.8**).

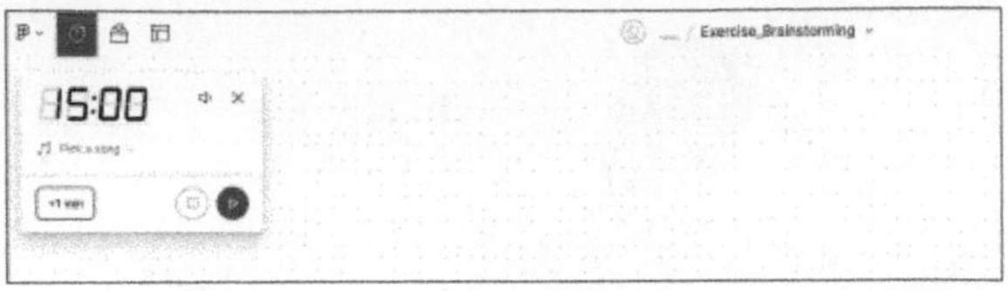

FIGURE 4.8 Figma's timer function. I chose 15 minutes for this brainstorm.

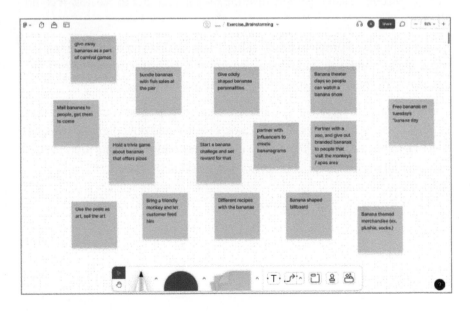

Next, you give the participants 15 minutes to think of ideas related to the problem to solve. For me, I would start diverging around the problem space and think of all the ways you could generate more revenue for the business. That could be marketing promotions, partnerships with other businesses, or even games people could play at the banana stand. Plenty of ideas could work (**FIGURE 4.9**).

FIGURE 4.9 The results of my 15-minute brainstorm. I came up with lots of ideas for the banana stand.

If I were doing this brainstorm in a group setting, I would then give each participant time to talk about their ideas with the group. This would allow everyone to share their ideas, feel heard, and possibly inspire the group to combine ideas or even generate new ones.

Here's a list of everything I came up with during the brainstorm:

- Give away bananas as prizes for carnival games.

- Bundle bananas with other sales at the pier, like fish.

- Give oddly shaped bananas personalities as a marketing ploy.

- Put on theater shows using the bananas.

- Give out free bananas on Tuesdays.

- Mail people bananas as a tactic for them to visit the store.

- Hold trivia competitions about bananas.

- Start a challenge around bananas that gets people excited and social.

- Partner with influencers to sell bananas.

- Partner with zoos; give bananas to people to feed animals.

- Use the peels as art and sell them.

- Bring a monkey to the store and allow people to feed it bananas.

- Create banana-based recipes.

- Advertise via a banana-shaped billboard.

- Sell banana-themed merchandise.

To take this a step further, I could group these concepts into themes to see if any strategies emerge from those themes. The benefit of this is that it may cause me to generate more ideas or combine ideas into a newer, stronger one. Possible themes could include:

- Repurposed bananas (recipes, peels, activities)

- Partnerships (influencers, businesses)

- Giveaways (promotions, bundles, prizes)

- Games (prizes, bananas as a theme)

- Branding (merchandise, billboards)

You could then work from these themes to think of new ideas, or combine themes to create stronger, multifunctional ideas (FIGURE 4.10).

FIGURE 4.10 The themes that emerged from sorting the ideas into different buckets.

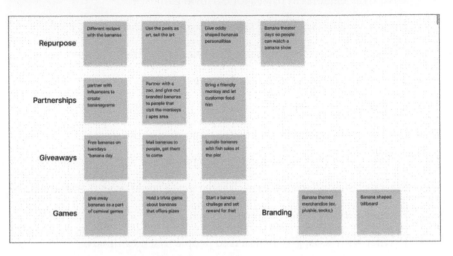

Brainstorming is a highly divergent activity that produces results that can be combined, remixed, and iterated on further. Hopefully, this exercise convinced you that there's always money in the banana stand.

How Do You Brainstorm Well?

As an ideation technique, many of the best practices[5] of ideation also apply to brainstorming specifically.

Set a Clear Problem to Solve

This is a crucial step to the brainstorming process, and the first—you have to establish the purpose of the session. Explain the context to the group, including what problem you are trying to solve with your brainstorming session.

Include Your Research

In addition to setting the context with the problem to solve, you can also include your persona in the exercise. Being able to connect with a persona during the brainstorm will help people think of solutions that incorporate your users' wants and needs.

Set a Time Limit

Establish how much time participants will have to think about solutions. Being upfront with time limits ensures participants focus on the task at hand,

---

5 www.interaction-design.org/literature/topics/brainstorming

and setting limits in thinking about ideas in addition to discussing them afterward prevents the activity from spiraling out of control. I usually give 15 to 30 minutes, but your problem may require more or less time, depending on what you are working on and how much time you have to devote to it.

Aim for Quantity

Since brainstorming is about finding the best ideas, you should focus on creating as many as possible. You don't know what the best ideas are yet—that's why you're brainstorming! Shoot for as many ideas as you can rather than thinking of the perfect, singular idea during the brainstorm. You want a wide range of ideas to choose from later.

Encourage "Crazy" or "Weird" Ideas

In brainstorming, no idea is too crazy. In fact, crazy ideas can create related ideas that are more feasible variations. Encourage your participants to think outside of the box, use a "magic wand" on the problem, or otherwise think of things that they may not believe feasible but would be amazing if they work.

Build on the Ideas of Others

Since brainstorming is a group activity, approach it with a mindset of collaboration. As people share their ideas, ask yourself whether you can build on those ideas to take them further.

Have One Conversation at a Time

To make sure everyone stays on track during your brainstorm, it's good to have one conversation at a time. This will allow the team to be respectful of each other's ideas and create the opportunity for participants to build off each other's ideas.

Take Notes

Make sure someone is taking notes and keeping things on track during your entire session. This could be the facilitator of the session, but it's sometimes better to have someone else do this while the facilitator focuses on moderating the conversation.

No Negativity

Remove judgment, criticism, and negative body language from the session where possible. Negativity prevents people from sharing their ideas and being valued, which reduces the effectiveness of your brainstorm and prevents the best ideas from coming through.

When Should You Avoid Brainstorming?

Brainstorming is one of the most common forms of ideation. However, it's not always appropriate. There are times when you don't need to use brainstorming.

You Don't Know What Your Problem Is

If you don't have a clear grasp on what you want to solve, then brainstorming will not be effective. You need to rely on other ways to understand your problem, and to perform that research before trying to think of solutions via brainstorming.

You Know Exactly How to Solve Your Problem

If you have a complete understanding of how to solve your problem, then you don't need to use brainstorming—you can instead focus on executing that solution, possibly using a visual ideation technique to explore different ways of implementing that solution.

You Won't Be Able to Use Ideas from Your Brainstorm

AUTHOR'S NOTE In this book, you will be using several ideation techniques. If you have been working on your project by yourself, it may be a fun exploration to invite several other people to participate in your ideation sessions.

If you are unable to use the ideas from a brainstorm, then you shouldn't have a brainstorming session. This may be because your roadmap is locked in for the foreseeable future, or you might not have the time to conduct the session and work on the ideas that participants generate.

Brainstorming Is the Quintessential Ideation Technique

Brainstorming is often confused for ideation for a reason. It's a powerful, reliable, common exercise that produces incredible results. It's the perfect ideation technique for the design thinking process, and one to turn to at the start of the ideation step of design thinking. If you need to generate concepts for your design solution, brainstorming is one of the best tools you can use.

Let's Do It!

AUTHOR'S NOTE This is a great time to go back to your persona and consider it while brainstorming. During the design thinking process, you will constantly refer to the artifacts you've been making to influence future design decisions, and the persona is one of the major ones to return to.

Let's brainstorm solutions for our solo traveler project. Let's start by taking another look at the problem to solve:

As solo travelers, our users want to feel informed and assured so that they can feel comfortable on their trip. How might we provide a way for our users to maximize their solo travel experience?

To brainstorm around this activity, you will want to create a working space for yourself (and your participants, should you choose to invite others along for the session). I suggest Figma, Miro, or even some sticky notes and Sharpies.

Alternatively, you can use the working space I established in Figma: https://tinyurl.com/asuxd-brainstorm

You'll also want to keep the tenets of good brainstorming in mind.

- **Diverge.** Think of wild and crazy ideas and try to come up with as many concepts as you can.

- **Don't evaluate your ideas just yet.** Focus on generating them over making decisions about them—decisions will come later.

- **Build off the ideas generated.** When looking back at the list, see if you can combine ideas, create themes, or otherwise find a way to enhance what you've thought of.

AUTHOR'S NOTE When using sticky notes and Sharpies, I recommend writing in all capital letters. It's easier to read from a distance.

AUTHOR'S NOTE Refer to the "Brainstorming" section in the appendix for examples to compare your brainstorming results with.

VISUAL IDEATION

Brainstorming and other forms of conceptual ideation help you figure out, at a really high level, some solutions that could satisfy the problem to solve. The purpose of conceptual ideation is to generate a wide range of concepts so that you can choose a few to move forward with.

To make those solutions more tangible for yourself and the team, however, you'll need some visual ideation to go alongside them. Visual ideation starts the process of taking a concept and bringing it to life with examples. Conceptual ideation, on its own, isn't enough to establish buy-in for the team and develop a clear path forward. You need to take the ideas generated during this step of the design thinking process and show what they could look like.

Several types of ideations help flesh out concepts further and depict the vision you have for a solution. One of the most effective and common forms of visual ideation is to draw out that solution via sketching.

What Is Sketching?

Sketching is an ideation technique that allows you to explore and communicate ideas visually. If two people talk about a concept without seeing a visual representation of that concept, they may end up imagining different things. It's much easier to see the vision of an idea laid out, as if the idea actually exists.

That's why you sketch—you take the representation out of your head, put it on paper, and have a conversation about what you think the solution should look like and how it should function. Additionally, by sketching, you can explore the idea further. This could possibly lead to a clearer sense of the solution's features and functionalities or, alternatively, help you see that the concept wouldn't actually work or be that impactful. Sketching helps you communicate, clarify, and explore the concept much further (**FIGURE 4.11**).

FIGURE 4.11 Sketches like these allow the team to debate the validity of the solution and its execution at a higher level, sooner than if you actually built it. (Chaosamran_Studio/Shutterstock)

Sketching is a way to explore and communicate ideas visually. It's abstract—just enough detail for everyone to get the high-level idea, yet specific enough to provide the gist of what you want to convey.

Sketching is also imperfect—it's not meant to be the final idea; rather, it's a concept. You don't spend time on details to make a perfect sketch to present; instead, you create rough versions of ideas to get a good sense of them. An added benefit of it being imperfect is that the idea still feels malleable rather than finalized and concrete.

Finally, sketching is iterative—you don't have to stick with the first drawing or first idea. Rather, you can keep redrawing and iterating on ideas until you feel they make sense to pursue further.

Why Do You Sketch?

You may turn to sketching for many reasons, including the reasons in the following sections.

Cost Effective

Sketching is extremely cost effective. You save time by thinking about the problem in the fastest way possible. Instead of building a complete thing or manipulating a digital tool, you can rely on sketching to build a concept in the lowest-effort way. Sketches are cheap, and this disposability lends itself well to the ideation process. When you're finished, you don't feel bad about throwing out a sketch. That means you don't feel bad about tossing out the work, either. The purpose of the sketch was to get you to a better sense of the idea rather than be attached to any specific thing you made during the sketching process.

Idea Definition

Since you turn to sketching to illustrate the first pass at your ideas, the sketching process causes you to define your ideas better. You must visually show your idea playing out, and going through the act of sketching your idea causes you to fill in gaps and better portray what you are thinking. As a result, you think more deeply about the problem and the solution you're trying to create to solve it.

Communicative

If you have an idea and want to communicate it to someone, how do you explain it? Do you discuss functionality and verbalize your thoughts? Yes, probably. But a sketch helps align and communicate very well, showing someone your thoughts rather than telling them. This lets you get your ideas out of your head and onto paper so you can show others and get everyone on the same page.

Collaborative

If you choose to, you can sketch as a group to flesh out ideas. You could involve stakeholders or other team members and do it together, to foster a sense of creation among the team and make sure everyone has a chance to be involved in the solution.

How Do You Sketch?

When you're ready to sketch, you'll need a few things at your disposal:

- Something to write with (pen, pencil, sharpie, stylus, and so on)

- Something to write on (paper, whiteboard, iPad, and so on)

- Tools to support the process:

  - Straight edge or a ruler

  - Eraser

  - Color (for emphasis)

For physical sketching, you could also invest in a UI stencil multipurpose tool to draw specific shapes and icons. UIStencils.com (**FIGURE 4.12**) is a great place to find these types of tools:

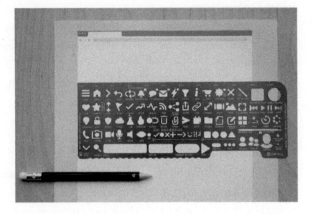

FIGURE 4.12 A sketching tool from UIStencils.com that makes sketching easier.

Conventions

When you're sketching, there are agreed-upon conventions that you can rely on to communicate your ideas. Using these conventions, you're able to speak a common language with others and transfer your thoughts to the page so that others can see what you're thinking of.

You can break down digital interfaces into common high-level components.

LINES

At the core of an interface is a series of lines. Lines divide content into separate sections, represent elements like text, or even combine to form shapes like boxes that hold text or circles that represent user profiles (**FIGURE 4.13**).

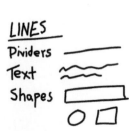

FIGURE 4.13 Common representations of lines.

For text, you can also use actual handwriting if you want to communicate a specific word or sentence.

CONTAINERS

Using a series of lines, you can create a container (**FIGURE 4.14**). A container holds content, like text, images, icons, or many other things an interface would want to represent. Depending on what's inside the container, you could have a button, a control (like a toggle or checkbox), or a card.

IMAGES

Images are represented in several ways (**FIGURE 4.15**), depending on personal preference. I've seen people use an X inside a container to communicate an image. I've also seen people draw a mountain with a circle to imply a picture. For specific images, like a profile picture, you can also use an avatar (a circle and a semicircle).

ICONS

Icons are a nice way to communicate aspects that are common across many products, like search, reviews, home, settings, notifications, and many more (**FIGURE 4.16**).

These elements are often combined to make an interface, like the one in **FIGURE 4.17**.

> **AUTHOR'S NOTE** With many design deliverables, there are multiple ways to communicate information. There's not always a "right" way to do something; rather, if your artifact communicates your point, then you did things correctly.

FIGURE 4.14 Common representations of containers.

FIGURE 4.15 Common representations of images.

FIGURE 4.16 Common representations of icons.

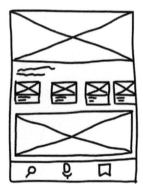

FIGURE 4.17 Combining various elements into a high-level sketch.

I haven't told you what this sketch is intended to represent. Yet you can get a sense of what I'm trying to talk about by looking at the common elements that exist in this sketch. It looks like a mobile phone (since it's a rectangle), with an image at the top (the big X in the rectangle), a few cards (the row of rectangles with Xs and text), another image (another X), and finally a bottom navigation bar with search, voice, and save options (the row at the bottom with icons). Perhaps this is a voice memo product, with the ability to record, search for notes, and look at bookmarked recordings. We're able to have that conversation because of the conventions that exist for me to represent my ideas.

Warmups

When sketching, it's good to do a few one- to two-minute exercises to warm up. I suggest taking a few minutes to draw some simple UIs to *stretch* your sketching muscles before diving into a more complicated sketching session.

Feel free to practice with any of these UIs to warm up. When re-creating these screens, try to stick to one to three minutes per screen.

Easy Warmup (Google Search)

An *easy* warmup could be a sketch without a lot of elements. This gives you the time to get right all the elements that are present on the page without worrying too much about the details (FIGURE 4.18).

FIGURE 4.18 Google's homepage.

Medium Warmup (Bing Search)

A *medium* warmup could be a sketch with a few more elements but still a lot of white space. While there's an image in the background and a few more elements at the bottom of the screen, this example is comparable to the previous one (FIGURE 4.19).

FIGURE 4.19 Microsoft Bing's homepage.

Hard Warmup (Yahoo Search)

A *hard* warmup could be a sketch with a lot of elements. This example has a lot of different components that come together to form a page (FIGURE 4.20). It can be challenging to draw all these elements in only a few minutes!

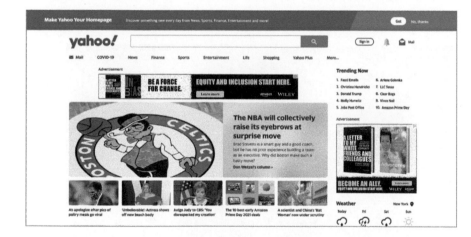

FIGURE 4.20 Yahoo's homepage.

Crazy 8s

After you've warmed up a bit, you'll be ready to start sketching ideas based on the concept you choose to visualize. It can be a challenge to know where to start, however—you'll be working from a blank canvas.

AUTHOR'S NOTE Many designers, me included, fear a blank piece of paper the most. It's hard to get started when you don't have a starting point.

To make it easier on yourself, I suggest a technique that's popular in the industry. *Crazy 8s* is a sketching technique that drives rapid ideation around a concept you want to explore (**FIGURE 4.21**).

To use this technique, follow these steps:

1. Get a piece of paper and fold it into eight sections.

2. Starting with the first section, draw one screen of your solution, or one idea you want to explore. Try to take around one minute to do so.

3. Move on to the second section, spending a minute visualizing your idea.

4. Keep moving from section to section as the time allows.

The goal is to fill up the page with visualizations of your idea—one visualization per section on the piece of paper.

When doing this exercise, you should time box yourself—this exercise is meant to be rapid-fire ideation, to drive the benefits of sketching. You can set any time limit you want, but eight minutes is a nice amount of time to spend (one minute per section). By the end of the exercise, you would have eight visualizations in eight minutes.

AUTHOR'S NOTE While the recommendation is eight visualizations in eight minutes, it's really difficult to fill up the page in that amount of time. It's OK if it takes you more than eight minutes for fewer than eight pictures—this is more of a guideline than a rule.

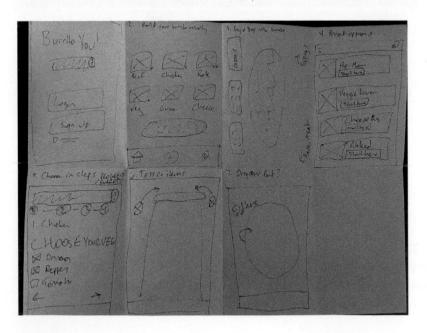

FIGURE 4.21 A crazy 8s exercise I did for a build-your-own-burrito app. I didn't fill up the entire page in the eight minutes, and that's OK.

For the crazy 8s technique, I've experimented with several additional areas of focus to help me develop my ideas. I've narrowed down my ideation process to focusing on one of two themes:

- **Divergent ideation**—How many different ways can you visualize a solution? This style of crazy 8s puts a focus on representing the idea in as many ways as possible.

- **Flow-based ideation**—Think of a journey your user will go on in your product. What would that journey look like? You can visualize each step of the journey, at a high level, to see what you come up with.

You don't have to be limited to a single crazy 8s session, either—you can, and should, do multiple rounds to better develop your ideas. For example, you could do one round of divergent ideation to explore different ways to execute the concept, then a round of flow-based ideation to better explore your favorite idea from the first round. It's totally up to you!

AUTHOR'S NOTE Feel free to do this ideation by yourself or with a team. If you do it with a team, be sure to present everyone's sketches for three minutes after each round.

Visual Ideation Gives Ideas More Definition

Visual ideation is the practice of exploring possible solutions in a visual manner. Sketching is an excellent visual ideation technique to turn to once you have a rough idea of some solutions to the problem to solve. Sketching helps us take high-level concepts and visualize them in a way that allows us to have more detailed conversations. Sketching allows us to get out of our heads and explore ideas to see if they could actually work. It's the perfect technique to use in the ideation phase of the design thinking process.

Let's Do It!

Let's make some sketches for the solo traveler project. Remember, this was our problem to solve:

> As a solo traveler, our users want to feel informed and assured so that they can feel comfortable on their trip. How might we provide a way for our users to maximize their solo travel experience?

Hopefully you have already completed your brainstorm to create ideas to sketch around. If you have, feel free to take one to three of those ideas and start sketching using the crazy 8s method.

AUTHOR'S NOTE Refer to the "Sketching" section in the appendix for examples to compare your sketches with.

If you don't have any ideas to sketch around, that's OK—you can try the crazy 8s method using any of the following prompts (which are also good for practicing the technique in general).

Give yourself eight minutes to work through any of the following prompts:

- Design an app to build your own burrito.

- Design a custom T-shirt-making website.

- Design an app that helps people decide where to get lunch.

- Design a mobile app that lets people find tasty recipes.

- Design an app that teaches kids a new language.

- Design an app that lets people discover new books.

RELATIONAL IDEATION—NEW IDEAS OUT OF EXISTING CONCEPTS

Brainstorming and sketching are two of the most common forms of ideation. The former allows you to generate multiple concepts that address the problem to solve, while the latter lets you visualize those concepts into something more concrete and tangible.

Relational ideation is yet another way to get your mind thinking about the problem space. Unlike the other forms of ideation, this ideation focuses on exploring what already exists in the hopes of kickstarting an idea that addresses the problem to solve. By exploring the relationships between things and looking through a different lens or from a different angle, you may observe something and gather enough momentum to think of an interesting solution.

Relational ideation is designed to get your brain making connections. It takes what currently exists and shifts the perspective, just slightly, to see if you can look at something from a new angle. Sometimes this will be related concepts, like with mind mapping, while other times it will be remixing ideas to make something new, like with SCAMPER. If you feel stuck in your ideation and want to try a different approach, give relational ideation a try.

Mind Mapping

A mind map is a diagram that explores how concepts are related to each other. Mind maps begin with a central theme or idea as the starting point.

From there, various themes or ideas extend outwards from the core idea to form branches. Those ideas could also have their own concepts branch out from them, creating what looks like a family history or tree. In this way, you can draw relationships between concepts in an effort to think about a problem space in a new way.

Let's look at a mind map for a hypothetical project—a business that sells merchandise at the beach (**FIGURE 4.22**). Let's say you're looking to figure out what things you could sell at the beach but aren't really sure what items to offer. Do you branch out into things to do on the beach, like games or sporting goods? Or maybe you start selling food? Perhaps you sell essentials, like towels or sunscreen. It feels like you could go in so many directions.

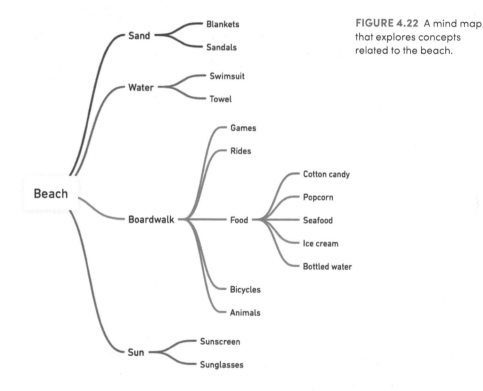

FIGURE 4.22 A mind map that explores concepts related to the beach.

Fortunately, if you want to explore the problem space—what do you sell—you can think of all the things that are associated with the beach as a start. From there, you can focus on themes for your store and the things you want to sell. A mind map would allow you to explore these themes and see what you may even be interested in selling.

To build this mind map, let's start at the core concept—a beach. From that concept, I branched into related ideas of things you would expect at a beach, like the sand, the water, the boardwalk, and the sun (FIGURE 4.23).

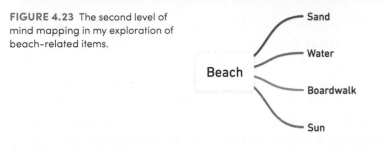

FIGURE 4.23 The second level of mind mapping in my exploration of beach-related items.

Each of those concepts also has related concepts, like blankets or sunglasses. I spent some time thinking about each branch and how ideas could be related to those sections, like in FIGURE 4.24.

FIGURE 4.24 The third level of mind mapping in my explora- tion of beach-related items.

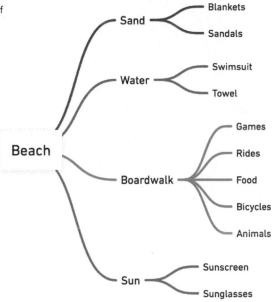

You could continue to explore this as much as you want, going deeper and deeper into related concepts as you progress through the mind map. I did so for the food category, and stopped there after I felt like I had a sufficient number of relationships.

At the end of this process, you would ideally have a lot of areas to explore. If you look at the first branches, those feel like themes—you could focus on the boardwalk, for example, and set up shop on or next to the boardwalk. You could offer food, or have rides, or even carnival games that passersby could play. Or perhaps you want to focus on beach essentials, and you open your business near the entrance to the beach, selling towels, blankets, and footwear.

With relational ideation, mind maps are used to explore relationships between ideas. When you think of something like the beach, what do you associate with it? That's where mind maps can help—to establish the links between one concept and related concepts.

When mind mapping, don't worry about being neat—this is an iterative exercise with the room for revision. Focus on getting your ideas out there and refine after you've explored the problem space.

Also, don't map out solutions—map out relationships. After you've established all the relationships, you can go back and think of some solutions related to those. For example, in our beach mind map, you explored all the elements and products related to the beach, but you haven't explored how you will sell them or to whom you will sell those items. Rather, you are establishing a comprehensive list of related elements, so that you have explored the problem space and have a list to work from once you start to think of solutions.

SCAMPER

The *SCAMPER* technique is another form of relational ideation. This technique allows you develop or improve products or services by relating concepts to form new ideas.

SCAMPER is an acronym made up of seven themes to guide ideation:

- Substitute
- Combine
- Adapt
- Modify
- Put to other use
- Eliminate
- Rearrange

Each of these themes is a prompt for you to think differently about a problem. To use this technique, you take a product or service and apply each theme in the list to that product or service. As you apply the themes, you can start to generate product ideas for the problem you are working on.

After going through each theme, you can look at the list of ideas you generated and compare them to the problem to solve. You may find a concept you want to explore further, and you could use another ideation technique, like sketching, to build from it.

SCAMPER is an excellent ideation technique that offers a lot of creative association potential. As a form of relational ideation, it allows you to generate concepts that you can explore further via visual ideation. Additionally, it allows you to improve upon concepts you may have already generated, which would improve the quality of the solution you want to explore.

Use SCAMPER when you want a new perspective to generate concepts or explore a solution even further.

Let's take a closer look at each theme in SCAMPER and think of how you can apply it to a product or service.

Substitute

What can be replaced? With substitute, you are trying to think of something that already exists and swap it with something else. You must break down the parts of existing products and see what elements can be replaced.

Can you change how something is made? Can you swap one part for another? Can you use different ingredients or materials to make it? Think about how a product is made, sold, distributed, and perceived, and how you can substitute something else in the place of those elements.

Let's look at a few examples.

- What if you took Airbnb but replaced houses with pets?
- What if you replaced the music in Spotify with ASMR audio?
- What if you substituted cashiers with touch screens?
- What if you replaced gym memberships with home equipment?

Some of these substitutions have already been made. Companies like Peloton, Tonal, and Mirror advertise themselves as an at-home gym replacement.

People now have the option to substitute working out at a gym with working out in their homes (FIGURE 4.25).

FIGURE 4.25 A person exercising in their home—a substitute for going to the gym. (Studio Romantic/Shutterstock)

Combine

What can be combined? With combine, you are trying to take two things that exist and put them together. Think of combine as a mashup of existing elements that could bring new life to an industry or solve a problem. You can consider anything from materials to processes, technologies, or even entire products. Sometimes, creating something new is taking two existing things and putting them together.

- What if you combine Spotify and virtual reality for digital concerts?

- What if you combine people who travel often and empty office space?

- What if you combine social networking with professional networks?

- What if you combine cabs and people who want to carpool?

Prior to ridesharing services really taking off, getting in a cab with a stranger did not sound like an appealing option. Having to wait for that stranger and not knowing where you were going or when you'd arrive at your destination felt like bad user experiences. However, with the advent of Uber and other ridesharing services (FIGURE 4.26), it's a common option to save a little bit of money and choose a carpool instead of taking a shorter, direct route to your destination. By combining different trips, all riders save a little bit of money at the cost of time.

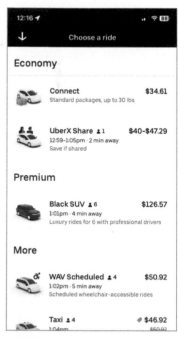

FIGURE 4.26 Uber's carpool option, UberX Share, combines riders so that each rider saves money.

Adapt

What can be added or repurposed? What about the current system can you enhance? With adapt, you look at an existing product and think of the things you can tweak or adjust to obtain a different outcome.

- Plane tickets could have concierge services where an airline representative takes travelers around the city for a day.

- Zoom could introduce low-latency video calls for large online gatherings to expand into the virtual conference market.

- Netflix could expand its content library with a community section featuring independent films.

- DoorDash could adjust its delivery service to include hardware or household supplies in addition to food deliveries.

DoorDash (and other delivery services) initially started as food delivery services. Since then, they have adapted their products to include more items for delivery, like groceries, alcohol, and pet items (**FIGURE 4.27**).

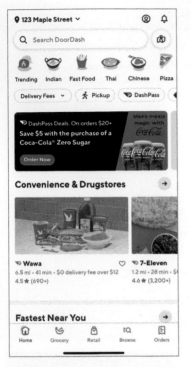

FIGURE 4.27 Doordash's bottom menu includes other categories for delivery besides food, such as grocery and retail options.

Modify

What can be changed? With modify, the focus is on minimizing, maximizing, or otherwise enhancing existing elements to create a new experience. If you dial down or dial up one element, what would happen?

- Smaller movie theaters could book private screenings and put more seats to use in a smaller space.

- Uber could maximize the types of goods it delivers via Uber Eats to generate more sales.

- Apple could minimize the number of components in its hardware to make the thinnest laptops possible.

Dayuse (**FIGURE 4.28**) is a hotel service that allows customers to book hotels for a few hours at a time. This could be perfect for travelers that need a few hours of sleep or rest between activities in cities they aren't staying at for very long.

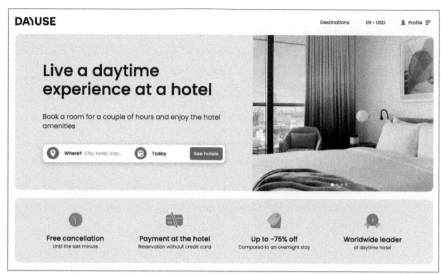

FIGURE 4.28 Dayuse.com's homepage, which advertises hourly hotel stays.

Put to Other Use

Can you use a product in a different industry or context? What would it be like to sell to a different customer? Or to use the product in a different way?

- Old phones have limited utility. Can you record audio tours on them and give them to travelers?

- Can you make a streaming service for children instead of adults?

- Can you repurpose old tablets and give them to children?

- Can you take discarded technology and turn it into art?

- What if you used virtual reality to show home renovations to new homeowners?

Nintendo, a video game company, is widely known for its creations. One of those products, the Nintendo 3DS, was originally intended to be a high-quality portable video gaming experience. Unexpectedly, the Louvre museum contracted Nintendo to use this technology for a completely different use than playing video games—they wanted the console to serve as an audiovisual visitor guide for guests of the museum (**FIGURE 4.29**).[6] Nintendo complied, putting their console to another use.

FIGURE 4.29 In 2012, the Louvre offered audio tours using 3DS video game systems from Nintendo—not Nintendo's original purpose when creating the console. (Trinochka/Shutterstock)

---

6 www.nintendoworldreport.com/news/29776/nintendo-3ds-audio-guides-available-at-louvre-museum

Eliminate

What can be removed or simplified? With eliminate, you try to take out certain elements and observe what would happen. What if you had access to only certain resources, or cut out a part of the process?

- Hotels have bathrooms for each guest. Can you consolidate to a single shared public restroom or even shared rooms?

- What if you removed the concept of ownership from a car, and instead rented cars to people when they needed them?

- What if Amazon removed the step for going to your shopping cart, and instead let you buy an item immediately from their site using your saved information?

- What if you eliminated cashiers from supermarkets and let people check themselves out?

Returning to an example in a previous chapter, eliminating steps in the process can help improve the user experience. Adding a "buy now" option to an e-commerce website allows the user to skip steps in the process, eliminating the need to go to a checkout page (FIGURE 4.30).

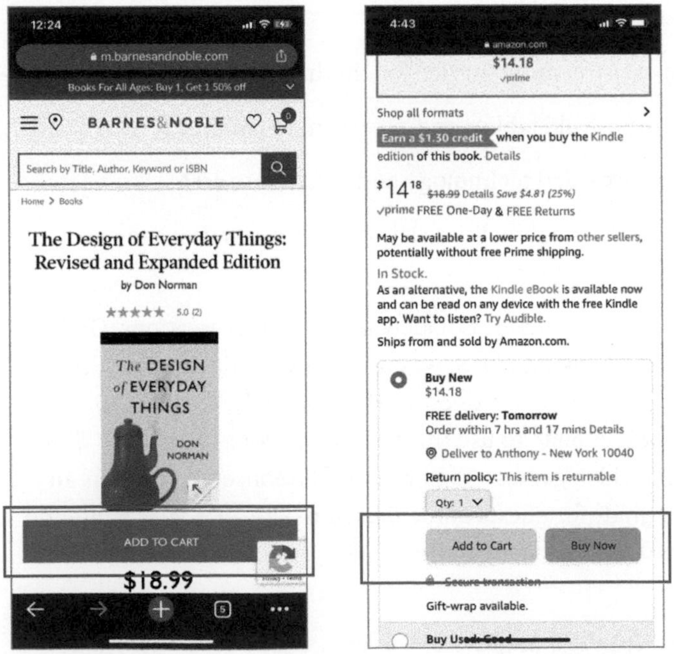

FIGURE 4.30 The product detail pages for the same item on two different websites.

Rearrange

What happens if you reverse or flip a process or flow? With rearrange, you take steps in the process and reorder them to produce something new.

- Museums ask for an entry fee. What if you collected payment when guests leave and ask them to pay what they think the experience was worth?

- What if you generated a list of items in a person's shopping cart, and every week asked them to remove items from it to confirm their order instead of adding items to it to build it?

- What if you messaged someone in a dating app before seeing their profile, then after several conversations, got to see what they looked like?

Lovetastic[7] is a dating app (**FIGURE 4.31**) that offers profiles, matching, setting search parameters, and more. One thing it doesn't offer, however, is photos—the premise of the app is that dating profiles don't contain pictures. Instead, the app hopes that people foster a connection first, then choose to meet and see each other's photos afterward.

Let's Do It!

Let's try a relational ideation technique for our solo traveler project. Remember, this was our problem to solve:

As a solo traveler, our users want to feel informed and assured so that they can feel comfortable on their trip. How might we provide a way for our users to maximize their solo travel experience?

For this exercise, try one of the following:

- Create a mind map related to the problem to solve. Can you come up with a mind map containing 30 things related to the problem space?

- Perform a SCAMPER related to the problem to solve. For each theme in SCAMPER, try to think of three or four ideas related to the problem space.

Once your ideation is complete, see if anything comes out of it that you want to incorporate into your project.

Dating innovation
Profiles do not contain photos

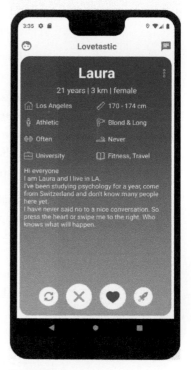

FIGURE 4.31 Lovetastic, a dating app with no photos.

AUTHOR'S NOTE Refer to the "Mind Mapping" section in the appendix for examples to compare your maps with.

---

7 https://play.google.com/store/apps/details?id=com.lovetastic.android

PRIORITIZATION

By the end of our ideation process, you should have generated tons of ideas to explore. You could have done this with brainstorming, lightning demos, mind maps, sketching, SCAMPER, or some other form of ideation. You could have done this as a team or as an individual. You could have done this for a specific problem, or to explore the design space more broadly for a solution. However you get there, you will reach a point where you need to figure out what you actually want to build.

The process of choosing what to build, and when, is called prioritization.

What Is Prioritization?

Prioritization is the process of determining what ideas you want to work on for your product. With respect to design thinking, it occurs when you need to choose which ideas to bring through the design thinking process from the ideate phase to the prototype phase.

Usually, prioritization is a team effort. It's uncommon for a single person to completely own the decision-making process for what to test or ship. In fact, it's common to bring in other voices during this process to gain their perspective. Stakeholders, mentors, directors, or others may come in at this step to share their thoughts and help push a direction forward. In these instances, it can be especially helpful to have a framework for deciding.

Let's explore several frameworks that will let you prioritize.

Dot Voting

Dot voting is one of the most common methods of prioritization, and it's simple—every participant gets a few votes, chooses the ideas they like the most, and puts a dot on each of them (**FIGURE 4.32**). At the end of the process, you tally up all the dots, and the ideas with the most dots get built.

Figure 4.33 is a sample brainstorm with a ton of options to choose from. For this brainstorm, participants were given three dots to vote with, and everyone used all their dots to vote for their favorite ideas. There were four votes for one idea (upper left), three votes for a second idea (middle), and two votes for a third idea (upper middle). Since those were the most popular votes, the team would pursue those opportunities first.

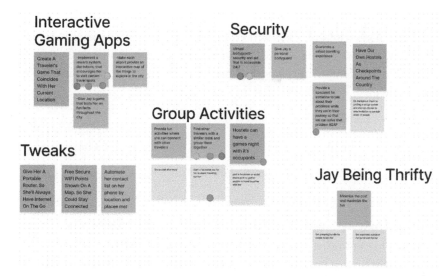

Dot voting has a lot of benefits that make it one of the most common methods of prioritizing.

- **Transparent**—Votes are cast at the same time in a clear, obvious way. It's obvious what ideas have the most votes and who voted for them.

- **Democratic**—Everyone has an equal voice, and the ideas that most people agree to are the ones that move forward.

- **Fast**—Since voting is done simultaneously (usually at the end of the session), there isn't a lot of time spent debating ideas or going back and forth on choosing what to build.

- **Easy**—You take a few dots, put them on what you like, and go from there. It's not a complicated or time-intensive method.

Dot voting is a great method to use when you're earlier in your ideation and trying to figure out what concepts to pursue. If you're deeper in the process— say, trying to determine what features you should implement for a specific idea, and when—dot voting helps less. Instead, you'll need a different method of prioritization to choose just how much of your product to build.

MoSCoW Method

If you have a good idea of the general thing you'd like to build but aren't sure how many features you should include or how to prioritize them, then the *MoSCoW method* might be the perfect method for you to try next. MoSCoW is an acronym:

- **Must**—The things you absolutely *must include*

- **Should**—The things you probably *should include* but don't have to

- **Could**—The things you *could include* but probably don't want to (yet)

- **Won't**—The things you know you *won't include* (yet)

Using the MoSCoW method, you can develop a sense of the things you immediately want to include and, just as importantly, the things you agree not to include so that you don't get distracted by the possibilities. The way the method works is you create a matrix of Must, Should, Could, and Won't (**FIGURE 4.33**), then map your ideas to that matrix to come to a consensus on what to build.

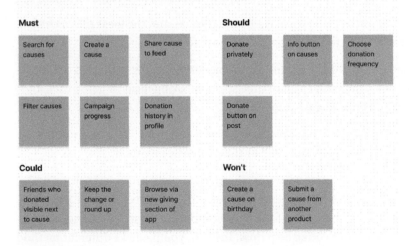

FIGURE 4.33 A MoSCoW that prioritizes which features to include for a solo traveler project.

MoSCoW - Adding causes to our product

Must

Search for causes	Create a cause	Share cause to feed
Filter causes	Campaign progress	Donation history in profile

Should

Donate privately	Info button on causes	Choose donation frequency
Donate button on post		

Could

Friends who donated visible next to cause	Keep the change or round up	Browse via new giving section of app

Won't

Create a cause on birthday	Submit a cause from another product

For this MoSCoW, I was trying to think of all the features I could include in the product I wanted to design. I had a ton of ideas after the group brainstorm and needed to pare down to choose which to pursue. If I'd had time, I could've pulled from other categories, but for the first visualization of the idea, I wanted to stick to the Must section of the MoSCoW prioritization.

This particular MoSCoW helped transition from brainstorming to sketching so that I could better visualize ideas on this project and move into the prototyping step of the design process.

The MoSCoW method of prioritization has a lot of benefits:

- **Collaborative**—Everyone discusses the placement of each idea in the matrix, leading toward a discussion of not only the ideas but the importance of them as well.

- **Aligns**—MoSCoW builds consensus and aligns teams, since there is open conversation about each idea.

- **Eliminates**—MoSCoW helps eliminate ideas, since it's just as important to decide what not to build as it is to decide what to build.

The MoSCoW method could be perfect for your prioritization needs, especially if you feel the need to discuss every idea from your brainstorm. However, if your team still can't decide on prioritization after trying MoSCoW or dot voting, you may just have to include most or all your ideas in your prioritization approach.

Cars Method

If you or someone on your team really wants to at least see each possibility, then the Cars method might be the correct approach. The *Cars method* is a method I've developed working in the industry to size product features and gain alignment from teams on what you should specifically focus on building and is an excellent method for exploring the design space.

This method usually works best with a specific idea that has a lot of potential features or variance. Essentially, it's broken into three groups, represented by cars that increase in both quality and cost:

- **Compact**—What's the smallest version of what you can build?

- **Midsize**—What are all the features needed to most likely satisfy the problem to solve?

- **Cadillac**—What's the biggest, largest version of what you could create that would be the dream product for your users?

To perform this method, for each large idea that comes out of your ideation, create a feature set that extends across each car size. What is the minimum viable product of your solution, the bare basics of what you can deliver on? That's your Compact—the least you need to do to satisfy the problem.

Next, ask yourself what you think is needed to create a really good experience—everything you feel would make this idea not only solve the problem but be delightful and enjoyed by users as well. That's your Midsize.

Finally, think about all the extra stuff from your ideation that you could include —the bells, whistles, and otherwise fun and crazy ideas you came up with. That's your Cadillac.

To prioritize, create a table that outlines the size, feature set, and vision of each category, like in TABLE 4.1.

If you were to try this method with Spotify, for example, Table 4.1 is a possible place where you could land for the first version of the service.

TABLE 4.1 The Cars Method for Spotify

SPOTIFY PRODUCT CONCEPT		
SIZE	FEATURE SET	VISION
Compact	• Search for music • Play songs • Song/album art	A lightweight version, allowing users to listen to music they don't own
Midsize	• Search for music • Play songs • Song/album art • Profile creation • Save songs into playlists • Song history • See what friends listen to • Group playlists	A more robust version, adding additional aspects to our product like account creation, library management, and social features
Cadillac	• Search for music • Play songs • Song/album art • Profile creation • Save songs into playlists • Song history • See what friends listen to • Group playlists • Ability to upload personal music for community • Data-driven playlists based on user preferences • Custom animated artwork for songs	The most robust possible version, adding additional aspects like community uploads, data tracking and recommendations, and microinteractions/animations

The first, Compact iteration of Spotify could be a place for people to search for music and play it, with no tracking or concept of saving a profile. Think of it as a jukebox that plays music—you can choose what you want to play, but you can't save your information or preferences. This is the barebones version of a freeform music listening experience that lets users select the specific music they want to hear.

The Midsize would add the ability to save playlists and interact with others on the platform. This would elevate the service to something very enjoyable— users could save their favorite songs, make playlists out of them, and share those playlists with friends. You're already at a compelling service based on the Midsize alone.

Can you elevate that further? If you upgrade to the Cadillac, you would add data tracking, recommendations, uploading, and custom animations. Now the service would listen to its users, make recommendations, build playlists for them, and even let them share their own music on the platform. It would even have delightful elements toward the fit and finish of the product, such as custom animations depending on the song you're listening to.

Spotify has all these features today. However, they didn't start at this point— they built toward it, over time, through iteration and product enhancements. This may have been their vision all along, but to get there, they needed to take one step at a time and prioritize the more important elements.

To use Cars in the design thinking process, you would go through this exercise, then propose these three options to the team and see which ones they thought were worth building. To validate our MVP, you may need only the Compact. Or you may have team members or stakeholders that want to see the Cadillac, or at least have it tested with users before discarding it. It's a method that can help bring around that alignment and have a conversation around what's important.

Cars is a method that has especially resonated with stakeholders because it shows them the entire problem space and all your thinking, then invites them into the process to determine which version to pursue. Are you trying to launch your product quickly, or are you uncertain how successful it will be? Let's deliver the Compact. Is this something you want to go all in on as a company and give 110% for? Let's go for the Cadillac. It frames the prioritization process like a menu, where key decisionmakers check off which features they want to order.

Conclusion

Generating ideas during this step of the design thinking process is one of the most fun parts about design. There are so many possibilities to explore, things to do for your users, and ideas to address the problem to solve.

It can be really challenging to move forward from a list of several dozen ideas. Luckily, you have many prioritization techniques that allow you to choose the *best* ideas to pursue. *Best* measures more than the quality of an idea—it can measure its feasibility or practicality as well. These techniques help you determine the best ideas to move forward with—best based on our constraints, that best address the problem to solve, that best enhance the lives of users.

Let's Do It!

After all the ideation you've done, it's time to prioritize some ideas from that ideation. For this exercise, you should apply one of the prioritization methods to one of the ideations you completed earlier in this chapter. Of the various ideation methods you've conducted, the easiest to prioritize would probably be your brainstorm. However, I leave the choice to you.

AUTHOR'S NOTE Refer to the "Cars Method" section in the appendix for examples to compare your cars method results with.

Choose whatever method of prioritization you'd like—dot voting, MoSCoW, or Cars. However, dot voting is a method you can't complete by yourself. I recommend inviting a few others to a prioritization session to see which ideas they find most interesting and why.

AFTER YOU IDEATE, YOU PROTOTYPE

This chapter began by introducing the concept of ideation—the process by which you generate ideas that could solve your users' problems. From there, you defined three types of ideation—conceptual, visual, and relational. You explored each type, including techniques to help you ideate across each type of ideation. You then learned what to do with all these ideas by learning how to prioritize ideas with techniques that are collaborative, easy, and transparent.

In the next step in the design thinking process, you will take the ideas you have prioritized and start bringing them to life further. It's time to visualize your ideas and prepare to get them in the hands of your users to test. To get feedback about your solutions, you need to test your designs with users. To test your designs, however, you need to complete a preparatory step first—you need to prototype your ideas so that users can interact with them.

PROTOTYPING SOLUTIONS

The fourth step in the design thinking process involves putting the solution together. Up until this point, you've thought of various ideas that could address the problem to solve. Through the ideation process, you've come up with a few key ideas that you want to take forward and test with users so that you can understand how the solution works.

Before you can test anything, however, you need to visualize those ideas in a way that others can see them. You need to represent ideas in a form that allows users to tangibly interact with them so that you can get the feedback you need to bring those ideas to life in a meaningful way, at scale. You've reached the point where you need to prototype.

Prototyping is an art—how do you fully represent an idea without actually building it? How do you give users a glimpse of what could exist, yet avoid spending too much time and energy creating that possibility? You want to show users what you intend to build yet allow for that thing to be transient so it can change and evolve after users provide you feedback.

Prototyping is also a science—how will your users progress through your idea? To test, you will need to structure an experiment for users to move through. You will need to gather evidence from the testing process, and the way you structure your prototype will influence the evidence you receive during the testing process.

Once again, art and science come into play in the design thinking process, and leveraging both allows you to develop a prototype that seeks to get you the answers you need most—will your solution work?

WHERE ARE YOU IN THE DESIGN THINKING PROCESS?

As you wrap up your ideation and have determined some ideas you want to test, you begin to transition from the ideate step of the design thinking process to the next step—*prototype* (FIGURE 5.1).

FIGURE 5.1 The Nielsen Norman Group design thinking process.

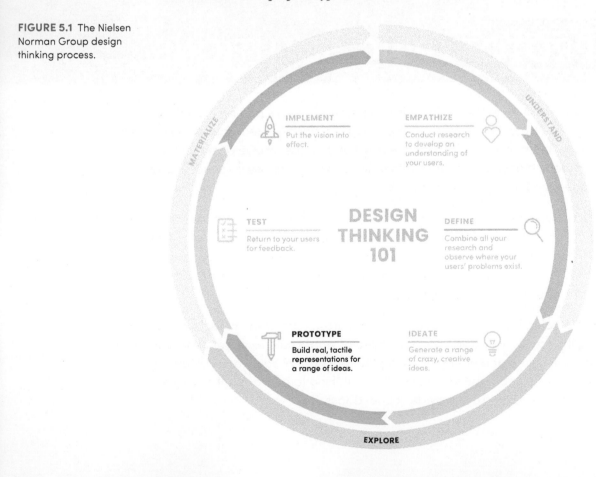

During the prototype step of the design thinking process, you must prepare for users to try out the ideas you thought of during the ideate step. The overall goal is to build a solution that will work for users; to get there, you need to represent that solution in a lean yet tangible way so you can create an experience for users to provide feedback on.

During the prototype step, you seek to understand the answers to the following questions:

- How do the ideas fit together?

- How do they function?

- How would a user flow from one step of the design to the next?

- Does the solution even make sense?

With answers to these questions, you will have a way for the ideas you've thought of to feel more real so that users can give you the feedback you need to build the final product. To get there, however, you'll need to create a flow for users to move through, design that flow visually, and create some sort of way for users to experience that flow so you can test it.

PROTOTYPING

To move on to the next phase of the design thinking process, testing, you need to visualize your designs in some way that allows people to interact with them. This is called making a prototype.

Prototypes consist of different forms of fidelity—low, mid (or medium) and high. *Low fidelity* is the initial sketching out of an idea. *Mid fidelity* is an in-between state that adds more context and improves the structure of the idea. *High fidelity* incorporates branding and the final visual design into the idea so that it feels like a real product. Each level of fidelity has its own purpose, and showing any of them to others can get different levels of feedback depending on what you want to learn.

Once you have completed designs that you want to test—whether they be low, mid, or high fidelity—you will be ready to make what you need to move on to the next phase of the design thinking process: the *prototype*.

What Is a Prototype?

During the design thinking process, you will hit a point where you must take your ideas and get them in the hands of other people to get feedback. You need information as to whether the ideas are usable, useful, and understood by the users you're trying to design for. To do this, you need a prototype.

A *prototype* is an interactive version of a design concept. It comes from the wireframes that you make during the prototype step of the design thinking process, and when all the wireframes are combined, you end up with a prototype to test with.

To create a prototype, you follow these general steps:

1. Start with a task flow—some high-level flow of how a user goes through our product. (More details in the "Task Flows" section.)

2. Make wireframes showing the key screens of that task flow. They could be low-, mid-, or high-fidelity—and each one has its own benefits.

3. Make those screens interactive—either by using digital tools that allow you to create clickable hotspots or, in some cases, by pretending to "be the UI" by using your hands and body to act out what you envision the system would do were it built.

Following these steps, you could create a prototype like the one in FIGURE 5.2.

This is a quick prototype for a car rental app concept I worked on. To create this prototype, I followed the same general steps I outlined before:

1. Start with a task flow—In this case, search for a car rental location, enter your trip details, then see a list of cars to rent.

2. Make low-, mid-, and high-fidelity wireframes—These let me confirm the foundation, layout, and visual design of my ideas.

3. Make it interactive—Because it's interactive, I can test this flow with users or show my team how my ideas function.

In mere seconds, you can use a prototype to demonstrate just exactly how you expect your ideas to play out. You add interactivity to the designs and show, rather than tell, people how they function.

Prototypes can be used in multiple ways, depending on the feedback you are looking for.

FIGURE 5.2 The steps in a prototype for a car rental app, made with Figma. The arrows represent where a user will click and what screen they will go to next.

Test with Users

For the design thinking process, the most common reason to make a proto-type is to test with users. Does the idea satisfy their needs? Does it address the problem to solve? The best way to learn if the ideas work is to try them out! Testing with users gives you this answer, and usually shows you questions that you didn't think of in the first place.

Pitch to Stakeholders

If you want to get mentor, client, or stakeholder approval of your ideas, a prototype can go a long way in showing how you expect your ideas to work. Instead of telling a client what will happen when their users use the product, you can show them. This works very well at multiple levels of fidelity—I've shown stakeholders interaction design at mid fidelity to explain how UI elements would animate on the screen before spending the time to create high-fidelity designs. Use prototypes to get executive buy-in.

Check Your Ideas

Prototypes are also an excellent internal tool to use as you design. I've used prototypes to test my ideas with myself, seeing how it feels to move from one screen to the next. This is especially important with micro-interactions, where I need to determine the exact animation that I want in my UI. Then, I take the prototypes I feel satisfy the design aesthetic I'm looking for to developers, to see if they are technically feasible and how difficult it will be to build.

Depending on what you're looking for, prototypes also have a lot of different possible levels of fidelity in addition to purpose.

What Types of Prototypes Exist?

Broadly speaking, there are four types of fidelity for prototypes. The one you choose to use depends on the time you have to build it, the stage of the design process you're in, and the feedback you're looking for.

Low Fidelity

Low-fidelity, or *paper*, prototypes (**FIGURE 5.3**) are used when you need more clarity on whether your approach even addresses the problem to solve. They are great at obtaining early concept validation and providing a general sense of how an idea can play out. Prototypes by nature are more about showing the vision for your idea and getting a sense for its product market fit rather than the specific usability of your product.

FIGURE 5.3 A low-fidelity prototype, where a researcher acts out each step in the UI. Full video at https://tinyurl.com/asuxd5-3a. (Chaosamran_Studio/Shutterstock)

Generally, these prototypes are theatrical in nature. Since you aren't using any digital product to transition from one state to the next, there needs to be someone playing the part of the computer for users as they test the prototype.

AUTHOR'S NOTE Another low-fidelity, paper prototype is available at https://tinyurl.com/asuxd5-3b

Mid Fidelity

Mid-fidelity prototypes (**FIGURE 5.4**) are used to test the structure of your solution. It's great for mid-stage concept validation, such as testing product market fit, but also good for getting a general sense of the usability for your product. Mid-fidelity prototypes are good when you have a decent idea of how a solution could play out and you want to test that structure.

FIGURE 5.4 A set of mid-fidelity wireframes in the context of a task flow that could be connected via a prototype.

High Fidelity

High-fidelity prototypes (Figure 5.2), or ones that have "final visuals," are used when you want to test your final designs with users or demonstrate your final concept to your team. These are good for late-stage validation and building alignment on visually representing your ideas. Usually, these types of prototypes are more about usability than about concept validation—ideally, at this stage of the process, you've got a good sense as to whether your idea has good product market fit.

These types of prototypes generally contain transitions and animations as well, to further convey that the product is like one you would experience in the real world.

Code

A fourth type of fidelity for a prototype is a *coded* prototype (FIGURE 5.5). These prototypes take in real data during a usability test and remember that data as the test continues. It's the highest form of simulation of the real product outside of building it. These types of prototypes are rare but extremely impressive, as they end up feeling exactly like the product you intend to build. In some cases, some designers work with UX engineers whose jobs are specifically to build working, functional prototypes to test, like at Google, Amazon, or Meta. These prototypes are sometimes called "functional prototypes," which start to lay the foundation for the code that will be used in the final product.

Thankfully, some digital tools exist to make coded prototypes if you don't know how to code yourself. For example, you can try the prototype in Figure 5.5 for yourself at https://tinyurl.com/asuxd5-6.

What Tools Can Help You Prototype?

For most of prototyping solutions, you can rely on the same tools you use to make wireframes (more about wireframes in the section "What Is a Wireframe?"). The most common tools in the industry to make wireframes today are Figma, Sketch, and Adobe XD. Each of these tools offers native prototyping solutions for designers to test out their ideas within the products themselves.

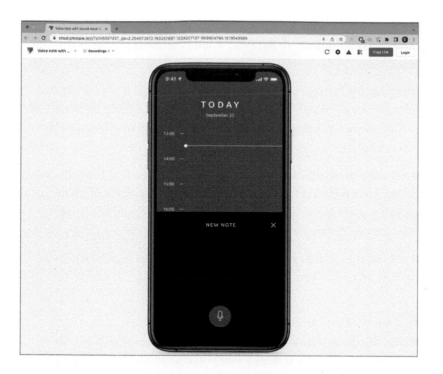

FIGURE 5.5 A prototype that accepts data from the user as they use the prototype. The user can record voice data, which the prototype translates into text and stores as a note in the prototype. (Made via Protopie.com.)

For more advanced prototype needs, such as microinteractions, responsive designs, or coded prototypes, you may need to branch out from these tools. Principle offers great motion options, Webflow offers excellent responsive tools, and both Protopie and Framer have excellent coding capabilities. Use these tools if your needs require it—though Figma, Sketch, or Adobe XD should often be able to fit your needs.

Choose the Right Tool for the Right Fidelity

The prototyping tool you choose to connect your designs and make them into a prototype depends on what you want to test.

If it's early on in your project and you want a vague sense of whether your idea works, you can use paper and low-fidelity designs.

If you want people to comment on the structure of your product and its architecture, mid-fidelity and a prototyping tool like Whimsical might be all you need.

If you're looking for feedback on the visual design and aesthetic of your product, you'll need high-fidelity designs and a dedicated wireframing software like Figma.

If you need people to experience the product with data as if it were a real finished experience, you will have to use a specific prototyping software like Protopie, or maybe even make the product with the help of someone who knows how to code.

I've tested using each of these levels of fidelity—sometimes on the same product. They all have their merits and downsides. Choosing which one depends on what you want to learn, the maturity of your product, and how many resources you can dedicate to the testing process.

Before you build anything, you should first figure out the logic of what you want to build. To do so, you'll need a task flow.

TASK FLOWS

A good first thing you should consider in the prototype step of the design thinking process is the logical steps a user will take in the product. In other words, you need to think about the flow of the designs. You can do this by creating a task flow.

What Is a Task Flow?

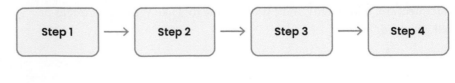

A *task flow* is a linear depiction of a single task performed by the user. It is the simplest, highest-level steps a person would take to get to a specific goal. Task flows essentially represent the paths a user would take to get from the start of the process to the end (FIGURE 5.6).

Task flows are excellent at showing simple, direct pathways to illustrate the high level of a solution. They are great at the abstract user journey in the context of a persona's goals and needs and help you determine the specific logic you'll need to account for in the solution to allow users to accomplish their tasks.

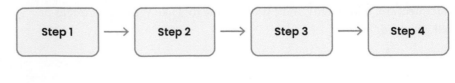

AUTHOR'S NOTE Usually, a user has multiple pathways to complete a task. Generally, it's best to start by imagining the easiest, most direct route from point A to point B. This is often referred to as the "happy path" and the one people most commonly design first.

FIGURE 5.6 The structure for a task flow, which is commonly represented with boxes and arrows. The user proceeds through each step in the flow until they reach the end.

Consider the task shown in FIGURE 5.7 for a user—paying a credit card balance in a banking app. To do so, you can think of the logical, high-level steps a user would need to execute to complete this task most easily (and happily).

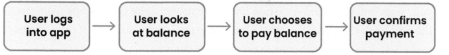

FIGURE 5.7 A task flow for a user to pay the balance on a credit card.

Let's break down this flow. Every task flow needs a starting point—usually, something like "the user opens the product" or "the user lands on our webpage." It's basic, but it helps orient the story and provides just enough context to imply the user is coming into the product from a specific entry point.

Next, you know the user is going to want to pay their credit card balance, so they'll need to find the balance in the product. You can represent this by saying "user looks at balance," so you know the user is seeing the amount they need to pay. You don't specify where the user is, however, because you haven't designed what that looks like yet. Are they in the middle of the home screen? Did they navigate to their credit card statement? You don't know—you're still figuring it out and can fill in that detail later.

Afterward, you say "user chooses to pay balance." Again, where are they? Some screen deeper in the navigation of the product? Or is everything happening all on the same screen and the user is on their homepage? You still don't know—you haven't designed it. You're still considering the high-level logic.

Finally, the "user confirms payment." Is this an email? Did they press a button? Again, you don't know—but you will, soon.

The way this flow is written doesn't prescribe how the actions are conducted—just that the steps took place. You know a user opened the product, saw their balance, made the choice to pay that balance, and confirmed that the payment was correct. These are the high-level actions a user needs to take to complete the task in the product.

I recommend starting your task flows at a high level, just like in this example. Creating a task flow at a high level allows you to make sure each step logically makes sense—especially as the tasks become more complex.

After you have a good foundation of the high-level steps required to get from point A to point B, you can start to apply more detail to the flow in later steps of the prototyping process.

Why Use Task Flows?

You use task flows to communicate the execution of ideas so you can move on to the specifics of how the system will operate. Additionally, task flows help align teams on what specifically will be built. If you think of all the steps your user will take, and illustrate how they move along those steps to get to the end goal, then you can have a conversation with your team if those steps make sense before you begin to create your designs.

FIGURE 5.8 shows a more detailed task flow for a cooking product. To make a new experience, it's common to do a lot of UX work involved with showing the structure of an experience before beginning to build that experience. This task flow shows how a user would move through the product on their first time visiting it—all without building a single screen to represent those steps.

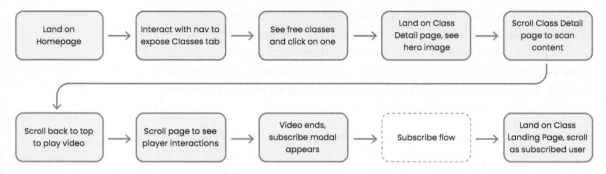

FIGURE 5.8 A detailed task flow describing how a customer discovers new content, watches it, and subscribes to the product because of it.

This task flow discusses only the happy path a user would take in the product. Abstracted out to its simplest form, those steps would be:

1. Land on the homepage.

2. See the content.

3. Interact with the content (for free).

4. Subscribe to the product (to access content more regularly).

The task flow doesn't go into branching paths of what a user could do throughout the product, like rewatch the free content, look for other pieces of content, or even look around the product more generally. Nor does it cover all the interaction design or use cases of those pages, like opening a menu, scrolling a webpage, or clicking a button. Rather, it shows the vision for what you wanted to build, without providing other choices for the user to move through. The purpose of this design artifact is to specifically communicate that to the team—how can someone, in the most basic sense, move through our product?

Task flows are perfect for the prototype step of the design thinking process. This is because a task flow allows you to get buy-in and organize your thoughts before you start designing. By creating a flow for your user, you can map out the specific screens you need to design before you begin putting pen to paper.

How Can You Construct a Task Flow?

The following guidelines will help you make a task flow for your product before you create any designs.

Think of the User's Perspective

When you think about your product and what you want to create, you need to think about how someone else will experience it. How does the user discover your product? How do they learn what it is? How do they go about using it? Why have they come to your product in the first place? Put yourself in the mindset of your user, who will have a different familiarity with your product than you do. Is this their first time? Have they ever heard of the features or functionality of your website? What do they need to know to accomplish the task at hand?

AUTHOR'S NOTE
Product Management can help here. Usually, they've defined some of what the user is looking to do in the product and created user stories—short descriptions of what users want to accomplish using your product. Task flows often come from these stories.

Create a Slice of the Product

A task flow focuses on a single goal. How do users onboard to the product? How do they create an account? How do they search for content? How do they pay for a service? Each of these elements is a different task. You are not thinking of the entire system but rather focusing on a single task in the system. Remember, you're building this task flow with the intent of usability testing a piece of the product. You don't need every piece of the product for the prototype.

Make a Single Path

Similar to a single piece of the product, you also want a single path through the product. Task flows aren't about all the decision points a user can make; rather, they are linear, single-choice flows that move sequentially through the product. They do not include decision points for users or branching logic—each step should play into the next one until the task is complete.

Apply Task Flows to the Prototype Step

Once you have created your task flow, think about the key screens you will need to design to support it. This will give you clarity and focus for the next element of the prototype step—creating wireframes to test. Let's take another look at the task flow from before (Figure 5.7):

For this task flow, let's list the key screens you will have to design.

User logs into app—You'll need what the user will see before, during, and after they log in. That can be covered by a login screen with two states (empty and filled) and a home screen that gives the user what they'll want to interact with most (things like balances and payment options).

- Login screen (empty state)

- Login screen (filled-in state)

- Home screen/dashboard

User looks at account balance—You'll need to show that information somewhere. Let's assume it's a common thing a user wants to see and take actions on and put it in the home screen. You can also assume they'll want to see more details on that balance by opening the account on a new page, but let's see if you need that once you start visualizing the product.

- Home screen/dashboard (focus on account balance)

- Detail view of balance (user clicks it from dashboard), if needed

User chooses to pay balance—You will need some sort of screen that indicates the user is about to pay their balance. Maybe this happens in a smaller pop-up window or on a brand-new page. Maybe it even happens on that detailed view you were talking about before. You're not sure yet! That's OK—you'll figure it out when you start drawing.

- Detail view of balance (user clicks on it from dashboard), if needed

- Balance payment screen

User confirms account payment—You need a confirmation screen where the user sees the choice to pay the balance. From that screen, you need the before, during, and after of that interaction—this could be that no payment option is selected, then the user selects that option, clicks pay, and the pay is confirmed. Maybe this is all on one screen that changes state a few times (like the login screen), or maybe they're all different screens. You'll see when you design.

- Balance payment screen (no payment type selected)
- Balance payment screen (payment type selected)
- Balance payment screen (user clicks pay)
- Balance payment screen (payment confirmed)

Now that you've thought about how the task flow will work, you can see every single step you need to sketch out to make the product work:

- Login screen
  - Empty state
  - Filled state
- Home screen/dashboard
- Detail view of balance, if needed
- Balance payment screen
  - No payment type selected
  - Payment type selected
  - User clicks pay
  - Payment confirmed

Looks like you have three screens for sure—login, home, and balance payment. Two of those screens have multiple states for you to think about as well.

Thinking through the flow in this way allows you to make the next part of the process—visualizing the designs—much, much easier. Once you have a clearer plan for what the user will do in the product, you can follow the plan to make sure you're designing each of these screens for the prototype.

Task Flows Make Prototyping Easier

At the beginning of the prototype step, you may be tempted to go straight to sketching out your designs. After all, you just came from the ideate step, which is full of exciting energy around all the possibilities you created for your users.

However, it's beneficial to take a pause and think through the logic of the solution you want to visualize. How will your users actually use the solution you want to build? Even a quick, high-level flow will allow you to map out the key screens you'll need to visualize in your prototype.

Knowing what the user needs to do at each step in the task you want them to test will help you design as well—you can avoid double work and going back to fix steps in your designs because you didn't realize you needed to communicate a key piece of information earlier in the flow. I've had to rework designs to fit things I didn't think about until I got to the end of a task.

By spending just a little bit of time making a task flow before you design, you can ensure you've thought through all the things your user needs to do in a task and will be well positioned to start sketching your ideas.

Let's Do It!

Let's make a task flow for the solo traveler project. You're going to think of a task related to the product that you want users to test. It shouldn't be too big, like building an entire trip itinerary. Nor should it be too small, like logging into an app. Try to aim for something that would have a few steps in it—something like three to five smaller elements to it.

Be careful when choosing this task—you're going to be working with it for a while. The next several exercises will build on this task flow, as you'll be taking it into higher levels of visual detail and eventually testing it with users. Don't worry too much, though—you can always adjust elements of the task as you go (or choose a new task to visualize once you get to testing).

For this exercise, I'd recommend you do two things. First, think of the high-level steps your user will need to take to complete the task. There shouldn't be too many of these—just the largest steps needed to go from one point to the next.

Second, think of all the screens you'll need to visualize that task. What will the user need to do to move from each step? You can make a list of each screen (and state of those screens), so you know exactly what you need to visualize in the next exercise.

If you don't want to use the solo traveler project, you can pick up any product and think about each step you would need to take to complete a task. First, open that product. Then go through each step to complete a single task. As you go through those steps, write down each action you had to take, or each screen you saw. That's the task flow.

Here are a few tasks you could practice this technique with:

- Use the search feature on Spotify to find a song to play.

- Create an account on Amazon to sign up for their platform.

- Change your profile settings in Netflix so you have a new name and picture.

- Upload a photo to Twitter and post it.

- Take a photo with your phone and send it to a friend.

By practicing this technique as a user, you will be able to put yourself in the mindset of a user and be better equipped to create more accurate task flows in the future.

AUTHOR'S NOTE Refer to the "Task Flows" section in the appendix for examples to compare your task flows with.

WIREFRAMES

When preparing to show your ideas to users near the end of the design thinking process, you need to take all the features and concepts you decided on during the ideation step and make them "real enough" for people to interact with, so they can give you their thoughts and opinions. To do so, you need to create what that will look like and how it will feel. To assist you in this process, you can make wireframes.

What Is a Wireframe?

Wireframes are a visual representation of what the user will see and do as they use the product solution. They communicate what the user will experience, without having to actually build a coded or fully functional experience. They are a shorthand version of what someone could expect to see in a product (**FIGURE 5.9**).

When thinking of the importance of wireframes in your project, think about it like a house. To build a house, where would you begin? Would you decide on a paint color or the type of curtains to buy? Most likely, you'd begin at the foundation, and consider the structure and layout of the house before choosing anything related to its appearance. (Ideally, you'd start even earlier and think about who would be living in the house in the first place!)

FIGURE 5.9 Wireframes for a car rental app. They give the recipient a sense of what's going on so that you can have a conversation about the direction of the product.

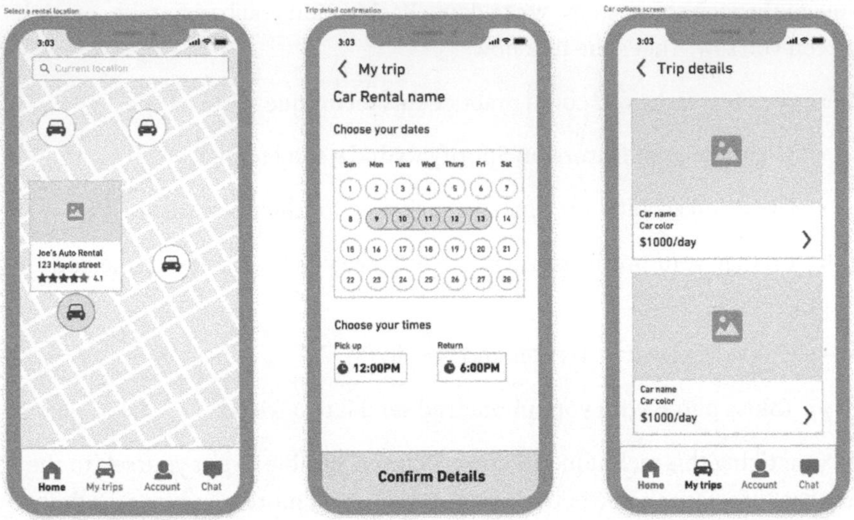

To build that structure and layout, you make wireframes—these allow you to visualize how the house could play out before you even start building it. Wireframes exist at three stages of fidelity:

- **Low fidelity**—the foundation of the house
- **Mid fidelity**—adding on the layout of the house
- **High fidelity**—adding on the appearance of the house

Iteratively, you make decisions at each stage of fidelity as you work your way to a completed house. Designing in this way lets you focus the conversation at each stage of the process. First, you stabilize your ideas by figuring out the foundation. Then, with a solid foundation, you determine how you move around the product via structure. Finally, when your product has a complete structure, you focus on its appearance.

Let's start at the foundation, with low-fidelity wireframes.

Low-Fidelity Wireframes

Now that you have a task flow to guide us for your prototype, you can start to visualize the steps in that flow a user will walk through to complete the task. One place to start could be at the final representation of each of these screens—a high-quality series of images that depict the final version of the prototype you intend to test with users.

WIREFRAMES ARE NOT PROTOTYPES

Wireframes are single, still, non-interactive images that represent the user experience. A prototype is an interactive experience made up of wireframes that connect to allow a user to navigate from one wireframe to the next. Just as there are low-, mid-, and high-fidelity wireframes, there are low-, mid-, and high-fidelity prototypes.

A fourth type of prototype exists—a coded prototype—that can be made one of two ways. The first is to use high-fidelity wireframes in conjunction with advanced prototyping software that stores variables used in the prototype, like a name, a number, or some other important piece of information needed to simulate the user's experience with more accuracy.

The second way to create a coded prototype is with actual code, relying on a software engineer to take the designs, put them into code, and create a "fake" product with a non-scalable code base designed specifically for testing the user experience. The benefits of this are to simulate the user experience most accurately without actually building everything else required to release the product. These forms of coded prototypes can call on databases to represent real, actionable content in the product and usually incorporate motion and microinteractions as a part of the testing process.

Rather than jump straight to the result, however, you should start smaller. Working at a lower fidelity would allow you to have conversations around where to place elements, what information to include, and how the user will navigate from one section to the next.

Over the next few sections, you'll dive into the different fidelities of wireframe design and explore the benefits of each—starting with low fidelity.

What Is a Low-Fidelity Wireframe?

A *low-fidelity wireframe* is a high-level representation of the overall idea of your product. It is your design vision, abstracted out to portray the basic structure of your experience to stakeholders, team members, or even users you want to test with.

FIGURE 5.10 is an example from a car rental service that lets you look for cars to rent in your area. Without too much explanation about the product, you can look at the wireframes and get a general sense of how the product functions and where the user is for each step of the process. The user starts on a map and finds a place to rent, then chooses their trip details, then browses available cars.

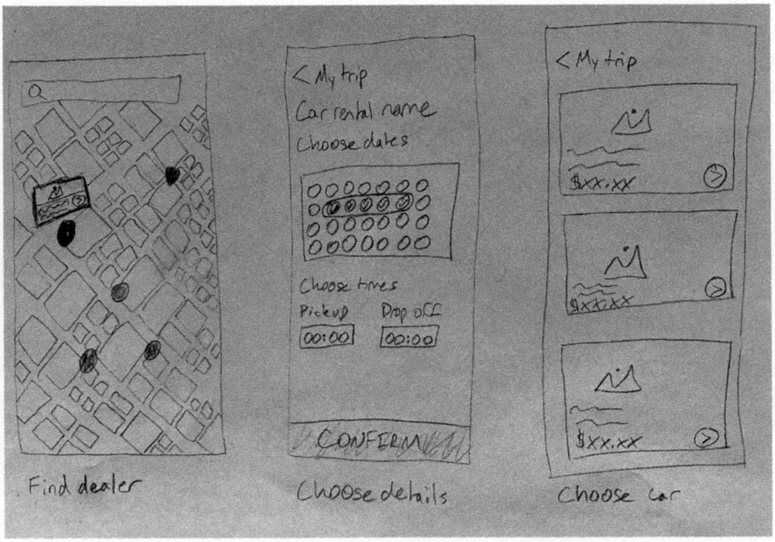

FIGURE 5.10 Low-fidelity wireframes for a car rental app. These sketches allow us to plan out a product at a higher level before starting to visualize it more clearly with increasing levels of fidelity.

To build a series of low-fidelity wireframes more easily, you can rely on a task flow to think of each key screen you need to demonstrate the high-level vision. For this project, I used the task flow in **FIGURE 5.11**.

FIGURE 5.11 A task flow that helped me build the wireframes for the car rental app.

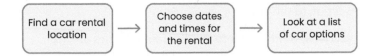

From that, I designed three screens that would let users complete this task: the map, the trip details page, and the list of car options to look at.

When Should You Use Low Fidelity?

When building your product, you should start with low fidelity. This is because low fidelity helps everyone on the team figure out the plan before committing to it. Product managers can see the start of an idea and offer their opinion on how it should function. Developers can look at a solution and start to weigh in from a technical perspective. Designers can debate interaction patterns and features that will enable users to accomplish their goals. By starting at low fidelity, every discipline involved in the creation of the product can weigh in before you choose a direction and have to go back later to fix it.

An added benefit of low fidelity is that it feels imperfect—it doesn't feel like the idea has been completed yet. You are still forming an opinion on the layout of elements and the specific way you want to address the problem to solve. Because of this, people realize the idea isn't fully formed and are more comfortable with debating it. It's still early. This makes the team less attached to the ideas and more able to have a more open conversation about the design of the product, which leads to further team alignment and a better product at the end of the process.

What Do You Normally Include in Low Fidelity?

For a low-fidelity wireframe, you want a high-level first pass at what you are thinking for the product. To accomplish this, there are several pieces of information you can include so you can avoid getting bogged down by details.

The product, divided by sections—How is the product divided into parts? Each screen should have a good sense of hierarchy—what elements are related and what elements are separated. Using lines and shapes, you can divide the product into common groupings and separations that make clear what elements within the wireframe are related to one another. Things like boxes to hold information, lines to divide one section of a screen with another, or even white space to allow for enough space away from elements is something that should be done at this stage to create the space needed in your UI.

AUTHOR'S NOTE
A good rule of thumb for low fidelity is that the wireframes should look like quick sketches of a real product—as if someone had abstracted out the core elements of an experience and drawn them on a piece of paper.

Navigational elements—How does the user get around? You should have a good sense of the pathways a user will need to get from point A to point B. Things like buttons, check boxes, arrows, or other elements that allow a user to move from screen to screen should be present.

Glimpses of content—What content is the user interacting with? These don't need to be fully fleshed out—you shouldn't include things like high-quality photos or complete copy, but you should block out the space needed for these elements. You can represent them using the sketching conventions discussed in Chapter 4—lines for text, lines (or a mountain) for images, and avatars for photos of people.

Best Practices for Low Fidelity

When designing low-fidelity wireframes, there are a few best practices you can follow to ensure you spend the least amount of time making something for the team to talk about.

Go fast—Low-fidelity wireframes are supposed to be fast—don't spend a lot of time making them. Rather, go for the broad strokes so you can show as much of the foundation of the idea with as little detail as needed.

Get physical—Generally, low-fidelity wireframes are done with paper or on a whiteboard, sometimes even with other team members present. This helps you move quickly and not have to worry about manipulating a digital tool. Sketching is the easiest way to get your ideas onto paper. Additionally, the act of drawing a digital product on paper makes the idea feel less real, since you are interacting with it in a physical medium.

Monochromatic—To maintain the theme that low fidelity is imperfect and still being formed, you should avoid introducing fidelity where you can. That means sticking to monochromatic color schemes to avoid distracting the eye and steering the conversation toward aesthetics. Black or gray and white work best, to give it that napkin sketch vibe and steer clear of more visual design conversations.

Simple shapes—As with sticking to a single muted color, be more abstract with the shapes and figures you include in the wireframes. Choosing to include icons, text, or other graphic design elements steers the conversation away from the foundation and gets people thinking about copy, visual representations, or other things that the team isn't ready to discuss yet. Avoid descriptive text where you can and use simple shapes to stay as high level as possible.

Start with Low Fidelity

Getting started with low fidelity is simple—all you need is a pen and a piece of paper. From there, you can start to sketch out the high-level ideas for your product (that came from ideation) using a task flow to think through each step a user will need to take to accomplish the task you want to prototype.

Low-fidelity wireframes have the potential to accelerate later stages of the process by figuring out the foundation first. If you take the time to make them, and make them right, you can build a stronger team alignment before you even start building your product.

Let's Do It!

Let's start making low-fidelity wireframes for the solo traveler project. Working from the task flow you created in the last exercise, make all the wireframes you'll need to allow a user to get from the start of the task to the end.

Alternatively, if you don't have a task flow to work from and still want to practice low-fidelity wireframes, you can try to make them based on the task flow you looked at earlier (Figure 5.11).

As another option, if you want to practice task flows and low-fidelity wireframing at the same time, you can try any of these prompts:

- Use the search feature on Spotify to find a song to play.

- Create an account on Amazon to sign up for their platform.

- Change your profile settings in Netflix so you have a new name and picture.

- Upload a photo to Twitter and post it.

- Take a photo with your phone and send it to a friend.

AUTHOR'S NOTE
Refer to the "Low-Fidelity Wireframes" section in the appendix for examples to compare your low-fidelity wireframe with.

Mid-Fidelity Wireframes

Low fidelity allows you to start thinking about the layout and positioning of the task flow. From that foundation, you get to add increasing amounts of detail and really start to flesh out the journey the user goes on in the product. Using mid fidelity, the fidelity of every aspect of your task flow increases. Things look crisper. The narrative tightens up and becomes easier to follow. The components look more like the real product. Everything starts to become much clearer.

It can be tempting to jump straight into high fidelity after sketching things out in low fidelity. However, if you take the time to explore mid fidelity for your product, you'll get your user experience in a better spot and make the transition to high fidelity all the easier.

What Is a Mid-Fidelity Wireframe?

A *mid-fidelity wireframe*, or medium-fidelity wireframe, is a more detailed representation of your product. It builds upon the basic structure of your sketches and lower-fidelity versions of your idea and begins to add more specificity. If a low-fidelity version of your product is the foundation of a house, then a mid-fidelity version is the layout and flow of that house.

CHAPTER 5   PROTOTYPING SOLUTIONS   221

Going back to the examples from the last section, imagine a car rental service that lets you look for cars in your area to find one to rent (Figure 5.10). A mid-fidelity version would build upon this structure and incorporate more detailed UI decisions, as shown in **FIGURE 5.12**.

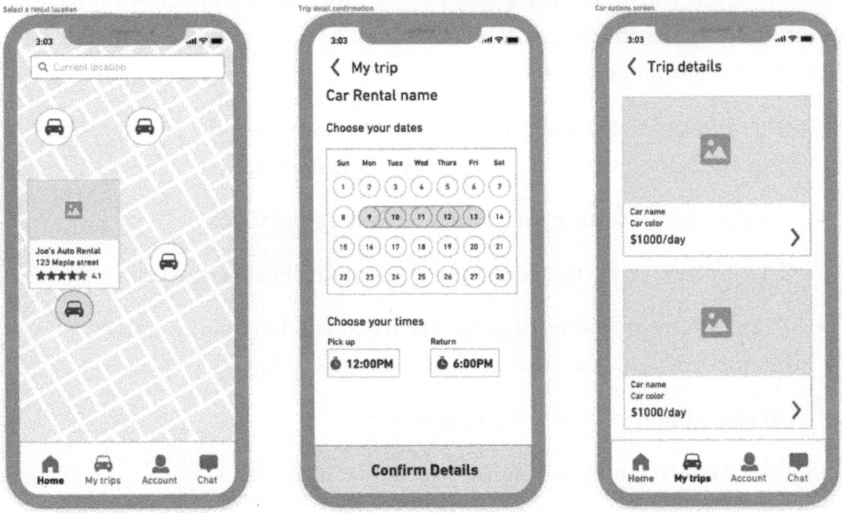

FIGURE 5.12 Mid-fidelity wireframes for a car rental app. Mid fidelity builds on low fidelity, adding more detail, structure, and polish.

When you compare the evolution from low fidelity to mid fidelity, you can see several things start to take shape. The mid-fidelity version looks more and more like a digital product—uniformity to spacing decisions, clearer copy, and UI components that look familiar, like a neatly spaced bottom app bar with icons representing portions of the app.

AUTHOR'S NOTE Some designers don't use the term *mid fidelity*—rather, what you call *mid fidelity* they call *low fidelity*, and what you call *low fidelity* they call *sketches*. The definitions can be challenging to agree to—a general trend that you should be aware of in this field.

However, this wouldn't be confused for a real application—it still "feels" like a fake product. These icons aren't a common style that you see in UI design. There's no color in the product. Things feel a bit too large in this interface. There's no polish to the map section; nor are there pictures of content in the product.

This is the power of mid-fidelity wireframes—this feels like it could be a product if you added a bit more detail. You can see your ideas forming, but they're still taking shape. By using this level of fidelity, you get to shift the conversation around the UI components you are choosing, the structure of the application, and the copy you're considering including.

This level of fidelity also helps communicate the vision to people outside the team. Showing this stage of the product to mentors or stakeholders allows them to provide pivotal feedback about the product unrelated to design-specific elements like color or typography. Presenting your work in this way keeps the conversation around structure instead of style.

What Do You Normally Include in Mid Fidelity?

Descriptive text—Start to think of the words you'll use to communicate with your users. You don't have to be perfect here, but you should start thinking of the titles of your navigation, the language in your calls to action, and the overall copy needed for the product. You can still use placeholder text, like lorem ipsum, if you don't have the words just yet, but make sure you work with whatever copywriters or UX writers you can at this stage to start figuring those things out (if your team has access to those resources).

Cleaner components—Bring in design best practices to increase the fidelity of your designs. Make elements more consistent—if you have a style for a type of component, like a button, use that style every place you have that type of button. Use a spacing system to make sure related elements have the same spacing from one another. Use white space to give your designs room to breathe and imply sections on a screen. The cleaner your designs, the easier they will be to follow.

More storytelling—As you add fidelity, the story of your task flow starts to take shape. It becomes clearer which screen the user is going to next, and where they last came from. A narrative starts to form—what are the finer details of the task the user is completing? Mid fidelity is the time for this narrative to be added to your designs, and you can use this time to produce a more descriptive story of using the product.

Best Practices for Mid Fidelity

When designing mid-fidelity wireframes, there are a few best practices you can follow to ensure you keep the team on track about the conversation you want to have at this stage of the design process—does your structure and layout work for the product?

Make it digital—A mid-fidelity wireframe needs to feel clean, deliberate, and precise. To accomplish this feeling, it's best to let go of pen and paper and make things digital. Use a wireframing tool to make things neat and look well laid out—it will look more real and help with the transition to high fidelity.

AUTHOR'S NOTE Lorem ipusm text is one of the ways you can put placeholder text into wireframes when you aren't ready to fill in what you specifically want to say. Many designers use this technique to mock up designs with incomplete copy.

Focus on layout and placement—A good mid-fidelity wireframe shifts the conversation from idea alignment to idea execution. It's not about what you're building but rather about how you are building it. What are you placing in your navigation? Where on the screen will you have interactive elements? How can a user move around the interface? It's time to have these conversations with the team and make these decisions if you haven't already.

Avoid color if you can—As with low fidelity, you want to avoid color where you can. The conversation isn't about aesthetics, like what specific colors you want in the product. Instead, you should stick to grays, black, and white to keep the theme of "it's not done yet" fresh in the minds of your team and stakeholders.

If you need to use color for a non-aesthetic reason, like emphasizing an element that can be interacted with (like a button), consider adjusting opacity, saturation, or brightness to imply interaction design, like a selected or disabled state.

Mid Fidelity Builds on Your Foundation

Low fidelity should feel like a napkin sketch. Mid fidelity should feel like a step away from the real thing. Use tools like Figma, Sketch, or the wireframing tool of your choice to bring the conversation from physical to digital. My personal favorite wireframing tool that's fast, easy, and simple to use is Whimsical.[1]

AUTHOR'S NOTE
Refer to the "Mid-Fidelity Wireframes" section in the appendix for examples to compare your mid-fidelity wireframe with.

Mid fidelity is a great step between initial visual exploration and final visual design. It's a bridge that connects the start of your ideas to the end product. By using this technique and creating mid-fidelity wireframes, you can focus the conversation on the structure and layout of your product. When that conversation ends, you'll be in a great spot to transition to the final stage of wireframing, high fidelity.

Let's Do It!

Let's start making mid-fidelity wireframes for the solo traveler project. Convert the low-fidelity wireframes you created in the last exercise to mid fidelity by adding the details needed to make things clearer.

Alternatively, if you don't have low-fidelity sketches, that's OK—use the sketches I provided from the last exercise and bring them to mid fidelity.

---

1 https://whimsical.com/

High-Fidelity Wireframes

With low and mid fidelity, you are figuring out the structure and layout of our product. What features and functionalities are you going to include? How does a user get around? How do you ensure you are staying consistent—in your language, your interactions, and your placement of the elements on a page?

When you move to high fidelity, you are putting the final touches on your product. You start to add color. You incorporate all the brand elements into the designs. You add the final flourishes to your product, like shadows, motion, and any other fit and finish you deem necessary to create the highest quality design you can.

The product isn't done yet—you still need to test your designs with users before you can ship your work. But with high fidelity, you get much closer to the final representation of the product.

What Is a High-Fidelity Wireframe?

A *high-fidelity wireframe* is the final representation of your product. It builds upon the work of earlier iterations to take your idea to its last stage before testing and building your product. It should look and feel like a real, completed product.

If a low-fidelity version of your product is the foundation of a house, and a mid-fidelity version is the layout and flow of that house, then the high-fidelity version is the aesthetics of the house.

Let's take another look at the car rental app in Figure 5.10, this time in high fidelity. The medium-fidelity version built upon this structure and incorporates more detailed UI decisions, as shown in Figure 5.12.

Going to a high-fidelity version of the product would take the foundation and structure laid out in low and mid fidelity and add color, typography decisions, images, iconography, and more to make it look more real, as in FIGURE 5.13.

When you move to high fidelity, it feels like you are looking at a real product. The wireframes have every detail needed for a real design, like copy, interactive states, and screens mocked up in real device frames. If you handed these designs to a developer, they could build them; if you handed them to a user, they could imagine using them.

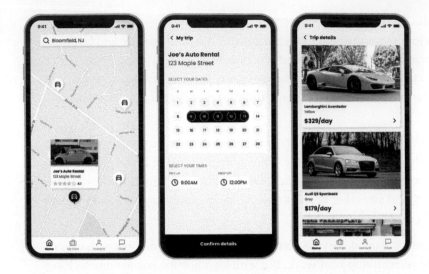

You've built up to this moment. You didn't start at high fidelity—there would simply have been too many decisions to make if you had. You could spend hours on typography, color, branding, and other visual design elements alone, let alone the rest of the decisions it took to get to this point. This is why you should break your design process down into stages to create your wireframes.

By using mid-fidelity wireframes, you can focus on the final visual design for this step of the process. You used mid fidelity to get alignment and figure out your structure. On top of that structure, you have moved to high fidelity, by adding the final details that allow you to realize a polished version of the product.

What Do You Normally Include in High Fidelity?

Color—You should no longer design in black, white, and gray. This is the time to add in the color you want to have in your product—any brand colors, inter active colors, or any additional visual fit and finish, like shadows, gradients, or other visual elements. Things shouldn't look like a concept—they should look like the real deal.

Typography—If you haven't decided on what typography you want to use yet, now is the time. You should have a clear, primary typeface you want to use in the final product, and that typeface should be aligned with the brand. It should be systematic—you should use the same font treatments for all your common elements. Buttons should use the same type. Headings on different

AUTHOR'S NOTE You can use more than one typeface, but for simplicity, I recommend sticking to a single font family unless you have a good reason to deviate—like branding, for example.

pages should be the same size, weight, and style. Ideally, you'll have built a style guide or some other way of keeping track of your type treatments across the product.

Imagery—In all the places you were using placeholder lines and mountains, you should now replace those with images that a user would see using your product. These images should be high quality and on brand with the rest of the product. If you don't have these images, that's OK—for prototyping purposes, you can use a stock library like Unsplash, or even generate images using AI if you must.

You should also have the iconography you plan to use in the product. You don't need to create these icons—there are plenty of free icon libraries you can leverage, especially for a prototype. When it comes to the final product, you may want to make your own set, but for now, use what you can to make prototyping easier.

AUTHOR'S NOTE I'm a huge fan of Feather icons—they look very clean, are systematic (they have the same weight across the icon set), and usually lead to a great result (https://feathericons.com/). (icons © Cole Bemis)

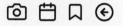

Best Practices for High Fidelity

When transitioning from mid-fidelity to high-fidelity wireframes, it's all about the look. Does it feel like a real product? Can people imagine using it? Does it follow the best practices and conventions for digital design? For high fidelity, you're trying to represent your ideas as if they already exist.

Make it real—Since this stage of the process is all about polish and presentation, then you should make it look as real as possible. Apply all your branding, like logos, colors, typography, and anything else needed to make that feel real. When presenting designs, it's a nice touch to mock up the wireframes in the device in which they will be used—that will help stakeholders and users see it in context.

Final visual design—At this point, all your design decisions should be complete. You should know how each component will look. You should have an opinion on spacing and layouts. You should be using photography and iconography that represents the product and the brand.

Final copy—All the words in your designs should be complete and approved. If you have a UX writer or copywriter, they should have seen your designs and worked with you to figure out those words. As you are presenting the final design, you need to make sure the copy is complete as well. No more lorem ipsum or other placeholder text in your designs—that will confuse users you test with and stakeholders you present to.

How Can You Get Started with High Fidelity?

Although I don't go too deeply into the tenets of good visual design (which is the subject of another book entirely), there are a few tips I can provide you to help guide you in the process from going from mid to high fidelity.

THE 60-30-10 RULE

A classic design rule that helps designers across all mediums figure out how to apply color in their designs is the 60-30-10 rule, shown in FIGURE 5.14.

FIGURE 5.14 A bar that represents the amount of color proportionally present in a product.

60%	30%	10%

The rule states that 60% of the design should be a dominant color, 30% should be a secondary color, and 10% should be an accent color. This works really well for interior design, for example—60% of the design would be the things in the room that take up a lot of space (walls, floors, couch, carpets), 30% would be things that have a smaller presence (curtains, side chairs, small tables), and 10% would be the small elements that add a touch of color around the room (throw pillows, artwork, lamps, and so on). You can apply this rule to UI design just as easily as you would for interior design. For UI design, this rule could play out like FIGURE 5.15.

FIGURE 5.15 Applying the 60-30-10 rule to a UI component.

Looking at an individual component in an example product, you can see that this card uses the 60-30-10 rule well: 60% of the component is white (the background of the card), 30% is blue (the interactive elements like the toggle, the slider, and the arrow), and 10% is black (the text).

If you apply this rule to the rest of the product, you could design every component with 60% white (backgrounds), 30% blue (interactive elements), and 10% black (text), as in FIGURE 5.16.

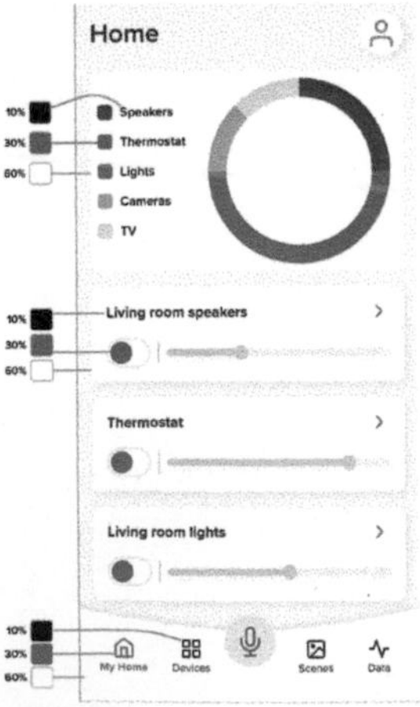

This is not a hard-and-fast rule—there are variations on this theme (some of the blues are lighter or darker in some sections, for example), but overall, it works pretty well as a general guideline to make a clear, aesthetically pleasing design.

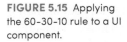

FIGURE 5.16 Applying the 60-30-10 rule to a UI design.

Note that the interactive color isn't always 30%—if you had a more text heavy news app, for example, perhaps 30% of the design would be black, representing all the news content users want to read, and 10% would be blue, representing the interactive elements they could interact with as they read the news.

USING VISUAL ELEMENTS FOR HIERARCHY AND SIGNIFICANCE

Color commonly indicates interactivity in UI design. Often, an interactive element is a high-contrast color that stands out compared to the background color and is usually the brand's primary color. This is because interactive elements are designed to stand out—the purpose is to let the user know that these elements can allow users to take action.

At first glance at **FIGURE 5.17**, I can see this element is interactive—not only can I tell that it is a card (the shadow suggests it's interactive), the copy in the card describes what I will do once I interact with it. Additionally, the color of the text at the bottom of the card suggests that it is interactive—that color is different from the rest of the text in the card (and most of the text in the product this is designed for), so the product is building the expectation that blue text means interactivity (this is reinforced by other interactive elements being blue as well).

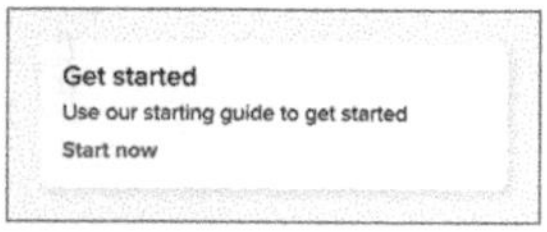

> **Get started**
> Use our starting guide to get started
> Start now

FIGURE 5.17 A card that uses color and shadow to imply interactivity.

The use of color can also establish hierarchy in the UI. The interactive color is designed to stand out relative to the rest of the UI. If you fill an element on the screen with more or less of that color, you can establish hierarchy, as in **FIGURE 5.18**.

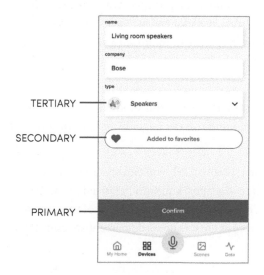

FIGURE 5.18 A UI that uses color on buttons to indicate the primary, secondary, and tertiary actions.

The dominant element on this screen is the large blue Confirm button at the bottom of the design. It is the primary element you want users to do on this screen—confirm their details. However, you also want to communicate other elements to the user, such as the ability to add this device to their favorites. If you also gave that button a blue background with white text, it would compete on the same level of hierarchy as the confirm button. You don't want that—you want it to be the second most important thing on the page. Therefore, you can make some of it blue, but not all of it, to let users know that it's an action they can take, but not as important as the confirmation action.

You can do the same to other interactive elements that you want users to have access to if needed but you assume aren't as important. On this screen, the "type" of device is a tertiary action—you intend to automatically detect that for users when they add their device to the app, but if they want to change it, allow them that option.

Other elements, like the name and the company text fields, are also interactive, but they don't need to have color in them. Their design (text boxes with labels) is a common UI pattern that users should be familiar with because they are so similar to those of other products. Based on previous experience, the expectation is that the user can tap those fields and enter text, as they can in other products.

SPACING SYSTEMS

In UI design, it's common to design systematically. You choose one or two typefaces and stick to those throughout the designs. You determine a series of colors and use the same ones throughout the product. You make decisions about icons and stick to the same visual style for those icons. It's good to have rules and principles to design by so that you can maintain a sense of rhythm and consistency in your designs.

The way you lay out your designs is no different. You should think systematically about how you space elements on the page. You should follow some sort of pattern in your UI, to position elements on the page using a common set of rules across the product.

Taking a quick look at an example (**FIGURE 5.19**), you can see how a spacing system can keep designs clear, consistent, and well balanced in the UI. Each element has consistent spacing distance from both sides of the screen throughout the design. Within components, there is consistent spacing of

FIGURE 5.19 Examples of spacing elements using a spacing system in a UI.

elements from the top, bottom, and sides. Furthermore, similar elements, like each card, are equally spaced from one another.

For a good rule of thumb, I suggest choosing a base value for spacing units (like the number 10) and spacing things out by multiples of that number. In that way, you'll be able to develop a more harmonious UI.

High Fidelity Represents the Final Product

You've reached the final visual detail you can test with—high fidelity. Low and mid fidelity were the foundations that got you here. Building off those designs, you can add the final fit and finish that gets you to high fidelity, which stands as a proxy for the final designs before testing.

Let's Do It!

Let's make the high-fidelity wireframes for the solo traveler project. Convert the mid-fidelity wireframes you created in the last exercise to high fidelity by adding the final touches to your product.

Alternatively, if you don't have mid-fidelity wireframes, that's OK—use the designs I provided from the mid-fidelity exercise and bring them to high fidelity.

When to Use Which Fidelity

So when should you use each level of fidelity for your projects? It can be tempting to jump straight into high fidelity, especially if you already have your branding and UI components ready to go. However, even with fully fledged design systems, it can be advantageous to design low- or mid-fidelity wireframes first. That's because people will see your work differently depending on the quality you present. Let's recap the likely reactions you will get from each fidelity.

Low Fidelity

If you present low-fidelity wireframes, people will see your vision. They won't provide feedback on UI or visual design because they won't see it. Conversely, they will have a harder time imagining your idea because there is less fidelity. People outside of the day-to-day workings of your project will have a difficult time looking at low fidelity compared to mid or high fidelity because they lack the daily context of working with the problem to solve.

AUTHOR'S NOTE It's common to use the numbers 4, 8, or 10 when determining the base value of your spacing system. These numbers are based on extensive research from top technology companies and years of experience of designers working in the field. Personally, I use an 8-point system for all my UI components except text, for which I use a 4-point system to have a little more flexibility.

AUTHOR'S NOTE Refer to the "High-Fidelity Wireframes" section in the appendix for examples to compare your high-fidelity wireframe with.

For users to test with, low fidelity is generally too abstract to get quality feedback. You may gain valuable insights around the value of your idea, but to gain great usability testing feedback, you usually need more fidelity for people to interact with your wireframes without you walking them through them.

Use low fidelity with immediate team members, early in the process, to get ideas out of your head and share them with others for feedback and alignment. You could use it with users as well if you want to learn more about their expectations for interacting with your idea early on.

Mid Fidelity

If you present mid-fidelity wireframes, people will see your ideas. You may get some feedback on visual design, but more commonly you will get feedback about the execution of your idea and the direction it's headed. This is the level of fidelity that helps build consensus across your team and outside of it. Internally, it helps everyone see the plan to complete the problem to solve. Externally, it helps build the context for those who aren't familiar with the problem or how you are trying to solve it. It also provides people the opportunity to influence the design before the design is "done."

For users, mid fidelity can be a great way to get some feedback about value proposition and usability. As it's a more complete version of your ideas, it will be easier for users unfamiliar with your ideas to understand them.

Use mid fidelity to present to team members for alignment and stakeholders for mid-project approval. Show mid-fidelity wireframes to developers, to confirm technical specifications before fully designing your UI. Additionally, use mid fidelity with users for some good insight on user expectations around the features and functionality of your product. In some cases, mid fidelity can also be used for usability testing, such as a mid-fidelity prototype with copy to explain interface elements and content.

High Fidelity

If you present high-fidelity wireframes, people will see the final execution of your ideas (even if that isn't your intent). You will get a lot of feedback about visual design, and if anything feels off visually, it may become the focus of the conversation. People will bundle aspects of your structure and your visual design into their feedback and may reject or approve an idea based on the combination of these elements. If you want feedback on the final idea this is the form of fidelity to present.

For users, high fidelity is the most common way to test your designs. Users aren't always familiar with the product design process, so seeing gray images, monochromatic wireframes, or incomplete copy can lead them to think the product is broken (at Nickelodeon, we couldn't test anything at grayscale for fear of scaring our younger users!). If you create the closest representation to the product you intend to ship, you will get the best feedback about it, from both a product market fit and usability perspective.

Use high fidelity when you want to show stakeholders the final (or near final) execution of your ideas. At this stage, you shouldn't have questions about the structure or layout; rather, it's about how the final product looks and how stakeholders can expect it to function. Additionally, use high fidelity when you want to confirm the usability of your product with your users.

Use the Right Fidelity!

I once created a series of high-fidelity designs that illustrated a new feature for a web product. We wanted to offer people the ability to print content from our website more easily, so I created a flow that illustrated how they would do so. Instead of using mid fidelity, I chose high fidelity.

I made my flows for our new idea and proceeded to present them to stakeholders. We had two options to consider—a print button at the beginning of the page, or a print button later on as the user browsed the content. We needed an answer around where we should put the button on the page, and approval for our design direction of the flow (not the visual design).

Unfortunately, in my haste creating the feature, I chose a subjective icon to communicate the print functionality. As a result, the room was confused about the choice of icon. Some liked it; others didn't. Stakeholders spent 20 minutes of meeting time discussing an element of the product that didn't matter at that stage—an icon's visual design—instead of discussing how the user would encounter or use the print functionality.

The impact of my decision to use high fidelity and a placeholder icon instead of mid fidelity and a clearer icon caused the team to focus on something completely irrelevant to the conversation at hand. I wasted all our time—all because of an icon.

Let's Do It!

Let's make a prototype for the solo traveler project!

AUTHOR'S NOTE
Refer to the "Prototype" section in the appendix for examples to compare your prototype with.

For this exercise, I recommend using your high-fidelity wireframes. Connect each step/screen of your designs into a prototype. You can use the tool of your choice, though I recommend using either Figma or the tool you built your high-fidelity wireframes in.

If you'd like to test with a different fidelity, go ahead—it's up to you. Alternatively, you can take the wireframes I've created and use those to test—though you'll have to import them into a prototyping tool first to do so.

AFTER YOU PROTOTYPE, YOU TEST

This chapter started at the beginning of the prototype step of the design thinking process. Fresh off your ideation, you came up with a task you wanted to test with your users. You went through every stage of fidelity—low, mid, and high—to visualize that task flow and represent everything users would see and experience as they moved through the task. Finally, you created a prototype from these visualizations so that you could test it with users to see how your designs perform.

That's where you're headed next—the next step in the design thinking process is to conduct user testing with your prototype. To do so, I'll be talking a lot about usability. I'll define what usability is. I'll discuss how to structure usability testing. I'll cover how to find participants, how to test with them, and how to analyze the results of those tests. Finally, I'll talk about presenting the results of those tests to others so you can share the feedback from testing with team members.

$$\Psi(x_b, y, z, t)$$

$$x = x_b$$

$$x$$

CHAPTER 6

TESTING YOUR DESIGNS

The fifth step in the design thinking process requires you to speak with users once again. Now that you have a prototype that represents your design solution, you must see how it performs with the people you've been designing for. Through the testing process, you evaluate the usability of the solution and determine if it will work for the target audience.

Testing is an *art*—once again, you must navigate conversations with users, which is an art form. You must use creativity and storytelling to describe the ideas and sell the vision of what you want to make so that users can see the full picture of what you designed. You must share your imagination with your users and bring them into the world you want to make.

Testing is also a *science*—you establish parameters for your test, to remain consistent across users. Use the same language when asking questions to different users, to reduce the variance in the tests. You track metrics, like time to complete a task or the level of ease using the prototype. You take this data, analyze it, and create averages and statements that evaluate the usability of the prototype.

Art and science come together when testing ideas, and you need to rely on both to discover whether the product idea will work.

WHERE ARE YOU IN THE DESIGN THINKING PROCESS?

As you wrap up the design work that you need to conduct for the prototype step of the design thinking process, you should have a good idea of the parts of the product that you want to test with users. You should have established the flows you wanted to design for, created various wireframes for the key screens of those flows, and put them together into a functional prototype. You did all this work for the next part of the design thinking process—*test* (FIGURE 6.1).

During the test step of the process, you wish to see how your ideas perform. You want to take the prototype created in the last step and test it with users.

FIGURE 6.1 The Nielsen Norman Group design thinking process. The fifth step of the model is test. In this step, you finally share your designs with users for feedback to see if your solution could address their wants and needs.

IMPLEMENT
Put the vision into effect.

EMPATHIZE
Conduct research to develop an understanding of your users.

UNDERSTAND

MATERIALIZE

TEST
Return to your users for feedback.

DESIGN THINKING 101

DEFINE
Combine all your research and observe where your users' problems exist.

PROTOTYPE
Build real, tactile representations for a range of ideas.

IDEATE
Generate a range of crazy, creative ideas.

EXPLORE

Your task during this step is to find users to test with, conduct the testing, and analyze the results. From those results, you'll make the needed revisions and shore up all the product's use cases as you head toward building it.

To support that goal when coming out of the test step of the design thinking process, you wish to have recruited users to test with, conducted testing with those users, and gained a better understanding of the designs.

But what are you trying to understand with the designs? Well, the main goal of testing is to determine the *usability* of the designs—how *usable* are the designs that you've made?

TESTING

Although you have the prototype you want to test with, you still aren't ready to do that testing just yet. To test, you need to plan what you want to accomplish with testing, define the testing criteria, and find the users you want to test with. From there, you can conduct testing and analyze the results so that you will know how successful your ideas will be before you launch the product.

One of the most common forms of user testing is a core component of the design thinking process—usability testing. Usability testing allows you to see how users interact with your product, and from there, you can form opinions on what works, what doesn't work, and what you can do to improve the user experience even further.

Are your designs easy to learn? Easy to use? Satisfying? The only way to determine this is to put them in the hands of other users and observe. The main purpose of the testing step is to determine how usable your designs are—to evaluate their *usability*.

What Is Usability?

Usability is a condition of the user's experience with a product or service. Usability.gov defines it as:

> *The quality of a user's experience when interacting with products or systems, including websites, software, devices, or applications. Usability is about effectiveness, efficiency, and the overall satisfaction of the user.*

Essentially, usability is a measure of a variety of factors, such as how intuitive a product is to use, how easy it is to learn, and how satisfying it is to users.

Looking back at Aarron Walter's hierarchy of user needs (FIGURE 6.2) from his book *Designing for Emotion*,[1] you can see that one of the core needs users have for products and services is that they be usable.

FIGURE 6.2 *Usable* is the third need that users have for a product.

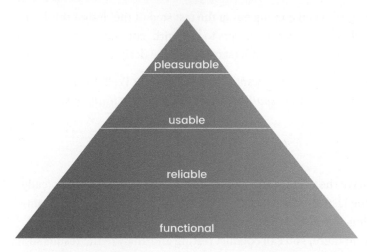

If a product is not usable, then it doesn't meet the core needs people have when trying to use that product. It might not function well, or it could be hard to use, or perhaps it has a learning curve that makes it difficult to pick up. Whatever the case may be, your products need to be usable so that you satisfy the needs of the users.

Usability is something that can be measured through observation and analysis. If people struggle to understand how to operate a product, or how to accomplish their goals within that product, then the product isn't as usable as it could be. Elements and their use could be more obvious. Information could be easier to access. The design could benefit from fewer steps or more intuitive steps without needing explanation. Or perhaps it can require less effort to use a product—this would improve its usability as well.

To better understand how a product can become more usable, let's look at a common household product that evolved over time to improve its usability: the phone.

In 1876, Alexander Graham Bell patented the first phone (FIGURE 6.3).[2] It was a curved device with two separate attachments—one for speaking into, and

---

1 https://abookapart.com/products/designing-for-emotion
2 https://en.wikipedia.org/wiki/Telephone#/media/File:Alexander_Graham_Telephone_in_Newyork.jpg

another for listening to the person on the other end of the line. It revolutionized the way in which we communicate. The product satisfied all the core requirements of the hierarchy of user needs:

- **Functionally,** you could call someone.

- The connection and conversation were **reliable**.

- The phone itself was **usable** via mouthpiece and receiver.

- It was **pleasurable** to use an innovative technology that enabled people to do things they could never do before.

FIGURE 6.3 Alexander Graham Bell placing a phone call from New York to Chicago in 1892. Image courtesy of Library of Congress.

Over the years, the design of phones has drastically increased their usability to further satisfy users' needs.

In the 1930s, phone design evolved greatly. The need for a separate speaker and input were condensed to a single handset that sat on top of the phone (**FIGURE 6.4**). It was clear when the phone was ready to receive a call because the device couldn't operate unless you took the handset off its cradle. A rotary dial for dialing someone's number improved the functionality of the product while indirectly adding satisfying tactile feedback, including sound and motion design whenever a number was selected from the wheel. Overall, this was a much more usable product than earlier iterations.

AUTHOR'S NOTE You can still consider tactile feedback in the digital products you design. On phones, for example, you can think about how haptics play into the user's experience—sending a vibration to signal the receipt of a message, for example, instead of relying only on sound.

Still, there was room for growth. In the 1960s, later versions of phone design improved upon the usability of earlier models even further. A touchpad replaced the rotary dial to improve the speed at which users dialed (FIGURE 6.5). The touchpad allowed for an additional character to be added, like a * or # key, increasing its functionality.

FIGURE 6.4 A rotary telephone, which iterated on the original telephone design to improve the usability experience. (Berthold Werner/Shutterstock)

FIGURE 6.5 The next evolution of phones, which updated the speed and functionality of the previous model. (Lawrence Roberg/Shutterstock)

Eventually, technology allowed for phones that could operate without needing a corded connection (FIGURE 6.6). The usability of the product skyrocketed—now, users could take their phones out of their homes or places of work and be reached anywhere. Core functionality like the touchpad and additional characters remained, but the improvements of connecting with others and not needing a landline to be connected allowed users to communicate from anywhere.

Phones are so much more powerful than they were in the early 2000s. A digital dial pad replaced the physical one (FIGURE 6.7). The mechanics of how our phones ring changed—choosing different audio effects or applying haptics, such as vibration. Phones can do other things, like receive emails, play games, or access the internet. The usability of phones has reached a level far beyond what Alexander Graham Bell envisioned when he patented the phone.

FIGURE 6.6 Phones eventually became portable, drastically increasing the usability of the user's experience by allowing someone to place and receive calls from anywhere. (W.Scott McGill/123RF)

FIGURE 6.7 Mobile phones evolved into "smartphones," incorporating applications far beyond placing and receiving calls, such as information retrieval, entertainment, and health tracking. (Lifdiz/Shutterstock)

Each iteration of the phone has improved its usability across different elements of the product. Some improved functionality, like making it easier to call someone mechanically, while others improved delight, by adding new functionalities that enhance the act of placing or receiving a call.

You can affect the usability of a product in many ways. This is because there are many elements of usability that you can adjust.

What Are the Elements of Usability?

When looking at the usability of a product, you can analyze six different metrics to understand the quality of our user's experience.

Learnability

How easy is the product to learn? Is there a high learning curve when first encountering the product? How complicated are basic tasks to perform? What is the novice's experience when encountering the product for the first time?

For phones, it's easy to learn how to use one. Someone provides you with a phone number, and as the user, you enter that number into the phone to call someone. You get immediate feedback if you performed the process correctly or incorrectly—you hear the person you intended to call, or you hear a noise that indicates you made a mistake. After you input your starting information, there is nothing else you need to do to operate the device—you just talk.

Ease of Use

How intuitive or easy is the product to use? How much "sense" does it make to operate? The product should be easily understood by the people who use it.

The design of phones has remained intuitive over the years. You input several numbers into the device to operate it. Then, once you have entered those numbers, you wait until the other person answers. Phones are designed to be lightweight and comfortable to hold and to fit near your ear. Using a phone just "makes sense."

Memorability

How memorable, or easy to remember, is the product? After the product has been used, how much of that product's operation is remembered by users when they come back?

Generally speaking, the core functionality of a phone is to place a call. Since this process is easy to learn and easy to use, it is easy to remember. A lot of the signifiers of using a phone are obvious and baked into the device. Even if a user doesn't remember how to use a phone, because it's easy to learn and use, the usability is still strong because of how intuitive they are.

Error Proof

How does the product handle errors? How often do users make errors using the system? How serious are these errors? And how easy is it to recover from them?

Entering the wrong number on a phone by selecting an incorrect character is easy and common. If this happens, the user can quickly start over by hanging up and trying again. Modern phone design allows for the ability to save contacts, which let users enter a number once, then select that saved contact whenever they wanted to make a call in the future. This feature helps prevent errors from occurring in the first place.

Efficient

How efficient can users be with the product? How fast can users accomplish their goal?

This area of phone design has improved dramatically over the years. Older phone design relied on a rotary dial to place a phone number. Users had to pull the wheel to a number, then wait for the wheel to reset before inputting the next number. Technological advancements in the mid-19th century allowed for this wheel to be replaced with a touchpad, speeding up the calling process significantly. The addition of saved contacts also improved efficiency, because users could make a single selection (the contact) rather than type out the entire phone number.

Satisfying

Is the product satisfying to use? Do users like using it? This is a bit more subjective because people have different preferences, but it is still a metric you can use to gauge the overall usability of the experience.

Phones can be very satisfying to use—hearing a loved one on a phone call is a magical experience, and one that doesn't happen with products like emails, written letters, or texts. Furthermore, modern phone design has included video capabilities that further improve this experience—now, you are able to dial a phone number and both see and hear the person you are trying to communicate with, from anywhere in the world.

These elements exist for any product or service—they aren't just related to physical ones. When evaluating the usability of your product, keep these six principles in mind to improve the overall experience for users.

How Do You Evaluate Usability?

To evaluate the usability of a product or service, you rely on various methods to conduct user testing and get a sense of the user's experience. There are many forms of user testing, including but not limited to:

- **Card sorting**—to user test the information architecture of the product

- **Task analysis**—to user test the difficulty of completing a task within a product

- **A/B testing**—to user test which version of a product users like more

The usability testing process can be broken into several high-level steps:

1. **Find users to talk with.** This could be past, current, or prospective users interested in your product.

2. **Ask users to perform tasks using the product.** This could be onboarding to the product, completing core objectives in the product, or something else.

AUTHOR'S NOTE It's common in the design industry to refer to usability testing as user testing because it's the most common form of user testing that occurs. They're technically different—"user testing" refers to any testing that occurs with users, whereas "usability testing" refers to evaluating the usability of a product and is a subset of user testing. Language is complicated; feel free to use either when referring to usability testing (I slip between the two from time to time myself).

3. **Observe users as they complete their tasks.** Take notes, ask questions, and record their interactions as they encounter problems, become confused or delighted, and work their way through the tasks.

4. **Synthesize results after all usability tests are complete.** Form opinions around the key insights of the tests.

This is the core flow of conducting usability testing—find users, see how they use the product, and analyze those results. There's a lot of nuances to conducting usability testing, however, which is what you'll explore in the next section.

USABILITY TESTING—PLAN AND DEFINE

Now that you have a better understanding of what usability is, it's time to start preparing for users interacting with the prototype. You need to work out a lot of logistics before testing, however. You must define what you want to accomplish, how you will conduct testing, and what you'll measure from the tests. To start, let's take a closer look at what usability testing is.

What Is Usability Testing?

Usability testing is a form of evaluating a product or service by testing it with current or potential users (**FIGURE 6.8**). The product could be an existing one, and you could test the usability of the current experience. Or the product could be a new one, and you could test the usability of the intended experience. It could even be a mix of the two, by testing a feature enhancement for a current product. Thankfully, no matter the product or objective, the general flow of conducting usability testing is the same.

1. **Create a test plan.** You need to define a test plan. The test plan outlines the scope of what you need to test. What is the purpose of the test? Why are you testing this element of the product? Who do you want to test it with? How will you test it with those people? How will you find those people to test with? The test plan incorporates all the elements of the test itself—the logistics behind the test, but also the business value and user needs that go into wanting to conduct the test in the first place.

2. **Define success.** You need to define what success looks like for that plan. You need to determine the metrics that you will evaluate the test against. What things do you want to observe during testing? Do you need to know how much time it takes to complete a task? If the information is clear or unclear? What about if users can "use" the feature? You could look at qualitative metrics, like satisfaction, or quantitative metrics, like time spent on a task. Whatever you decide, you want to know this upfront, before conducting the testing, so that you can record the data that informs those metrics.

3. **Recruit users.** You can find people to test with. You need to recruit all the users you want to test the product with. Are you going to recruit current users? New users? Do people need to have context of the product for you to gain accurate data, or do they need context of the problem so they have accurate needs? You must figure out who you want to test with, how you'll find them, and work out the logistics of the test itself.

4. **Conduct testing.** Once you're ready to test, you must conduct the testing. You need to coordinate times and places to meet, in addition to making a prototype to test with. You will have the people recruited go through the flows and let you know what they are experiencing as they do so. You'll observe their actions and ask them questions about the user experience of the product.

5. **Analyze results.** Once you have enough participants go through the prototype, you'll look at the results. You'll analyze common patterns and draw conclusions that support or reject the initial hypotheses. You'll take these results and share them with the team, and from those results, you'll form opinions on what to do with the product going forward.

This is the flow of usability testing. No matter the product, the process, objectives, and outcome remain the same: define a test plan and metrics, find people to test with, conduct testing, then analyze the results.

At Kaplan, I oversaw the user research for our product—a SaaS platform that allowed universities to take their curriculum and put it online for students and teachers to conduct courses. I was responsible for the design of the teacher experience—what it was like to roster students, assign materials, and observe grades. I constantly had to conduct usability testing to inform the design decisions I made for the product. For example, I was working on a feature that allows teachers to view the overall performance of students across multiple tests and classes. To support this work, I wanted to conduct usability testing of the feature with teachers, to see if my designs helped support their problems, such as seeing all the tests at once and understanding, as quickly and efficiently as possible, how students were doing. I created various mock-ups that portrayed the new experience, like the one in **FIGURE 6.9**.

FIGURE 6.9 A wireframe for a teacher's dashboard of student progress. This wireframe was a part of a prototype I used to test my ideas (https://tinyurl.com/asuxd6-9).

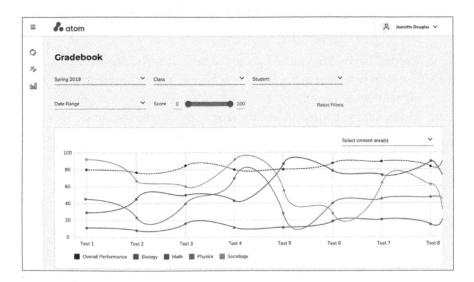

To support my hypothesis that this was a more usable solution than the previous one, I followed the usability testing process and planned to conduct usability testing. I created a test plan—test with six teachers who are familiar with the old UI. Then, I defined metrics—I would observe how quickly they could complete tasks as I took note of whether they were more satisfied using this UI compared to the old one. After that, I recruited teachers by emailing existing users of our old UI and seeing if they wanted to participate in a test. Then, I conducted the test with those users, scheduling time to meet over a video call. I took notes, and afterward, synthesized my notes into a findings document that I shared with the rest of the team, in order to validate the direction we wanted to take the product.

By relying on the usability testing process, I was able to successfully conduct usability testing and drive positive outcomes for the users I was designing for.

Creating a Test Plan

Our first step when conducting usability testing is to create a test plan. As mentioned, this is the blueprint for how you will conduct your tests—not just the actual tests themselves, but the vision for why you need the testing, the process for how you will do the testing, and the people you want to test with.

What's the Purpose?

First, you must define the purpose of your test. Why are you doing this test? How does it benefit the business or your users? The purpose of the test helps you structure what you need for the test, but also helps to convince team members why you should invest time and money into testing.

From the Kaplan example I provided earlier, I helped convince the team that we needed testing by defining the testing purpose—understanding whether the planned revisions to our UI would help teachers better understand the overall performance of their students. The previous UI looked like FIGURE 6.10:

The original UI was usable, but we felt like we could improve the user experience. I defined the purpose of the test for our redesign:

- Easier to navigate?

- More enjoyable to use?

- More meaningful to use (for example, better features, enhanced quality of life)?

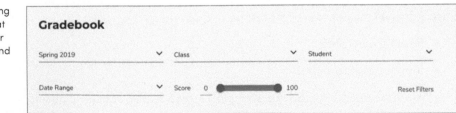

CLASS SUMMARY				
HOME /				

CLASS AVERAGE (Diagnostic Tests)
1101
TOTAL SCORE

CLASS AVERAGE (Last Test Taken)
1114
TOTAL SCORE

DOWNLOAD

CLASS CODE	STUDENT NAME	DIAGNOSTIC TOTAL SCORE	MOST RECENT TOTAL SCORE
		1010	—
		1120	1090
		1130	1140
		1110	—
		—	—
		1100	1100

Asking myself these questions and defining the purpose of the test, prior to testing, allowed me to structure my test so that I could try to find the answers to these questions.

What's the Scope?

After you define the purpose of your test, you need to define the scope. What are you going to test? Are there specific flows you want to learn more about? What do you need users to do in the test so that you can gain the information you're looking for?

For Kaplan, I needed to understand the flow of a teacher searching for a group of students and looking at their test results. To accomplish this goal, I created a task flow for searching for students, selecting that group, then viewing the test results (FIGURE 6.11). Then, I made a series of wireframes that mocked up this flow and put them into a prototype.

FIGURE 6.11 The beginning section of the task flow that allowed users to search for a group of students and find their test results.

Gradebook

Spring 2019 ⌄	Class ⌄	Student ⌄

Date Range ⌄	Score 0 ●──── 100	Reset Filters

The first step in this flow was to allow users to select a class—much like they would when looking at student test results. I mocked up a wireframe at the beginning of my prototype that asked them to find a class. This allowed my users to get in the mindset of reviewing results prior to seeing those results, which helped sell the vision of my prototype.

Who Is Your Audience?

After you have a sense of the scope of your testing, you need to define who you want to test with. Do you have personas that define the type of users you want to speak with? Do you know what types of users will use the product? These are the people you need to find so you can test with them. Perhaps they currently use the product, and you can email a slice of the user population to find the right ones to speak with. Or maybe they've never used the product, and you need to find brand new users to test an onboarding flow with. It all depends on the scope of the test.

For Kaplan, I needed to test with current users of the product. After all, we were enhancing our existing UI and wanted to know if teachers thought it was an improvement, so it was crucial that we talk with existing users to understand that metric. Fortunately, because we had an existing product and were redesigning it, I was able to speak with current users of our product and test with them.

Moderated vs. Unmoderated

Once you have the high-level details figured out, you move on to more logistical components for usability test. You have a choice between a moderated test and an unmoderated test. Moderating a test means that you are present with the users, asking them questions and interacting with them as they take the test. Unmoderated usability testing means that you structure a test with a predetermined series of questions along a set flow for users to complete, then rely on a software to do the testing for you (plenty of tools are available online that provide unmoderated testing).

Unmoderated testing has its benefits. It's easier and faster than scheduling interviews with users and moderating those interviews yourself—you won't be in the room as the user tests the product, so your time is freed up to do other tasks. Because you aren't in the room, you'll see how someone would interact with your product without you guiding them as they test it, so you remove some bias as well. It's a cheaper alternative for teams that don't have dedicated research resources to spend time and money testing with users directly.

Moderated testing also has its benefits. By being in the room with users, you can ask them follow-up questions or provide clarity in places they get stuck. This will let you get better data from the test. Additionally, by being in the room with users, things may come up unrelated to the test that you are curious about. I've had several usability tests turn into user interviews, where I started asking deeper questions about my user's needs that helped shape other parts of the product.

There's no right or wrong way to choose between moderated and unmoderated—it all depends on the needs of your test. If you have a straight-forward flow and need to spend more time on other parts of the product, then choose unmoderated. If you need to ask specific follow-up questions about parts of the flow you want to test, then choose moderated.

For Kaplan, we needed to moderate the test—I needed to know just how the new UI improved upon the old experience, which required asking follow-up questions based on users' responses. I contacted teachers using the product and scheduled times for us to meet to talk about it.

Remote vs. In Person

As with the digital tools that allow you to conduct testing without modera-tion, you can also conduct testing without being in the same physical space as your users. Remote testing allows you to use conferencing software to test with people all around the world by video. Additionally, digital prototyping tools usually have some sort of sharable link that lets test participants inter-act with the prototype as if they were interacting with the real product. As a result, you can test with anyone, from anywhere in the world.

Being in person does have its benefits, though. For example, low-fidelity paper prototypes can't be tested remotely. Furthermore, some tools, like eye-tracking software, are expensive and need to be installed in specific usability labs to operate at scale, which requires people to come into the office to test. Finally, some users don't test well remotely and are better to test with in person. Working at the children's media network Nickelodeon, for example, it was difficult to test remotely, because children were more likely to veer off task unless a trained usability professional was in the room with them keeping them focused.

For the Kaplan usability test, I chose to test remotely. We didn't have a dedicated usability lab, and participants were located across the United States, so it made the most sense to conduct sessions over the internet.

Hardware/Software

To actually conduct the test, what will you need from a tools perspective? What device will you test on? What additional hardware do you need to conduct the test, like eye-tracking machines? For example, it's a good idea to at least record the session for your notes. It's also a good idea to test on the device the product will exist on; for example, if making a mobile app, it's advised to test on mobile devices.

What software will you use to conduct the test? If it's remote, do you have the conferencing software you need? What did you use to build your prototype, and is that easily shareable? Some wireframing tools are actually very difficult to test remotely, since they require local installation to function. Other wireframing tools provide links that let you share with others directly and easily.

> **AUTHOR'S NOTE** Tools change all the time. As of this writing, it's common for me to use Figma to manage all wireframing and prototyping needs for a user test. This may change in the future as technologies continue to improve.

For Kaplan, I needed to allow users to control the prototype directly, so I used a combination of Sketch to wireframe and Marvel to prototype so users could access the prototype on their computer instead of me using a screen share.

Roles

When conducting testing, it's helpful to decide roles for the facilitation of the test. Who will be talking with users directly? Who, if anyone, will take notes? Assigning these roles beforehand ensures a smoother testing day. It's very helpful to have one person serve as the *primary* by interacting with the user during the test and facilitating the conversation while a *secondary* takes notes and chimes in as needed.

> **AUTHOR'S NOTE** It's a really good partnership between product and design to have people from both disciplines participate in user testing. It helps with team building and developing a shared context around the users both departments are designing for.

For Kaplan, I was fortunate to work with a product manager who was very involved in the process and wanted to attend testing, to better his understanding of our users' needs and make a better product. I served as the primary, walking users through the test, while he served as a secondary, taking notes and asking questions that I missed.

Defining the Test Metrics

After you define the test plan, you need to figure out what things you want to track during the test itself. This is where metrics come into play. The metrics you choose for your test help you compare across users and evaluate the test as a whole. The purpose is to choose metrics that allow you to validate your assumptions and help you feel more confident in whatever direction you choose for your product after the test.

For whatever metrics you choose, it's important to be able to compare results across different users. A common metric to aim for is an *analysis anchor*, which is some statistic or observation that creates a normalized opinion from test to test. This could be something like a user satisfaction score, where at the end of each test, each user ranks how satisfied they are by the product. At the end of all the tests, you could take the average of that score and produce an overall satisfaction metric for your prototype.

Generally speaking, metrics can be divided into two groups—quantitative and qualitative.

Quantitative

Quantitative metrics are numerical insights from your test. They could be based on time, such as how long it takes a user to complete a task. Or they could be based on completion, such as the number of users who completed the task successfully without assistance. Essentially, they are metrics that make it easier to compare results across users, since they are based on numbers and usually associated with some sort of scale (**FIGURE 6.12**).

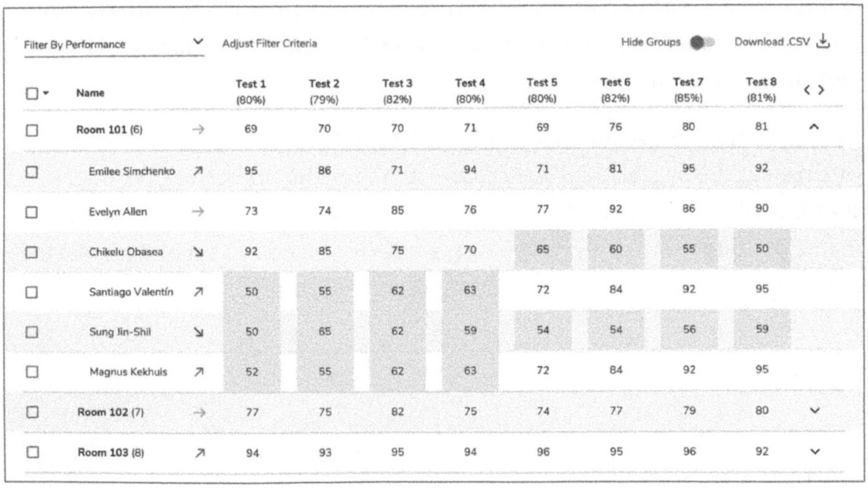

FIGURE 6.12 A wireframe for a teacher's dashboard of student progress. This wireframe was a part of a prototype I used to test my ideas.

	Name		Test 1 (80%)	Test 2 (79%)	Test 3 (82%)	Test 4 (80%)	Test 5 (80%)	Test 6 (82%)	Test 7 (85%)	Test 8 (81%)	
☐	Room 101 (6)	→	69	70	70	71	69	76	80	81	∧
☐	Emilee Simchenko	↗	95	86	71	94	71	81	95	92	
☐	Evelyn Allen	→	73	74	85	76	77	92	86	90	
☐	Chikelu Obasea	↘	92	85	75	70	65	60	55	50	
☐	Santiago Valentín	↗	50	55	62	63	72	84	92	95	
☐	Sung Jin-Shil	↘	50	65	62	59	54	54	56	59	
☐	Magnus Kekhuis	↗	52	55	62	63	72	84	92	95	
☐	Room 102 (7)	→	77	75	82	75	74	77	79	80	∨
☐	Room 103 (8)	↗	94	93	95	94	96	95	96	92	∨

At Kaplan, I observed various quantitative metrics associated with the usability test. I looked at how many people could recognize the information in the table—a binary, yes-or-no metric that I was able to convert into a percentage after all the tests were complete. I also looked at how long it took them to go through the first part of the flow to get to that table—another numerical metric I was able to convert into a statistic called time on task. These metrics helped compare rates and results from a quantitative perspective and let us better understand the performance of our designs.

Qualitative

Qualitative metrics are based on what people say or how they feel. When using your prototype, users will make comments about the designs that you can then interpret for your results. A user may say, "This was easy to do" or "I don't understand what I'm looking at." As the researcher, you must interpret these statements and, in some cases, dig a little deeper to get the meaning behind them. Qualitative statements are harder to work with because of their subjectivity and potential lack of clarity when reviewing results. However, they are some of the strongest data points you can use when sharing your results with the team to move forward.

When testing at Kaplan, I would observe what users said about the UI and follow up as needed to get a better sense of what they meant and what they wanted from the product. For example, users mentioned that they didn't understand the arrows that were in the table I designed. I intended for those arrows to show trends in a student's performance, but teachers didn't understand when those trends started or ended. After hearing that feedback again and again, we decided to remove that feature, to avoid confusing our users. This qualitative feedback helped us improve the product once we were ready to release it.

Tracking Common Metrics

Here are some common quantitative and qualitative metrics for you to consider in your usability tests:

- **Successful task completion.** Did users complete a task?

- **Critical/non-critical errors.** Did users make an error they couldn't recover from? Did they enter the wrong data or go to the wrong place?

- **Error-free rate.** How much did the user complete without making an error?

- **Time on task.** How long did it take the user to complete the task?

- **Subjective measures.** What score would users give their own satisfaction? Ease of use?

- **Likes, dislikes, recommendations.** What did users enjoy? What would they want changed? Added?

Use these metrics as a starting point for defining the things to track and observe during your tests.

Starting with Your Goals

It's tempting to jump straight into usability testing once you have your prototype complete. However, you should take the time to think about what it is you want to accomplish. What will you test? How will you test it? And what will you track? Answer these questions before you test your prototype with users. Sometimes, the answers to these questions will even cause you to rethink your prototype and restructure your test. It's always good to be thinking one step ahead before moving on in the process.

Let's Do It!

Let's prepare for usability testing your prototype with users. Before you test, it's good to come up with the structure of that test so that you can ensure a well-run experience for yourself and the users you test with.

AUTHOR'S NOTE Refer to the "Usability Testing: Plan and Define" section in the appendix for examples to compare your plan with.

For this exercise, I'd like you to come up with a plan for testing. Answer the following questions:

- **Purpose**—What do you want to accomplish with your test?

- **Scope**—What part(s) of the product will you be testing, and what are their flows?

- **Audience**—Who will you be testing with?

- **Moderation**—Will you be there, or will you use an external service to do the testing for you?

- **Remote**—Will you be present with the users, or will you connect virtually?

- **Software/hardware**—What technologies do you need to test with? Do users need to bring devices to test on?

- **Quantitative**—What metrics will you track for quantitative results?

- **Qualitative**—What metrics will you track for qualitative results?

USABILITY TESTING: RECRUIT AND CONDUCT

Once you've figured out all the logistics of your test—what you want to test, the type of people you want to test with, and how you'll conduct the testing—it's time to find your users and test your product with them.

How Many Users Should You Test With?

Some confusion exists around the appropriate number of users to test with. Some may feel that testing won't be statistically significant unless you test with dozens of users. Others may feel that you need to test with even more users, to make sure that you capture all the different types of personas that use your product.

It all depends on the type of testing you are doing. For something like A/B testing, you do need a lot of users to best understand the analytical metrics that come out of that testing. But for usability testing, you don't need very many users at all.

The Nielsen Norman Group has done significant research into the number of users required for usability testing. If you are strictly testing the usability of a simple flow, you can get away with as few as five usability tests.

FIGURE 6.13 is a graph from the Nielsen Norman Group that shows the percentage of usability issues found with a group of usability tests compared to the number of users that tested a flow.[3] It shows that testing with just five users uncovers about 80% of usability issues with your product. As you add more users to the test, those increases become marginally beneficial—fewer and fewer usability problems are uncovered.

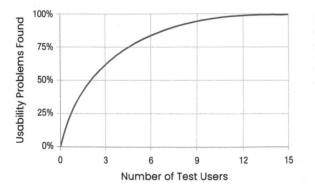

FIGURE 6.13 A study conducted on the number of problems found during usability testing relative to how many people tested the same experience.

---

3 www.nngroup.com/articles/why-you-only-need-to-test-with-5-users

For usability testing, I recommend scheduling six to eight users to test with. This is because you are targeting five good usability tests. Some users may cancel, be poor test participants, or not give you the feedback you are looking for. I find that six to eight users put me in a good spot to hit most of the usability issues with whatever I test.

> ## ONE SIZE DOES NOT FIT ALL USABILITY TESTING NEEDS
>
> The correct number of users for a usability testing session has been debated for years in the industry. Some say that five is far too few users and that you need statistical significance to uncover all the usability problems in a flow. Others say that it depends on product complexity, and that some products, such as lifesaving software, have harder flows to work through than others do. The truth is that one number will not satisfy all your testing needs. There's an even greater degree of complexity when you start to think about multiple flows, or the same flow with different personas. You could argue that a flow should be tested with multiple people that satisfy each persona, increasing the amount of testing required significantly. A great deal of research has been done on this topic, which you can read about in the article "Five, ten, or twenty-five—How many test participants?" at www.humanfactors.com/newsletters/how_many_test_participants.asp.
>
> For the purpose of the exercises in this book, six to eight users might work. In the field, you will need to adjust the number of people you test with based on your constraints, your product, and the needs of your organization. There truly is no magic number of people to test with for every single usability test.

Where to Find Users

Once you align on the number of users you're looking to test with, you must find those users. You have a variety of methods available to find users.

Internal Methods

Internally, you may already have a pipeline for sourcing testers. Many organizations have sales development representatives or customer support professionals that talk with real-life users daily. Reaching out to these individuals, establishing relationships with them, and asking if they have any prospective users to test with is a great way to develop a user testing pipeline for short- and long-term projects. It's even beneficial to attend calls with these users proactively, hearing directly from the customer what they need from your product.

You may also have in-product opportunities to contact customers. Some companies run engagement surveys that appear as users interact with the product. Users who opt into these surveys could be great individuals to talk with about the product—they have already proactively agreed to provide feedback to the company.

For products with email subscribers, it could be beneficial to contact those recipients to see if they want to participate in usability testing. Sometimes, you can also segment a list of emails into different user groups. You could leverage this capability and create a subset of users that you want to talk with, prescreening for any demographic information you want before reaching out to users.

Any of these methods could be successful for your testing needs. These are the users that already use your product and have context around it. Additionally, they are most likely invested in making your product better—after all, they use it, and they want it to solve their problems. They may not need much convincing to be involved in making it better.

External Methods

If you don't have access to any users internally, you can always seek out users externally. Various products exist where people sign up to get paid to conduct usability testing for other companies. Services like Usertesting.com, Maze, and UsabilityHub offer a wide demographic of users to choose from for user tests. Generally, this testing is unmoderated and asynchronous—a company posts a user test online, and individuals participate on a first-come, first-served basis to complete the test (for a small fee). This is an excellent way to get quick usability feedback about your product.

Do-It-Yourself Methods

If your company lacks the resources for external software to recruit users, you can always find them yourself. Screener surveys that gauge a candidate's potential for usability testing your product can be sent online in community forums, social media, or other places. This is a very common method for those working on lean budgets or personal projects.

One extreme version of this method is to conduct guerilla testing. This is a form of usability testing where you go to a physical location and try to find users at that location. It could be a coffee shop, park, bookstore, or even around your office if you want some quick testing results. This method can work really well for recognizability of UI elements in your product, such as what an icon means or if some copy makes sense.

Preparing Your Script

No matter how you find your users, once you have them, you'll need a strong test script and a good approach to asking test questions as users move through your product. You can divide your test script into three sections—pre-test, during test, and post-test.

Pre-Test

At the start of the usability test, it's generally good to ask a few simple-to-answer questions just to get the user ready for the test. This is to break the ice, confirm some background information on your end, and prepare for the actual product testing. Questions like "what is your profession?" or "how do you use our product?" allow the user to begin to open up and provide good context for their familiarity with the product. These also help prime the user and get them thinking about the flow you're going to show them next.

Good pre-test questions include:

- What is your profession?

- Are you familiar with our product?

- How do you use our product?

- Any questions related to the test's functionality (for example, "how do you usually look for content?" if you are testing a search feature)

- Any questions related to the test's subject matter (for example, "how often do you watch TV?" if you are testing a streaming service)

During Test

Once the usability test starts, it's good to ask questions about your product, its potential, and whether or not it makes sense. These types of questions are geared toward evaluating your idea and confirming a user's understanding of it. This is where you should be uncovering the answers to the metrics you defined earlier in the process as well.

Good during-test questions include:

- What would you expect to happen after taking that action?
- Did that match your expectations?
- Where would you look for that?
- Would you expect to be able to do that?

Post-Test

At the end of the usability test, you will have the opportunity to wrap up the session and gain overall information about your product. This is the perfect time to ask about a user's impressions, their general satisfaction, and any additional features or functionalities they would want from your product.

Good post-test questions include:

- On a scale from 1 to 5, how satisfied were you with this product?
- On a scale from 1 to 5, how confident would you feel using this product?
- If you could add anything to this feature to make it even better, what would you include?
- Is there anything else you'd like to share?

Facilitating the Test

With all your preparation out of the way, you've finally arrived at the actual test. This is when you conduct the usability test with the user and lead them through the product using your script. Let's talk about a few ways you can facilitate the test to ensure you and your user have a great experience.

Framing the Session

First, you'll want to frame the test session. Explain why you're here and why the user is here, in addition to what you hope to accomplish. This lets the users have a greater understanding of the session itself.

Make sure your user is comfortable—give them the opportunity to ask any procedural questions before starting the test. Ask if they need water or are ready to begin before jumping into your script.

Set expectations for your user as well—tell them that you are testing the product, not them, and that you want to understand how the product is performing, not how *they* perform during the test.

Additionally, ask them to speak out loud as they make decisions and move around the test. This will give you a glimpse into their thought process. Also encourage users to verbalize the decisions they make during the test, which gives you crucial data for how they would move around your product in the real world.

Before jumping into the script, ask permission to record—explain how it's helpful for the team, and that the purpose of recording is for your notes and to share only with your team.

When setting the stage with users at the start of a usability test, I use the following structure:

> *Hi there! I'm a designer working at [company] on [product]. I'm looking to test some new options for an enhancement we are considering adding to our product. Today, we're going to walk through testing those options. This is a usability test, but it's a test of us and our user experience, and not you and your thinking process.*
>
> *As we move through the designs, I'd like to ask you to think out loud so I can see the reasoning behind your decisions and get a sense of how we can make our product even better.*
>
> *Before we begin, would you mind if I record this session? It'll only be used to share internally with my team later.*

AUTHOR'S NOTE It's rare, but if a user doesn't want you to record a session, that's OK—respect their intent and take notes as well as you can during the session. Hopefully, you have a note taker with you while you facilitate the test.

Conducting the Test

Once you have started to record and are ready to work through your script, keep in mind a few additional techniques to ensure a great testing session.

Allow the user to lead you through the test. Don't answer questions right away or jump in if they get stuck. You won't be there in real life as they use the product, so watch for when they get confused and if they can course correct. It's useful data for making sure any enhancements you make to the product are beneficial.

As you go through the test, make sure you understand the user's intent and choices as they make them. Ask clarifying questions like "why did you go there" or "what did you mean by that" to get a deeper understanding of their thought process. If you get an answer you didn't understand, request that they elaborate on it.

Good clarifying questions include:

- What did you mean by that?

- Can you elaborate?

- Can you provide an example?

- Why?

At the end of the test, make sure to wrap up any additional questions you may have, like overall satisfaction or ease of use. You should also provide a few minutes for your users to ask questions as well—not only is this a nice gesture, but their questions can influence what you decide to enhance about your product coming out of the test in addition to influencing what you may want to work toward next. Then, thank them for their time and move on to the next test!

Usability Testing Makes Things Better

Usability testing can be a stressful process. Do users like your product? Do your designs make sense? Can people actually use what you made? I usually go into usability testing with a lot of excitement, a little bit of anxiety, and every so often, some concern. Laying your bare designs in front of your users is a stressful process.

Even though it's difficult, it's often rewarding. You learn so much about why someone comes to your product, how they view your designs, and what really works for them. When you do make intuitive, meaningful designs that positively impact others, it's an incredible feeling. When you don't, you learn what you can do better so that you can accomplish that goal.

Besides, it's much better to find out how well your product performs in a test scenario than to release it without trying it out first. Trust me—you'd rather have a less impactful result in testing than in the real world!

Let's Do It!

Let's recruit and conduct users for your usability testing! You can use any method you'd like to find users, including:

- Paid services, such as UserZoom or UserTesting

- Social media, such as LinkedIn or Facebook

- Online communities, such as Discord or Slack

- Guerrilla testing, such as in coffee shops or parks

- Friends and family, such as via texts or phone calls

It doesn't matter so much where your users come from, just that they are the type of user you are designing for. The closer they are to your persona, the better. Aim for six participants to make sure you get enough feedback.

If you've completed the screener survey exercise in Chapter 2, "Using Empathy as a Design Tool," this will be a lot easier for you! You could reach out to the participants that you've already interviewed and ask if they'd like to test your prototype. Alternatively, you could copy the questions in that screener survey and send it out again to find new users to test with.

AUTHOR'S NOTE Refer to the "Usability Testing: Recruit and Conduct" section in the appendix for examples to compare your plan to recruit testers and conduct the test with.

After you find your users, test with them! Make a testing script for your prototype and walk through the test with them. As you test, make sure you:

- Record each session (with permission!).

- Capture the metrics you want to track.

- Always ask "why" to get more clarity if you don't have it based on the response.

Good luck and have fun!

USABILITY TESTING: ANALYZE RESULTS

Once you've completed all your usability tests, you should have a good sense of what works and what doesn't. You have either participated in the tests directly, observing results firsthand, or have seen the results of unmoderated tests, seeing the points where users struggled or were able to succeed. From this alone, you should have ideas on what to approve and what to improve upon.

However, you can do better. You can take the results and think critically about how to take them further, to gain an even better understanding and share results broadly with the team. Luckily, there are several methods you can use to create easy-to-digest insights that help steer your product in an even better direction.

In my professional work, these insights have been a crucial part of usability testing. Often, it wouldn't be enough for me to say "we should include or remove this element from our product" without any reason or data to back it up. Sometimes, other team members would want to include specific elements in the product that directly went against users' wishes. To help avoid these scenarios, you need evidence to prove why you should or shouldn't do a certain thing for your users. Satisfaction scores, feature usability analysis, and even direct quotes from users all help you do the most important aspect of your job: advocate for the user.

Scoring Scales

If you think back to the metrics you defined at the start of the usability testing process, you chose certain metrics that work on a scale, like asking users the question "on a scale from 1 to 5, how satisfied were you using the product?" These metrics are often referred to as scoring scales, analysis anchors, or the *System Usabilty Scale* (SUS).[4] They allow you to take a subjective measure by providing the user with a scale where they self-rate the metric you want to capture.

Look at the unmoderated survey shown in FIGURE 6.14 that is administered after a usability test.

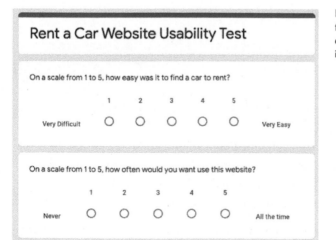

FIGURE 6.14 Two questions about a user's product experience after participating in a usability test.

These are examples of what could be asked after a usability test. These two questions ask the user to self-select a score based on the ease of use and the desirability of the product. In these examples, the higher number a user chooses, the *better* an outcome you get for your product. You want your product to be both easy to use and desirable, which is the reason you are testing it.

---

4 www.usability.gov/how-to-and-tools/methods/system-usability-scale.html

One benefit of capturing information this way is that you get to take a qualitative metric—an opinion—and convert it into a quantitative result. This allows you to compare the result more easily between users and create an average score for how *easy* or *delightful* your product may be.

You can use these scales for many different aspects of the usability test—they could rank individual features, comment on overall satisfaction, or provide an opinion on the usability of your product.

Stoplight Chart

Scoring scales can play well into other analysis artifacts coming out of usability testing. One of these artifacts, a stoplight chart, is a visual representation of key insights gathered from your usability testing. A stoplight chart is a great way to display a high-level view of areas of strength and opportunity from your testing.

FIGURE 6.15 is an example stoplight chart from a usability study I ran for a solo traveler app.

FIGURE 6.15 A stoplight chart for a round of usability testing I conducted.

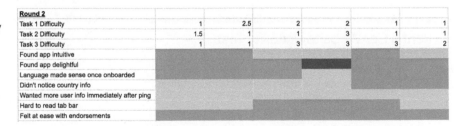

Round 2						
Task 1 Difficulty	1	2.5	2	2	1	1
Task 2 Difficulty	1.5	1	1	3	1	1
Task 3 Difficulty	1	1	3	3	3	2
Found app intuitive						
Found app delightful						
Language made sense once onboarded						
Didn't notice country info						
Wanted more user info immediately after ping						
Hard to read tab bar						
Felt at ease with endorsements						

At a glance, your eye is drawn to the green, yellow, and red boxes in the chart. These represent observations from each test and are meant to signify the high-level impression regarding aspects of those tests. Green represents a positive result, yellow a mixed result, and red a negative result.

The columns of this graph represent users—in this example, I tested with six people. The rows represent aspects of the prototype, such as specific UI components, content items, or features that I tested.

By organizing the data in this way, you can clearly see what worked well and what could be improved upon. For example, the app was delightful for most users (row 5, five of six users thought so). Additionally, there's an opportunity to improve upon the app's *ping* feature, which lets you search for nearby users (row 8, all users had mixed opinions about it during the test).

Looking at the columns of the chart, you can also see some users had an easier time with the test than others. U4, the fourth user, had a particularly difficult time compared to the rest of the cohort. Perhaps this user is outside the target demographic, or something happened during that test that made it more difficult for them. This is a great example of why I like to test with six to eight users—it's possible that this user is skewing the data.

One last thing to note about this stoplight chart is the second to fourth rows. Each of these is a scoring scale, asking users to rank how difficult each task was to complete. This scale is from 1 to 5, with 1 being easy and 5 being difficult. Adding up the numbers, you can see that the second task was the easiest, and the third task was the most difficult. To improve upon the product, you might want to focus on the third task and see why it was harder to complete.

Pull Quotes

Scoring scales and stoplight charts are excellent at gaining key insights that can be compared across users and across aspects of the product. This data helps galvanize the team and provide direction on where to focus next.

You can supplement these analysis artifacts and build an even stronger case for how you can advocate for your users by using pull quotes. *Pull quotes* are direct statements made by users during the test. As a user interacts with your product in a usability test, it's best practice to encourage that they speak out loud and verbalize their thoughts. During this usability testing process, they will become surprised, excited, or frustrated, and say so. As a researcher, it's your role to understand (and ask) why they feel that way. In these moments, users provide you with research gold—their exact feelings, in their exact words. These quotes are so powerful—they let you in on how your users feel, and with that, you can express those feelings to others on the team and show them the reasoning behind your decisions.

Let's look at an example. I'm a designer working on a project to make an app for solo travelers in new countries. After usability testing, I come to the team and say, *"Users were very concerned about safety."* What's your reaction? Do you believe me? I've told you what our users said—they are concerned about safety in the context of the app. But maybe it feels flat, or perhaps you don't believe me.

AUTHOR'S NOTE Since color alone is not the best indicator to rely on from an accessibility perspective, you can add iconography to a stoplight chart to make things clearer for your audience. A set of icons—checkmark, slash, and close (or whatever you prefer)—can accomplish the same goals as using green, yellow, and red colors. You could even use icons and color!

What if I shared some quotes from the users instead?

> *I try to go with a group. An established travel group because I felt safer.*

> *In general, it's common sense not to go out in a strange city on my own and start drinking. Unfortunately, that is sort of my reality as a woman that travels. I definitely have more freedom to do those things in groups than alone.*

> *Safety is something we always think about.*

If I told you the key insight—users feel concerned about safety—it has a level of impact, sure. But the level of impact is magnified greatly by including quotes. Quotes drive empathy—it's one thing for a researcher to state an insight, but that insight is taken to another level when it's backed up by pull quotes.

It's so much more powerful for a user to say, in their own words, exactly what they mean. The best way to advocate for your users is to let them speak directly to your team, through pull quotes. When trying to advocate for the user, why not let them do it?

Analyze and Summarize Your Results

You finally know how users feel about your product. You've conducted usability testing and gotten great feedback about what works with your designs, what doesn't, and what potential they have. You can aggregate the results and make statements about the usefulness and quality of the designs, and by doing so, you'll know how helpful and successful they are.

This is extremely important knowledge—and information you shouldn't keep to yourself. Now that you have the results of your testing, it's time to share them more broadly. The product team, along with other teams in the organization, should know how the designs performed and what users want from the product. It's time to capture all the user feedback and present the usability testing results.

Let's Do It!

Now that your usability testing is complete, it's time to look at the results! Ideally, you've captured audio and video recordings from each test. Look back at those results and create a stoplight chart that captures all that feedback. The goal is to create a table that allows you to develop averages and capture general sentiment about aspects of your product.

You can put plenty of things in a stoplight chart to demonstrate product feedback, including:

- Scoring scales, such as a net promoter score (a survey that asks users to rate how likely they would be to recommend a product) or a system usability scale (a standard questionnaire that measures the usability of a product)

- Completion rates (what percentage of users completed a task; how long did it take them)

- Error rates (how many errors happened and at what points)

- Task-specific measures (questions you had about a specific part of your prototype)

- Qualitative metrics, such as what did users like, dislike, want to add to the product

AUTHOR'S NOTE Refer to the "Usability Testing: Analyze Results" section in the appendix for examples to compare your analysis with.

The exercise of making a stoplight chart will set you up very well for the next step in the process—presenting your findings.

USABILITY TESTING: PRESENTING FINDINGS

You're almost finished with the test step of the design thinking process. You've developed a testing plan, found users to test with, conducted the testing, and gotten some insightful results. Even if the results weren't what you initially wanted to hear, it's great feedback to improve the quality of your product before launching it to the wider public.

Now that you have your usability testing results, it's time to share those results with other members of your organization—both those working on the problem to solve directly and those working on related problems.

AUTHOR'S NOTE Even if you are working alone on a project, it's good to take the advice in this chapter—preparing a summary of your testing results will allow you to go back to your results more easily in the future when looking at the history and evolution of your product. Additionally, the tips in this chapter are very helpful for those making a portfolio or case study from their work.

Why Should You Share Your Results?

At the end of the usability testing process, it's common for teams to analyze their results and make product decisions that are in favor of the users they are designing for. Product teams will take the insights from usability testing and apply them to their product's vertical.

Unfortunately, it's less common for these teams to share their learnings organizationally. Individual teams can work in silos, impacting their specific product vertical, blind to the fact that a user's experience with a product applies to more than one aspect of that product.

In some cases, individual teams can even forget to share testing results among the team. On various projects, I've seen product managers and designers work on a feature and ask developers to build it without providing the specific context from usability testing results. This context allows developers to better empathize, and even potentially generate ideas or weigh in from a technical perspective to make the product even better.

Outside individual teams, sharing results with stakeholders helps facilitate the product development process. Illustrating to key decision makers the impact of a feature and how it performed can open the door for continued support of that feature or even generate new ideas for the product.

Other teams benefit from shared research results as well. Not only do they see how users feel about the product, but they can also see how teams conduct research, inspiring those teams to conduct research themselves.

I've had each of these scenarios occur in my working experience. I've been on individual teams where I conducted usability testing and by sharing the results with the team, everyone had a greater understanding of the impact of what we were building, which renewed everyone's efforts and improved morale. I've shown stakeholders the results of research, highlighting key insights combined with pull quotes to demonstrate the value of a feature or the reason we chose to remove functionality from the product. I've even shared my testing results with other teams and had deep conversations on the best ways to conduct democratized research—research done by teams, to empower individuals to perform usability testing rather than rely on a third party or a different part of the organization. Sharing research results is extremely beneficial to cultivate a strong research practice in addition to a stronger appreciation for the user's perspective.

How Can You Share Testing Results?

Luckily, sharing testing results doesn't have to be so complicated. If you're following a good usability testing process, you will already have a lot of what you need. Key metrics you tracked during testing and core insights coming out of testing go a long way for sharing results. The challenge here is organizing all that information for people who won't be as familiar with the problem as your immediate team is.

Summary Sheet

One good way to share testing results is in a high-level summary document. This can be informal and short—essentially, it's a report of what you plan to do after testing is complete. Organize your insights, throw a few key metrics in there, and you're good to go—it could even be a single page.

FIGURE 6.16 is an example from a project I worked on for the solo traveler app. I conducted multiple rounds of testing and wanted to keep the team informed of updates to the project as I moved along. To do so, I analyzed all the usability testing and created a high-level, one-page document detailing results and next steps.

Usability Testing Round 2
For our second round of usability testing, we tested *3 tasks with 6 participants.*

Summary Insights:
- Average Difficulty of tasks:
  - Task 1 - 1.58 out of 5
  - Task 2 - 1.42 out of 5
  - Task 3 - 2.17 out of 5
- As a whole, users found the app delightful and intuitive. Users could envision the app's purpose and see it fitting into their lives.
- Users had issues with our app terms / language at first, but once learned, found it intuitive.
- Users had to orient themselves in the app at first, but once situated, found it intuitive.
- Users were unclear what happened after they accepted a ping request, and wanted more to that flow.
- Users wanted to more immediately see the results from sending a ping. To see user information at a glance, and sort it.
- Users also wanted to know more about the radius of a ping.
- Users felt at ease with the endorsements feature.

Planned Revisions from Round 2:
- Revise copy in app to be less confusing.
- Add an overlay for ping results so users can see all info at a glance.
- Build more to accept a ping flow.
- Build out more to the endorsements flow.
- Make all wireframes high fidelity.

FIGURE 6.16 A sample report of usability testing results.

First, I made sure everyone knew the structure of the testing I conducted. I informed them the stage of testing I was in, in addition to the number of participants I tested with.

Then, I wrote down the insights of the test itself. I started with key metrics, such as task difficulty and high-level takeaways, such as whether users found the app easy to use or delightful. After that, I commented on specific insights as they related to the test, such as issues with certain tasks or aspects of the app that were confusing.

Finally, I concluded with the planned revisions based on the test itself. I made sure the team knew what I wanted to work on, based on the observations I saw during usability testing.

That's the flow of a good summary sheet:

1. What was the test structure?

2. What are the metrics, or analysis anchors I must compare across tests?

3. What are the high-level takeaways from the test?

4. What needs to change?

5. What are the next steps?

That's all you really need to share with other teams to have an effective summary of your research results. Straight and to the point—just the results themselves and what you plan to do about it (and a little bit about test structure too). This is information you are probably planning to use for your immediate team anyway, so taking some time to collect it and share it with others can really help foster understanding and best practices for usability testing among all teams and individuals at your organization.

If you go a step further and include a bit more information, you can build upon this foundation to make a truly powerful share-out of your research results.

Presentation

As effective as the summary sheet is, I have found an even more effective method for sharing usability testing results: making a presentation. This method is more time consuming, but the visual nature of it makes it more digestible for those who have less context around the project. Additionally, it has a lot more room for you to present and arrange information in a way that helps get your point across.

Beyond being visually appealing (which is part of the job of being a designer), it allows for something I refer to as the *three pillars* of usability testing results: the part of your interface where the insight was made, the insight itself, and a pull quote supporting the insight.

FIGURE 6.17 is a presentation I made for an NFT marketplace. In the marketplace, users could purchase tokens that correlated to real eSports players, similar to a fantasy sports marketplace like DraftKings. We were tasked with redesigning the interface to introduce new features and make the system easier to use. For our project, we designed and tested several versions of the product.

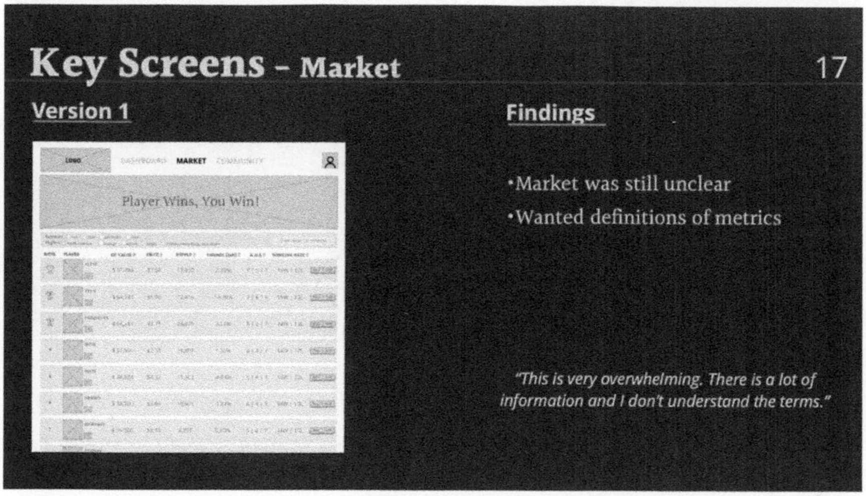

FIGURE 6.17 A part of a presentation with the *three pillars* in action—the screen, the findings, and a quote that captures the user's sentiment.

For this presentation, I wanted to walk stakeholders through our design thinking process. To do so, I showed the first version of our UI (a mid-fidelity wireframe we used for usability testing) and paired it with the insights learned during testing. To support those insights, I included a quote that illustrated where the insight was coming from.

Using the three pillars method, I was able to do the following:

1. **Contextualize** what part of the product we were talking about.

2. **Explain** what we learned about that part of the product.

3. **Build empathy** and prove our point by including what users said about it.

This method builds context, establishes a learning, then illustrates the impact of that learning. It's usable for any situation from usability testing, provided you've set up the test to generate this data and have recorded the data during the testing process.

To go a step further, you can apply the method to iterations, as shown in **FIGURE 6.18**.

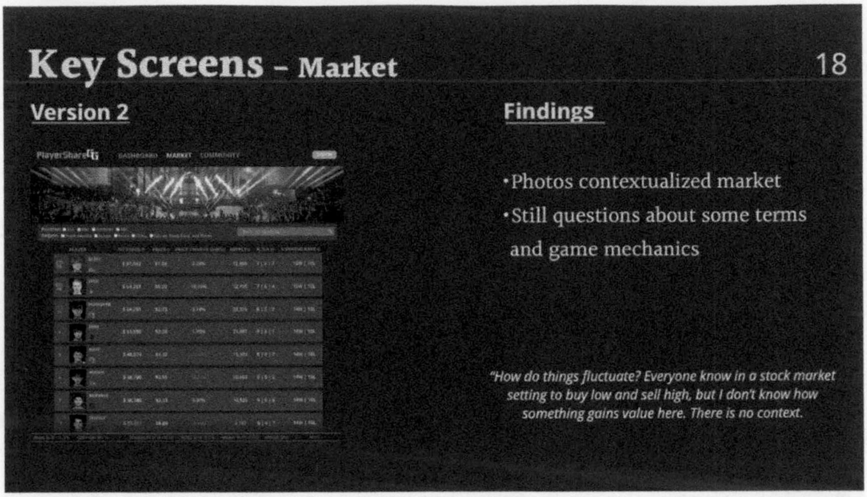

FIGURE 6.18 Results from the next round of testing for the feature in the example in Figure 6.17.

This is the next iteration we had for the same feature—this time, we were able to reduce confusion, but not eliminate it. For users, it went from not understanding the product to not understanding the market—an improvement, but one that still had room for growth. But the three pillars format still applies—picture, insights, quote.

It helps to add context to the presentation as well, including an introductory slide that explains testing methodology.

FIGURE 6.19 shows the number of prototypes created, across the number of tests conducted, and how many iterations there were on the core concept. This helps contextualize the usability testing process for people who weren't there to participate in it.

In addition, you should have a slide that explains next steps, after presenting all your insights, as shown in **FIGURE 6.20**.

Here, we explained that we were headed to our MVP and working out a few more features before designs were complete. Additionally, we descoped several elements and explained to the client that they should focus on certain aspects of their product first, then revisit others later.

That's all you really need for your presentation: an introduction to the testing process, however many *three pillar* statements you want for each finding you wish to share out, and a conclusion explaining what happens next.

Share Your Test Results

It may not be top of mind for you to share your results with others in your organization. After all, how does that benefit you directly? You already have the results—you can just incorporate those results into the product and not waste time preparing summaries of your testing results or getting as detailed a presentation.

Trust me when I say that this is a *really* important part of the process. Documenting the results of your testing will benefit you in so many indirect ways. People will be able to apply the learnings of your testing to their projects, creating a better product. Directors will feel more confident in the decisions you make, as they will be backed by data and testing. Teammates will be inspired by your knowledge and consider you an expert in your domain space. Finally, you'll be contributing to a culture of knowledge sharing and teamwork—which will pay dividends in the future as you all continue to work together toward your ultimate goal: improving the lives of the people you design for.

AFTER YOU TEST, YOU IMPLEMENT

This chapter started at the beginning of the test step of the design thinking process. Prototype in hand, you defined the purpose and scope of your usability testing as you began to plan what you wanted to learn about your designs. You established metrics, found users to test with, and conducted usability testing to better understand whether your designs worked. Even better, you may have discovered whether your ideas address the problem to solve by asking users directly if your solution would work for them.

From here, there's only one step left in the design thinking process—it's time to make your product real. In that step, you'll learn how to implement your designs. You'll work from a set of user stories to make sure you're capturing all the use cases of your product. You'll think systematically, determining which elements of your designs can fit into a system that you create. Finally, you'll learn what it's like to communicate your designs to others so that they can be developed.

$$\psi_{n\ell m}(r, \theta, \phi) = \sqrt{\left(\frac{2}{na_0}\right)^3 \frac{(n-\ell-1)!}{2n[(n+\ell)!]}} \, e^{-r/na_0} \left(\frac{2r}{na_0}\right)^\ell L_{n-\ell-1}^{2\ell+1}\left(\frac{2r}{na_0}\right) \cdot Y_\ell^m(\theta, \phi)$$

$$H = T + V = \frac{\|\mathbf{p}\|^2}{2m} + V(x, y, z)$$

$$\left[\left(\omega^2 - \alpha - \frac{3}{4}\beta z^2\right)^2 + (\delta\omega)^2\right] z^2 = \gamma^2.$$

CHAPTER 7

IMPLEMENTING YOUR DESIGNS

The sixth and final step in the design thinking process brings everything together into an end-product solution. By this point, you understand more about your audience and the problem to solve, have explored what you could build to solve that problem, and begun to materialize that solution through testing it. Now, you must implement your designs.

Implementation is an *art*. To implement, you must be a master communicator. How do you clearly communicate your ideas to others? How do you learn the working styles of the people you need to collaborate with to build your designs? How can you express your ideas so that they are implemented correctly? It's not enough to blindly deliver specifications to others and expect them to advocate for and build the designs; you must first think about how those people will approach creating the product.

Implementation is also a *science*. By following certain procedures while implementing, you can set up your designs so they can scale. You are expressing knowledge—in this case, the knowledge that allows someone to re-create your vision at scale. This step requires precision—exact specifications need to be delivered that cover all use cases for your product, not just a single flow. To do this, you rely on systems to share your designs—not just systems that express all these use cases, but systems that express the components that the designs are built upon.

By using art and science, you can bring the project together, share it with others, and implement your solution.

WHERE ARE YOU IN THE DESIGN THINKING PROCESS?

As you leave the test phase of the design thinking process, you have tried your ideas with users in order to understand how the designs function. You should know whether users are able to use the designs, and whether the product could solve the user's problems. Ideally, you have a good sense of what works, what needs to be revised, and what needs to be removed to create the product you want to build. Given all this knowledge, you're ready for the last step in the design thinking process—*implement* (FIGURE 7.1).

During the implement step of the process, you are working toward completing your designs. You've spent the rest of the design thinking process understanding what the problems are and exploring how to solve them. Now, you are tasked with making the solution a reality.

The implement step should have a solid foundation for the product. You should have a system that allows you to design easily and consistently. You should have a way for your designs to be built by developers. Finally, you should have a framework for future enhancements. These systems will allow your team to build the product and deliver it at scale—not just for a few usability tests, but for every person who wants to use the product.

How can you be sure the product will meet all the needs of the users? Until this point, you have built for one (or perhaps several) flows, depending on your tests. To scale, you need to think of all the use cases for the product. One way for you to structure the designs and deliver a solution that works for users' needs is to take inventory and track all use cases via user stories.

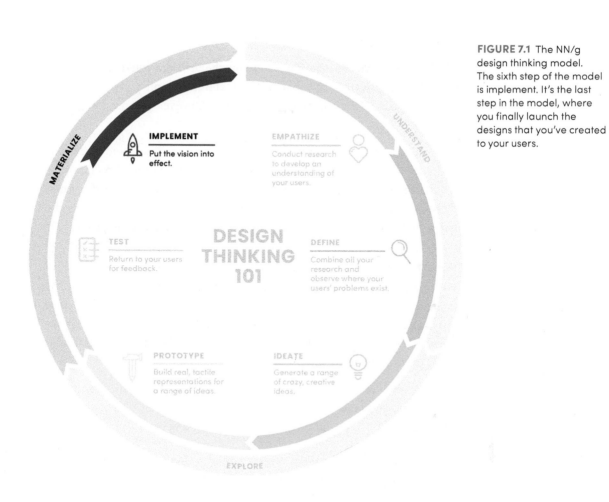

Within the figure:

IMPLEMENT
Put the vision into effect.

EMPATHIZE
Conduct research to develop an understanding of your users.

MATERIALIZE

UNDERSTAND

TEST
Return to your users for feedback.

DESIGN THINKING 101

DEFINE
Combine all your research and observe where your users' problems exist.

PROTOTYPE
Build real, tactile representations for a range of ideas.

IDEATE
Generate a range of crazy, creative ideas.

EXPLORE

IMPLEMENT

Now that you have a completed, validated design approach, you need to build the product. This is the last step of the design thinking process that will get you across the finish line—delivering the product solution so the team can implement it.

How do you deliver your designs, though? What can you do to ensure your design intent is honored across the product? What do you hand off, and how do you do so? During implementation, you leverage statements about your users' needs, diagrams that communicate how users move through the product, visual guidelines for building the product, and documentation that explains how all the pieces fit together.

To start, let's talk about your users first—through a process artifact called *user stories*.

USER STORIES

You know what you're building. You know the problem you're trying to solve, the designs that solve that problem, and the people you are solving the problem for. To implement those designs, however, you need to get a lot more specific.

Until this point, a lot of your work has been about the vision and direction of the solution. That vision is important, and something that should remain the North Star of the solution. To accomplish that vision, you need to know the steps you must take to get there. That's where user stories come in—the individual tasks users take within a product to accomplish their goals.

What Is a User Story?

To ensure all the features and functionalities that users need are captured in the requirements of a product, product teams often create user stories. A *user story* is an informal, general explanation of a software feature written from the perspective of the end user. Essentially, it describes the solution from the user's point of view.

Imagine you were working on a financial retirement platform. To accomplish users' goals, you may write user stories like the ones in FIGURE 7.2 to describe core needs users have and tie them to features you believe will solve them.

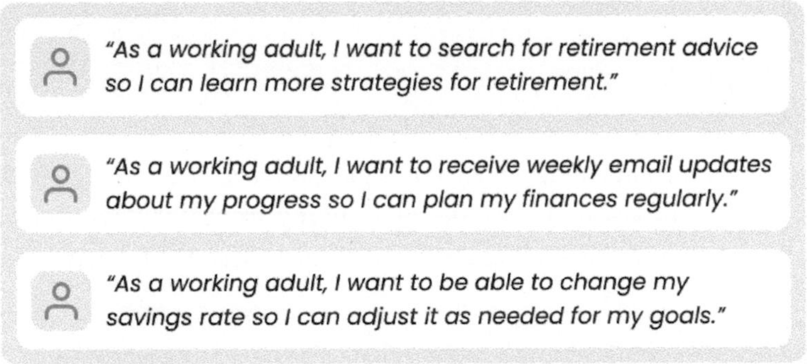

FIGURE 7.2 Several user stories for a financial services product.

"As a working adult, I want to search for retirement advice so I can learn more strategies for retirement."

"As a working adult, I want to receive weekly email updates about my progress so I can plan my finances regularly."

"As a working adult, I want to be able to change my savings rate so I can adjust it as needed for my goals."

Let's say that in your design thinking process, you saw that users wanted to search for financial information to plan for retirement. Maybe you learned this in a user interview, it came up during a usability test, or it was a feature from another product. Regardless of how you discovered this information, you've decided that you want to put this functionality in your product.

To communicate the need and the desired functionality for your product, you could create a statement that captures what you aim to make, who you aim to make it for, and why. That statement would look something like the one in **FIGURE 7.3**.

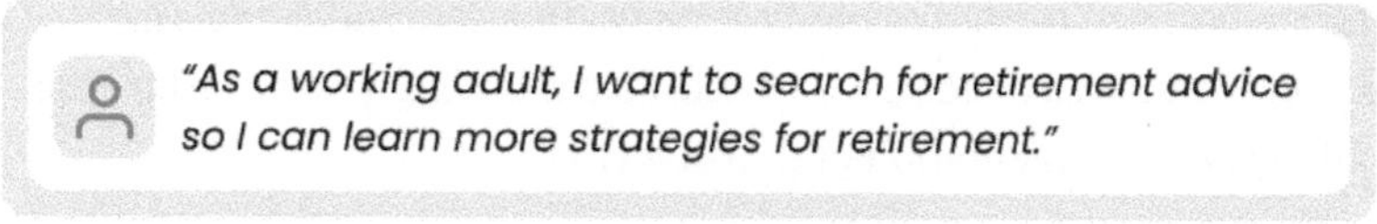

> "As a working adult, I want to search for retirement advice so I can learn more strategies for retirement."

FIGURE 7.3 A user story centered on search functionality for a product.

This statement helps align the entire team around your vision. You know who you are designing for—a target user. You know what they want—the ability to search for advice. Finally, you know why they want it—to better prepare for retirement.

By writing these statements, you can better empathize with your users. Additionally, you can better understand the user's perspective while creating your product for them.

To write a user story, you can use the formula in **FIGURE 7.4**.

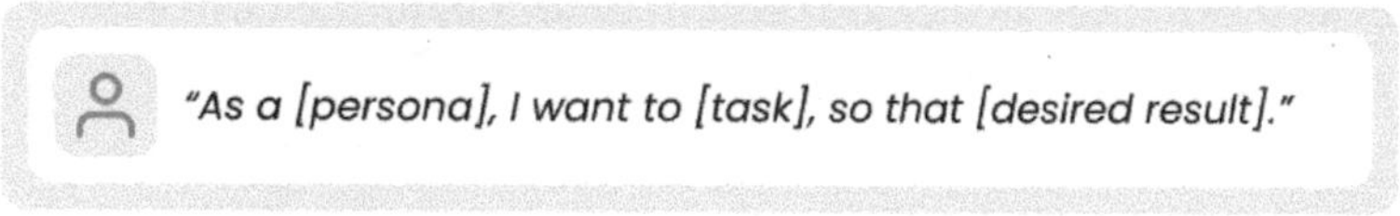

> "As a [persona], I want to [task], so that [desired result]."

FIGURE 7.4 The formula for writing user stories.

As a [persona]...

This part of the formula comes from the perspective of the user and frames the solution through their eyes. It is crucial for user stories—you are writing the product requirements through the lens of the user. Leveraging your user research and referencing the persona or user you defined earlier in the design thinking process keeps you grounded in the user's needs. You can make statements like *"would Jane/John ask for this feature?"* or *"what would Jane/John want to do here?"*

...I want to [task]...

This next part of the formula outlines the high-level description of the solution. It explains, at a glance, the specific thing you will focus on for your persona. Generally, this is the feature or functionality you are looking to create to address the problem to solve.

...so that [desired result].

This final part of the formula is the problem to solve, the issue that you encountered in your research.

Putting all these elements together, you get a short, specific, and goal-oriented statement from the user's point of view. This statement explains the work to be done in a clear, concise way while also allowing you to be flexible with designing the implementation of that solution.

How Do You Create User Stories?

Using the formula, you can create all the user stories you need for your product.

First, you need to understand the goals of your personas. What do they want? What do they need? Ideally, you figured this out during the empathize and define phases of the design thinking process—though some of this may have come out in testing as well.

Let's say that one of the high-level goals of our users is to retire (**FIGURE 7.5**). They are coming to your financial platform to save money for retirement. You can then break down the various ways users have communicated why they want to achieve this goal, or how.

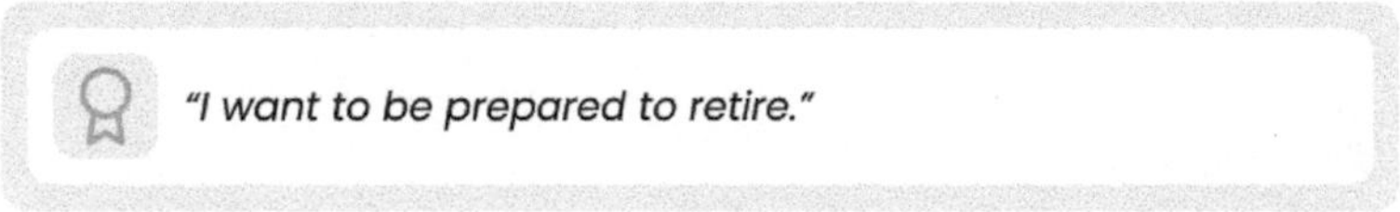

AUTHOR'S NOTE Usually, user stories are written by product managers looking to build the product by combining all the disciplines involved in its creation—design, engineering, editorial, and more. While designers don't normally write user stories, they absolutely influence them, either directly, by advocating for the user, or indirectly, by improving the business's understanding of the user with design thinking.

FIGURE 7.5 A user's goal.

"I want to be prepared to retire."

The goal can become a larger initiative that helps frame the specific things you will do to help users accomplish the larger goal with the product. Often referred to as an "epic," you can get a bit more specific (**FIGURE 7.6**) about what you will do to support users' larger goals.

FIGURE 7.6 An epic, which is a collection of user stories based on users' goals.

"Enable me to grow my savings with a retirement account."

For this financial product, you could have an epic that allows users to grow their retirement savings using a retirement account through your service. This would accomplish the main goal—be prepared to retire.

To accomplish this epic, you can break it down even further (**FIGURE 7.7**). This epic is ambitious and contains many smaller parts. How do you enable users to grow their savings? Luckily, you can support this epic with a bunch of smaller user stories.

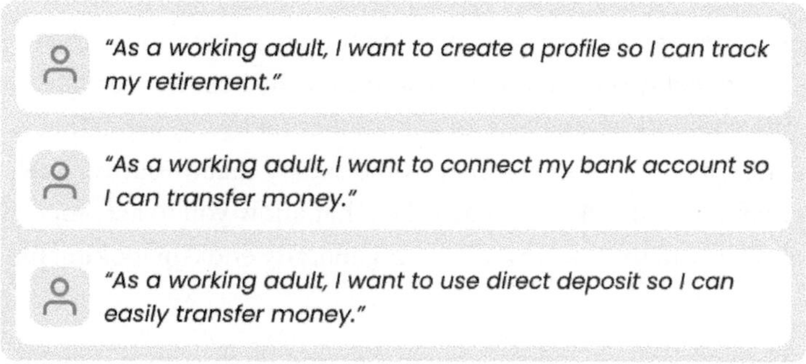

"As a working adult, I want to create a profile so I can track my retirement."

"As a working adult, I want to connect my bank account so I can transfer money."

"As a working adult, I want to use direct deposit so I can easily transfer money."

FIGURE 7.7 Several user stories that relate to users' goal of retirement.

Using the framework for writing user stories, you can create a series of short, specific, actionable initiatives that support the epic and, in turn, support the user's original goal—be prepared to retire. For your financial product, you need to allow users to create an account, connect a bank account, and even support automatic payments into that account, all in the effort of having them be prepared for retirement.

Putting it all together, it could look like **FIGURE 7.8**.

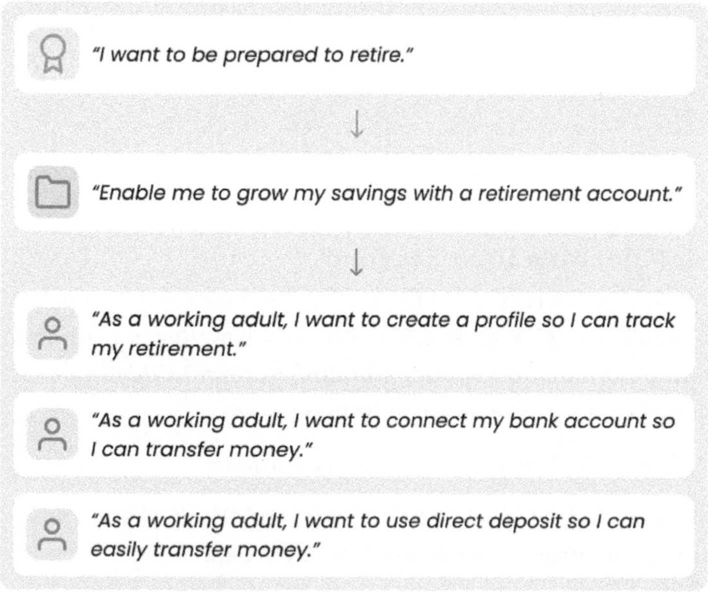

"I want to be prepared to retire."

↓

"Enable me to grow my savings with a retirement account."

↓

"As a working adult, I want to create a profile so I can track my retirement."

"As a working adult, I want to connect my bank account so I can transfer money."

"As a working adult, I want to use direct deposit so I can easily transfer money."

FIGURE 7.8 A user's goal, which leads to an initiative (an epic) based on several user stories that will allow users to accomplish their goal with your product.

Each element of the user's goals supports the next. The first element, the high-level goal, or *initiative*, is the core user need. Next, the specific product feature, or *epic*, is an aspect of that user's need. Finally, the functionalities of that feature, or *user stories*, are the pieces you need to create in order to support that aspect of the user's needs.

This is how user stories are constructed on product teams. You start with an initiative, usually driven by some market opportunity the business recognizes (via user research, competitive analysis, or some other method). From that initiative, you embark on various epics that would satisfy that initiative. Each epic has smaller components, called user stories, that allow you to accomplish the goals of that epic (and thus the initiative). It generally ends up looking like **FIGURE 7.9.**

In this way, you can organize all your ideas for the product into an actionable plan to build it.

FIGURE 7.9 A goal, or initiative, supported by several epics, which are composed of many user stories.

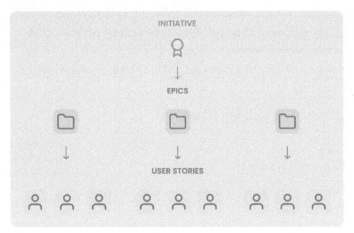

How Do You Prioritize User Stories?

You can use user stories to structure all the work to be done for your product. Those stories can roll into epics, those epics into initiatives. But as a business how do you know what initiatives to pursue in the first place? Which epics should you follow? What user stories are most important?

You could use a few methods to prioritize your user stories:

- **MoSCoW:** Standing for *Must, Should, Could,* and *Won't,* you can use this technique to categorize each user story by group.

- **Priority:** Using a system like *High*, *Medium*, and *Low* you can assign a weight to each story to emphasize the importance of each story.

- **Effort:** Using a system like *Extra Small*, *Small*, *Medium*, *Large*, and *Extra Large* (as if you were talking about T-shirt sizes), you can assign a number of resources to each story to help prioritize.

Sometimes, these prioritization methods can be combined. For example, a user story may be something that Must (MoSCoW) be built for the product, and it may be Large (Effort). In that case, it would be something the team would start on sooner, since it's a resource-intensive necessity for the product and needs to be built at some point, so starting it sooner would make sense.

Usually, user stories are written and prioritized when requirements are scoped out for a project to be developed—so often, they come when it's time to deliver designs to developers. This is because this process helps efficiently build products and ensures no functionality is missing from a feature.

SEQUENCES OF EVENTS

The sequences of events aren't "one size fits all" for all projects or organizations. Often, user stories can come before you start creating designs for a project. Other times, they come after, as you have seen in this book.

For existing products that are receiving smaller enhancements, user stories usually come before designing—there are fewer unknowns (you already have a product), and as a result, less ideation and exploration needs to take place to determine what tasks users want to complete in the product.

For "net new" experiences (like a new product or feature), user stories can often come after designing, when it's time to implement a solution—there are a lot more unknowns, like what things do users want and whether a solution even works for them. It doesn't make sense to write detailed user stories that tie into code developers need to write—you don't necessarily even know what you're building yet. As a result, user stories come after once you're clearer on the solution you're looking to build.

User Stories Give Implementation Structure

User stories help you make sure you're building the right features and functionalities for your users. They allow you to establish a user's goals, create initiatives that support those goals, and determine mechanics in the product that facilitate those initiatives. User stories allow you to cover all use cases, push for the right features, and keep the user front and center as you implement your designs.

It can be challenging to know how to write user stories, which ones the business wants to prioritize, and what's most important for your users. Thankfully, as designers, you can rely on other team members to help you create and prioritize your stories. Usually, defining these user stories and deciding what epics and initiatives to focus on is a team effort, with Product leading that effort. As a designer, however, it's important to understand how this all plays out, so you can do what you do best—advocate for the users in those stories.

Let's Do It!

Let's make some user stories for our solo traveler project. Be sure to use the formula in **FIGURE 7.10** to frame your thinking.

FIGURE 7.10 The formula for writing user stories.

"As a [persona], I want to [task], so that [desired result]."

AUTHOR'S NOTE Refer to the "User Stories" section in the appendix for examples to compare your user story with.

I won't be prescriptive about how you visualize this—that's up to you. You could use Microsoft Excel, Word, Figma, or even a piece of paper if that helps you think through the logic of each task your users need to accomplish in your solution.

Don't worry about making epics or initiatives at this point. You could go the extra mile and include those as well if you'd like. Alternatively, it could be a good thought exercise to start from epics or initiatives and filter down to the stories you want to include. I'll leave that up to you as well.

FLOW CHARTS

As you move through the implement step of the design thinking process, you will need to explain the logic of your product to your partners so that you can build the designs correctly. You'll need to map out how a user moves through the product—the steps they need to take so that they can complete their tasks. Not only will you need the *happy path*—the path users take to accomplish their goals most commonly and easily—you will also need the *unhappy paths* as well—the paths where additional logic may be needed, like an error form if a user makes an incorrect selection, or a subscription process for users who aren't logged in to the product.

Some of this may sound familiar based on the work you did in Chapter 5, "Prototyping Solutions," regarding task flows. This is because task flows are a subset of a broader class of design deliverable that we'll discuss next—flow charts.

What Is a Flow Chart?

When designing an experience for users, you must create various ways those users will move through that experience. You must think about how they onboard to the product, move through specific features, and complete the tasks that they came to the product to perform. To support this thinking, you can create *flow charts* to visualize the paths users take as they move through the product.

Looking at the flow chart in **FIGURE 7.11**, you could imagine the user (represented by the circle) moving through the flow from the left side of the diagram to the right side. As they move through the flow, they reach a choice (represented by the diamond in the middle of the diagram) and must decide which way to go through the experience. They eventually reach the end of the task, represented by the oval on the right of the diagram. A *flow chart* helps show how someone moves through any process, from the real world to digital.

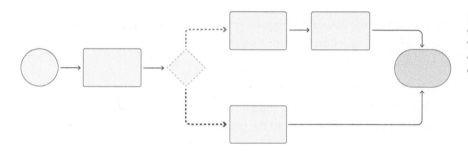

FIGURE 7.11 A high-level overview of a flow chart, which is a series of steps a user takes through an experience.

When thinking through ideas and explaining how a product functions, you can use several types of flow charts to visualize how a user moves through the product.

You'll hear people refer to flow charts as task flows, user flows, wireflows, flow diagrams, and more. As with many other concepts in the industry, the terms are commonly used interchangeably. I offer these brief definitions to help describe the nuance between different types of flow charts—some flow charts are less specific, while others are quite detailed.

- A **task flow** keeps the flow at a high level.

- A **user flow** explores various paths a user could experience depending on their choices.

- A **wireflow** ties your flows to your designs.

Each can have different levels of fidelity and description as well. The names of your artifacts are important, so that you can define a common language among the design thinking process with your peers. However, don't let the names of the deliverables get in the way of what's more important—the information you are trying to communicate with your artifacts.

Let's take a closer look at each type of flow chart.

What Is a Task Flow?

We discussed task flows in Chapter 5. As a reminder, and in context with other types of flow charts, a *task flow* is the most abstract version of a flow chart. It is a linear depiction of a single, specific task performed by the user (**FIGURE 7.12**).

FIGURE 7.12 A simple task flow.

Essentially, a task flow is the high-level steps a person would take to get to a specific goal. A task flow is simple, sequential, and non-branching—just the single series of steps from point A to point B.

FIGURE 7.13 is a task flow for a user to discover, explore, and sign up for online cooking classes. It depicts, at a high level, how a user would go from landing on a homepage to subscribing to the product. There's a clear, linear path the

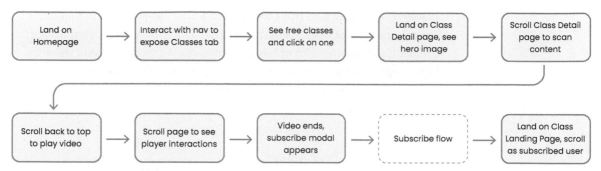

FIGURE 7.13 A more detailed task flow.

user would take to accomplish this goal—they would land on the homepage, interact with the premium content for free, and at the end of that interaction, they would be prompted to subscribe. When they do, they land back on the content page, ready to consume more content.

Task flows are an excellent place to start when considering how your product functions. They are a great way to organize your thoughts and identify the high-level steps your user will take as they move through your product. When beginning to ideate a new feature, or trying to figure out how all your designs could logically flow together, it's a good idea to make a few task flows to flesh out your ideas and sequence how your product works.

Task flows are good to have around when you're ready to deliver the product as well, because they set the stage for more detailed flow charts that are useful for developers—user flows.

What Is a User Flow?

A *user flow* is a more detailed task flow (**FIGURE 7.14**). It includes all the ways a user can move through a process to complete a task. If a task flow outlines the *high-level steps* a user takes to get from point A to point B, then a user flow outlines *each possible step* a user can take as they move from point A to point B.

FIGURE 7.14 A task flow that depicts the high-level steps a user takes to buy a MetroCard.

FIGURE 7.15 is a user flow from the New York City subway system that outlines the process of buying a MetroCard to pay for the subway. Purchasing a MetroCard requires a lot of inputs from users. A task flow would show the *happy path* a user would take through this process—showing the single high-level steps required to complete this task.[1]

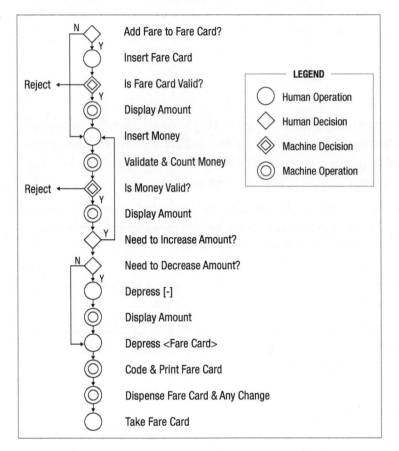

Unlike with a task flow, you are looking at multiple possibilities in the user flow. What if the user's card isn't valid? What if they insert the wrong amount of money? What if you need to give them change because they put in too much money? There are so many alternative cases you need to consider when designing a robust, fully functional system. That's where user flows can help you find each of the states you need to design for.

---

1 Link to image is this: https://en.wikipedia.org/wiki/Flow_process_chart#/media/File:Subway_Fare_Card_Machine_Flow_Process_Chart.jpg

FIGURE 7.16 is a flow chart I created for a solo traveler project (like the one in this book!). Users can send "pings" to other users nearby to communicate and meet up for various reasons. One of the core use cases I considered was the ability to meet up to share a cab.

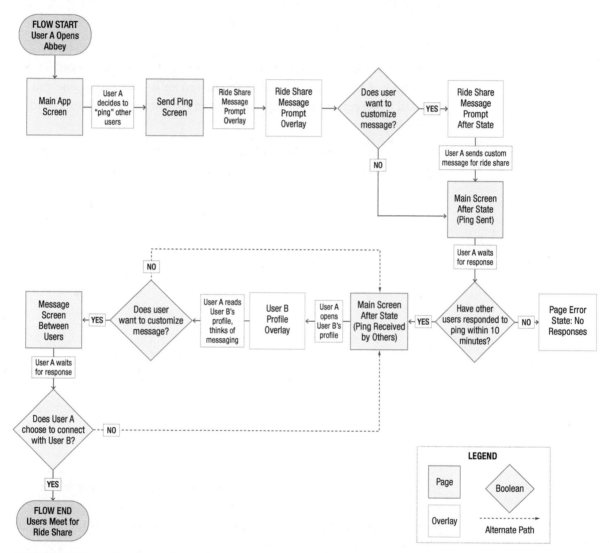

FIGURE 7.16 A user flow for a solo traveler app.

This user flow shows all the logic within that process, and how the system will respond as a result. For example, a user could send a "ping" to meet up, and someone might respond. Or it's possible no one receives that ping because no one is around. Or perhaps people see it, but no one chooses to respond to it. Each of these logical possibilities is covered in the user flow in Figure 7.16. That's the intent of a user flow—to cover the entire system, not just an individual piece of it.

User flows allow you to explore all the logical possibilities in a process. You must think of each possible scenario and design for it—this makes sure you cover all use cases and avoid any dead ends in your product when users end up using them.

Good user flows include a key, or legend (**FIGURE 7.17**), that explains what each symbol represents in the flow.

FIGURE 7.17 The structure of a user flow, which includes a legend that explains what each symbol in the flow means.

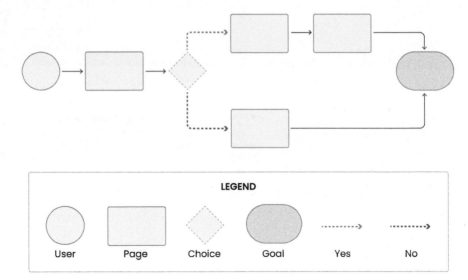

You need a legend because if you don't have one, it's a lot harder to follow along. With all the branching logic, it's easy to lose your place or the part of the process you are in, and having symbols helps reduce the cognitive load of whoever's reading the flow.

What Is a Wireflow?

If you want to take the concept of a user flow one step further, you can mock up each step in the process and show exactly what the user sees in the flow. Referred to as a *wireflow*, it allows you to show the specific, screen-level instances of how a user would complete a task (FIGURE 7.18).

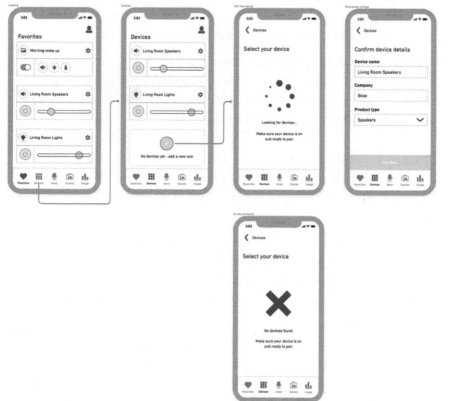

FIGURE 7.18 A wireflow for an app that controls smart devices.

Wireflows build on user flows. You take the same logic from a user flow, except instead of symbols, you show the screens a user would interact with, the places where the user would interact on those screens, and where those interactions lead. Additionally, you would use annotations to explain what's happening at that moment in the wireflow, to provide additional context to what the user's currently doing.

In Figure 7.18, you can see a wireflow for a smart device app. In it, you can navigate to your devices page, add a new device, and try to pair it to your app. This wireflow represents a slice of a user flow—you can see the *happy path* where the app can find the user's new device, and the "unhappy path" where the app fails to find the user's new device.

Note that wireflows can exist for any level of fidelity—you can use them during ideation as you work in low or mid fidelity, or you can use them during implementation of your ideas as you work in high fidelity.

Wireflows are excellent at walking through a task, step by step, to illustrate the workflow. Visualizing your ideas in this way helps you see, screen by screen, what a user will experience when you build it, and presents the user journey in the context of specific screens.

Which Flow Chart Should You Use?

If you're unsure which version of a flow chart to use in your projects, ask yourself what would be helpful to visualize to organize your thoughts and align the team.

If you're early in the process, use a task flow to lay out the general, high-level steps. This will let you organize a sequential, logical way for users to go through your product. This is helpful to share with the team during the planning stage, to make sure everyone is on the same page about their vision for the product.

If you're headed to development and you want to make sure you've covered all the possible states in your product, then make a user flow. This will let you uncover edge cases and ensure you don't miss error states, empty states, or anything else that a user may experience in your product. Share these user flows with your team to make sure that you're not missing any states and that developers have a good understanding of each state they need to account for.

If you're looking to present your ideas to the team as a complete design, use a wireflow. This will let you walk through the product as if you were the user and will show everyone what each screen will look like so that the team can align on the execution of the user experience. This could be early, such as if you are iterating for usability testing, or later, such as if you are pitching your designs to stakeholders for approval.

No matter the stage of the design thinking process, flow charts are excellent tools for organizing your thoughts, building alignment, and making sure you cover all your bases as you implement your designs.

Flow Charts Facilitate Implementation

Flow charts help you take the product across the finish line. Although they were useful earlier on in the prototype step of the design thinking process to think of your flow for users to test, they return here for a different purpose: to capture all the logic in your product. Flow charts allow you to think of all the edge cases in the product. What happens when the user isn't signed in, but needs to in order to access their shopping cart? Or if a user submits a request for a driver in a rideshare product, but no one responds? You need to think through all these cases to have a successful user experience for your product, and flow charts allow you to visualize and represent those possibilities.

Let's Do It!

Let's make a flow chart for the solo traveler project. You have three options to choose from:

- Task flow
- User flow
- Wireflow

Which should you choose? Well, if you've been following along with the exercises up to this point, you've already experienced making two of these for your project. In the "Task Flows" section of Chapter 5, I asked you to make a task flow. In the "Prototyping" section of Chapter 5, I asked you to visualize and connect that task flow, which is essentially a wireflow.

Let's experience what it's like to make a user flow—all the logic needed to implement a solution. You can start fresh with a new flow or use the task flow/wireflow from Chapter 5 as a starting point for your user flow. Remember that you'll want to think about all the steps and logic required to implement your designs. Are there error states? Extra steps not fully captured by the flows you've already created? Conditional logic, such as, a user being a free or premium customer? Think about all the possibilities and visualize them in a user flow—you'll need to account for those when the product is created.

AUTHOR'S NOTE Refer to the "User Flow" section in the appendix for examples to compare your user flow with.

STYLE GUIDES

When your testing is complete and you're ready to start implementing the product, you will need to make sure your branding and visual guidelines are ready as well. You may have some high-fidelity designs that you've tested already, or you may still be in a lower-level fidelity and not fully sure what your product looks like visually. No matter the case, it can be beneficial to create some high-level view of what your product will look like.

To accomplish this, you can make a quick guide, called a *style guide*, that globally represents your product's visual design.

What Is a Style Guide?

A *style guide* is a short document (**FIGURE 7.19**) that shows branding and visual design decisions such as typography, color, icons, photography, and more to help give a sense of what the product feels like.

FIGURE 7.19 A style guide for a car rental app.

Documents like this help show others the vision of what you are creating. You can use them to pitch a direction for your product, get buy-in or approval from stakeholders, or even use it as a feedback document to make sure you're on the right track.

Style guides help drive UI decisions as well, because they combine brand elements with UI elements, showing how the branding would apply to the product.

The result feels like a mix between a moodboard and a UI sheet. You have brand elements, like photography and color, which would be used in a moodboard, but you also have UI elements to be used in the product, like buttons, icons, and cards.

What Goes into a Style Guide?

Style guides can vary depending on the needs of the product you are working on. Generally, there are common elements across products that can be valuable to share at a high level using style guides.

Imagery

Imagery helps to set the tone of the product. It can include images you intend to use in the product, images that inspired you initially during the product's creation, or images that convey the feeling of the product. Essentially, these are the things that make the product feel a certain way and are related to it somehow (**FIGURE 7.20**).

FIGURE 7.20 Images are often used in a style guide to convey the tone of the product.

For this car rental app, some of our brand values include luxury, movement, and travel. These images help to convey those principles and set the tone for the rest of the style guide.

Typography

The typography section (**FIGURE 7.21**) of a style guide is used to communicate the typefaces, fonts, sizes, and use cases of the text in the product. Best practice is to name the typeface, then show examples of its font weights and how those could be applied to the product.

For the car rental app, we are using Poppins, a geometric sans serif font. The design would benefit from something that feels wider, like a car, and something that is round, like a car's wheels. Poppins is a popular, common font to use in design, and feels at home in this product.

FIGURE 7.21 Typography is commonly included in a style guide to show the text used to communicate with users.

Color Palette

The style guides should also include the colors (**FIGURE 7.22**) that you intend to use in the product. This is more than just the brand's colors—it should also include some UI states, like active or inactive colors, in addition to system statuses, like success, warning, or error (commonly green, yellow, and red, respectively).

FIGURE 7.22 Color values for a style guide. Among other reasons, color is often used in style guides to make sure assets are created using the same color values.

For the car app's color section, there is the background color (white), several grays to indicate UI status (like inactive or unselected), and the primary color, black. Black in this app is an indicator of luxury—the app is intentionally branded toward a higher-end consumer who wants to rent a luxury car for a trip. Using this color scheme carries that feeling throughout the product.

Iconography

As you move on to iconography, you start to incorporate UI elements into the style guide. Icons (**FIGURE 7.23**) help convey feeling in the product, and the choices you make with them greatly influence the user's experience.

FIGURE 7.23 Iconography used in a style guide. Generally, a style guide contains a link to download icons so that everyone can access the same resources.

Here, the icons are a lightweight-stroke icon set called Feather Icons. They are a set of open-source icons that are customizable and applicable to many use cases and industries. They are excellent for this application because they are rounded like the typography and they feel luxurious, which is the intended feeling when trying to influence users to think about cars.

UI Components

UI components (**FIGURE 7.24**) help show how all the other design decisions outlined in the style guide come together to form in-product elements that users can interact with. Showing the UI components allows others to imagine what it would be like to use the product.

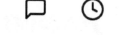

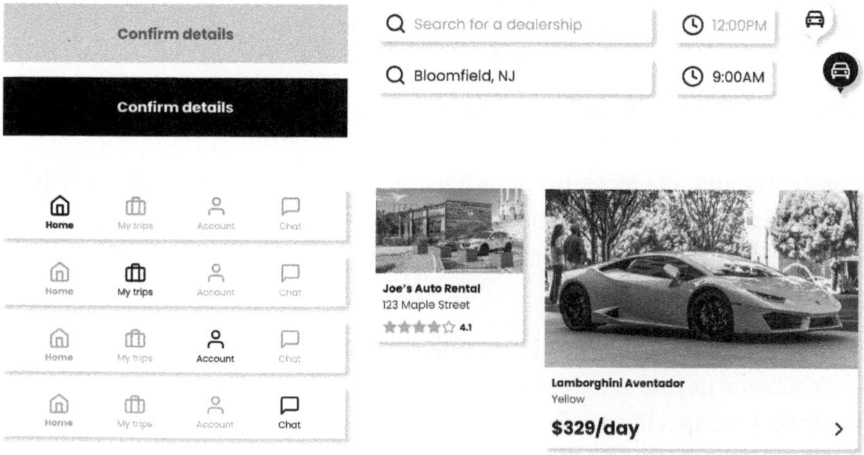

FIGURE 7.24 While not all style guides include UI components, it's helpful for a designer to communicate the elements of a design that are commonly repeated in the product, such as buttons, search fields, and cards.

For the car rental app, there are components like buttons, text fields, navigation bars, and cards. These will be the most common and crucial elements in the product to navigate and interact with. Users will have to enter a lot of information in text fields, they will browse a lot of cards to look at car dealerships and cars they can rent, and they will need to move around the app using the app's navigation bar at the bottom of the phone.

Mockups

Including mockups in your style guides can be helpful (if you have them). These tie everything together and show how the UI components shared previously play out when combined (FIGURE 7.25).

FIGURE 7.25 Mockups for a style guide. Mockups are rare, but they're helpful for those who aren't familiar with how all the elements combine in the product.

For the car app, the mockups show how the navigation, cards, and text fields combine into the user's experience with the product. Imagine clicking a card for a car dealership (on the left) and seeing the cars available from that dealership (on the right).

This is just one way a style guide can play out. You may want to include different elements in your style guide, such as spacing or grid lines, or UI components that are specific to your product, like a graph. Use this framework as a guideline for creating a style guide for your product.

Style Guides Portray Your Brand

Although you may be tempted to rely on the product itself to communicate the visual design decisions that have been made, the product can only go so far. As you add features and functionalities to the product, it is easier for your visual design to become out of sync. Deviations in the color, size, and shape of your UI components is a common side effect of not having a style guide to point to for basic design decisions. Having a high-level view of all the visual design logic you apply to your product is a crucial component to scaling your designs and implementing your product.

Let's Do It!

Let's create a style guide for the solo traveler app. Create a one-page document that shows, at a high level, the visual-design decisions for your product.

Your style guide should include the following information:

- Color
- Typography
- Iconography
- Imagery (if applicable)

Your guide could also include UI components, like a bottom app bar, header, cards, buttons, or anything else that is a consistent and common pattern in your product. If you'd like to show these in context, like with a mockup or two, all the better.

AUTHOR'S NOTE Refer to the "Style Guides" section in the appendix for examples to compare your style guide with.

Practice It!

If you like this layout and want to apply it to your project, feel free to use the following template to get started.

https://tinyurl.com/asuxd-styleguide-template

I also recommend you search Figma's Community section for style guide templates, so you can see different options for how to lay out your style guide.

DESIGN SYSTEMS

Style guides allow you to define the visual identity of your product. They communicate, at a high level, all the broad aesthetic decisions you make around color, typography, imagery, iconography, and even some UI components. Style guides affect more than the product—they extend to branding, marketing materials, social media presence, and more.

A style guide's effect goes wide across the product and the channels that promote the product. However, its breadth comes at the sacrifice of its depth. A style guide cannot capture all the applications of visual design to a product. You may know your typography from a style guide, but do you know how it is used in the product? At what font weight, size, or line height? You may know your colors, but do you know when to apply each one, where, and how?

That's the benefit of a design system. Where a style guide broadly captures the visual identity of a product, a design system provides the documentation and pieces that allow the product to be implemented consistently and at scale.

Designing for Consistency and Scalability

As you move through implementing your designs and creating a product, your visual design should stay consistent throughout the user's experience. This is a key element of a good user experience—you are creating patterns and establishing a visual language with your design choices. The colors you use indicate functionality, like interactive text or disabled states. The shapes and shadows you use for buttons suggest brand values and establish aesthetics. Ideally, you stay internally consistent with those choices—for example, if you decide the buttons are blue in one part of your product, then they should remain that same shade of blue throughout your product.

This matters for the implement step of the design thinking process. When you build your designs, you need a roadmap explaining your visual design choices. Ideally, this is baked into each screen you produce and share with developers. Sometimes, however, you lose consistency in your design deliverables.

Perhaps you select a slightly different shade of blue for your buttons over the course of a flow. Maybe you increase the font weight here or there, for things to look nicer. Or perhaps you change the size of text, and in one section of your product your headings are larger than the headings of another section. It is very easy to lose consistency as you scale, especially if you are moving fast or among different teams.

If you design without a system, then over time, it becomes harder and harder to remain consistent. It takes longer to design, because you must remake your design decisions, like the appropriate size of text for a section or a color for an interactive component. If you could design without having to make these decisions, you would be able to move faster, stay consistent, and increase the scalability of your design process.

From a development perspective, engineers will also want to build systematically. They will ideally establish a style in code, and then apply that style unilaterally throughout the product wherever it applies to the design. That way, if there is ever a need to change the design, by changing that style, the change applies to the entire product. This speeds up development, avoiding situations like "hard coding" sections of the product only to go back later to update them (or, commonly, never go back at all).

For these reasons, and more, it is beneficial to adopt a design system. A *design system* is a set of reusable components that combine to form experiences. They are governed by common standards, have a clear set of documentation, and in some cases, even have a set of principles that accompany why they were made and how to use them.

To use design systems in your projects, you must start at the foundational concept of understanding them—atomic design.

AUTHOR'S NOTE
Building a product using variables and systems is extremely important. For one of the products I worked on, the developers hard coded the navigation instead of relying on a system that would allow them to swap links in and out of the bottom app bar. Users wanted a change in the navigation pattern, but the company couldn't deliver on that change until a year later.

What Is Atomic Design?

Atomic design, first conceptualized by Brad Frost, is a methodology for creating design systems. Borrowing concepts from chemistry, it asks you to think about the products you create on a molecular, or "atomic," level. Atomic design reduces products down to their smallest components and builds on top of those components by connecting them to form larger ones.

Another way to think about it is to imagine a product as a series of building blocks (**FIGURE 7.26**) that combine to form an experience. Each block plays off others, allowing you to take smaller elements and combine them to form a larger experience.

FIGURE 7.26 A design system is made of up smaller pieces that combine to form a larger experience. (sukiyaki/Shutterstock)

Pulling from a predefined set of blocks, or components, allows you to stay consistent and deliver comparable experiences across different parts of the product easily, quickly, and at scale.

AUTHOR'S NOTE As with all the other times I've noted it, the definitions can vary from person to person. Some might say a singular property, like an instance of color, is actually a *token* rather than an *atom*, and that the combination of several tokens, like in a button, is an atom. In Brad Frost's original definition, singular properties like a color were considered atoms. The definitions shift as the industry's understanding of design and the ability to communicate it improve and evolve. As long as you can communicate your decisions, you'll be good.

Atomic design is also made of up several components, broken into five categories, from smallest to largest:

- Atoms
- Molecules
- Organisms
- Templates
- Pages

Atoms

In chemistry, atoms are the basic building blocks of matter. In design, *atoms* are the smallest, most individual elements in a product.

When designing a product, the smallest expression of that design is considered an atom—an element with a single property. These are the things like the colors in your UI, the text on the screen, or the icons used to take actions within the product (**FIGURE 7.27**).

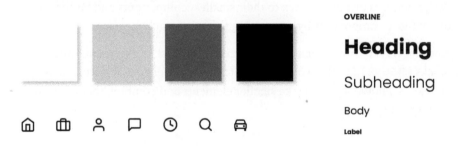

OVERLINE
Heading
Subheading
Body
Label

FIGURE 7.27 The most basic form of an atom in atomic design—color, typography, and iconography.

Atoms can also be represented a little bit more complexly, like combining several properties into a single component. A button has several properties, like color, shape, text, icons, elevation, curvature, and states, but it's still small enough that some refer to it as an atom (**FIGURE 7.28**).

Confirm details
Enter text

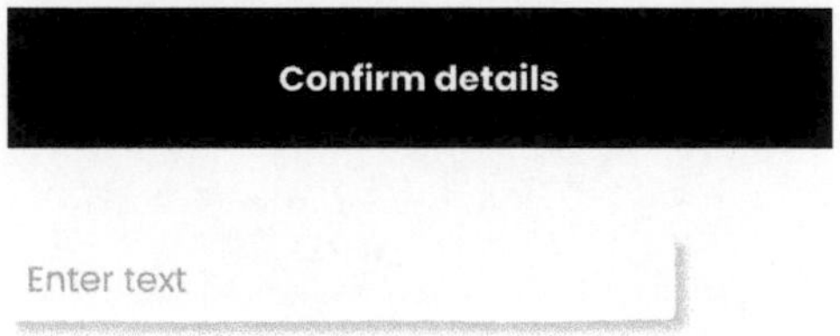

FIGURE 7.28 More complex atoms that take on multiple properties, like color, shape, space, typography, and elevation.

Molecules

When you start to combine these atoms into larger forms, you get *molecules*—instances of multiple design decisions that turn into compound elements.

When you take atoms like color, typography, and icons and put them together, you start to form UI elements that have more functionality. Perhaps you create a navigation bar, or a form field with an icon, or an interactive timer component (FIGURE 7.29). You can start to see smaller atoms influence the design of your components and combine like building blocks to create larger, more complex elements in a design.

FIGURE 7.29 A series of atoms combined into molecules, like a navigation bar, a search field with text and icons, or a time picker.

Organisms

Once you have stronger building blocks to use in your system, you can start to form organisms. *Organisms* are collections of molecules that combine to form more complicated, distinct sections of an interface.

This is where parts of your UI combine to form more complex components. You can use several molecules in tandem to form organisms, which start to look like real, contextual parts of your product. This is where a design system can start to feel less like a style guide and more like a style guide applied to a product—you see the product starting to form into recognizable pieces in a user experience (FIGURE 7.30).

FIGURE 7.30 Several examples of organisms, like cards or a date picker.

Templates

Using enough organisms, you can start to form the overall skeleton of your product by creating templates.

Templates show your layouts in action, taking the core idea of atoms, molecules, and organisms and putting them together to form the structure of an experience. Templates provide context for how all the individual parts play together to form an experience.

The templates in **FIGURE 7.31** show where the pieces would go but don't include the data that would power those experiences. Rather, templates show how the pieces would fit into the experience without actually pulling in the data that powers the end user experience—like the metadata in a card (pictures, prices, reviews, and so on).

FIGURE 7.31 Several templates for a product. They outline the logic of how the pieces combine to form a user experience.

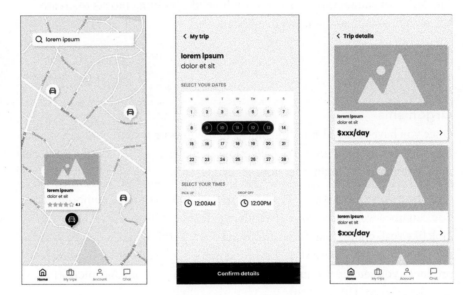

Pages

Once your templates are established, you can add the real-world data to create pages.

Pages show real or representative content to fully demonstrate the actual user experience. You can use pages to test real content, observing what the product would look like with actual data (**FIGURE 7.32**). Pages are the final form of the product in action.

Atomic Design in Action

When you put all these concepts together, you get a systematic process for how you can think about building your product (**FIGURE 7.33**).

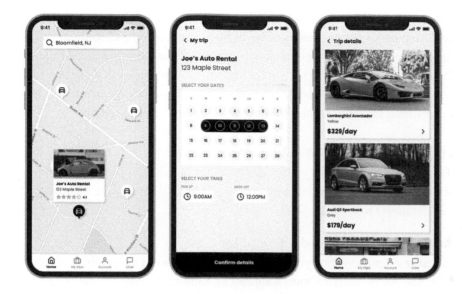

FIGURE 7.32 The pages that power the end user experience.

FIGURE 7.33 The stages of atomic design, from atoms to molecules to organisms to templates to pages.

Zooming out and combining each step of atomic design, you can see how each step builds off the previous one. To build pages full of real content, you need templates to understand their structure. For templates, you need organisms to lay out your designs. To make organisms, you need molecules that can combine into distinct elements of your interface. To make organisms, you need atoms, the foundational building blocks of your design system.

How Can You Make a Design System?

To use a design system for your products, you can follow a process to understand what you have, create a common language for it, then make a series of smaller pieces to build it.

Audit the Current Product

To make a design system, you must first know what's in your product (if you have one you're working from). Conduct an audit of the visual patterns and make a list of your atoms. What do your buttons look like? What colors do you use? What typography do you have, and where? How is it applied?

To support this work, it helps to take screenshots of all the flows in your product. This will let you take stock of all the UI components you've created and systematically work your way through each screen until you have a clear sense of all your design decisions.

If you built your product from a style guide, that helps as well! Leverage the design decisions from that artifact as they are applied to your product and incorporate them into the design system.

Establish Your Visual Language

After you have a good sense of the design decisions you've already made, it's time to form opinions on what you want to do for your product moving forward. To create a set of atoms that's consistent and easy to pull from, unify design decisions in your UI. Think about your colors—how many different grays do you need? Do you need different typographic treatments for similar sections of your product? Do you have a consistent set of spacing? These small, tiny decisions will filter through the rest of the process, and it's important to form an opinion on all of them before moving to the next step.

Create a Component Library

Once you have decided your visual language, you need to use wireframing software (like Figma) to make the actual atoms, molecules, and organisms that will power your product. Start small—create atoms for color, typography, iconography, and spacing. Build off that—make buttons from color, type, and space. Make form fields from color, type, space, and icons. Keep combining those smaller elements into larger ones until you have a library of all the components commonly used in your product.

Create All the States of Each Component

When building your component library, don't forget to include other states—a button isn't always active; a form field isn't always empty (**FIGURE 7.34**). You will need each of these states to create pages for your final designs, so make sure you think about them as you build atomically.

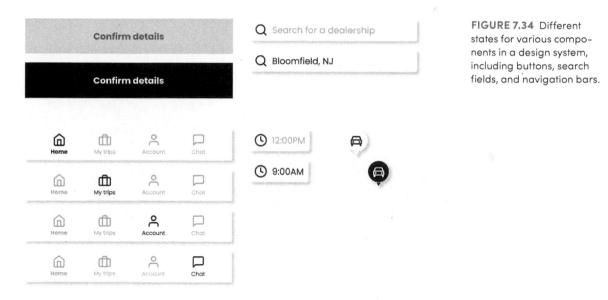

FIGURE 7.34 Different states for various components in a design system, including buttons, search fields, and navigation bars.

What Systems Can You Look at Today?

Many organizations use design systems to build their products. Some organizations have designers and engineers that specifically work on these systems as their primary job function. These systems are robust not only in the number of components they have, but also in having a deep philosophy behind why they made the design decisions they have.

Many companies offer both their philosophies and components to the public, to showcase the strength of their design prowess in addition to helping the community and pushing forth the design craft. These public facing resources are invaluable—you can learn a lot looking at any of these systems to understand what companies do and why they do it.

Examine the images in the following sections to see some examples of established design systems and explore what's possible when using design systems to build products.

Material by Google

Google is one of the companies that lead the design industry regarding design systems documentation and structure. It makes its entire design system's logic and structure public facing, allowing anyone to view its design decisions, observe its specifications, and pull code to implement its design patterns (**FIGURE 7.35**).

FIGURE 7.35 A sample page from Google's design system, Material. Available at https://m3.material.io/.

Carbon, by IBM

Like Google, IBM also provides its design documentation and components for the public to see and use. Both companies have a similar structure to their pages, offering guidelines, components, community resources, and blogs that discuss case studies and updates regarding the system and its implementation patterns (FIGURE 7.36).

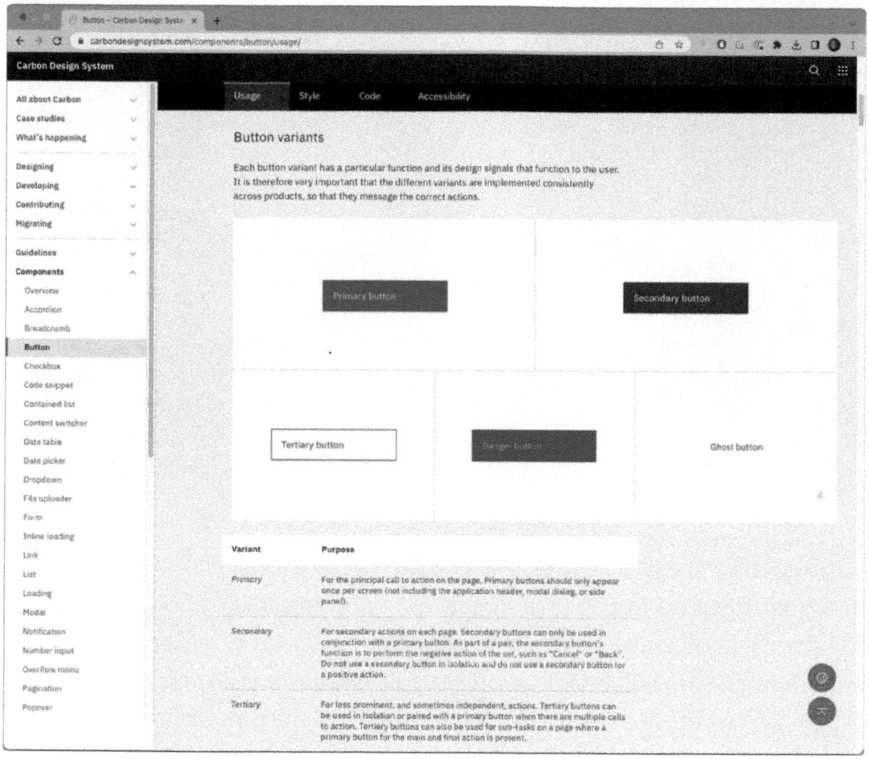

FIGURE 7.36 A sample page from IBM's design system, Carbon. Available at https://carbondesignsystem.com/.

Polaris, by Shopify

Similar to Google and IBM, Shopify also offers its design system to the public, including the same content as the other two (and various other companies as well). Interestingly, Shopify offers upcoming designs (in the form of alpha and beta components) in addition to older designs (marked as legacy or deprecated components). Seeing the history of the system allows additional context into the decision making of the company and helps us understand where it's been and where it's headed (FIGURE 7.37).

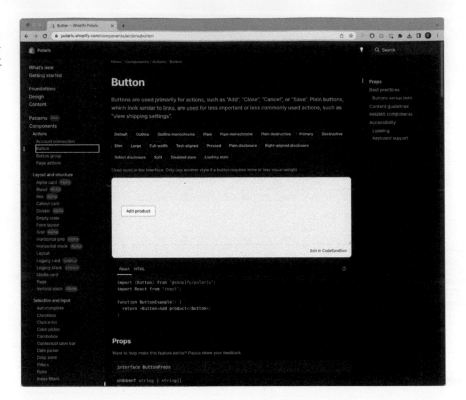

FIGURE 7.37 A sample page from Shopify's design system, Polaris. Available at https://polaris.shopify.com/.

Design Systems Improve Implementation

Design systems allow you to design the product consistently and at scale. Having a common visual style in your product will lead to better user experiences—you will have less internal inconsistency, a clearer visual language, and more flexibility to make changes to the product as it evolves. Even if your product is small or just getting started, it's important to create a system in which you design it.

Let's Do It!

Let's start creating a design system for the solo traveler app. You should already have all the pieces you need in your designs.

1. Find the elements you use consistently—things like styles, buttons, navigational elements, cards, or anything else that repeats across your solution.

2. Organize these elements and turn them into components in your design software.

   Depending on your design software, they may also be called *symbols* or a different word entirely. Essentially, what you're doing is creating a "master" instance of each design decision.

3. Once you've created your master components, go back to your designs and replace the individual elements with copies linked to your master components.

   That way, if you ever change the master component, your designs will update automatically—just like they would in code.

DELIVERING DESIGNS

You've reached the final point of the implement step in the design thinking process. Now that you've done all the work in understanding the problem to solve, and you feel that your designs solve that problem well, you need to prepare your design decisions in such a way that others can easily build them and make them real.

It's finally time to deliver your designs to developers.

Delivering Your Designs

You've ideally been communicating with developers this entire time. You've ideated possible solutions, discussed technical feasibility, and kept a strong dialogue going as you tested your designs with users. At some point, though, developers will need to see the actual designs, fully specified, so that they can build them.

There are plenty of tools you can use to do this—Sketch, Adobe XD, Figma, and other wireframing tools make this process a lot easier than it was in the past. Each of these tools offers some way for developers to "inspect" the design so that they can take that blueprint and apply it in code.

In the example in FIGURE 7.38, you can see a preview of what this looks like for a developer using Figma. A developer can select any element in your design file and look at all the properties they need to build it. They can pull colors, shadows, icons, images, and even animations, if you add them, in the code format they require in order to put it into the product (at the time of this writing, in CSS, iOS, or Android).

This is an extremely powerful workflow option for product teams. In the past, you would have to write specification documentation for every single screen and each component, as shown in **FIGURE 7.39**.

FIGURE 7.39 A specification document that outlines the functionality of a component in a design.

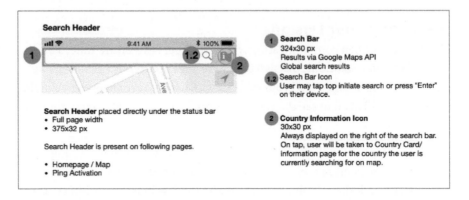

In this example, the designs were annotated to provide not only functionality but also pixel sizes so that developers could put those into code. Although some places have the need for robust documentation, like the example in Figure 7.40, many companies now remove this step from the workflow, letting designers focus more on actually designing the product. If a developer needs to see a specification, they can go into the file where the design was made and look themselves.

Because developers (and other team members, like product teams) now have a direct line to the files, it's important that you structure them in a way that makes the most sense for an observer. People looking at your work might be seeing it for the first time, or they may lose context of where they are in the user's journey. In fact, after several weeks away from a particular flow, *you* might forget too. That's why the structure of your design file, and how you deliver it, plays such a huge role in implementing your designs.

AUTHOR'S NOTE Design systems help too! If you use the same button in multiple places, you can have a centralized documentation system that reduces overhead for everyone involved. A developer will pull the design system button and put it into the product. No rewriting specifications every time you create a button (or any other design system component).

How Should You Structure Your Content?

Depending on the size of your product and the portion of the product you work on, you may want to structure your file in different ways. One way to structure it is to create pages based on milestones, like so:

- Initial brainstorm Month/Date/Year

- MVP Month/Date/Year

- Release 1.0 Month/Date/Year

- Release 2.0 Month/Date/Year

This form of organization lets you see the product's evolution over time and works really well if you don't have a lot of features. If you're working on a lightweight, early-stage product and rushing to a minimum viable product release, then this could work well.

Alternatively, you could organize by feature, like so:

- Feature 1

- Feature 2

- Feature 3

- Brainstorming

This schema lets you stay organized by initiative and revisit these pages when it's time to update a feature or add new functionality to one.

Another way to organize could be by user role, like so:

- User role 1

- User role 2

- User role 3

This structure may work nicely for a platform that changes slightly, depending on who's signed in.

Any of these (or even other) schemas can work for storing your files. It's up to you how you organize, and it will drastically vary by the product you work on, how mature it is, and how much content you must design.

How Should You Organize Your Screens?

When preparing your files for implementation, it's valuable to organize screens in a logical, easy-to-follow way. After working with several design teams and seeing how each team chose to organize, I have found that the most efficient, effective way to organize designs is based on flows, then states.

Organizing by flows (user flows, user stories, or otherwise) allows you to show each step (**FIGURE 7.40**) in the *happy path* of a user trying to accomplish a task. If there are deviations from that happy path (error states, loading states, and so on) you can capture those directly after illustrating the happy path.

FIGURE 7.40 The structure to organize your screens in a design file. It starts with the user story, followed by each sequential step in a flow.

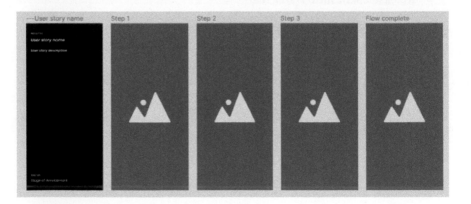

This is a sample structure for how you can break down a file into easy-to-follow, digestible stories that other team members can follow. By using user stories, for example, these flows can tie directly to product initiatives and developer tasks to complete, which improves the ability to track designs and follow along without having context on the inner workings of your project file.

First, list out an artboard that shows high-level project details, as shown in **FIGURE 7.41**.

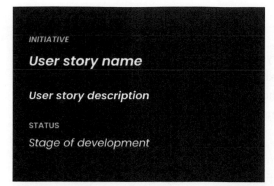

The details of a user story at the start of a flow. This provides clarity and context for the screens that come after this.

Four pieces of information are detailed in this summary sheet:

- **Initiative**—What feature, epic, or project is this flow related to?

- **User story name**—What user flow, or user story, does this flow relate to?

- **User story description**—What is the actual user story? What are the details of the task the user is trying to accomplish?

- **Status/stage of development**—At what point in the design thinking process are you with this flow? Is it still being designed, ready to be built, or already in the product?

Filled out, the summary sheet could look like **FIGURE 7.42**.

FIGURE 7.42 The filled-in user story summary.

For this flow, you are working toward the MVP of a car rental app. The user story is to search for nearby dealers. The description is the user story as written by a product manager, as it appears in the project management software you use to build the product. The status is that this flow is ready to be built by developers.

After you list out the details in your summary sheet, you then list each step the user takes in the actual product to complete the task. Choose the steps that outline the happy path—the path without any problems or navigation to a part of the product outside the current task. If there are deviations, you can show them later.

For this user story, you have four screens (**FIGURE 7.43**) that illustrate the happy path—the empty state of the search screen, the user searching a location for car dealerships, the search results, and a selected state showing a car dealership the user is interested in.

FIGURE 7.43 The screens that show the flow for the user story in Figure 7.42.

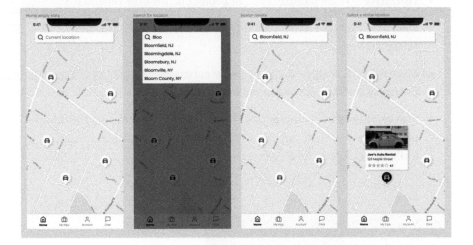

Since that's all you need for this flow's happy path, this flow is complete. You would need to show unhappy path moments in a later section of the file (for example, if there are no search results in a geographic area, or the user misspelled a location) but that's not necessary in this row.

Putting this all together, you'd get something like **FIGURE 7.44**.

Figure 7.44 shows a single row of signs—a summary sheet describing the user story, and four screens that depict the user's happy path toward completing that story.

If you follow this logic for all your user stories, it would look something like **FIGURE 7.45**.

FIGURE 7.44 The combined user story and flow. Delivering designs in this way makes things a lot clearer for the reader.

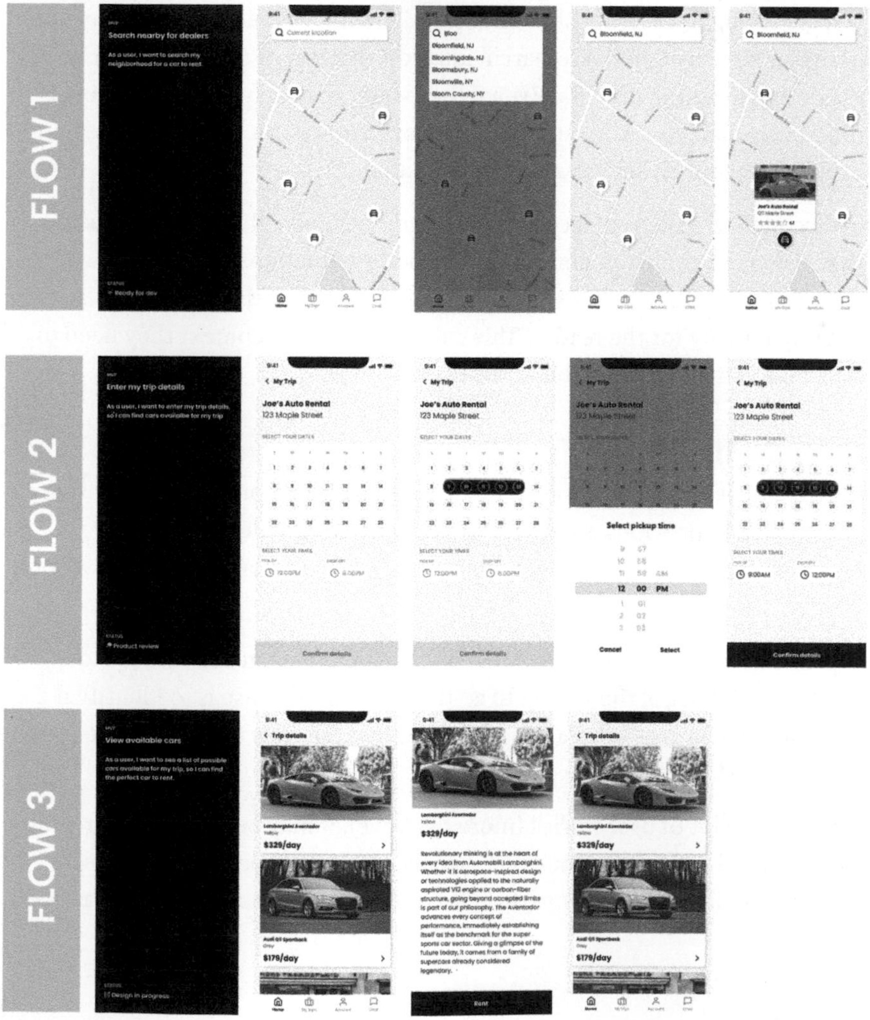

FIGURE 7.45 An example of how a design file could be structured to make the designs clearer for the reader, even if they have no context about the project.

Here, you can see that this initiative has multiple flows, with different screens, each of which all our team members can follow easily. You establish context (the user story, the description, the stage of development) and follow that up with each step in the flow for the user to accomplish their goal.

If you structure your pages and your screens in an organized, clear way for anyone on the team to follow, then implementing your designs will be easy, consistent, and frictionless for everyone involved.

Provide Specifications and Context

To deliver your designs, you must provide not only their specifications but also the context around them. You can't assume people understand what you are trying to accomplish with the designs you've created. They may not have been involved in the research, ideation, testing, or any other part of the design thinking process. Even if they were, they may have seen things differently than you. You need to take your vision, put it down on paper, and explain to people what you are trying to build.

To accomplish this, you need to have clearly defined deliverables that show that vision. To show someone how your design functions, root it in the people you design for. Take a user story, illustrate the flow for that story, and lay that out sequentially for the reader. This will give them the context they need to understand the vision and build the design.

Let's Do It!

AUTHOR'S NOTE Refer to the "Delivering Designs" section in the appendix for examples to compare your delivery designs with.

It's time to deliver your designs! Using both the user stories and the designs you created in previous exercises, lay out your design files so that they clearly show how a user would accomplish each user story you made for your product.

If you're missing a few screens to do this, that's OK—you can create those screens now. Part of the reason to go through this exercise is to identify if anything is missing—after all, it's better to find out now than when the product launches!

If you have a lot of user stories (more than five), it may be difficult to create the flows and screens for each one. I challenge you to see if you can create all of them, but if not, then try to do at least three so you can get some practice.

THE END OF THE PROCESS?

After you deliver your designs and your product is built, you have officially ended the design thinking process. You've hit every part of the process. You started by empathizing with users and understanding their needs. You moved on to define the problem to solve so that you could ideate solutions to that problem. You built prototypes of your ideas, tested them with users, and finally, finished implementing your designs with developers. You've completed the process for the product that you wanted to build, and ideally, created something that helps improve the lives of the people you've been designing for this entire time.

So, what happens next? Let's take another look at the model from the Nielsen Norman Group (FIGURE 7.46).

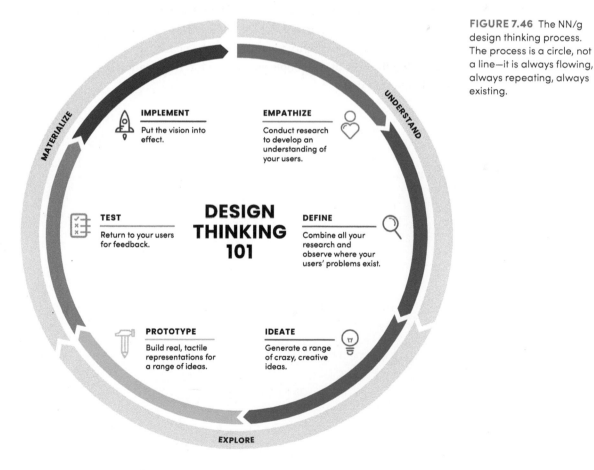

FIGURE 7.46 The NN/g design thinking process. The process is a circle, not a line—it is always flowing, always repeating, always existing.

I could have written about a lot of design thinking models that have similar processes. I chose this one for a specific reason—its cyclical nature. Other models are represented as lines, as if design thinking starts at the project's kickoff and ends once the product is complete.

That's not how design thinking works—at least, not for me. You can always improve the experiences you create by going back to the start and repeating the process. You can take your current product and evolve it further, enhancing the user experience with new features and functionalities. You can improve the understanding of your users by speaking to them again, showing them what you built, and interviewing them about their future needs. You can find new problems to solve, then try to solve them by ideating new possibilities and testing them.

Other models assume that once you implement something, you're done. And you could be if you want to be! But the Nielsen Norman model of design thinking offers the possibility to continue—the chance to keep iterating and improving the lives of the people you design for. Personally, that's a chance I'm thrilled to take.

CHAPTER 8

WHAT'S NEXT?

Now that the design thinking process is over, you've completed a full end-to-end design thinking exploration for a user problem. You've understood your users, defined the problem to solve, created a design solution for them, prototyped it, tested it with users, and built the specifications for implementing it.

So, what do you do now that the exploration is over? That depends on what you want to do. You may be completely satisfied with the knowledge you've gained throughout this process and ready to move on to a new problem. Or you may want to iterate on your solution based on the valuable information you learned during testing. Or you may want to add to the product you've made by exploring another side of it or by developing the features even further.

Before you move on, though, you should know a few things about what happens after the design thinking exploration ends. Our memories are fickle and fade easily—you should write down what you've done so there's a record of all your work, both good and not so good. You may want to share this work with others, so you should be aware of how to give and receive feedback about designs. You might even want to work in the industry, or if you're already here, you might benefit from some advice on how to navigate it.

321

Let's talk about a few final points before moving on to the next project—starting with how to document all the amazing work you've done thus far.

WRITING A CASE STUDY

To work in user experience design professionally, you need to demonstrate that you are a subject matter expert in design. In some way, shape, or form, you need to show potential employers or clients that you can perform design tasks that lead to positive outcomes for the businesses and users you design for.

There are several ways you can do this. You can give talks demonstrating your design expertise, advocating for design thinking or some other element of user experience design. You can write, by posting articles online or publishing novels showing your knowledge of design. Or you can open a design file and talk about the work as you walk through screens or flows of completed designs.

All these methods can be successful, especially as you progress in your career. But there's one method of showing your work that is the most successful, helping convince teams that you're the right candidate for the job—and that's writing a case study.

What Is a Case Study?

A *case study* is an in-depth walkthrough of an in-progress or complete project. A case study could be about plenty of topics. You could write a case study about a feature, like how you added something to a product. You could write a case study about a process, like how your team operates and performs work. You could write a case study about a system, like a design system you created, modified, or oversaw. The number of projects that could be discussed has no limit.

FIGURE 8.1 is an excerpt from a case study[1] that I wrote while working at Kaplan, an education company. I was part of a team creating a feature for teachers to look at the progress of their students over time using data visualization. In this case study, I cover various elements of the project, from business goals to design process to outcomes and more. A good case study covers all elements of a project that prospective employers or clients will want to see.

---

1 https://medium.com/atom-platform/designing-gradebook-d94d6bf82295

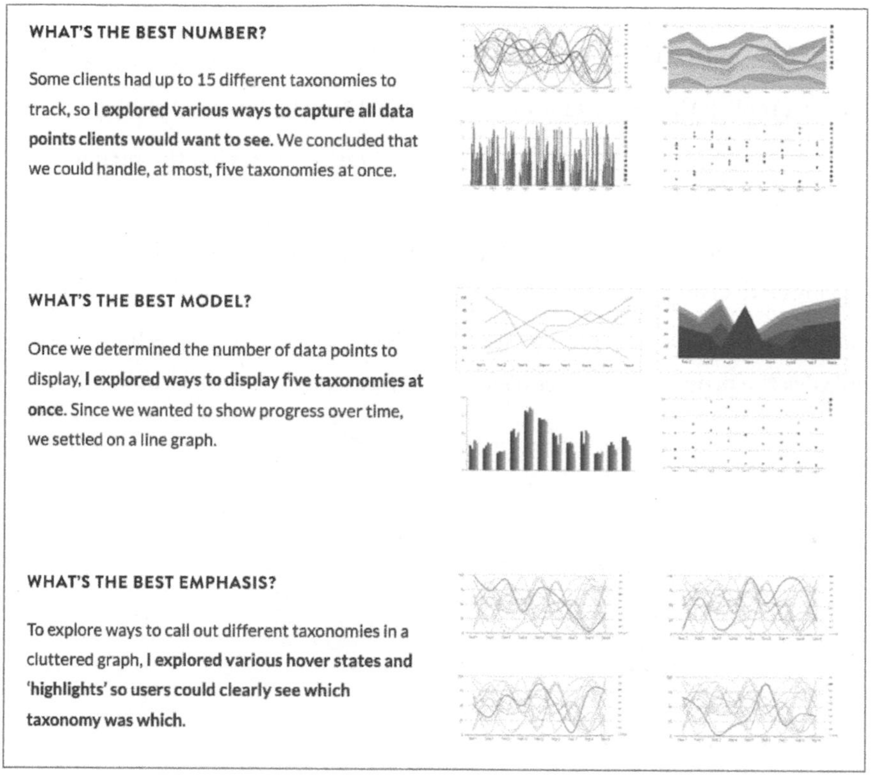

WHAT'S THE BEST NUMBER?

Some clients had up to 15 different taxonomies to track, so **I explored various ways to capture all data points clients would want to see.** We concluded that we could handle, at most, five taxonomies at once.

WHAT'S THE BEST MODEL?

Once we determined the number of data points to display, **I explored ways to display five taxonomies at once.** Since we wanted to show progress over time, we settled on a line graph.

WHAT'S THE BEST EMPHASIS?

To explore ways to call out different taxonomies in a cluttered graph, **I explored various hover states and 'highlights'** so users could clearly see which taxonomy was which.

FIGURE 8.1 A portion of a case study debating alternatives for data visualization models.

But how can you connect all the project elements? How can you structure your case studies so that people can easily understand the story of a project they never participated in? Let's take a closer look at how to structure case studies and how you should approach writing them.

Show Your Process

A *good* case study mentions the process the designer went through to deliver the project. A *great* case study walks through that process, showing each step of the project from start to finish. You don't need a ton of detail about your process, but as you walk through each moment in your case study, the reader should have a sense of where they are, what you did, and how you approached the project.

Explaining your process is important—demonstrating that you have a standard approach to design helps show employers that you have a plan for conducting design and implies that you will use this plan to solve their problems.

Showing your process gives employers an example of how you work and promotes confidence that you can do the work.

To accomplish this sense of process, I do two things in my case studies:

- I show my process upfront, to set expectations for what the reader will read.

- I walk through each step of that process, providing more detail about the decisions I made along the way.

FIGURE 8.2 is an example of my case study process, which, generally speaking, follows the process you've been learning since the start of this book.

FIGURE 8.2 A portion of a case study detailing the process for completing the project.

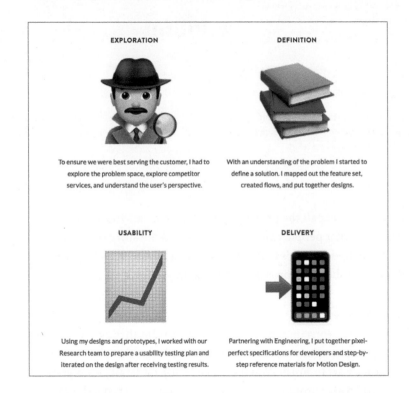

EXPLORATION

To ensure we were best serving the customer, I had to explore the problem space, explore competitor services, and understand the user's perspective.

DEFINITION

With an understanding of the problem I started to define a solution. I mapped out the feature set, created flows, and put together designs.

USABILITY

Using my designs and prototypes, I worked with our Research team to prepare a usability testing plan and iterated on the design after receiving testing results.

DELIVERY

Partnering with Engineering, I put together pixel-perfect specifications for developers and step-by-step reference materials for Motion Design.

The six steps of the Nielsen Norman Group design thinking process (**FIGURE 8.3**) work well for structuring your case study and taking someone clearly through your process. Let's see how each step can map to a story.

1. **Empathize**—Who are the users? What are their wants and needs?

2. **Define**—What's the problem you solved? How did the users solve this problem prior to using your solution?

3. **Ideate**—What solutions did you think would work? Which ones did you pursue?

4. **Prototype**—How did the prototype look? How did it function?

5. **Test**—How did the solution perform? What did users think?

6. **Implement**—How was the solution built? What is the final product?

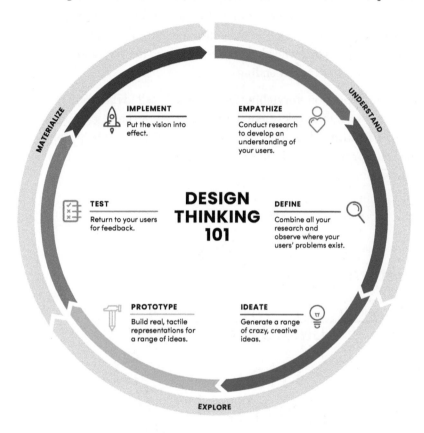

FIGURE 8.3 The NN/g design thinking model. It maps well to a case study's structure and storytelling.

Add an introduction (a high-level overview of the project, including the business goals) and a conclusion (how the project went and any next steps coming out of it), and you have a strong, compelling overview of your work.

In my case study example in Figure 8.2, I cover each of the questions from these steps across four separate sections—Exploration, Definition, Usability, and Delivery. Then, once I set the expectations for what will be discussed, I break out my case study into those sections and discuss each one in more depth.

Tell a Story

A case study walks a reader through the most important elements of a project. It has a beginning, a middle, and an end. It has an introduction to the project, a series of tasks performed to complete the project, and the outcome of that project. Essentially, it's a story.

Treat your case studies as if you were writing a short story about your project. Define the protagonist—you, the designer. Define the antagonist—the problem you needed to solve. Provide all the great elements of storytelling within your journey—where you traveled, who you met along the way, and how the actions you took led to a happy ending.

One of the most common storytelling frameworks is called the *hero's journey*[2] (**FIGURE 8.4**). It's a framework where the protagonist, the hero, goes on a journey. Along that journey are moments of challenge, friends that help along the way, and transformation amidst deep despair. Eventually, the hero prevails, and returns home to journey again.

FIGURE 8.4 The hero's journey—one of the most common and compelling forms of narrative in modern media.

Return
(Gift of the Goddess)
Call to Adventure
Supernatural aid
Threshold Guardian(s)
KNOWN
UNKNOWN
Threshold (beginning of transformation)
The Hero's Journey
Atonement
Mentor
Helper
Challenges and Temptations
Transformation
REVELATION
Abyss
death & rebirth
Helper

---

2 https://en.wikipedia.org/wiki/Hero%27s_journey

You can apply this framework to any design-related case study.

If you take the design thinking model from the Nielsen Norman Group and combine it with the hero's journey, you have the perfect model for writing a case study (FIGURE 8.5). You start with a call to action—the project goal, or the problem to solve. You empathize with users and define the problem. You absorb so much information and agonize over what to do for your users—so you ideate. You emerge, reborn and renewed, understanding finally what it is that might help your users, so you transform your solution as you prototype and test. When it's time to return home—to finish the project—you implement your solution successfully and save the day.

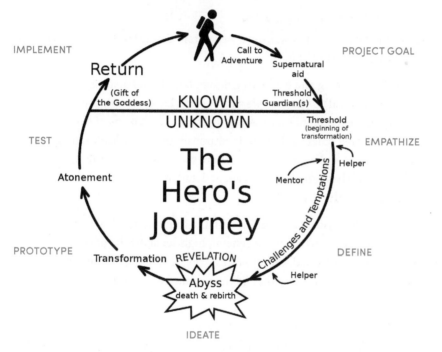

FIGURE 8.5 The NN/g design thinking process superimposed on the hero's journey.

Presenting your work is a journey—one that you went on, and one that you should bring your audience along on as well. Consider the following questions as you try to write your case study's story:

- **Call to Adventure**—What was the problem you were initially asked to solve?

- **Threshold Guardians**—What did the business want?

- **Helper, Mentor**—Who were your users?

- **Challenges, Temptations**—What did your users want?

- **Abyss**—What did you consider creating to help them?

- **Transformation**—What did the solution look like?

- **Atonement**—How did your solution work when usability tested?

- **Return**—Which solution worked, and what did you deliver?

AUTHOR'S NOTE It may take some time for you to adjust to thinking about your work in this way. That's OK! You've probably encountered this format before without even knowing it—many movies follow this narrative format, including *Star Wars*, *The Wizard of Oz*, *The Lord of the Rings*, *The Matrix*, and plenty of movies from the Marvel cinematic universe.

When you look at the events of a case study through this lens, you can see how storytelling can naturally fit into the presentation of your work.

Design for Non-Readers

The unfortunate truth of writing a well detailed case study is that, sadly, people probably won't read it.

The reality of hiring and evaluating design talent (and just reading long-form content in general) is that people simply don't have enough time to read everything presented to them. A recruiter looks at dozens of candidates a day. A manager must balance their daily responsibilities in addition to figuring out who to hire and when. Colleagues are so focused on doing the work that they also don't have the time to read, in detail, every word a designer writes in their case study.

People approach your case studies with the intent not to learn every detail of what you did but to learn the general, high-level results of your work. The intent comes from different places—the people that you work with, the people you want to work with, and the people that want to follow your work in the industry.

For those who work alongside you, they will want to know the implications of your work. What does this study lead to for the business? What are the outcomes of this project on their specific work areas? What can they learn from this work that can be applied to their own work?

For those who are looking to hire you based on your work, they are looking to see whether you are able to solve the problems of their organization. Are you able to do design? Are you able to do it in the way they want you to do it? Are you able to do it for the specific problem they are trying to solve?

For those who follow along with your work, they want to see your successes. How are you doing? What are you working on now? What is the result of that work?

These are the questions a reader of your case studies will have, and this is what they will look for in your case studies. As a designer of user experiences, it's up to you to design an experience in a way that's best consumed by the audience you are designing for. In this case, you must learn to communicate clearly with the readers of your case study.

To communicate an effective case study, you're supposed to write a detailed, compelling story for those who want to read every detail (and some people will). But if people don't want to read your story, then how are you supposed to communicate that story to your readers? Well, as with any other design problem, you must understand your users' needs. You must think about how they want to use your product, and design for their behavior and goals.

People don't read word for word on the internet. They scan, skim, and way-find through content online, looking for information they want to engage with, then spending time with that information until they're satisfied.

Our information superhighway functions just like a real-world highway—and so should your case studies (**FIGURE 8.6**).

FIGURE 8.6 A good case study should read like a highway—the reader should be able to travel through it quickly, but also have plenty of stops along the way to take in the view should they choose to. (Doug Meek/Shutterstock)

People consume content, especially long-form written content, like they would drive on a highway. They scroll at breakneck speeds, passing through each section on a page like exits on a highway. If they see an interesting stopping point, they'll take that exit, spend some time there, then keep scrolling to the end of the road.

You should design your case studies like a highway. You should use clearly labeled exit signs with interesting, easy-to-understand rest stops that explain what a reader will find if they happen to stick around for a few minutes.

FIGURE 8.7 is a section from my case study about an education platform. I've structured it such that the reader never needs to actually read in order to understand what's happening in the project.

First, I use engaging headlines that describe the step in the process. I title this section "Viewing Grades (Anyway You Want It)" for several reasons:

- It explains the step in the process for the user (they can view grades in multiple ways with this feature).

- It tells a story—viewing grades any way the user wants is more engaging than saying something like "grade customization."

- It references a popular rock song, demonstrating my personality and adding levity to the process of reading my case study.

After the headline, I show three subsections that further explain the point in the story. Each subsection is a single headline with descriptive text and a supporting image explaining that section.

The reader could scroll past all of this if they don't care to read it. As they scan the page for the next "exit sign" on the case study highway, however, they will read each headline and be drawn to each image. As a result, they'll know what this entire section is about, without having to read any of the additional content. Should they choose to stay a while and learn more, they have that additional context—from both the supporting body copy and the details of each image.

To help people to understand your case study without reading it, use headlines and engaging images that tell the story at a high level.

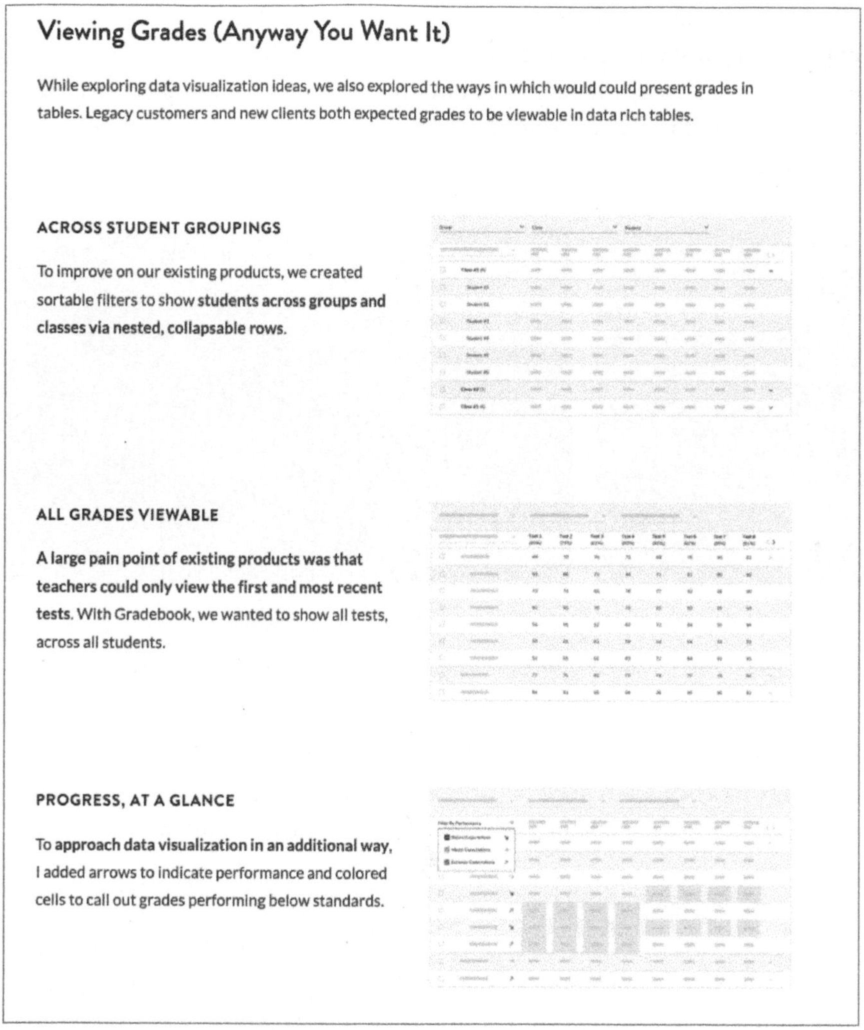

Viewing Grades (Anyway You Want It)

While exploring data visualization ideas, we also explored the ways in which would could present grades in tables. Legacy customers and new clients both expected grades to be viewable in data rich tables.

ACROSS STUDENT GROUPINGS

To improve on our existing products, we created sortable filters to show **students across groups and classes via nested, collapsable rows.**

ALL GRADES VIEWABLE

A large pain point of existing products was that teachers could only view the first and most recent tests. With Gradebook, we wanted to show all tests, across all students.

PROGRESS, AT A GLANCE

To **approach data visualization in an additional way,** I added arrows to indicate performance and colored cells to call out grades performing below standards.

FIGURE 8.7 A portion of a case study discussing the different ways a design solution could visualize student grades.

Communicate Through Images

Since people don't read, or don't read a lot (unless they're interested in the content), your headlines and your images will be telling most of the story. To design a compelling case study, you need compelling images to support it.

This doesn't mean you need the most progressive, aesthetically pleasing images possible for your case study. Rather, your images need to be clear, easy to follow, and enough of the story for a reader to fully understand what's happening at that moment without having read anything before or after that point.

FIGURE 8.8 is a moment in one of my case studies[3] that clearly shows the impact of my work. By creating a before and after of the UI, I can show exactly what I added, where it went into the product, and how it integrated with the rest of the user experience.

BEFORE LAYOUTS

AFTER LAYOUTS

THIS IS NEW!

FIGURE 8.8 A case study image that communicates a new feature by relying on product screenshots over text.

This is a perfect example of how to use images to structure your story moments. Provide context, show progress in an individual moment in the process, and use clear labeling to explain where you are in the story.

Demonstrate Expertise with Case Studies

Writing a case study is very difficult. Although it may sound easy to explain a project to someone, it is some of the hardest work you can do when preparing a way to share your work. Figuring out the story you want to tell, in addition to telling that story in a clear, concise, and engaging way, requires a skill set that takes time and effort to develop.

A well-written case study is worth the effort. A view into your process, how you design, and examples of designing successful products are the most convincing ways for you to get a job. I've used my case studies time and again to receive job offers at top tech organizations, Fortune 500 companies, and start-ups looking for a founding designer to take their product to the next

---

3 https://medium.com/vimeo-engineering-blog/enhancing-vimeo-events-with-layouts-7b9611c7b296

level. In the job interview process, nothing beats well-written, easy-to-follow case studies.

CREATING YOUR PORTFOLIO

As a designer in the industry, you'll be expected to demonstrate your ability to design. Unfortunately, people won't take a promise at face value—they need to see your work to have a good understanding of your ability to do the job they want you to perform.

As a result, the industry has evolved to require a designer to *have done* work to show that they *can do* work. What this requirement means varies from organization to organization. Some places want a designer to have a fully fleshed-out case study that illustrates their end-to-end design process. Others are comfortable with designers opening a working file and walking through a problem. No matter the way you show off your ability to design, the fact remains that you still need to, in some way, show off your ability to do the work.

Most often, a company will require a designer to share their work in advance prior to scheduling an interview with that designer. That's why it's helpful to have a well-written case study that speaks for itself and shows your expertise. You will need to demonstrate your work across multiple projects, so it's ideal to have multiple case studies, but if you don't, then having a main one that you can point to first is the next best option.

The collection of your case studies and other works is most commonly referred to as a *portfolio*. You can create and distribute a portfolio in many ways, and it's up to you to determine what works best for you. Each way has its advantages and disadvantages.

Highly Visual, Emphasis on the Work

For designers who want to do stunning visual design, there are platforms where companies specifically look for the best visual design examples and resources to be inspired and hire from. These platforms are excellent at highlighting truly amazing visual work.

FIGURE 8.9 is an example from Dribbble, the leading platform for visual design examples.[4] You can see UI design that looks modern, clean, and

---

4 https://dribbble.com/shots/17292758-Music-Learning-App

stunning. This particular example showcases a few visual designs, with short descriptions of them. When it comes to visual designer roles, Dribbble is a great place to post your work.

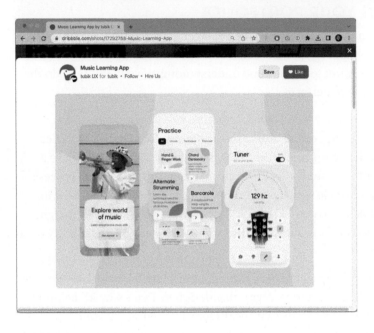

FIGURE 8.9 A product screenshot from Dribbble, a leading portfolio website.

Pros:
- Quick and easy
- Emphasis on visual design
- Puts your work in a place people look for it

Cons:
- Visual only
- Hard to show end-to-end process
- Less professional-looking—not a custom web presence, for example

Common platforms: Dribbble, Behance

If you're targeting more generalist roles, like UX designer or product designer, then these platforms aren't the best for hosting your portfolio. This is because many companies want to see more than just visual design for these roles—they want to see the end-to-end process, not just a few screenshots. These platforms don't easily accommodate long-form content, like an entire case study that includes research, iteration, and working with developers. There are better alternatives for showing that type of work.

A Bare-Bones, Personal Digital Presence

If you want to showcase your end-to-end process, you can think of the term *MVPort* (minimum viable portfolio), not to be confused with MVP for minimum viable product or with MVPr for minimum viable prototype—we live in a world of acronyms! Perhaps you don't have the time for or interest in making a custom website, or you don't want to develop the expertise to work in a website editor, or you don't know how to code. That's OK—these things aren't expected in a designer, especially one just starting out. The real emphasis should be on the quality of the work—not how the work is presented online.

To get up and started, especially as a junior designer, there's nothing wrong with using a bare-bones website editor. Within a few clicks, you can upload content online, lay it out on a page, and have a fully functional website.

FIGURE 8.10 is a screenshot from the landing page for UX Folio, a platform that allows designers to quickly and easily build a portfolio online. These platforms for online portfolios provide templates, mockups, and the ability to embed prototypes, among other features that help designers easily put something online.

FIGURE 8.10 UX Folio, a bare-bones editor that allows designers to create their own portfolio with ease. (UXfolio LLC)

Bare-bones editors are valuable for speed and ease of use. They come at a cost, however—customization. Without the ability to fine-tune certain elements of the portfolio, designers can feel frustrated and limited with how they are able to build their website. Furthermore, without the ability to adjust how information is laid out, you lose an edge in differentiating yourself from others if you rely on a templated experience.

Pros:
- Fast
- Easy
- Custom domain name/presence

Cons:
- Flexibility
- Professionalism (compared to other options)
- Uniqueness—relying on templates means you look the same as everyone else

Common platforms: Adobe Portfolio, UX Folio

A Customized, Curated Experience

For designers who want a more customized, curated experience but still don't want to code, website editors allow you to take a more flexible approach to building a website. A designer can start with a template, or start fresh, laying things out on a page anywhere they want without knowing how to code.

These website editors allow designers a great deal of customization, and the ability to make truly stunning websites. The customization available on these platforms allows designers to edit layout, typography, animation, and other design elements to truly elevate the portfolio experience.

Squarespace (**FIGURE 8.11**) is a leader in website editor services.[5] They have dozens of templates for users to get started and offer the ability to adjust many elements of their websites. Squarespace provides custom animations for interactive elements, offers plenty of typefaces to adjust the typography of their websites, and automatically adjusts the size of the website across different viewports. Additionally, it has a community dedicated to enhancing Squarespace features with custom code blocks.

---

5 https://tepito-fluid-demo.squarespace.com/

FIGURE 8.11
An example portfolio built using Squarespace, a common website editor. (© Squarespace 2023. https://www.squarespace.com/website-design)

Despite all this flexibility, website editors can be inflexible in some ways. You can change a lot, but not everything. There can be limited options for typography, for example, forcing users into a small number of available styles.

Additionally, users must learn how to use the service—the learning curve isn't steep, but it's still present, and it takes some time to figure out all the nuances. There are professionals who specifically build Squarespace websites for a living, which should be an indicator of the complexity of the platform.

Still, website editors are perfect if you want something custom but don't want to go all out and build your own website.

Pros:
- Easy to begin
- Tons of customization
- Compelling templates and micro-animations

Cons:
- Hard to master
- Learning curve
- Sometimes visually limiting—without ability to style content how you want or place it where you want

Common platforms: Wix, Squarespace

Going All Out

If you want to go all out for your portfolio and make the most compelling experience possible, you won't be able to get that from a website editor. Award-winning portfolios are custom made, allowing the designer to freely express themselves as they see fit.

There's no way around making an experience like this—you need to know code, to some extent. You don't need to know a lot of it, and you can leverage pre-existing code or other templates provided by services that offer full control, but it's hard. There's a lot of work that goes into making a custom site, just as much as doing the case study work itself, if not more so.

The benefit of making this investment is that you will have a best-in-class portfolio—and that in itself is just as powerful as the case studies in that portfolio. By making a portfolio that looks and functions like its own best-in-class product, you'll demonstrate your ability to design by having people see it directly in action, via your portfolio.

Webflow (FIGURE 8.12) is a leader in this space.[6] Webflow enables people to create custom animations, layouts, and anything else as if you were a developer. The best, most progressive and impressive portfolios come from Webflow, WordPress, Semplice, and other editors that require users to work directly with code.

FIGURE 8.12 An example portfolio built using Webflow.

Making these experiences comes at a steep price—the learning curve is the highest among tools like these. People try to use these platforms, hit a wall, and abandon them due to their difficulty. It's easier to spin up a Squarespace website than a custom Webflow one. But the results speak for themselves. The

6 www.blaiseposmyouck.com

decision is how much flexibility you think you need relative to the investment you want to make.

Unlike website editors that force you into a semi-on-rails experience, custom editors allow you complete flexibility—including the freedom to create a broken or unusable experience. If you go down this route, be prepared to think of all the ways the experience can fall apart when a user interacts with it.

Pros:
- Ultimate control and flexibility
- Stunning visual design and motion possible
- Community templates to make it easier

Cons:
- Ultimate ability to make a mistake
- Huge learning curve
- Some knowledge of code required

Common platforms: WordPress, Semplice, Webflow

But I Don't Want to Make a Website

Another, less intuitive option for having a public-facing website that shows your work is to not have one at all! You don't need a website to be your portfolio. You can create a presentation deck or PDF that has all your work without hosting it online on another service. You can even "post" it online if you want, saving the presentation to Google Drive or Dropbox and posting a link in your social media profiles that directs people to it. In fact, most people will find your portfolio through social media or through a link you directly send to a company. Does it matter where it "lives" online?

I've seen designers create case studies in Keynote, Microsoft PowerPoint, Google Slides, or even Figma and save them as PDFs that they send directly to companies. You have complete creative control over the visual design using this method—there's no limit to the way you lay out and display your work. However, there are two restrictions worth mentioning in this method.

- You can't include motion—because it's a static document, you won't have the ability to show elements moving in and out of the page. You may be able to include GIFs or video, but you will need to use them sparingly, lest the document becomes larger and larger in file size and unusable.

- The reader must scroll through the deck top to bottom—they don't have the flexibility to move around a website to click the things that interest them. The way you lay out the deck will be the way every user experiences it. This can be a benefit or a detriment. On the one hand, users can't go to the case study they want to read first. On the other hand, because they must move through each page one at a time, chronologically, you completely control the narrative.

FIGURE 8.13 is an example from a portfolio PDF I created during the job-seeking process. I had complete control to present my work the way I saw fit. I was able to use any size for images, use whatever fonts I felt like, and adjust the content into whatever layout I needed to.

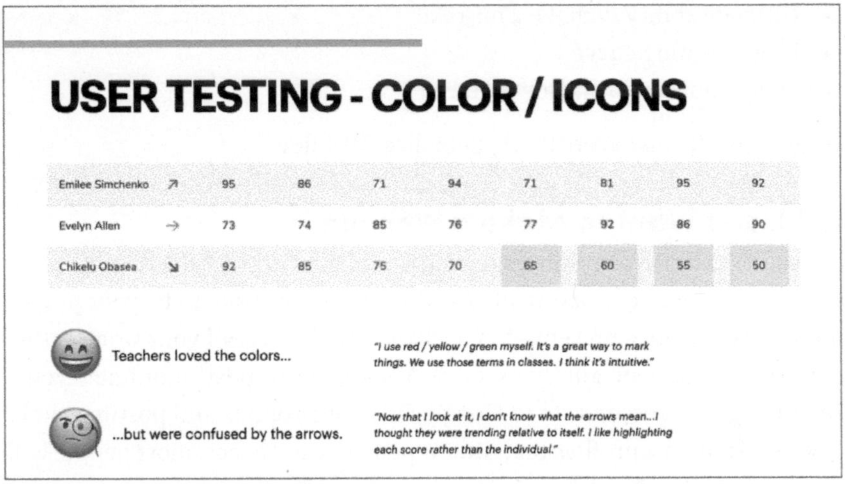

FIGURE 8.13 A portion of a case study depicted in a presentation rather than on a website.

USER TESTING - COLOR / ICONS

Emilee Simchenko	↗	95	86	71	94	71	81	95	92
Evelyn Allen	→	73	74	85	76	77	92	86	90
Chikelu Obasea	↘	92	85	75	70	65	60	55	50

Teachers loved the colors...

"I use red / yellow / green myself. It's a great way to mark things. We use those terms in classes. I think it's intuitive."

...but were confused by the arrows.

"Now that I look at it, I don't know what the arrows mean...I thought they were trending relative to itself. I like highlighting each score rather than the individual."

The biggest issue with portfolio PDFs is that they may be perceived as junior or immature. The industry expects designers to have a digital presence online. After all, wouldn't a digital product designer have a digital website to showcase their digital work? Not having a website feels weird in the context of the profession and compared to peers.

Still, portfolio PDFs can be very successful for candidates who don't want to post their work online or don't feel confident in creating a website. I've seen colleagues use portfolio PDFs to great success. Some people don't want to have a digital presence, or don't like sharing their work for anyone to see, and that's OK. If you don't want a website, you don't need one—if you can tell your story in a compelling way and get your quality across, you can use whatever format you like.

Pros:

- Full customization
- Full control over the user experience
- Easy to create (no code or editors required)

Cons:

- Limited interaction design (motion, hover states, video)
- Can look unprofessional relative to peers and other options
- Harder to have a digital presence

Common platforms: Keynote, Google Slides, Figma

Where Should I Put My Portfolio?

So, with all these options you have, what's the best one? What's the optimal way to showcase your work?

The truth is, there isn't a "best" way to show your work. It all depends on your goals and resources. If you don't have time or money, make a PDF. If you're trying to get into a top tech company, go all out and code your own site. A one-size-fits-all answer does not exist for how to show your work online.

What you do need to do, however, is show your work. You can't post a few pictures online and expect to get hired for an end-to-end design role. Companies need to see more than just your designs—they need to see your process.

The platform you choose to show your process doesn't matter—not as much as the content. A great case study in a PDF will always beat a great website with no context for the design process. Hiring managers need to see how a candidate will use their design skills to solve the problems they are hiring them to solve. If you don't demonstrate your work through a good case study, it doesn't matter how stunning your portfolio is.

GIVING FEEDBACK

Once you find yourself in a position where you are working with other designers, you will have to learn how to communicate with the rest of your team in the context of discussing design decisions. Designers will share their work with you, hoping that their ideas align with the rest of the team and help support the organization's vision of improving users' lives with their products. As a member of that team reviewing their work, it's up to you to provide your honest and fair feedback.

AUTHOR'S NOTE Creating a prototype as a portfolio website is becoming an increasingly popular trend as designers seek speed and customization to share their materials. Although this is something you can do, I advise against it, as it comes across as a less professional website experience. After all, if you're going to create a prototype of a website experience, why wouldn't you just create a website instead? Plenty of tools are available online that allow for this, and as a digital designer, you should be aware of them.

This is easier said than done. Design is a challenging field to participate in. Things can be subjective, there's not always a one-size-fits-all solution, and there are constant exceptions to the rules. Furthermore, the way in which designers invest themselves in their work and create new experiences is quite an emotional process. As a result, it can be hard for them to take feedback, especially when that feedback comes across as critical or judgmental.

Despite these challenges, there are ways you can navigate the feedback process so that you communicate clearly and kindly with other designers in a way that gets what you all want—what's best for your users.

How Do You Provide Feedback to a Designer?

Imagine you are working on a project with another designer, and they show you the latest iteration of their work (FIGURE 8.14).

FIGURE 8.14 A proposed design solution for a car rental service. How would you critique this design?

Lamborghini Aventador
Yellow

$329/day

Rent

Revolutionary thinking is at the heart of every idea from Automobili Lamborghini. Whether it is aerospace-inspired design or technologies applied to the naturally aspirated V12 engine or carbon-fiber structure, going beyond accepted limits is part of our philosophy. The Aventador advances every concept of performance, immediately establishing itself as the benchmark for the super sports car sector. Giving a glimpse of the future today, it comes from a family of supercars already considered legendary.

How would you respond? What would be an appropriate way to critique this work?

It's possible you may want to respond with any of the following critiques:

- *Those colors make no sense.*

- *The text is a mess!*

- *There's no balance, my eye is going everywhere.*

- *What were you THINKING!??!*

This initial assessment is accurate—the color, typography, and layout of this design are confusing. It doesn't follow good visual design principles, and overall, the design feels imbalanced. However, if this is exactly what you say, then it won't be received well by the designer, and they won't be able to adjust their work based on your critique.

This example critique is missing actionable feedback. It's missing the context of the designer who made these design choices. Most importantly, it's missing the empathy of a critique balanced by the right amounts of evaluation, tone, and attitude.

Giving critiques on a design is difficult for anyone to do. It takes knowing good visual design in addition to knowing good communication techniques that allow everyone involved to work together, hear the feedback, and act on it.

Let's talk a bit about how to critique designs.

What Is a Critique?

A *critique* is a detailed analysis and assessment of a piece of work—whether it be a theory, media, or a piece of design. To critique something is to evaluate it in a detailed and analytical way.

Critiques can be positive, negative, or neutral.

Imagine the forms of feedback about this sweater (**FIGURE 8.15**).

- *I love that sweater!*

- *I hate that sweater!*

- *That's a normal sweater.*

FIGURE 8.15 A purple sweater with a snowflake pattern. (Pakhnyushchy/Shutterstock)

Each of those statements may look like a critique. The statements analyze an object and include an assessment of it—in this case, a sweater. However, none of those statements are helpful. They're more like opinions—they don't explain the reason behind their analysis, nor do they explain any sort of actionable or helpful feedback that can elevate the object to improve it even further.

- *I love that sweater! Purple makes it feel royal, and the pattern reminds me of winter. I could imagine wearing this during the holiday season, next to a warm fire.*

- *I hate that sweater! It has too many patterns on it, which cause my eye to dart all over the place. I think there should be fewer.*

- *That's a normal sweater. It has sleeves, it's made of wool, and it's large enough to fit over clothes. It looks warm and comfortable—just like a sweater should be.*

When you add context to those opinions—the reasons behind the statements—you can take opinions and convert them into critiques. This helps provide direction to what would otherwise be a statement. Now, the designer understands the why behind the statement that was made.

Still, these latest critiques lack several characteristics of what makes a critique really good. Let's dive into a few tenets you can use to give and receive good critiques.

Giving a good critique requires inquisition, explanation, and specificity. You may have opinions, and feel those opinions strongly, but opinions alone don't justify (or motivate) others to act on those opinions. To provide great critique, you need to make sure you give feedback in a fair, balanced, and communicative way.

Ask Clarifying Questions

When critiquing someone's work, it's good practice to try to understand their perspective. Often, a designer makes a choice not out of randomness or mood, but rather a deliberate decision based on a factor they've already considered. When critiquing work, it helps to get that context from them.

Let's take another look at the design shown in Figure 8.14:

Imagine that your critique started with this:

> You: *I noticed you used red text for the price—what was your reasoning behind that decision?*
>
> Designer: *Well, red is a bold color, and I wanted to emphasize the price, because it's some of the most important information on the page.*

Now you have context for why that design decision was made. With that context, you can shift the feedback in a way that helps solve the design problem, rather than critique the choice the designer made.

AUTHOR'S NOTE As with asking a user "why" after they make a statement without context, be sure to ask a designer "why" when critiquing a design so that you know the reason behind the design.

Provide Context, Not Just Opinion

Once you have the designer's context, you should return the favor and provide your own. With mutual understanding, the conversation becomes less about the specific design choices and more about the outcomes around the purpose of the design in the first place.

Imagine you replied to the designer with the following:

> You: *Got it. I understand you want to draw emphasis to that part of your design, but red is often used in UI as a warning or error. I'm concerned that a user may think something is wrong when seeing it in red.*

If you look closely, a few things are accomplished in that feedback:

- Acknowledged their perspective (*I understand that...*)

- Explained your perspective (*red is often...*)

- Provided your opinion (*I'm concerned that...*)

That's a great way to structure feedback. Now, the designer has context—they are aware of the design principle that's being affected by this design choice, how it affects the user, and a way to think about fixing it.

Offer Exploratory Questions

Ask questions in your feedback. Asking questions in your feedback prevents you from being prescriptive and solving the problem for the designer.

Imagine you followed up your feedback about the price's color with the following:

> You: *Is there another way you can add emphasis to that part of the page, without using color?*

You can emphasize the part of that page without color—you could use whitespace, alignment, size, font weight, a different typeface, or any other visual design principle to make that part of the page stand out. But you know what? It's not your design—it's theirs. You should point out the problem, ask them to think critically about it, then see what they come up with.

Here are a few reasons why this is a great approach to giving feedback:

- It gives the designer agency around the solution—they get to think of it!
- It asks the person with the most information around the problem to think of a solution—they know the context best.
- It focuses on the problem—by exposing the problem, you can think of solutions that are problem-centric.

If you give a person a fish, they'll eat for a day. If you teach a person to fish, they'll eat for life.

Talk About the Good

In critique, it's common to focus on only the things wrong with a design. You're providing feedback on something and trying to fix the problems with it—why would you talk about the things that work?

Well, it's really important to celebrate the wins in a design. Mentioning what works in a design not only improves the morale of the person who designed it, but also gives them an understanding of what does work. With that understanding, they can apply the learnings from the elements that do work to the elements that don't.

Let's look at the design again and find some positive things to double down on for an iteration:

> You: *The choice of imagery is strong. When I see that car, I really want to rent it. I think using imagery in this way will incentivize users to want to rent it too.*

> You: *The typeface works really well with the brand. Poppins has a wide, rounded feel, like a car, so that really helps push the concept forward.*

Putting It All Together

At a high level, here is how this critique played out:

- A positive element (and why)

- A clarifying question

- A negative element (and why)

- A question to spur creativity

- Another positive element (and why)

When you put it all together, here's what you get:

1. Start with a positive statement to kick off the critique and establish a safe, friendly space.

   You: *The choice of imagery is strong. When I see that car, I really want to rent it. I think using imagery in this way will incentivize users to want to rent it too.*

2. Ask a clarifying question about part of the design that doesn't make sense to you.

   You: *I noticed you used red text for the price—what was your reasoning behind that decision?*

   Designer: *Well, red is a bold color, and I wanted to emphasize the price, because it's some of the most important information on the page.*

3. Digest the designer's response and follow up with your perspective, while providing context and being clear about the problem.

   You: *Got it. I understand you want to draw emphasis to that part of your design, but red is often used in UI as a warning or error. I'm concerned that a user may think something is wrong when seeing it in red.*

4. Ask the designer to think of an alternative, without providing one.

   You: *Is there another way you can add emphasis to that part of the page, without using color?*

You end with another positive aspect of the design, explaining why it works.

You: *I do think that the typeface works really well with the brand. Poppins has a wide, rounded feel, like a car, so that really helps push the concept forward.*

And that's the process!

Admittedly, this design has a lot more to critique. However, with the tenets established for giving critique, you'll be off to a great start to have the rest of that conversation with the designer.

RECEIVING FEEDBACK

Receiving critique can be even harder than giving one. When others evaluate your designs, it can feel like they are evaluating you. Negative comments about your decisions can hurt deeply, despite those comments not being directly about you. Furthermore, the feedback you receive might not be the type you are looking for. To receive critique well, it requires setting expectations, providing context, and trying not to take things personally.

How Do You Receive Feedback as a Designer?

To ensure you establish the best environment for a design critique, you can use the following roadmap to conduct your critique:

- Establish the context.
- Request specific feedback.
- Clarify that feedback.
- Summarize all provided feedback.

This roadmap creates a common understanding about the design, focuses the feedback on what you're specifically looking for feedback on, makes sure you understand the feedback you're given, and aligns the team on the expectations that come out of that feedback.

Describe the Situation

To start the critique, it's important to provide the context of your designs. When looking at the work, people won't have a clear understanding of the user's journey or the point in the product they are going to be looking at. Even if they do have that context, by describing the situation, you are setting the stage for the specific instance where the user will see these designs.

Imagine a designer shows you the design in FIGURE 8.16, without context:

Lamborghini Aventador
Yellow

$329/day

Rent

Revolutionary thinking is at the heart of every idea from Automobili Lamborghini. Whether it is
aerospace-inspired design or technologies applied to the naturally aspirated V12 engine or
carbon-fiber structure, going beyond accepted limits is part of our philosophy. The Aventador
advances every concept of performance, immediately establishing itself as the benchmark for
the super sports car sector. Giving a glimpse of the future today, it comes from a family of
supercars already considered legendary.

FIGURE 8.16 A design to be presented by a designer. You may not agree with the decisions, but you should wait to hear what the designer has to say before providing your feedback.

Do you know what you're looking at? Is it clear where you are in the user's journey? Do you have any context about this product?

Instead, what if the designer told you the following, then showed the design?

> Designer: *Hello! Today, I'm going to show some new designs for the product detail page of our car rental website. At this point in the user's journey, they will have found a car they want to rent and are looking over the specific details of that car before committing to renting it.*

When you provide the context before showing the design, you let the audience know where they are in the user's journey, and this sets the tone for what they're about to look at.

Set Expectations

After your audience has a good understanding of the situation, it's important to set the expectations for the type of feedback you are looking for. Start by describing what, specifically, you want feedback on. This will focus the attention of the people critiquing your work and prevent them from providing feedback on elements that are in flux or that you don't need feedback about.

> Designer: *We are going to see early-stage work around the choice of typography and layout for this page. Specifically, we're looking at the decisions around the typeface, the color choices of the text, and the general way the information on the page is positioned.*

When you ask for specific feedback, you can ask the audience for help around the areas you are focused on. This allows you to get feedback on the problems you are trying to solve, rather than feedback on elements of the design you can't control or haven't focused on yet.

Imagine you presented your design and didn't ask for this feedback. It's possible you could get feedback on the image, the content, or the interactivity. At this stage in the design process, you've explicitly said what you are working on and looking for feedback about. By setting this expectation, you avoid conversations around elements you aren't working on or, in some cases, can't control—like the content of the images, the text describing the car, or the actions the user can take on the page.

Ask Clarifying Questions

When receiving feedback about your designs, make sure you understand where the feedback is coming from. If you don't, you won't know how to fix it, and you may end up making the same mistakes.

In the car rental example, imagine you receive the following feedback:

> Critiquer: *I don't like the font—it doesn't make sense for this product.*

Do you know how to act on that feedback? It's clear you need to change the typeface, but to what? Let's see if you can find out.

> You, the designer: *Could you elaborate on why the font doesn't make sense for the product?*

> Critiquer: *Well, we're a brand about elegance—that font looks more playful than elegant.*

Now you have some context—the person critiquing the designs thinks you need a more elegant typeface. When you go back to design, you can think about finding a typeface that appears more elegant (bonus points for asking the critiquer what they think "elegant" looks like).

Summarize

At the end of a critique, it's important to summarize all the feedback. Summarizing all the feedback you're given during a critique has many benefits.

First, it allows you to make sure you're capturing all the feedback. It's easy to let important comments slip through the cracks; by summarizing the feedback, you make sure you've captured all the opinions.

Additionally, summarizing the feedback gives people the opportunity to follow up with clarifying comments. As you list each piece of feedback, the audience gains the opportunity to clarify the feedback further or add to it. This will give you more direction when you begin to act on the feedback after the critique.

Finally, summarizing all the feedback gets everyone on the same page and aligns the team. When you list every piece of feedback, you confirm the results of the meeting and create a list of action items to work on. This establishes expectations for what will be revised in the designs.

Don't Take It Personally—It Doesn't Have to Be Scary

When you receive feedback about your designs, try not to take it personally. It's important to release the emotional attachment you have to your work. After all, you aren't designing for you; you are designing for your users. You should do the best you can to do right by them.

Additionally, when people are critiquing your designs, they aren't critiquing you. They too are advocating on behalf of the people who will interact with and experience your designs and are trying to do right by them.

Critique isn't a battle. You don't have to defend yourself or argue about your design choices—the people critiquing your designs are offering their perspectives. Hear what they have to say, try not to take it personally, and thank them for their advice.

You are not your designs.

As someone receiving feedback, it can really hurt. We come up with what we think is an amazing design, just for every single element to be pulled apart, scrutinized, and analyzed. Receiving feedback requires setting expectations, following up for clarification, and a tough skin.

By following these principles, you'll be able to take something potentially scary and painful and make it a productive, meaningful conversation that helps both sides do what's best for your users.

WORKING WITH OTHER DISCIPLINES

Building products is a team sport. You can design individually, providing flows, creating UI components, and laying out beautiful, well-thought-out user experiences. But without people to build those experiences, craft their

AUTHOR'S NOTE You don't always have to act on the feedback you receive. The people providing this feedback are sharing their perspectives, not their orders. Even with my managers and directors, I've listened to their feedback and not incorporated it into the product. At times, I've been able to convince them of my perspective by going back to my desk and creating examples of what I believed was right, which contradicted the feedback they provided me. People are trying to help when offering their feedback, which goes a lot further than the alternative—silence.

futures, or provide you the support and funding to actually make them, you can't go further than wireframes. You can't take your ideas and make them into a reality for your users.

You need partners along the journey to help you make amazing experiences for other people.

The partners you work with should really be viewed as such—as partners. You should adopt a mindset where you work alongside and with other people, instead of working for them or them working for you. You need to develop strategies to communicate effectively with your partners so that you can all accomplish your goal: making the best thing possible.

Working with Engineering

When working with engineering, use the following tenets to guide your interactions with developers:

- Constant communication.

- Speak their language.

- Deliver everything.

Following these guidelines, you'll be able to develop a healthy, strong, and deep relationship with your engineers.

Constant Communication

When working with engineers, it's important to establish a good, consistent working relationship. Too often, designers and developers view the communication between each other as *handoff*—designer makes some designs, "hands them off" to developers, and they go and build it.

Handing off a design to a developer (**FIGURE 8.17**) without any prior communication isn't the best way for us to build products.

FIGURE 8.17 A relay race where one runner hands a baton to the next runner. This is not product development. (William Perugini/ Shutterstock)

Engineering should be involved in all aspects of the product creation process. They should be able to weigh in at the start of a project to help influence design direction based on informing the team what's possible or more feasible than other potential solutions. They should be involved during the project so that as design thinks of solutions, they share them with developers to get feedback. Too often, they are involved only at the end of the process, when you finalize your solution and begin to build it.

I've been on teams where developers are involved early. At Nickelodeon, whenever we created a new episode of interactive content, we had a kickoff with product, engineering, design, and animation, all working together to map out the interactive moments in our product. Design presented several options for what we wanted to create, and every other discipline weighed in on what was possible, what options were more feasible than others, and what they would investigate post kickoff to determine its complexity. Having all these perspectives in the room at the start of the project heavily influenced the end user experience in a positive way.

Developers should be involved in all stages of the process, early, frequently, and consistently.

Speak Their Language

There's an age-old question in product design that keeps circulating throughout the industry—do designers need to know how to code (**FIGURE 8.18**)?

FIGURE 8.18 Lines of code powering a product experience. (BEST-BACKGROUNDS/ Shutterstock)

I believe the answer to this question is confusing, which is why it keeps recurring in the industry. It can be helpful to know how to code, for sure. A basic knowledge of CSS, HTML, or any other coding language can help a designer understand what's possible, what's easier to implement, or even communicate with developers about the solution they build.

That's the real preliminary value to "knowing how to code." Developing "conversational" fluency so that you as a designer can "speak the same language" as an engineer is the ideal to strive for. You don't need to go into the code yourself to make something—that's what the engineer is for. However, to communicate effectively with that engineer, and to know what's possible, it's very valuable to be able to speak the same language by having a baseline understanding of code. Knowing how the product is built, mechanically, from a coding perspective, allows designers to design more effectively.

Deliver Everything

When you're pitching ideas to stakeholders, product managers, or even other designers, they mostly care about the higher-level items—things like the user's journey, or the *happy path* someone has through the product. The finer details, like error states, loading states, or other unhappy paths don't matter as much as the core, common overall user experience.

These other states matter a lot more to the people who must actually build them—developers.

When working with developers and delivering designs, be sure to include designs that cover all scenarios. This can be all the states of a page, like when it's partially loaded, has an error, or is fully loaded with content. It could also be things like all the states of a component—what happens when it's disabled, enabled, and interacted with.

Additionally, you should label and structure your deliverables in a way that helps a developer do their job. Being clear and comprehensive in your documentation will make it much easier for a developer to build the product.

Things that really help a developer do their jobs effectively can include style guides, component sheets, or other forms of documentation that explicitly define all the states of a design element or flow (FIGURE 8.19). For the people physically creating those states in the product, it helps to have things laid out in a way that helps them build it.

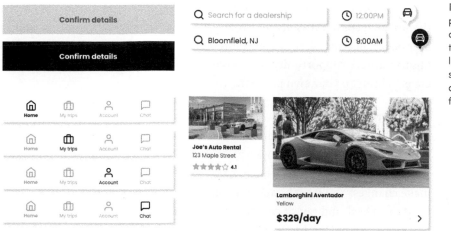

FIGURE 8.19 A set of components for a car rental app. The set includes multiple states to components, like active and inactive states for buttons, or empty and filled states for text fields.

Working with Product

When working with product managers, it's important to recognize that you two are a team. Almost joined at the hip, you both take actions that drastically affect one another as you advocate for the business and the user.

Use the following principles to navigate the relationship with your product managers:

- Think strategically.

- Track improvements.

- Be partners.

These principles lead to great teamwork, product excellence, and excellent collaboration across product and design.

Think Strategically

Product managers shape the product's future. They synthesize all the information they receive from the business, users, developers, and other sources to produce a plan for the product's roadmap. They have a heavy influence on how a product evolves over time.

As a designer, you should be involved in this evolution. The people designing the product should define how it's created and improved. Think about the ways you can have an impact on the planning process.

You can perform competitive research, looking at the marketplace to identify feature gaps or areas of opportunity for the product. You can investigate user needs, hearing directly from customers or looking at metrics. You can observe areas of opportunity within the organization, pulling from other areas to bring to your own product.

Track Improvements

As you work on a product over time, you will recognize elements that need to be fixed or revisited. You'll notice parts that weren't implemented in the way you envisioned. You'll hear feedback from users that will encourage you to make changes. You'll get better at design, and designing for this product, and want to go back and revisit decisions you made in the past or that were made before you started working on the product.

It's OK to want to update and revise the product—this is something you should actively seek out! The reality of the situation, though, is that you won't get to make all the changes you want to. The business will have to invest in specific initiatives and won't have the time to clean up or enhance all the things you want to, to make a better user experience.

So, what can you do? As designers, you can create a backlog (**FIGURE 8.20**) of potential product enhancements.

FIGURE 8.20 A UX backlog keeping track of all the elements of the user experience design wants to revisit and improve.

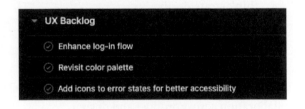

Much like engineering has a backlog for product improvements, you too can create a backlog for the user experience enhancements you want to add to the product. There's no guarantee you'll address any of these things, but when engineering bandwidth frees up, you can turn to the backlog and pull elements out of it for developers to work on in their down time. Having a list of items ready to go helps when teams are between projects.

Be Partners

You and your product manager are partners. A designer's primary stakeholder is the user. A product manager's primary stakeholder is the business.

Combined, a designer and a product manager represent the interests of the people who produce the product and the people who use the product. You're a dynamic duo (**FIGURE 8.21**) coming together to solve problems for the business and for users. You should work together to accomplish this!

FIGURE 8.21 A designer and a product manager are partners and work on behalf of the users they design for and the business they serve. (ASDF_MEDIA/ Shutterstock)

You can find plenty of moments to partner up. You can both conduct competitive research, debating which businesses have the largest impact on the industry and why they have the competitive advantages they do. You can interview users together, with one person walking through a prototype and the other taking notes. You can present to leadership together, with the product manager explaining the strategic value of a solution and the designer explaining its functionality.

Dozens of opportunities will present themselves to work together with your product manager to make amazing experiences.

Working with Leadership

Too often, designers believe that they work for the leaders of their company. This is not the correct perspective. Designers work for their users, to create great experiences for the people they design for. Designers do this with the permission, guidance, and approval of leaders in their company so that they may continue to design on behalf of their users.

Designers may work *for* leadership, but as a mindset, it's healthier and more productive to think that we work *with* leadership, to help them accomplish their goals.

At a high level, I strongly recommend following a consultant + lawyer mindset when working with leadership. Present designs for "the court" as lawyers would, relying on evidence and data to sway opinions. Then, show your designs as a consultant, explaining what option you think is best. Finally, invite them into the conversation, asking them what they think is best based on everything they heard.

To adopt this mindset, use the following guidelines:

- Be a consultant.

- Rely on facts.

- Ask for their opinion.

Be a Consultant

Leadership hires designers because they are subject matter experts. They have a specific skill set around analyzing, understanding, and designing the experience people have with their product. You are an expert in your field.

Leverage this expertise by adopting a consultant mindset. As a consultant, you would work with a client by understanding their needs, diverging around the problem to solve, and presenting a variety of options that could solve the problem (FIGURE 8.22). Do this for your product, and present that thinking to leadership, like a consultant would.

FIGURE 8.22 As a designer full of expertise, act like a consultant—understand your clients, determine what they need, and deliver it. (AboutLife/Shutterstock)

When presenting designs, show the best options you came up with, and explain why those options work. Each option will have its own advantages and disadvantages. Leadership will analyze those advantages and disadvantages to determine the path forward they feel is best for the business.

As a consultant, you should give them that opportunity. Combine that chance with your perspective, and you truly work with leadership to determine the best path forward.

Rely on Facts

People are moved by proof. Evidence is difficult to argue against. Well-structured arguments rely on data, analytics, or other indicators of truth. It isn't enough to say what path we should take without some sort of evidence to back it up.

Adopt a lawyer's mindset (**FIGURE 8.23**). A lawyer wouldn't go to court without proof—if they did, they would lose their case, and their client would suffer. The user is your client. Don't go to court without evidence to argue on their behalf.

FIGURE 8.23 As a designer presenting your case, adopt a lawyer mindset—gather your evidence and use it to deliver your arguments. (buritora/Shutterstock)

When presenting designs, show the proof you have for why you think they're best. Use click-through rates to indicate where people interact the most in your product. Mention feature requests to advocate for changes. Show competitive analysis to explain what alternatives already exist in the marketplace. Use data to illustrate why you made the decisions you did for each option you present. Then, ask for feedback.

Ask for Their Opinion

When presenting to leadership, keep in mind that they are the decision-makers. It's their vision, their product, their business. You don't get to choose the direction you move forward in—rather, you influence it, through options, evidence, and arguments.

Present your work through this lens. Offer all the information you've gathered—your research, your data, and your designs. Then, ask them what they think. After seeing the case you've made, what do they believe is the path forward? This moment of co-creation, where leadership sees all the options you've created for the business and the data behind them, allows them to make an informed decision based on the business's trajectory.

By providing the paths, the data behind them, and the opportunity to weigh in, you can work with leadership to craft the best user experience.

Working with Others

Building products is a team sport. You can't do everything yourself. You need to work with other departments to make products. You need developers to help you build a functional experience. You need product managers to prioritize and shape the experience's future. You need leadership to provide you with funding, direction, and support.

Luckily, you can navigate each of these relationships. You can find ways to work *with* each of these parties, instead of working *next to* or *through* them. By focusing on these moments of collaboration and co-creation, you can develop a working cadence that lifts everyone up and helps you make an excellent user experience.

CHOOSING A ROLE IN THE INDUSTRY

User experience design is a wide field, with so many different facets that go into creating an experience—researching people's problems, architecting a solution, making that solution visually appealing, and more. As a designer, you could focus on being responsible for all these elements of the user experience for the product you work on—and those roles exist, especially in smaller companies. Alternatively, you could specialize, focusing on one specific element of the user's experience.

You're fortunate enough to have the option to choose your path in this industry. You can participate in plenty of different ways in the user's experience, setting aside the type of company you want to work for, the industry you want to work in, and the team you want to work with.

Let's look at all the different ways you can grow your career.

Product Designer—Do It All

A *product designer* is expected to hold their own across all elements of designing the product. At any moment, a product designer will be expected to research, structure, and visually design the experience of the product they work on.

This is an excellent role to get started with in the industry—because the expectation is that you'll be working on everything, you get the chance to explore what sides of user experience design you really appreciate. A "jack of all trades" position like this gives you the chance to really explore the field and dip into parts of the process you won't get in more dedicated, specialist roles like motion designer or UX writer. However, this can be a double-edged sword.

For people who want consistency, want to focus on one specific thing, or would feel overwhelmed being responsible for all elements of the user's experience, then this role might not be for you. You will need the ability to jump between contexts, as one day you'll be talking to users about their problems and another you'll be delivering design specifications to developers. This role requires a lot of soft skills around navigating the workplace, in addition to the hard skills like research and design.

Looking at the qualifications for a product designer at Meta (**FIGURE 8.24**), you can see the need for multidisciplinary skill sets. Meta's ideal product designer has experience in interaction design, visual design, strategic thinking, and end-to-end design experience, among other critical skill sets. This is to be expected—a product designer is expected to handle themselves at any point during the design thinking process as they support the products they work on.

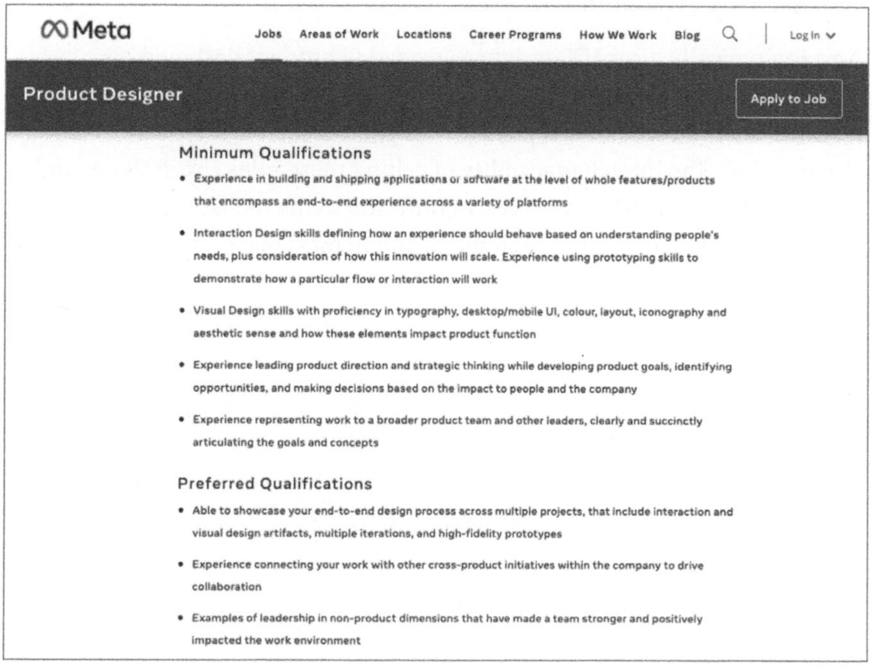

FIGURE 8.24 A product designer job posting from Meta.

∞ Meta   Jobs   Areas of Work   Locations   Career Programs   How We Work   Blog   🔍 | Log In ∨

Product Designer   Apply to Job

Minimum Qualifications

- Experience in building and shipping applications or software at the level of whole features/products that encompass an end-to-end experience across a variety of platforms

- Interaction Design skills defining how an experience should behave based on understanding people's needs, plus consideration of how this innovation will scale. Experience using prototyping skills to demonstrate how a particular flow or interaction will work

- Visual Design skills with proficiency in typography, desktop/mobile UI, colour, layout, iconography and aesthetic sense and how these elements impact product function

- Experience leading product direction and strategic thinking while developing product goals, identifying opportunities, and making decisions based on the impact to people and the company

- Experience representing work to a broader product team and other leaders, clearly and succinctly articulating the goals and concepts

Preferred Qualifications

- Able to showcase your end-to-end design process across multiple projects, that include interaction and visual design artifacts, multiple iterations, and high-fidelity prototypes

- Experience connecting your work with other cross-product initiatives within the company to drive collaboration

- Examples of leadership in non-product dimensions that have made a team stronger and positively impacted the work environment

UX Designer—Focus on the Structure

The expectations for a *UX designer* are quite similar to those for a product designer—own the end-to-end experience of the product you work on. In fact, there's a misconception in the industry that the jobs are the same; the terms are used interchangeably and often describe the same role.

The distinction between the two is that UX designers are, on average, more likely to focus on the structure of an experience rather than its visuals. A UX designer may have the support of a visual designer to create a team of two specialists focusing on a product.

This is something I've experienced in the industry personally—I was a UX designer at Food Network, where I paired with visual designers to create experiences. I focused on conducting research, crafting user journeys, and creating mid-fidelity wireframes so that a visual designer could focus on the branding, typography, and UI design of those experiences. With our powers combined, we were able to bounce ideas off one another as we each brought our specific skill set to the product. The sum of our efforts was greater than if either of us had worked on the product individually.

Although this distinction exists in some companies, it is more common to expect a UX designer to also perform visual design, especially as that designer become more and more senior.

Amazon typically hires UX designers instead of product designers (**FIGURE 8.25**). However, looking at their job descriptions, you see the same requirements you would for a product designer: research, structure, and visual design. The interchangeability of calling these roles UX designer and product designer continues to create confusion in the industry for those not familiar with the nuance between them, and in most places, there's no difference between the two.

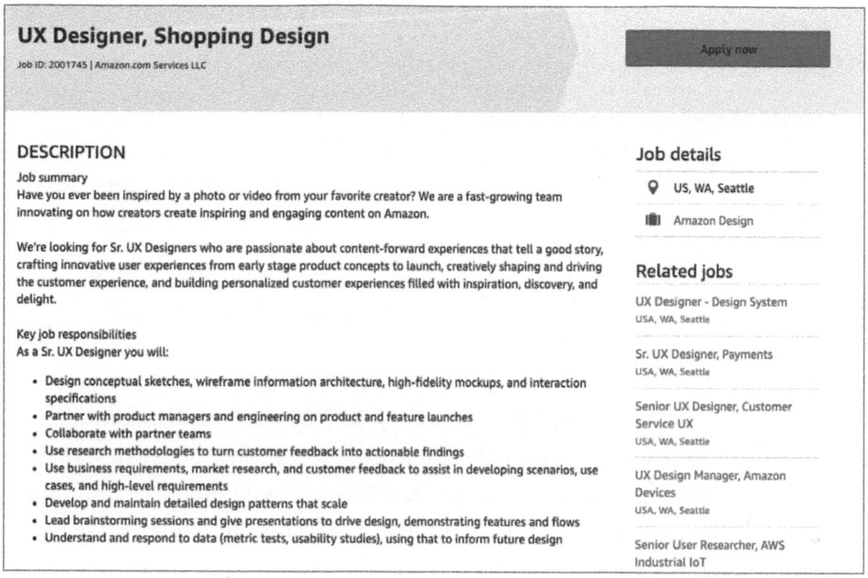

FIGURE 8.25 A UX designer job posting from Amazon.

UX Designer, Shopping Design

Job ID: 2001745 | Amazon.com Services LLC

Apply now

DESCRIPTION

Job summary
Have you ever been inspired by a photo or video from your favorite creator? We are a fast-growing team innovating on how creators create inspiring and engaging content on Amazon.

We're looking for Sr. UX Designers who are passionate about content-forward experiences that tell a good story, crafting innovative user experiences from early stage product concepts to launch, creatively shaping and driving the customer experience, and building personalized customer experiences filled with inspiration, discovery, and delight.

Key job responsibilities
As a Sr. UX Designer you will:

- Design conceptual sketches, wireframe information architecture, high-fidelity mockups, and interaction specifications
- Partner with product managers and engineering on product and feature launches
- Collaborate with partner teams
- Use research methodologies to turn customer feedback into actionable findings
- Use business requirements, market research, and customer feedback to assist in developing scenarios, use cases, and high-level requirements
- Develop and maintain detailed design patterns that scale
- Lead brainstorming sessions and give presentations to drive design, demonstrating features and flows
- Understand and respond to data (metric tests, usability studies), using that to inform future design

Job details

📍 US, WA, Seattle

💼 Amazon Design

Related jobs

UX Designer - Design System
USA, WA, Seattle

Sr. UX Designer, Payments
USA, WA, Seattle

Senior UX Designer, Customer Service UX
USA, WA, Seattle

UX Design Manager, Amazon Devices
USA, WA, Seattle

Senior User Researcher, AWS Industrial IoT

Visual or UI Designer—Make It Look Good

A *visual designer* is a bit more straightforward a role—expect to be in charge of the visual design of the product. Be an expert in color, typography, graphic design, illustrations, and other attributes that lead to stunning, visually appealing experiences. If you want to be involved in user experience design but don't want to think about product roadmaps or conduct research, then this role may be for you.

As far as the distinction between visual designer and UI designer, a visual designer may be more responsible for non-product specific needs at an organization, such as marketing materials, illustrations for a website, or some other graphic design needs the organization has. A UI designer would be expected to work more on the product and may go so far as to create stylized icons, logos, or other highly visual product elements.

Looking at available UI designer roles on LinkedIn (FIGURE 8.26), you see a focus on visual design elements like typography, color, and iconography. This is to be expected—UI designers are generally best in class with the visual aspects of a product.

FIGURE 8.26 A UI designer job posting on LinkedIn.

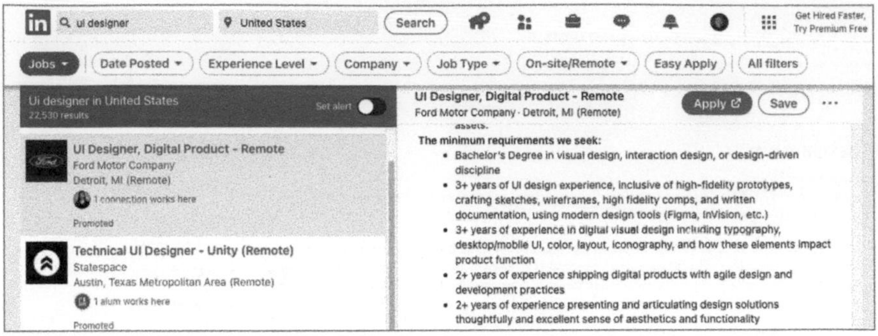

UX Researcher—Become an Expert on Your Users

If you don't want to do any visual design work, even at lower fidelities, then UX research may be for you. *UX researchers* focus heavily on understanding users' needs across the life cycle of a product. A UX researcher is an expert on research methodologies, conducting interviews with users, and delving deeply into the needs and motivations of the people they design for.

A UX researcher can be expected to conduct user interviews, develop personas, conduct usability testing (using another designer's wireframes, for example), or do anything as it relates to understanding more about their users. UX researchers have a significant, though indirect, impact on the evolution of a product—by finding out more about the problem space, they discover the information that leads an organization to the decisions it makes when crafting the user's experience.

You can see in FIGURE 8.27 the minimum expectations for a UX researcher at a company like Google—there is no mention of performing visual design tasks. Rather, the emphasis is on research, usability, and psychology.

FIGURE 8.27 A UX researcher job posting from Google.

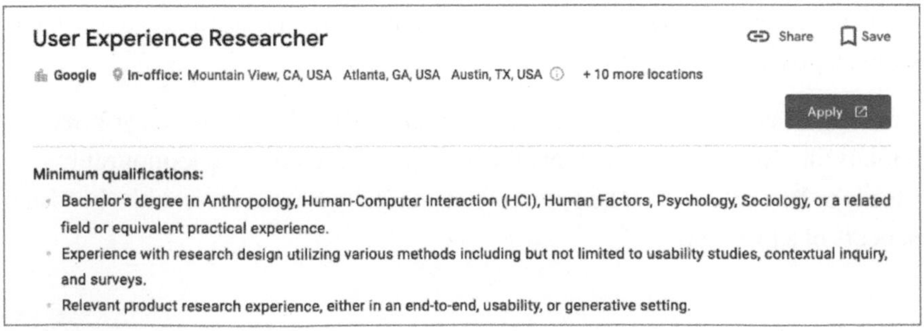

UX Writer—Craft the Perfect Copy

UX writer is a more specialized role in the industry. UX writers focus on how the product communicates with users through copy—anything that requires text, such as buttons, labels, headlines, and more. UX writers have a heavy emphasis on things like information architecture, where the taxonomy of the product ends up affecting how users understand groupings of product elements. UX writers cover anything and everything regarding copy—not its visual design, like typography, but rather its content.

Looking at a job posting from Spotify for a UX writer (FIGURE 8.28), you see tons of requirements around copy. They expect UX writers to own content, emails, notifications, brand stories, and other elements of the product's copy. A UX writer is involved across the product's end-to-end life cycle, but in a different capacity than a product designer would be. Instead of laying out a flow, a UX writer lays out the story of that flow through the use of words.

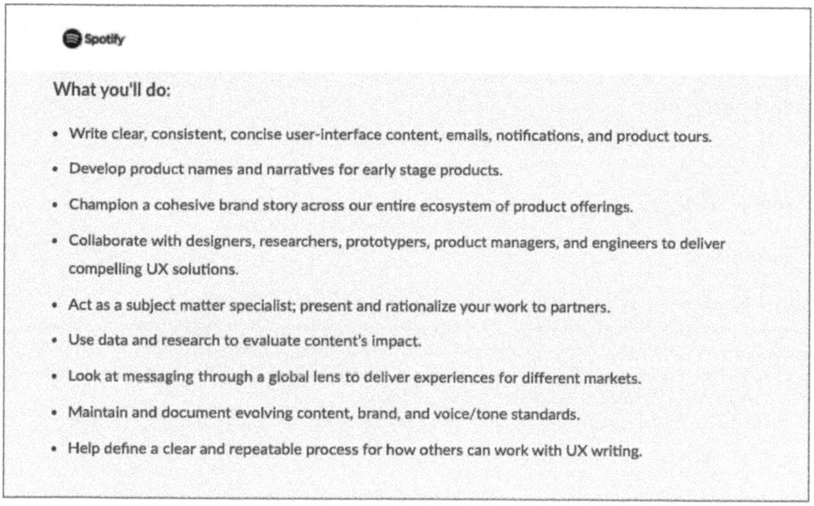

Spotify

What you'll do:

- Write clear, consistent, concise user-interface content, emails, notifications, and product tours.
- Develop product names and narratives for early stage products.
- Champion a cohesive brand story across our entire ecosystem of product offerings.
- Collaborate with designers, researchers, prototypers, product managers, and engineers to deliver compelling UX solutions.
- Act as a subject matter specialist; present and rationalize your work to partners.
- Use data and research to evaluate content's impact.
- Look at messaging through a global lens to deliver experiences for different markets.
- Maintain and document evolving content, brand, and voice/tone standards.
- Help define a clear and repeatable process for how others can work with UX writing.

FIGURE 8.28 A UX writer job posting from Spotify.

Design Systems Designer— Unify and Scale Your Product

A *design systems designer* is similar to a UI designer in that they both focus on the UI of the product. They are both expected to be best-in-class for creating and maintaining excellent visual design standards for the user's experience. The difference between them, however, is how they apply their visual design skill set.

A UI designer is more likely to work "vertically" on a product, focused on a specific side of the product, doing feature-oriented work. A design systems designer is more likely to work "horizontally" across the product, impacting each product area as they work on UI across multiple features. A design systems designer focuses on designing the systems companies use to create user experiences. They make components to be used across teams, and at scale, so that as new problems arise, the designers working directly on those problems have a set of resources readily available for them to use.

A design systems designer focuses on scale, consistency, and flexibility. They create UI that can be used across different contexts and make sure that a company represents a consistent UI across all of its products. These roles are more common at larger, more established companies that have many different products and a need to unify how they are presented to users.

At Microsoft, a design systems designer (FIGURE 8.29) is expected to support "cross-platform experiences"—an indication that this role covers multiple product areas. They write guidelines for how to use components, create components for use across these product areas, and have a large focus on consistency and patterns.

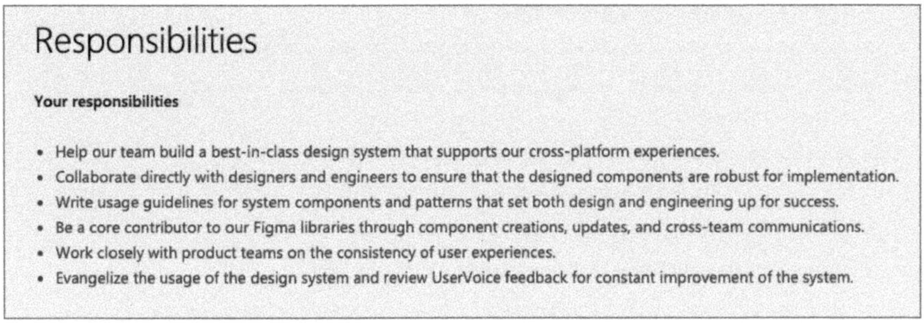

FIGURE 8.29 A design systems designer job posting from Microsoft.

Responsibilities

Your responsibilities

- Help our team build a best-in-class design system that supports our cross-platform experiences.
- Collaborate directly with designers and engineers to ensure that the designed components are robust for implementation.
- Write usage guidelines for system components and patterns that set both design and engineering up for success.
- Be a core contributor to our Figma libraries through component creations, updates, and cross-team communications.
- Work closely with product teams on the consistency of user experiences.
- Evangelize the usage of the design system and review UserVoice feedback for constant improvement of the system.

Motion Designer—Create Stunning Animations

A *motion designer* is a specialist in how animation behaves in a product. This role is expected to have a wide range in understanding movement, whether it be on a small scale, like tapping a button, or a large scale, like how a website uses parallax effects as the user scrolls the page. Motion designers create animated icons, loading states, and transitions, and sometimes even lean into marketing materials, like promotional videos, animated logos, or other video needs an organization has.

In terms of product work, a motion designer would be expected to take a nearly complete product and provide animated effects that truly elevate the product to a best-in-class user experience. As a result, these types of roles are normally found in organizations that have not only the budget to afford world-class polish, but also the desire to put that attention to detail into their products.

It's no surprise a company like Apple wants motion designers (**FIGURE 8.30**). Apple's products have hundreds of microinteractions and other moments where motion is applied to enhance the user's experience. A motion designer at Apple would be expected to work on motion across the company, from marketing materials to in-product animations and specific video needs.

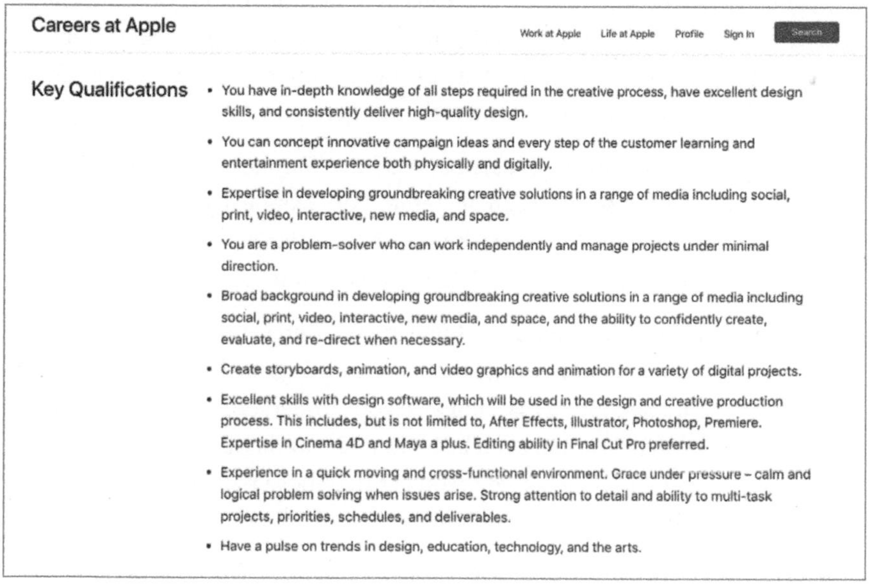

Careers at Apple

Work at Apple | Life at Apple | Profile | Sign In | Search

Key Qualifications

- You have in-depth knowledge of all steps required in the creative process, have excellent design skills, and consistently deliver high-quality design.
- You can concept innovative campaign ideas and every step of the customer learning and entertainment experience both physically and digitally.
- Expertise in developing groundbreaking creative solutions in a range of media including social, print, video, interactive, new media, and space.
- You are a problem-solver who can work independently and manage projects under minimal direction.
- Broad background in developing groundbreaking creative solutions in a range of media including social, print, video, interactive, new media, and space, and the ability to confidently create, evaluate, and re-direct when necessary.
- Create storyboards, animation, and video graphics and animation for a variety of digital projects.
- Excellent skills with design software, which will be used in the design and creative production process. This includes, but is not limited to, After Effects, Illustrator, Photoshop, Premiere. Expertise in Cinema 4D and Maya a plus. Editing ability in Final Cut Pro preferred.
- Experience in a quick moving and cross-functional environment. Grace under pressure - calm and logical problem solving when issues arise. Strong attention to detail and ability to multi-task projects, priorities, schedules, and deliverables.
- Have a pulse on trends in design, education, technology, and the arts.

FIGURE 8.30 A motion designer job posting from Apple.

Grow Your Career in Design

These are the most common roles you will find in the industry as they relate to user experience design. Some roles require extensive visual design knowledge, seeking best-in-class practitioners of aesthetic experiences. Others require deep psychological expertise, requiring professionals to know the inner workings of their users. Some roles require a broad skill set across all the disciplines of user experience design, seeking generalists instead of specialists.

No path is better than another. Different people like different parts of the design process. Some want to focus on a specific part. Others want to experience it all. Think about what you want for your career as you explore all the opportunities you have in the field of design.

WHERE DO YOU GO FROM HERE?

This may feel like the end of your journey. You've seen firsthand the art and science of UX design. You know what it is like to conduct the design thinking process end to end—and you've done it yourself. Trust me when I say this is only the beginning—you can take your learning in any direction you'd like.

You now know the design thinking process, which means you can apply it to any problem you choose to work on. You can make an entirely new product or take the process and apply it to the product you currently work on. Or you can apply it to one of your favorite products and make that product even better! What you choose to work on is up to you.

As for the techniques you have learned, you have only scratched the surface. Every technique we discussed can be iterated on, can be learned more deeply, and can even be modified by you to be improved. Like a carpenter, each of the tools you learned are yours to pick up, polish, and apply as you see fit.

You can even learn new techniques, focusing on a subset of UX to specialize in. You can learn more about research, becoming a specialist in user research. You can learn more about UI and improve your understanding of what makes a great digital design. You can even learn to code, and not just design experiences but implement them as well. You get to choose the path of your own education, and the possibilities are both wide and deep.

I showed you the door to design—it's up to you to walk through that door and make your path your own.

I can't wait to see you in the industry!

Cheers,
~Anthony

WHAT GOOD LOOKS LIKE

As you work through the "Let's Do It!" sections of Chapters 2 through 7, you might benefit from seeing what a good result looks like. I've included examples of how I would approach each exercise presented in the book. These examples are some of many possibilities of what your exercises could look like.

In design, we are influenced by our experiences—what we see, what we consume, what we come across. As a result, there's no singular "answer" for a problem—rather, the way to think about what good looks like is whether your answer addresses the problem you are trying to solve. If it does, great! If not, then iterate on it until you feel confident your answer will help the people you design for.

The references here are not intended to be the *correct* answers; rather, they are *possible* answers, or the answers I happened to arrive at when I worked on each exercise. Use these examples as a guide or a reference—not a solution.

CHAPTER 2: USING EMPATHY AS A DESIGN TOOL

Surveys

Finished with your survey? Great! Maybe it starts with something like
FIGURE A.2.1.

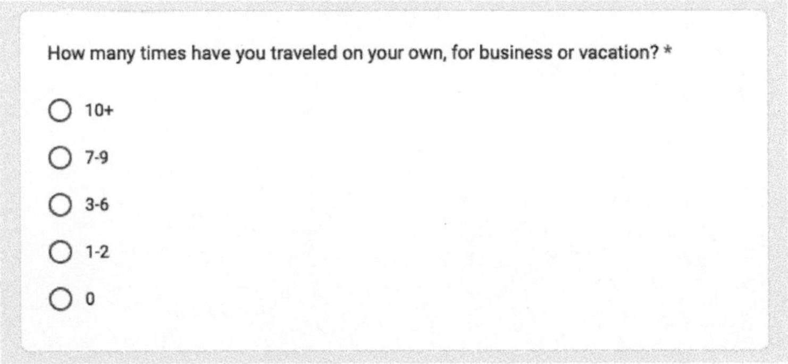

FIGURE A.2.1 A closed, single-response question to determine how frequently the respondent travels.

How many times have you traveled on your own, for business or vacation? *

○ 10+

○ 7-9

○ 3-6

○ 1-2

○ 0

I start by asking how often the respondent travels on their own. If they don't travel a lot by themselves, then they won't be a good interview candidate.

Next, I ask what products they use when they travel (FIGURE A.2.2). I do this to inform the competitive analysis in the future (more on this later), but also to get a sense of how this person likes to travel. Do they seek out hotels? Do they seek out social interaction? Knowing where they browse helps us get into the mindset of how they like to travel. This question also helps us in a future competitive analysis informing us of which products to analyze based on how many people select those products here.

I then collect demographic information (FIGURE A.2.3). This helps me avoid asking this later and keeps me informed for a future step in the process—the persona, which is a representation of our target audience. You'll learn more about personas in Chapter 3.

Finally, I ask for the respondent's name and if they will be interested in participating in an interview (FIGURE A.2.4). By asking upfront, I can filter out the people who don't want to participate in the survey, saving me time later.

From here, I would send this survey via social media and to friends to find participants to talk with. Hopefully I'll get enough people interested in an interview!

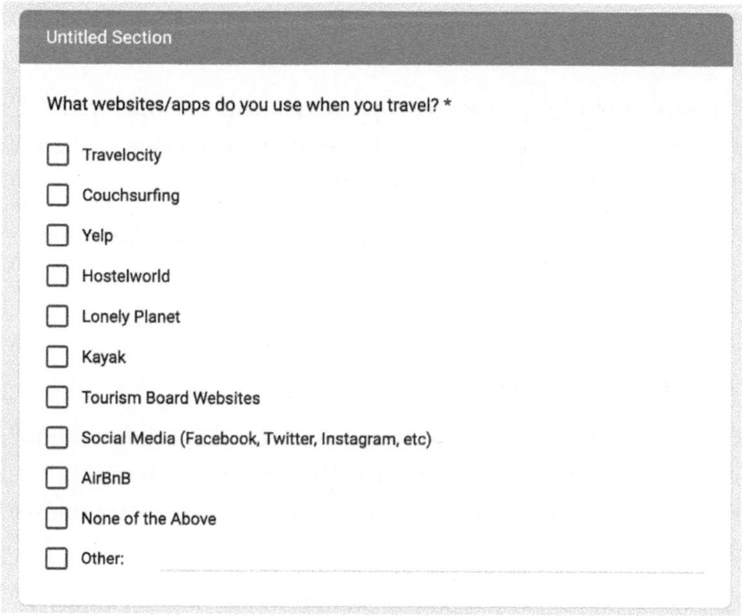

Untitled Section

What websites/apps do you use when you travel? *

- ☐ Travelocity
- ☐ Couchsurfing
- ☐ Yelp
- ☐ Hostelworld
- ☐ Lonely Planet
- ☐ Kayak
- ☐ Tourism Board Websites
- ☐ Social Media (Facebook, Twitter, Instagram, etc)
- ☐ AirBnB
- ☐ None of the Above
- ☐ Other: _____

FIGURE A.2.2 A closed, multiple-response question to determine the online products the respondent uses.

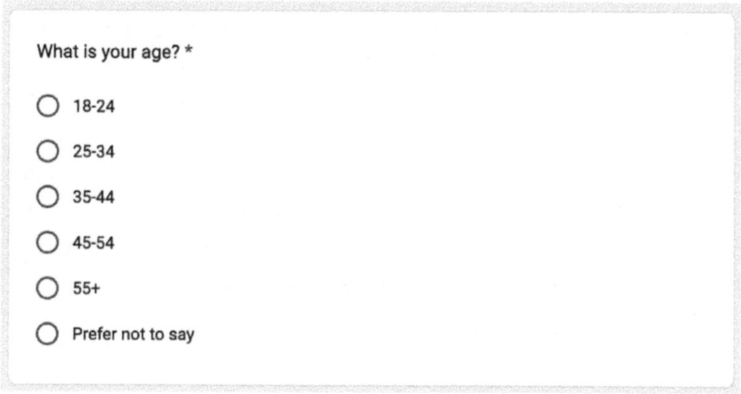

What is your age? *

- ○ 18-24
- ○ 25-34
- ○ 35-44
- ○ 45-54
- ○ 55+
- ○ Prefer not to say

FIGURE A.2.3 A closed, single-response question to determine the respondent's age.

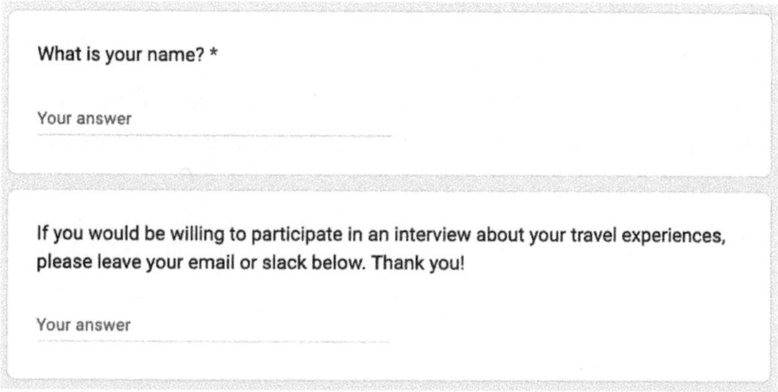

What is your name? *

Your answer

If you would be willing to participate in an interview about your travel experiences, please leave your email or slack below. Thank you!

Your answer

FIGURE A.2.4 A set of open-response questions that allow us to follow up with the respondent.

Interview Script

Let's look at how your script could have played out.

Ideally, the screener survey found good people to talk with—people who often travel alone. So, I focus on their experiences of traveling alone to better understand their wants and needs from solo travel.

Two of the first questions I can ask (after asking for permission to record) are the following:

How often do you travel?

How often do you travel alone?

Why is this? It's because I want to prime the participants into thinking about travel. A simple, easy icebreaker question like "How often do you travel?" helps ease the participant into the conversation and gets them in the mindset of the problem area: travel.

Next, I can ask about a time when the participant traveled alone. A question like this will be very open ended and lead to many different possibilities, so I need to be agile in the response and follow up on anything interesting this question might reveal.

When was the last time you traveled alone?

Be sure to respond to this question for follow-up information. The story that they tell can lead anywhere, and there may be some interesting information in that story. I'd have a few follow-up phrases to keep in mind, such as "tell me more about that" and "go on" to promote conversation.

Next, I want to know more about the factors they consider when traveling alone. Ask it in the following way:

What factors do you consider when traveling alone?

It's important to ask the question in a neutral way, not saying anything about positive or negative attributes. If the participant goes negative, figure out why. If the participant goes positive, also figure out why. A good follow-up here is "Why is that?"

Next, I can start to ask for some of the "normal" things people do when traveling alone. To that end, probe for information about how they spend their time while traveling alone.

How do you spend your time when traveling alone?

This should lead to some more stories about their solo travel experiences. As with the last question, I want to follow up on anything interesting that comes out of this answer. I'd make sure to ask why and probe for more information.

The last two questions probably provided a lot of information and stories to think about. Some of that information may have been positive or negative, but there's no way to guarantee that. To really get at the joys and pain points of solo travel, ask for that information. These next two questions are flexible—I might get these answers from the last questions I asked, or I might have to ask these to make sure I learn the positive and negative elements of solo travel.

What do you like about traveling alone?

What do you dislike about traveling alone?

The next couple of questions are secondary. They relate to the core problem but start to explore other verticals around solo travel. I can ask about whether the participant tries to be social during solo travel experiences. This can provide insight into possible product features or help me find ways to remove blockers in the travel experience.

Do you try to meet new people when traveling alone?

Next, I probe into how people prepare for a solo trip. By discussing how they do their research, I can learn whether the solution needs to handle the actual experience while on the trip or the parts of the experience before the trip as well.

How do you do your research on a travel destination?

Lastly, give the participant time in the conversation to bring up anything they'd like to discuss. Offer them the opportunity to share something that's off script—you may learn something that wasn't even on your radar.

Is there anything else I haven't asked that you think is important to talk about?

Putting it all together, you end up with the following script:

Hi there! I'm a designer working on a personal project exploring solo travel experiences. I'm looking to learn more about your thoughts and opinions on traveling alone. I'm going to ask you some questions today about your experiences with solo travel. Overall, this should take around 30 minutes. How does that sound? Do you have any questions before we begin?

Great. One last thing—before we begin, would you mind if I record this session? It'll be used only to share internally with my team later.

1. *How often do you travel?*

2. *How often do you travel alone?*

3. *When was the last time you traveled alone?*

4. *What factors do you consider when traveling alone?*

5. *How do you spend your time when traveling alone?*

6. *What do you like about traveling alone?*

7. *What do you dislike about traveling alone?*

8. *Do you try to meet new people when traveling alone?*

9. *How do you do your research on a place you are traveling to?*

10. *Is there anything else I haven't asked that you think is important to talk about?*

Data Set

I've put together an exercise that will allow you to practice affinity mapping in addition to seeing what a sorted, organized data set looks like. If you'd like extra practice (or you don't have a data set of your own), try sorting the data in this file: https://tinyurl.com/asuxd-affinity. If you'd like to see the groupings and insights, then remove or delete the rectangle that's blocking the solution. Have fun!

As for the exercise itself, I'm going to go through this data set and show you how I grouped all the information. I wrote out observations for all my users and organized them by participant, as in **FIGURE A.2.5**.

User 1

I consider costs	I like places I can meet other travelers	Would like to connect with others with similar interests
I want a platform to meet other travelers in same situation	I like that hostels are "catered toward meeting"	I use Google and Yelp reviews
Transportation is a big stressor	I do research for what others have done	I have traveled for half a year solo
I didn't want to put myself into unsafe situations	I ask others for opinions about where was safe	I like bus tours for safety

User 2

I use common areas in hostels to meet	Hostels are cheap and preferred	I like meeting other travelers
I want to meet others to share rides	The hardest thing is wanting to meet other people	What can I do at night?
I want to meet people who have been vetted	I don't like taking a bunch of buses and trains	I sightsee alone often
I let the experience guide me	It's a challenge if you don't speak the language	I usually take notes when I travel
I want to experience things, but also be safe	I check ratings of places based on safety	I am a budget traveler

User 3

I'd like to see who's in the area and meet them	I like to talk to strangers about their experiences	A map of London was essential to navigate
I try to meet a local for advice on the area	I stay longer if I know someone in the area	It would be nice to be able to speak the top words of a language where I go
You need to know and respect the local customs and codes, like clothing	I schedule personal travel around work events	I like to live the day like a local
Safety is always on my mind	I am very concerned with hotel safety	I go with an established group
Safety is very important when traveling abroad		

User 4

I have more freedom in a group than alone	I made close friends with hostel travelers	My best experience with strangers at a hostel outing
I review places with Google and Yelp	I use Instagram for travel inspiration	I am worried about navigating the transportation system
I look for food and drink wherever I travel	There are all these cultural norms to follow	I travel domestically and abroad
Is travel safe?	Is my lodging safe?	I would not go out on my own

User 5

I have a bad sense of direction and need a map	I want to experience the city like a local	I want to push out of my introvert shell when traveling
The language barrier is a source of stress when abroad	I like doing outdoor activities when traveling	Traveling solo is all about going with the flow
Biggest concern is safety	I keep my phone on data for Google Maps, so that I can get out of a sticky situation	I love couch surfing / Airbnb because you get to know the host
Hostels are not safe because anyone can steal your stuff	I stay at places where people are vetted and verified	I hate being picked out of the crowd as a solo tourist

User 6

Maps are important to me	Exchanging information in person is really valuable	I wish I could pinpoint where others are so they could give me tips
I research by walking around	I stay at Airbnbs because it is safe and private	I prioritize based on that day's mood
I choose travel based on food	I like to stretch my money	The language barrier is tough when you're alone
I don't always know someone in the area where I travel	I like to take notes when I travel	I prioritize based on even and exhibit schedule
I only want to travel to safe places	I like hostels because they are cheap	

FIGURE A.2.5 All the data points from my interviews across different users.

From this data set, I started looking for themes across different insights. I found related data points and put them together into groups. I repeated this process, shuffling around data points from group to group until I settled on a few groupings that made the most sense.

I made a few small groups that felt like themes but didn't have a lot of data points in them. Those groupings are in FIGURE A.2.6.

FIGURE A.2.6 Several smaller themes from my user interviews.

Travel history

I have traveled for half a year solo

I sightsee alone often

I travel domestically and abroad

Cost

I consider costs

I am a budget traveler

Hostels are cheap and preferred

I like hostels because they are cheap

How I prepare

I do research for what others have done

I usually take notes when I travel

I schedule personal travel around work events

Flow

Traveling solo is all about going with the flow

I prioritize based on that day's mood

I let the experience guide me

Generally, people had some similarities in how often they traveled, how they prepared, and how they thought about costs while traveling. They also had a few thoughts around "going with the flow" when traveling alone—having some flexibility in their schedule to act spontaneously was important to them.

Some insights around the mechanics of travel surfaced as well—from transportation to language barriers, to the technology people used to facilitate travel (FIGURE A.2.7).

Transport

Transportation is a big stressor	I like bus tours for safety	I don't like taking a bunch of buses and trains
A map of London was essential to navigate	I have a bad sense of direction and need a map	Maps are important to me

Language

It would be nice to be able to speak the top words of a language where I go	It's a challenge if you don't speak the language
The language barrier is a source of stress when abroad	The language barrier is tough when you're alone

Tech

I use Google and Yelp reviews	I review places with Google and Yelp
I use Instagram for travel inspiration	

FIGURE A.2.7 Additional smaller themes that emerged from my affinity map exercise.

Two much larger themes dominated a lot of the insights from the research—the first around social interaction, as shown in **FIGURE A.2.8**.

For the social category, a lot of users were interested in socializing, though there were some challenges around making that happen. There are 23 different insights here, so with a little massaging, I could break this out into more detailed information regarding the nuances of their thoughts around social interaction. For the first pass at this data set though, this is a good place to start.

Social

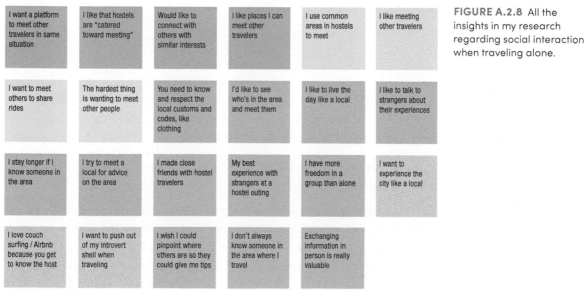

I want a platform to meet other travelers in same situation	I like that hostels are "catered toward meeting"	Would like to connect with others with similar interests	I like places I can meet other travelers	I use common areas in hostels to meet	I like meeting other travelers
I want to meet others to share rides	The hardest thing is wanting to meet other people	You need to know and respect the local customs and codes, like clothing	I'd like to see who's in the area and meet them	I like to live the day like a local	I like to talk to strangers about their experiences
I stay longer if I know someone in the area	I try to meet a local for advice on the area	I made close friends with hostel travelers	My best experience with strangers at a hostel outing	I have more freedom in a group than alone	I want to experience the city like a local
I love couch surfing / Airbnb because you get to know the host	I want to push out of my introvert shell when traveling	I wish I could pinpoint where others are so they could give me tips	I don't always know someone in the area where I travel	Exchanging information in person is really valuable	

FIGURE A.2.8 All the insights in my research regarding social interaction when traveling alone.

There were also a lot of insights around safety, seen in **FIGURE A.2.9**.

Safety was top of mind for a lot of participants. Traveling alone in a new location by yourself is a scary thing, so people wanted to feel safe while exploring. Sometimes safety concerns prevented travelers from maximizing their travels, which was a frustration for participants.

This one ended up a little large as well, at 19 insights. On a second pass, I could probably break this out into multiple subcategories as well.

FIGURE A.2.9 All the insights around safety from my interviews.

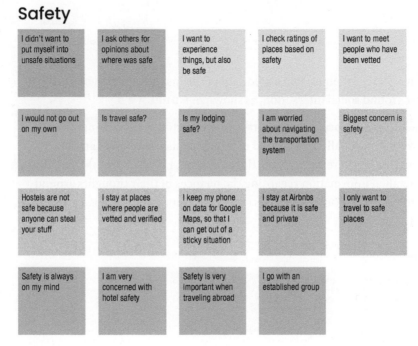

Safety

I didn't want to put myself into unsafe situations	I ask others for opinions about where was safe	I want to experience things, but also be safe	I check ratings of places based on safety	I want to meet people who have been vetted
I would not go out on my own	Is travel safe?	Is my lodging safe?	I am worried about navigating the transportation system	Biggest concern is safety
Hostels are not safe because anyone can steal your stuff	I stay at places where people are vetted and verified	I keep my phone on data for Google Maps, so that I can get out of a sticky situation	I stay at Airbnbs because it is safe and private	I only want to travel to safe places
Safety is always on my mind	I am very concerned with hotel safety	Safety is very important when traveling abroad	I go with an established group	

Finally, there were a few insights I didn't really know what to do with, and that's OK. I can always make a Parking Lot and leave them there or come back to them later as shown in **FIGURE A.2.10**.

Putting the exercise all together, I ended up with the affinity map shown in **FIGURE A.2.11**.

This is good for a first pass. The social and safety categories are a lot bigger than the others, so I would probably want to break those out a bit more into more granular sub themes. From there, I would want to come up with I Statements for each section, such as "I like to go with the flow" for the Flow section or "I am conscious of how much I spend" for the Cost section.

Parking lot

What can I do at night?	I hate being picked out of the crowd as a solo tourist	I like doing outdoor activities when traveling	I look for food and drink wherever I travel	There are all these cultural norms to follow
I research by walking around	I choose travel based on food	I like to take notes when I travel	I prioritize based on even and exhibit schedule	

FIGURE A.2.10 Several insights that didn't feel like they fit anywhere. On a future pass, maybe I'll be able to find a home for a few of them.

If you'd like to see where I eventually landed for this affinity map, look at this exercise (which you can do yourself!) https://tinyurl.com/asuxd-affinity.

Affinity mapping is an iterative process where you can refine and massage the information into different interpretations. I hope this exercise inspired you to examine your own data set and explore different mappings of the insights you gathered on your interviews!

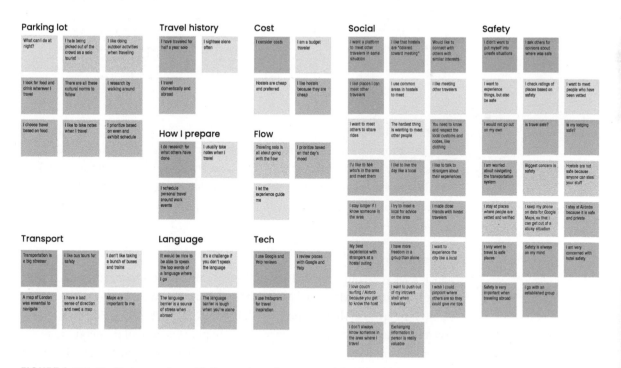

FIGURE A.2.11 The first pass of my affinity map based on my user interviews.

CHAPTER 3: DEFINING THE USER'S PROBLEMS

Persona

Based on the data set in the affinity mapping exercise, you may have created a persona that looks like the one in **FIGURE A.3.1**.

This is Jay, a solo traveler who seeks to maximize her trip and experience things like a local does. Let's look at each section of this persona to understand more.

"I want to experience things just like a local!"
Bio
Jay is a young professional who likes to solo travel around the world during her vacation time. She loves to set her own schedule as she explores new countries, experiences local food, and immerses herself in different cultures.
While traveling alone, she enjoys meeting other travelers and locals, not only to share a cab or an experience, but to feel safer in a new, unknown space.
Jay
Age: 28
Job: Copywriter
Favorite travel apps:
lonely planet
Skyscanner
couchsurfing
airbnb
Goals
• Have a blend between the tourist and the local experience
• Experience all she can on her trip
• Enjoy her trip based on her own schedule and preferences
• Share experiences and info with other travelers and locals
• Break out of her comfort zone and try new things
Frustrations
• Finding people who want to do the same things as her
• Finding people who she can trust
• Unsure how to approach others to join her
• Feeling like she can't do certain activities due to fears of safety
• Staying connected to the people she's met on her travels

FIGURE A.3.1 A persona based on research done for a solo traveler project.

Name/Photo

For this project, a lot of the user interview participants were women. This persona photo captured how they felt about travel—excited, outgoing, and thrilled to experience new places. The name felt appropriate as well—it didn't link to anyone we interviewed, and it was simple enough to represent the target audience.

Overview

Jay is a 28-year-old copywriter—additional information that represented the user interview participants. Most of the participants were between the ages of 25–35, so Jay is in that age range. Additionally, a lot of the participants relied on couch surfing and hostels over hotels, in part because of monetary reasons, so a high-paying profession for Jay wouldn't match the budget the target user would have for travel. While none of the user interview participants were copywriters, that profession would match the budget for the persona for Jay.

Quote

Although not necessary, a quote can really help flesh out the top things a person is looking for in an experience. This quote sums up what Jay is looking for—a travel experience that reflects how locals experience their location. It's ideal if this quote is a real quote from the interview, but it's OK if it's not.

Background/Bio

In the user interviews, people said they loved to travel alone because it allowed them freedom and flexibility. People had the choice to do what they wanted, when they wanted, with no constraints around any travel partners. People also expressed that they wanted to experience things like local residents do, which is a huge part of the travel experience for them.

Additionally, people enjoyed meeting new people during a trip—not just locals. Sharing experiences with others, in a safe way, is an important part of the solo traveler experience.

Likes/Goals

A lot of Jay's likes/goals come from the *I statements* in the affinity mapping exercise. Statements like "I want to experience things like a local" and "I want to meet other people" really came forward. Research showed that users wanted to connect with others and have local experiences during their travel. Additionally, being able to experience things on their own schedule was important.

Dislikes/Frustrations

A lot of these also come from the *I statements* in the affinity mapping exercise. Statements like "Safety is a top priority for me" and "Cost is a factor in my trip" help show what gets in Jay's way (and what you can design for). Research found that when traveling alone, people sometimes felt unsafe in their environment and would make decisions primarily with safety in mind. However, social connection allowed these people to feel safer and enjoy their trip more fully. A lot of the stories around not being able to enjoy a trip to the fullest came down to connecting with others and feeling safer.

User Journey Map

Based on the user interview data and the persona generated from the solo traveler project, a user journey map might look like **FIGURE A.3.2**.

This user journey map represents one example of how our persona could move through their user experience. Like the persona itself, the journey is not necessarily real, yet it is a representation of a real user journey. It's built from stories heard during user interviews, insights gathered from affinity mapping, and goals that real people had.

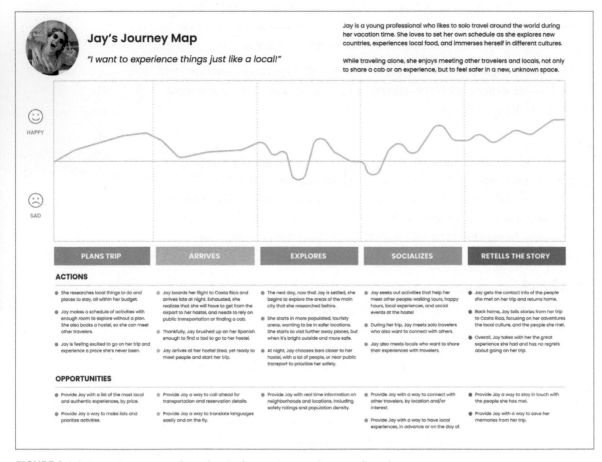

Jay's Journey Map

"I want to experience things just like a local!"

Jay is a young professional who likes to solo travel around the world during her vacation time. She loves to set her own schedule as she explores new countries, experiences local food, and immerses herself in different cultures.

While traveling alone, she enjoys meeting other travelers and locals, not only to share a cab or an experience, but to feel safer in a new, unknown space.

HAPPY

SAD

PLANS TRIP	ARRIVES	EXPLORES	SOCIALIZES	RETELLS THE STORY

ACTIONS

• She researches local things to do and places to stay, all within her budget.	• Jay boards her flight to Costa Rica and arrives late at night. Exhausted, she realizes that she will have to get from the airport to her hostel, and needs to rely on public transportation or finding a cab.	• The next day, now that Jay is settled, she begins to explore the areas of the main city that she researched before.	• Jay seeks out activities that help her meet other people: walking tours, happy hours, local experiences, and social events at the hostel	• Jay gets the contact info of the people she met on her trip and returns home.
• Jay makes a schedule of activities with enough room to explore without a plan. She also books a hostel, so she can meet other travelers.	• Thankfully, Jay brushed up on her Spanish enough to find a taxi to go to her hostel.	• She starts in more populated, touristy areas, wanting to be in safer locations. She starts to visit further away places, but when it's bright outside and more safe.	• During her trip, Jay meets solo travelers who also want to connect with others.	• Back home, Jay tells stories from her trip to Costa Rica, focusing on her adventures the local culture, and the people she met.
• Jay is feeling excited to go on her trip and experience a place she's never been.	• Jay arrives at her hostel tired, yet ready to meet people and start her trip.	• At night, Jay chooses bars closer to her hostel, with a lot of people, or near public transport to prioritize her safety.	• Jay also meets locals who want to share their experiences with travelers.	• Overall, Jay takes with her the great experience she had and has no regrets about going on her trip.

OPPORTUNITIES

• Provide Jay with a list of the most local and authentic experiences, by price.	• Provide Jay a way to call ahead for transportation and reservation details.	• Provide Jay with real time information on neighborhoods and locations, including safety ratings and population density.	• Provide Jay with a way to connect with other travelers, by location and/or interest.	• Provide Jay a way to stay in touch with the people she has met.
• Provide Jay a way to make lists and prioritize activities.	• Provide Jay a way to translate languages easily and on the fly.		• Provide Jay with a way to have local experiences, in advance or on the day of.	• Provide Jay with a way to save her memories from her trip.

FIGURE A.3.2 A user journey map based on Jay's experiences when traveling alone.

If you recall, Jay is a solo traveler who seeks to maximize her trip and experience things like a local does. She loves to travel alone, but even when she does, she still wants to connect with others along the way. She likes to travel on her own terms, yet still participate in activities with others from time to time on her trip. I took this information and created a story for Jay that matches her habits, wants, and pain points and reflects how she experiences travel.

Let's explore Jay's current state and how she experiences her user journey as she prepares for and goes on her trip.

Persona/Background

Jay's journey map starts with her photo, quote, and bio. Although this information is included in the persona, it's good to include here as well—not everyone on the team may have read the persona, and by including it here, they don't have to go find that artifact. Instead, the journey provides a brief description of who Jay is so that people seeing this journey have the information they need.

Phases

Jay's journey takes places over five phases: planning, arrival, exploration, socialization, and recall. Essentially, Jay's user journey follows her before, during, and after her trip. Jay's user experience extends beyond the actual trip—she must prepare for it beforehand and wants to relive it afterward. By looking at the entire journey, design opportunities may surface that will enhance her experience during her trip, such as by helping her prepare for the trip or by more easily saving memories from the trip.

Actions

I decided to tell a longer story with Jay's actions rather than using quotes in this section. There's no single right way to make a user journey map (or most design artifacts), and I wanted to use a more narrative format for this journey map, since there's a lot to express about Jay's journey. Some stories end up longer than others to communicate all the research and insights done from user interviews.

Jay starts by planning a trip to Costa Rica. She does research ahead of time to find local activities to participate in and book a hostel, all budget friendly (all user research insights).

AUTHOR'S NOTE A single set of user interviews can result in multiple journeys, and a single user journey may have multiple interpretations. We can tell many stories based on what we've learned from user interviews, in different ways. This is how user experience design can be more subjective and more like art, as opposed to times when it is more methodical and more like science.

Then, she gets on her flight and arrives in Costa Rica late at night. Tired and unfamiliar with her surroundings, she struggles to find a cab to her hostel. Once there, she relaxes and prepares for the bulk of her trip—exploring Costa Rica. These were also insights from our research; participants mentioned how they struggled with transportation and communication.

When Jay starts to explore Costa Rica, she begins visiting the tourist attractions—in part because that was her research, but also because it's safer that way. She is still not feeling fully comfortable in the area and wants that extra layer of safety before she branches out more. This was also reflected in our research—participants felt less safe when traveling alone, yet they still wanted to explore and see the sights.

Finally, Jay starts to socialize. She meets people through her hostel, activities, and exploration. She connects with other travelers and locals, which enhances her trip greatly. We also saw this in our research—participants wanted to meet others so that their trip could be enhanced.

Finally, Jay's trip ends. She records the contact information of those she met and heads home. She recalls the trip by talking about it with others and looking at photographs. She had a great time and wants to share her experiences. This was also a part of our research. People talked fondly of their travel experiences, outside of the several times they didn't feel safe.

This story didn't happen—at least, not as it's depicted in this journey. Rather, this is a representation of the stories we heard in our interviews, and that's OK. I'm not trying to tell a story that actually happened, but rather represent the general idea of the stories that occurred so that I can empathize with the persona and get a sense of how people travel.

Thoughts/Feelings

Jay's thoughts and feelings are represented by an emotional curve in the graph. For the most part, she has a great trip—she loves to travel and enjoys both preparing for a trip in addition to talking about it after. However, Jay has a few rough spots during the trip. Sometimes, she doesn't feel as safe, or transportation is a hassle, or she had an experience that didn't meet her expectations or even a social interaction she didn't like as much as other elements on the trip. Therefore, her emotional curve fluctuates between these experiences. In a few spots, it dips from happy to sad, but for the most part, she had an amazing time on her trip and remembers it fondly.

Insights

Finally, I have a section dedicated to possible opportunities based on the story in the journey map. Since Jay does a lot of up-front research, for example, perhaps a product that helps her do that research would help her in her journey. Once Jay starts to explore a new place, she's concerned for her safety; perhaps some features that identify how crowded places are or rank them by their perceived safety would make Jay feel better. Furthermore, since Jay likes to socialize so much, maybe an app that helps her socialize more easily would be right up her alley. Now that I have a story to work from, I can see where Jay thrives and where Jay struggles and start to think of ways to enhance her user experience.

Problem Statements

Let's look at a breakdown of generating a problem statement for the solo traveler project, going through the same steps you did in this chapter.

In the solo traveler project, the research from interviewing solo travelers revealed that travelers feel nervous while traveling alone. They feel they don't have a lot of familiarity with their new surroundings and feel that having some good resources around where they are would help them feel safer. Seeing this problem, you want to write a problem statement that will help you design. Let's give it a shot:

As a [traveler], I want [information] so that [I can travel well].

This problem statement could help you design something for the users. But it lacks substance. You don't have a lot of context around the user. The user needs are quite broad. And the goal is too ambiguous. Let's get more specific:

As a [single female traveler], I want [to be informed about my safety] so that [I don't have to worry about being in a bad situation].

This allows you to be a lot more targeted, focusing the solution on solo female travelers. You need to provide them with safety information. You can empathize, because you don't want the solo travelers to be in a bad situation. However, the statement made some assumptions that would have constrained the design. The statement assumed the travelers were female—you spoke with a lot of female travelers in the user interviews, for example, so that bias is in the problem statement. Don't assume that for the design solution.

Additionally, the need is very specific—for travel, it's possible that people want more than just information about safety. You may want to broaden that aspect of the problem statement as well.

Let's try again:

> As a [solo traveler], I want [a detailed country guide] so [I can travel well].

This problem statement is closer, but it makes an assumption about the solution. The user and goal are broader, but a product solution is included as a user need. Users might not want a detailed country guide. Let's try again:

> As a [solo traveler], I want [to feel informed and assured] so that [I can travel well].

This one doesn't assume a solution—rather, it focuses on the needs heard in the research. The user interviewees expressed that they felt unsafe when traveling alone. To feel safer, they expressed that they wanted information and assurance about their environment.

Let's try one more adjustment to the problem statement to see if you can take it a bit further:

> As a [solo traveler], I want [to feel informed and assured] so that [I can feel comfortable on my trip].

Here, the goal is adjusted. The last iteration had a good sense of the user and their needs, but this one really amps up what good looks like for the user. If you enable users to feel comfortable while traveling, then you'll have created a great design solution.

The problem statement is in a good spot. Let's see if you can pair it with a How Might We statement:

> As a [solo traveler], I want [to feel informed and assured] so that [I can feel comfortable on my trip].

> How might we provide a way for our users to maximize their solo travel experience?

Here, the problem statement is applied in a design prompt by asking "how might we?" Now, the project team will design to make users feel comfortable so they can maximize their solo travel experiences.

Competitive Research

We could have picked any of the techniques we covered for our competitive analysis. For our purposes, since we're headed into ideation on a new product idea, I'd lean toward starting with a lightning demo to gather inspiration and start giving me some ideas.

So, for the solo traveler project, let's look at products that are related to travel. Let's start with one of my favorite travel products, Airbnb (**FIGURE A.3.3**).

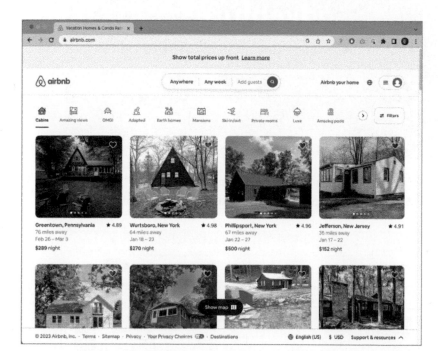

FIGURE A.3.3 Airbnb's landing page.

Looking at Airbnb, it has some very interesting filters at the top. It's rare to be able to sort by such specific and interesting things, like "amazing views" or "OMG!" It's a fun, playful way to get people excited about travel. Let's add that to the board.

Thinking more about our persona and our research, recall that a lot of travelers we spoke to rely on hostels. Let's check out a hostel website.

Hostelworld.com has an interesting option called "roamies" (**FIGURE A.3.4**). Sounds a lot like our persona, Jay! Clicking that link took me to a page that promises adventure in a small group. That's exactly what Jay is looking for, and perfect inspiration for our project.

FIGURE A.3.4 Hostel-
world's roamies option,
designed for travelers who
want to experience adven-
tures in small groups.

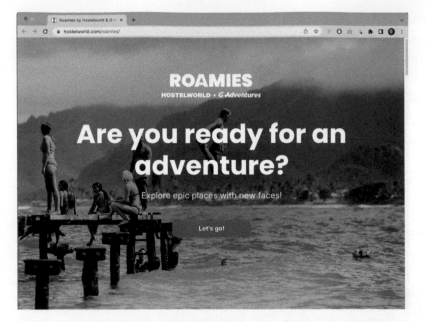

Let's explore some other travel inspiration. I'm a big fan of Tripadvisor
(**FIGURE A.3.5**), so perhaps they'll have something that inspires us.

FIGURE A.3.5 Tripadvisor's
home page.

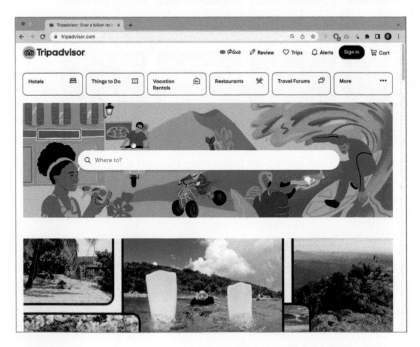

I love the imagery here—there's a lot of energy, excitement, and exploration coming from the illustrations and real-world photography being used on this site. It makes me want to travel.

We've looked at some related areas, so let's start to diverge a bit more from companies that offer travel experiences to the actual travel experiences themselves. A lot of travel blogs exist, so let's see if we can find one that gets us inspired.

After some searching for a travel blog, I came across a website called The Travel Episodes (FIGURE A.3.6). It has amazing photography that makes me want to go travel and backs it up with some compelling text to describe their journeys. Looking at this presentation of content makes me feel like going on an adventure.

FIGURE A.3.6 The Travel Episodes has incredible photography and writing to get me excited about travel.

What else can we search for? Jay mentioned she wanted authentic experiences, so let's look for examples of those too.

A company called Withlocals (FIGURE A.3.7) offers private, personal experiences with people that live in the area a traveler is visiting. This service would be perfect for Jay to spend an afternoon experiencing things like a local would.

FIGURE A.3.7 Withlocals.com offers travelers experiences with locals.

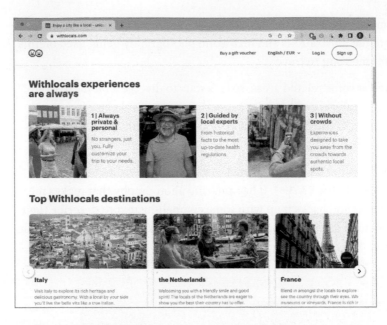

Let's see if we can find one more example to inspire us.

Searching another one of my favorite travel sites, Lonely Planet (**FIGURE A.3.8**), I learned they have a feature that creates travel itineraries based on activities, like being outdoors or seeing cultural wonders. It seems like a really cool way to think about travel, and I feel compelled to add it to my board.

FIGURE A.3.8 Lonely Planet allows travelers to select an activity and then recommends a destination.

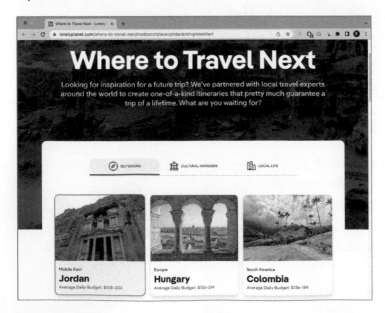

Putting our board together, we get FIGURE A.3.9.

Now that we have our mood board, we can start to get inspired for our ideation. We found fun ways to search, like with interesting filters or by choosing an activity before a destination. We found experiences, like guided tours from locals or small group adventures. We were also inspired by the design of the products we observed, like stunning imagery or compelling text. We could use all these elements in our eventual design solution—whatever it may be.

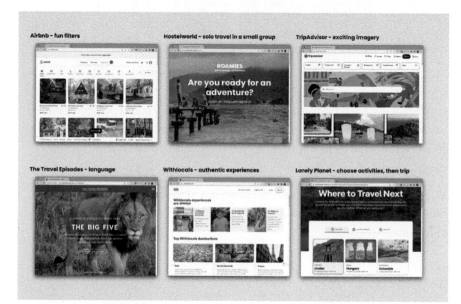

FIGURE A.3.9 Our lightning demo mood board.

CHAPTER 4: EXPLORING IDEATION TECHNIQUES AND TOOLS

Brainstorming

Working from the problem statement, I gave myself 20 minutes to generate the list of ideas shown in FIGURE A.4.1.

FIGURE A.4.1
Concepts generated from my brainstorm.

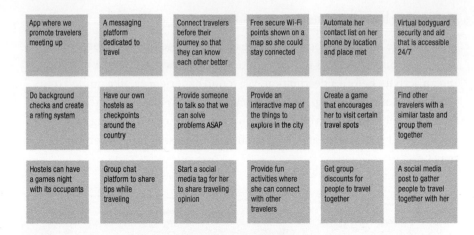

App where we promote travelers meeting up	A messaging platform dedicated to travel	Connect travelers before their journey so that they can know each other better	Free secure Wi-Fi points shown on a map so she could stay connected	Automate her contact list on her phone by location and place met	Virtual bodyguard security and aid that is accessible 24/7
Do background checks and create a rating system	Have our own hostels as checkpoints around the country	Provide someone to talk so that we can solve problems ASAP	Provide an interactive map of the things to explore in the city	Create a game that encourages her to visit certain travel spots	Find other travelers with a similar taste and group them together
Hostels can have a games night with its occupants	Group chat platform to share tips while traveling	Start a social media tag for her to share traveling opinion	Provide fun activities where she can connect with other travelers	Get group discounts for people to travel together	A social media post to gather people to travel together with her

That's a ton of ideas to think about! Not all of them would necessarily lead to a product you want to create—for example, you may not practically be able to provide a virtual bodyguard service. However, you could provide a mentor experience, such as a local who shows travelers around for a few hours. By seeing an idea and building off of it, you can create a new experience that might actually work for users.

But you're not ready to evaluate the ideas just yet—that will come later. For now, let's groups these into themes (**FIGURE A.4.2**) and see if anything else comes up.

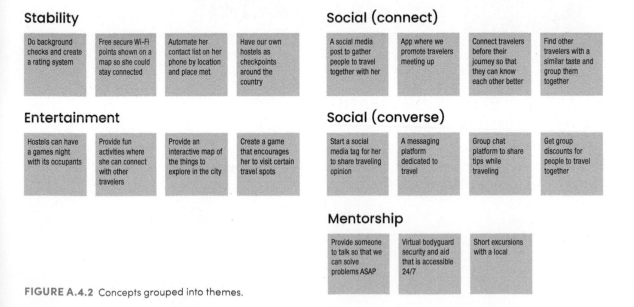

Stability

Do background checks and create a rating system	Free secure Wi-Fi points shown on a map so she could stay connected	Automate her contact list on her phone by location and place met	Have our own hostels as checkpoints around the country

Entertainment

Hostels can have a games night with its occupants	Provide fun activities where she can connect with other travelers	Provide an interactive map of the things to explore in the city	Create a game that encourages her to visit certain travel spots

Social (connect)

A social media post to gather people to travel together with her	App where we promote travelers meeting up	Connect travelers before their journey so that they can know each other better	Find other travelers with a similar taste and group them together

Social (converse)

Start a social media tag for her to share traveling opinion	A messaging platform dedicated to travel	Group chat platform to share tips while traveling	Get group discounts for people to travel together

Mentorship

Provide someone to talk so that we can solve problems ASAP	Virtual bodyguard security and aid that is accessible 24/7	Short excursions with a local

FIGURE A.4.2 Concepts grouped into themes.

While creating the themes, I took the idea about a local showing users around—it felt like a potentially interesting idea that might be valuable to have in the product. Let's look at the themes a little more closely:

- **Stability**—Jay is concerned around traveling by herself, so making her feel more secure would enhance her trip.

- **Entertainment**—Jay wants to maximize her trip, so including possible activities for her to do in new places could enhance her experience.

- **Mentorship**—Jay wants to connect with others, especially locals, to learn more about the places she goes. This could help her do so (and provide her security as well).

- **Social (connect)**—Jay likes traveling alone but still wants to meet people. This would let her connect to them.

- **Social (converse)**—Jay wants not only to meet others while traveling but also to share experiences with them. This theme would allow her to do so.

From these themes, you could start to combine different ideas and think of possible solutions to the problem to solve. You could even brainstorm again, using the themes as a guide to focus the ideation. You have so many possibilities!

Sketching

For this exercise, I was inspired by the brainstorming session around the problem to solve. From that session, I saw a lot of ideas around socialization and exploring things like a local, two things that our persona Jay really values. Jay wants her trip to be her own—to explore things as she wishes, to opt into activities that she wants to participate in. At the same time, she wants to connect with others—other travelers, and people who live in the areas she visits.

Jay would benefit from a short-form, flexible, customized way of connecting with other people—mostly around activities. See the sights, book a tour, have drinks with friends—something that she can opt into with as much or as little time as she chooses to dedicate to it, all on her schedule.

To satisfy this need, I decided to explore a product that would let Jay meet up with others and have short excursions in the areas she travels to. Maybe see a show, do a walking tour, eat some local cuisine, whatever she wants to do.

For our sketching exercise, I used the crazy 8s method (FIGURE A.4.3) to visualize some of these options. First, I folded a piece of paper into eight sections, then I timed myself for eight minutes and drew some possibilities.

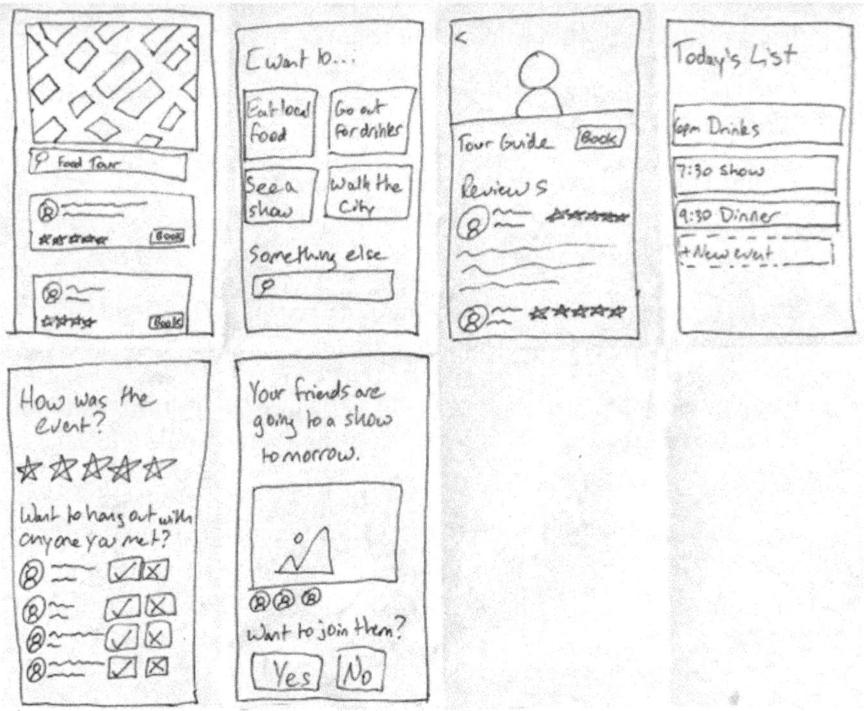

FIGURE A.4.3 The sketches from my crazy 8s activity.

For this exercise, I couldn't fill up the paper with the eight minutes I gave myself. That's OK—you don't need a full piece of paper to start exploring the idea. You could also give yourself more time if you really want to have those eight ideas.

Going from left to right, starting at the upper-left corner, I began by thinking of how Jay would use this service. I thought of a map view, with a search she conducted looking for food tours. You see a map, a search bar, and some results of the search with reviews of each of those tours. She has the option to book one if she likes.

The next sketch shows Jay searching by topic, in some sort of card view. This could be filters, or a way into the search screen you saw in the first sketch—I'm not sure yet. That's OK too—this is an exploration. There are a few pre-populated search topics that are most common for our users, and a search bar in case Jay wants something else.

The third sketch shows the profile of one of the locals—a tour guide that offers experiences in this product. The guide has a picture, a name, reviews, and the ability to book for an activity. It would probably help confidence and safety (things Jay cares about) if you add a piece of verification, like a check-mark or a label that says this is an authentic user of this product.

The fourth sketch shows Jay's calendar—the things she has signed up for and plans on doing that day. It's like other calendars, so I didn't feel like doing anything too special here—the app may or may not need some custom cal-endar options. Perhaps you could use a native phone app instead of a custom calendar option in the product.

The fifth sketch asks for a follow-up from Jay after an event. This type of feedback will help you know what events to recommend to Jay at a later date, signals the quality of the events to other users, and allows Jay to rate her favorite activities. It's also the perfect moment to foster additional connec-tion, sharing the profiles of everyone who was in the event with her. If Jay meets someone and doesn't get their contact info, she can follow up here and make friends during her trip—another of her goals.

Finally, the last sketch shows an event some of her friends are going to. It's a way for Jay to reconnect with those friends and continue experiencing things with others.

All these sketches are participatory for Jay—none of these are things she must do. Rather, they serve to satisfy her needs to connect, on her terms, with the people around her for local, authentic experiences.

Overall, not a bad ideation session for eight minutes, right?

Mind Mapping

For my additional ideation exercise, I chose to build off the idea that I've been working from for the last two exercises: a travel app that allows people to connect with others for activities. I realized I don't have too many activi-ties planned out to populate the app with, so it's hard to contextualize what people will actually do when using the app to find events. It's hard to build without content, so I figured I should think of some activities to help tell the story of using the product and sell the vision of creating it.

I need to generate a lot of ideas based on relationships between concepts. Sounds like a mind map would be perfect for this exercise. For this exercise, I used a product called Whimsical[1]—it's one of my favorite digital ideation tools.

I started by listing out the beginning point for the mind map—the concept of an activity. From there, I began to think of activities that someone could do on a trip. I thought of one or two, like going to a museum or eating some food. I realized I'd need some higher-level categories for each activity to fit into, so I wrote down three categories to capture the basic ideas I was coming up with: Move, See, and Eat (**FIGURE A.4.4**).

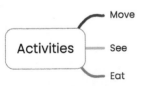

FIGURE A.4.4 The next step for my mind map was high-level categories.

Next, I started to slot some activities into each of these categories (**FIGURE A.4.5**). I had museums and food, and I started to think of more and more things to do:

- Sit on a bus
- Walk around a city
- Watch a show
- Visit a museum
- Have an authentic meal at a local's house
- Meet friends for drinks
- Eat street food

FIGURE A.4.5 The next iteration of my mind map, with more activities filled in.

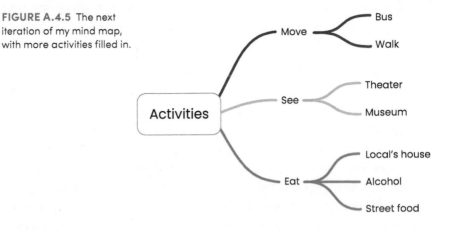

---

1 www.whimsical.com

As I filled in these activities, I realized I needed another level of hierarchy for some of the categories. There were really two types of movement—one where the person is doing the moving (like walking) and one where the person is being moved (like being on a bus). Additionally, there were multiple types of activities in the Eat category—locations and types of food. I split out these sections and filled them in with more ideas (FIGURE A.4.6).

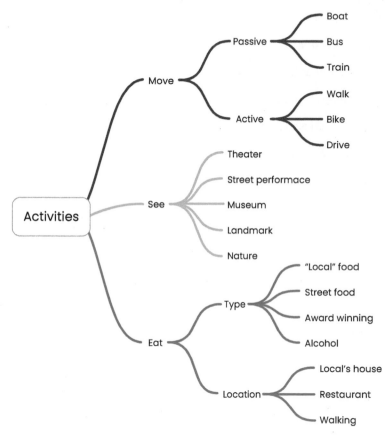

FIGURE A.4.6 My mind map, split out into greater detail and with even more activities.

I could have kept going at this point, thinking of more categories and ideas that fit into those, but this felt like a good start for some of the content that could find its way into my product. The purpose of this ideation was to think of things that Jay could choose from when on her trip, and I came up with 18 different ideas across three major themes. This felt like a successful ideation that fit into the rest of the work I've done for this project.

Car Method

For this exercise, I wanted to think of all the things that could be added to the product idea we've been working on in this chapter. I decided to use the Cars method to think of the smallest, largest, and middle ground options for this product.

I started by listing all the features I could think of for the product:

- User profile creation

- Payment processing

- Calendar view of user's activities

- Verified tour guide profiles

- Search for activities to participate in

- See list of participants

- Ability to friend people after an activity

- Suggest activities based on friends

- Rate activities

- Suggest activities based on user's reviews

- Custom activities created by and sponsored by the company

From this list, I grouped things by related concepts and shifted a few things around. I came up with the following categories:

User related:

- User profile creation

Activity related:

- Search for activities to participate in

- Verified tour guide profiles

- Calendar view of user's activities

- Payment processing

- Custom activities created by and sponsored by the company

Social:

- See list of participants

- Ability to friend people after an activity

Recommendations related:

- Rate activities

- Suggest activities based on friends

- Suggest activities based on user's reviews

Some things felt more critical than others to the product functioning well, so I moved a few around and split out each section into what felt like logical cutoff points for a small, medium, and large size for the product.

Compact:

- User profile creation

- Search for activities to participate in

- Verified tour guide profiles

- Calendar view of user's activities

- Payment processing

Midsize:

- Rate activities

- See list of participants

- Ability to friend people after an activity

Cadillac:

- Suggest activities based on friends

- Suggest activities based on user's reviews

- Custom activities created by and sponsored by the company

Finally, I put all these ideas together in a one-page table (TABLE A.4.1) to make it clear what features I'm recommending based on how much I want to invest in the product. Note that the table uses colored bullets to show the compounding features.

TABLE A.4.1 Features I'd Propose for This Product

SIZE	FEATURE SET	VISION
Compact	• User profile creation • Search for activities to participate in • Verified tour guide profiles • Calendar view of user's activities • Payment processing	A lightweight, simple version of the product that allows users to create an account and participate in activities
Midsize	• User profile creation • Search for activities to participate in • Verified tour guide profiles • Calendar view of user's activities • Payment processing • Rate activities • See list of participants • Friend people after an activity	A more mature product that includes social features allowing users to connect more easily
Cadillac	• User profile creation • Search for activities to participate in • Verified tour guide profiles • Calendar view of user's activities • Payment processing • Rate activities • See list of participants • Friend people after an activity • Suggest activities based on friends • Suggest activities based on reviews • Custom activities created by and sponsored by the company	The most developed version of the product, using data to power recommendations and content created by the company to introduce even more activities for users to participate in

Note that this is a list of ideas—you aren't committed to these at this point. Rather, this is a form of prioritization that will help you in your design thinking process. You could visualize each version of the product, as outlined here, then see which would produce the best user experience relative to the cost to build it.

CHAPTER 5: PROTOTYPING SOLUTIONS

Task Flows

For my task flow, I wanted to think about one of the core aspects of the product I built—the ability to find and book experiences. The way I've designed and prioritized my product coming out of ideation was to have Jay socialize with others through the context of experiences. By allowing Jay to find and book experiences with locals and other travelers, she could directly connect with others and potentially develop those connections further should she choose to after an activity.

Therefore, one core pillar of my product is finding and booking experiences—and that's the flow I want to start with. I'll be approaching the next few exercises in this book looking to make this flow as good as I can—from planning it out to visualizing it to eventually testing it with users.

FIGURE A.5.1 outlines the high-level steps Jay would need to take to book an experience using my product. To book an event, Jay would take the following steps:

AUTHOR'S NOTE A product is more than one task flow. Realistically, to test all the aspects of my product I'd want flows for the other things in it as well—things like creating an account, managing Jay's schedule, and connecting with people after an activity is over. For now, though, I want to focus on a single aspect of the product to make things less complex (though those other elements of the product are still on my mind).

Search for an event

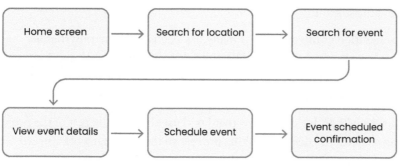

FIGURE A.5.1. A task flow for finding and booking an event in the app I'm designing.

Home screen—First, Jay needs to be in the product. I had her start at the home screen, though if I make the next step accessible from anywhere in the product (such as putting it in the bottom navigation of the app) then she could start from a lot of places. For simplicity (and testing my eventual prototype), I decided to start here.

Search for location—Next, Jay needs to search for an event, so she would interact with some search call-to-action (such as, a button that says search in the navigation of the app). To find an event, however, she first needs to start from a location—that way, the product can narrow down the results and not force Jay to look in a lot of different places she might not be going to. This will make it easier for the product to surface relevant results and for Jay to look through them.

Search for event—Once she's selected a location, Jay needs to select an event to look at so she can book it. There may be multiple sub-steps here, such as selecting from a category of events to look through or typing in an additional search query to find the specific event she wants to attend. At this level of planning, however, I can simplify and look at a higher-level picture of the steps Jay needs to take.

View event details—After Jay finds an event that's interesting to her, she will need to see its details to make the decision as to whether she wants to go on the event. Here, the product can satisfy her wants and needs by showing reviews, other friends that are attending the event, who the tour guide is, how long the event is, and so on—all the details she needs to decide.

Schedule event—When Jay has made up her mind and wants to attend the event, the product needs to allow her to schedule it. Again, this may be multiple steps—choose a date, choose a time, look at her schedule, and book it. For planning purposes, I can stay a little higher level with this one as well and say that she "schedules" it.

Event scheduled confirmation—Finally, Jay needs confirmation that her event has been booked. This could be multiple steps, like a confirmation screen and viewing it in some sort of calendar, or even something as simple as a pop-up window or a notification. I'll figure that out when I start designing.

Now I have my high-level task flow that I will use through the rest of the prototyping phase of the design thinking process so that you can work toward making the prototype.

Low-Fidelity Wireframes

To make low-fidelity wireframes, I need some sense of the steps a user will take in my product. Looking back at the last exercise, I made a task flow that maps out the steps Jay needs to take to book an experience, as shown in Figure A.5.1.

To visualize these steps, I made some sketches using the crazy 8s method of folding a piece of paper and giving myself all the time I needed to draw each step in the process, as shown in **FIGURE A.5.2**.

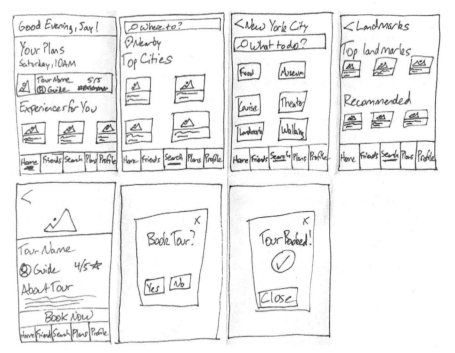

FIGURE A.5.2 Low-fidelity wireframes that represent how Jay might book an event in my product.

These sketches represent the task flow from the last exercise. However, I've added some more detail now that I need to start thinking about where the content and interactions will be on each screen.

1. Home screen—For the home screen (the first box in Figure A.5.2), I thought it'd be nice to greet Jay with a welcome message whenever she opens the app. There's also a preview of her schedule (the next event coming up) and some recommended events she might want to investigate. She can use the navigation at the bottom of the screen to get around the product too—things like a "friends" section for the people she meets during an event, a search option, a calendar (her "plans"), and a profile to manage her settings and presence in the app.

I want Jay to search for an event; to get there, she'll click the search option in the bottom navigation.

2. Search for location—The search screen starts by asking for a location to narrow down the results. Jay can type one in the search box, hit the pin beneath it to search nearby, or tap one of the cards to search based on popular locations. I haven't figured out the content yet, but that's OK—I'll get there.

To progress, Jay needs to search for a specific city. In this example, I went with New York City.

3. **Search for event**—The next screen shows more options for a New York City–based search. Jay can type in the search box, or she can choose a category, like Food, Museums, or Walking. For this flow, I decided for Jay to choose Landmarks.

4. **Select an event**—Once I got into visualizing the task flow, I realized there was another sub-step I wanted to sketch out for the eventual prototype to make sense. Within the category results, Jay needs to browse for an event that she wants to participate in. To do so, she looks at a list of Top Landmarks and Recommended Landmarks. Choosing one of these cards would take her to the next step in the flow.

5. **View event details**—After selecting an event from her options, Jay can now see all the details of that event—the name, the tour guide, the ratings, and more details about the tour. She has a lot of information that helps her make up her mind. If she feels good about the experience, she can book it by tapping the Book Now button at the bottom of the screen.

6. **Schedule event**—I didn't go into too many details in this wireframe— rather, I said to myself "she'll book it somehow" and represented that using a modal. In reality, she would need to choose a date, a time, and compare that to her schedule. To visualize the concept, however, this was all I needed at this level to make sure the task flow was working and could be represented.

If Jay says yes, she'll see her booking confirmation in the next screen.

7. **Event scheduled confirmation**—As with the last wireframe, I decided to broadly represent the concept of confirmation using the same modal with a check mark. In one way or another, the product would communicate to Jay that she has indeed booked the event. This might be a notification, a pop-up, or some other interaction pattern that clearly lets Jay know she's all set for the event.

There are plenty of details I still need to figure out—the specific content that goes into each screen, the registration details, and the visual styles of some of these elements, such as what icons represent the navigation best. That comes later. For now, I've accomplished what I needed to for low fidelity— begin visualizing the product, make sure the flow makes sense, and have just enough information and detail to move on to the next phase of prototyping: mid fidelity.

Mid-Fidelity Wireframes

Let's continue with my app—the traveler's app that allows people to book experiences and connect with attendees. The low-fidelity wireframes looked like Figure A.5.2.

I went into Whimsical to convert these from low fidelity to mid fidelity. **FIGURES A.5.3** and **A.5.4** show where I landed.

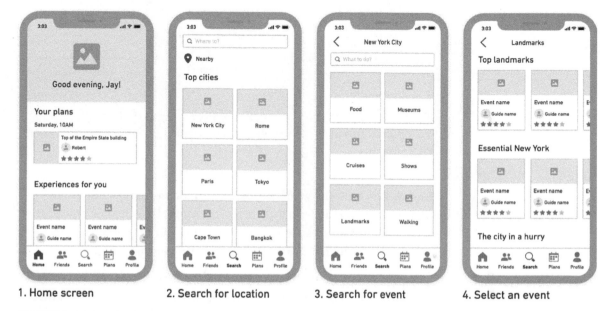

1. Home screen   2. Search for location   3. Search for event   4. Select an event

FIGURE A.5.3 Mid-fidelity wireframes for my traveler app.

1. Home screen—The home screen has the same information as the low fidelity version but has a bit more detail around the spacing and the quality of the image—it's easier to follow than the sketches from before. I've also made some choices around the icons that I'd like to use to represent each option in the navigation.

2. Search for location—On the search page, I've filled in some of the places Jay can choose without having to type into the search box. I decided to look up the most popular cities in the world and put them as options in my prototype—it adds some realism to the flow that you can see is taking more shape.

FIGURE A.5.4 My
mid-fidelity wireframes
for my traveler app.

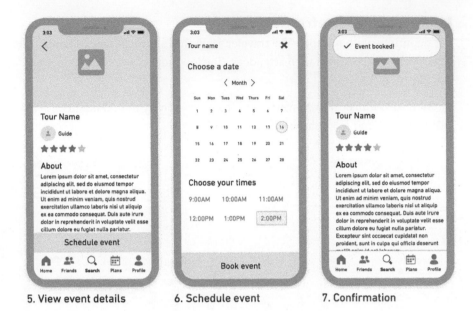

5. View event details   6. Schedule event   7. Confirmation

3. Search for event—As with the last screen, I focused on the things Jay would search by and added a little more specificity. Jay would technically be looking at multiple results, so I made everything plural. "Shows" sounded more appropriate than "Theaters," so I made that change as well.

4. Select an event—For this screen, I added some categories so I could get a sense of what types of events that Jay would be able to choose from. Things like "Top Landmarks" and "Essential New York" made a lot of sense to me as the things someone might want to do the most when visiting New York City. I added a category called "The city in a hurry," assuming Jay might not want to spend all her time on a tour.

5. View event details—This screen stayed mostly the same between the low- and mid-fidelity versions—I added some more structure to the page to figure out its layout and filled in the description with lorem ipsum placeholder text.

6. Schedule event—This is the page that got the most updates. Instead of the modal from before, I fleshed out the details of confirming the date and time. This screen will probably have multiple states in my prototype, so I may need to make a few more screens that represent each selection the user makes while testing the flow. That can come at the last step before making the prototype.

7. Confirmation—Finally, this screen changed a bit as well. It's the same screen as the event details screen, except there's a notification at the top of the screen that shows Jay she booked the event. I felt like I could reuse design elements to communicate this to the user and I don't need anything too wild here—a simple banner notification will do.

Now that I have my mid-fidelity wireframes, I can move on to the next step, high-fidelity wireframes.

High-Fidelity Wireframes

To create my high-fidelity wireframes, I used my mid-fidelity wireframes as a starting point (Figure A.5.4).

From here, I was able to re-create each of these screens (using Figma) in high fidelity (FIGURES A.5.5 and A.5.6) because I had a good blueprint for the content, functionality, and sections of the product I was trying to design.

Did you notice how each screen from the mid-fidelity version made it over to the high-fidelity version without much change? This is because I spent so much time in planning the details of each screen in low and mid fidelity. When I got to high fidelity, it felt like all that was left to do was to "color it in" by choosing images, content, and iconography that reflected my goals for the product.

1. Home screen—I added the content Jay would expect to see—things related to the city she's currently visiting, New York. She sees her next plan, which is to visit the Empire State Building. She also sees some recommended experiences—a row of cards that are Experiences for you and a row of cards that are the Best of New York.

2. Search for location—On the search tab in the bottom navigation bar, Jay can see locations she can search by. I've taken the content from the mid-fidelity wireframes and added more imagery to support the idea of those locations. These images will ideally entice Jay to explore different places and get excited about the possibility of traveling to them.

3. Search for event—Similarly for this page, I've added pictures of the things Jay can do once she searches by location—in this case, New York City. These images give Jay a sense of what to expect and continue to foster that sense of excitement.

Jay's looking for something to do related to the famous places in New York City, so she taps Landmarks.

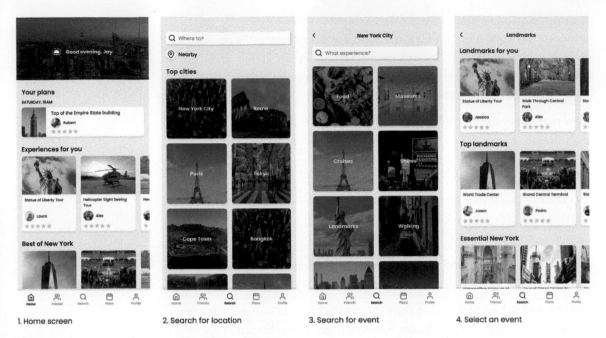

1. Home screen   2. Search for location   3. Search for event   4. Select an event

FIGURE A.5.5 My high-fidelity wireframes for my traveler app.

4. Select an event—For this screen, I added a lot more content so it could feel more real—the mid-fidelity wireframes didn't have a lot of content planned out for this screen.

Here, Jay can see a lot of different landmarks to consider—places like Central Park, the World Trade Center, and Grand Central Terminal. Jay has a lot of options! She decides to check out the Statue of Liberty tour.

5. View event details—When designing this screen, I realized I'd left out a few possible details that could make the product feel more real and be beneficial for Jay—things like the ability to save the tour for investigation later (the bookmark beneath the picture) and the amount of time the tour would take to complete (the clock beneath the tour guide photo). These help Jay plan her trip.

Jay reads the description of the event, looks at how much time it would take, then proceeds to schedule the experience by tapping the button at the bottom of the page.

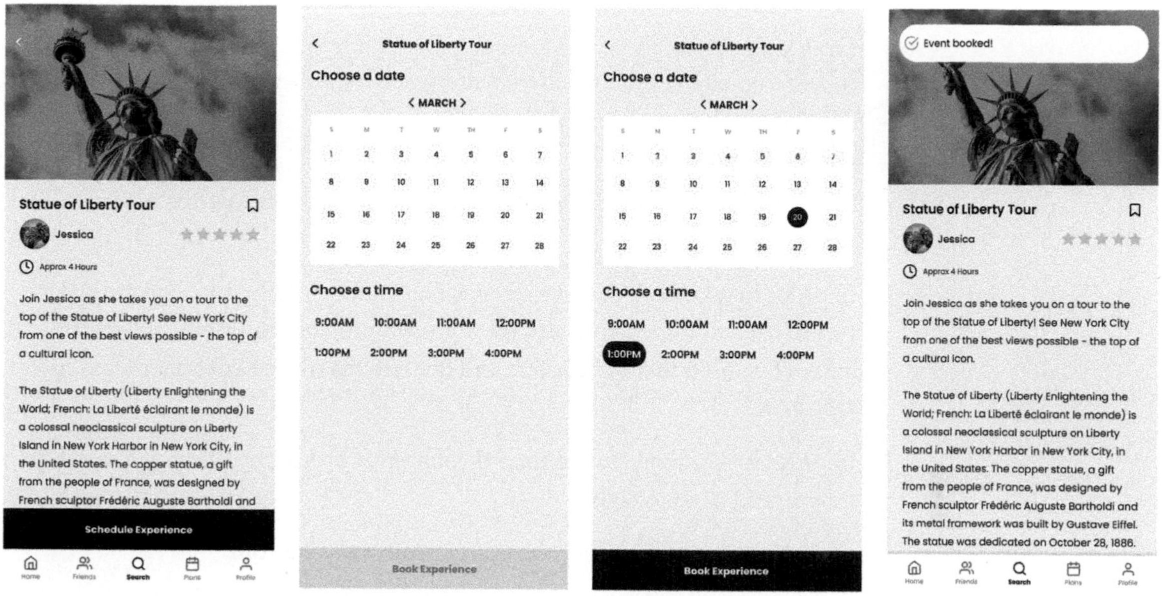

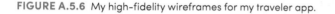

5. View event details   6. Schedule event   7. Select schedule details   8. Confirmation

FIGURE A.5.6 My high-fidelity wireframes for my traveler app.

6. Schedule event—This is the first of two screens needed in the prototype to communicate what's happening. The first of these is the empty state for scheduling an event—no dates or times are selected. Jay would first choose the date that works for her, then choose the time from that date (and times would reset based on each day's availability).

7. Select schedule details—Jay proceeds to choose a date and then a time to book the experience. As she selects each option, those selections are reflected by changing color (from no color to a black fill). This is to communicate to Jay that she has made a selection and that the system has registered that selection.

After selecting her options, Jay proceeds to tap the button at the bottom that says Book Experience.

8. Confirmation—On the confirmation page, Jay sees a notification at the top that lets her know her experience has been booked. The notification would slide in, then slide back out after a few seconds. If she taps it, she can go to her Plans to see all her booked experiences—but that's not a necessary thing I need to design for my prototype, so I left that out for now.

That's it for my high-fidelity wireframes! This is enough to start testing the experience. Now, there's just one step left before this step of design thinking is over—connecting all these screens together into a prototype.

Prototype

From the last exercise, I have my high-fidelity screens (Figures A.5.5 and A.5.6).

In order to take each of these screens and connect them into a prototype, I went back to Figma and used their prototyping capabilities to select the points I wanted the user to click and the screens those clicks lead to, as in FIGURE A.5.7.

In order for someone to progress through this prototype, these are the steps they would need to take:

1. **Home screen**—Click the search icon at the bottom.

2. **Search for location**—Click the New York City card.

3. **Search for event**—Click the Landmarks card.

4. **Select an event**—Click the Statue of Liberty Tour card.

5. **View event schedule**—Click the Schedule Experience button at the bottom.

6. **Schedule event**—Click the calendar.

7. **Select schedule details**—Click the Book Experience button on the bottom.

8. **Confirmation**—No inputs required (it's the end of the prototype).

And that's it! My prototype is ready for usability testing.

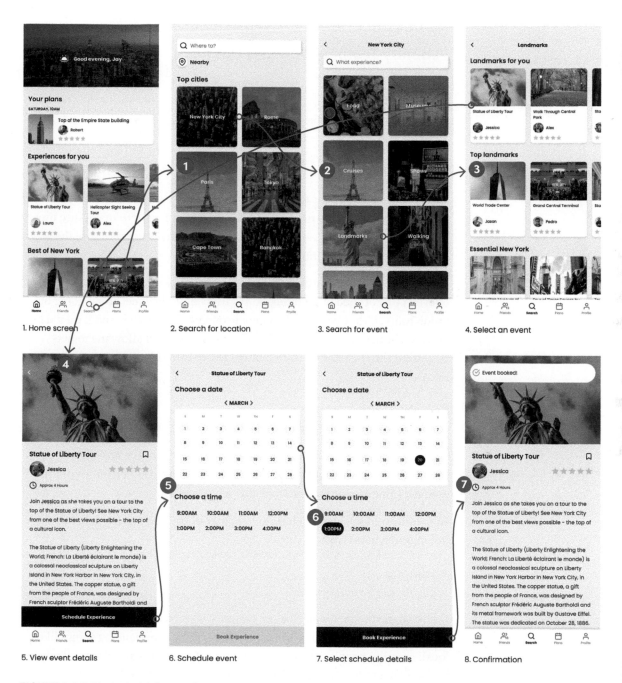

1. Home screen

2. Search for location

3. Search for event

4. Select an event

5. View event details

6. Schedule event

7. Select schedule details

8. Confirmation

FIGURE A.5.7 The high-fidelity wireframes, connected by arrows that indicate where someone clicks and where that leads to.

Usability Testing: Plan and Define

For my version of the solo traveler project, I created the prototype in Figure A.5.7.

Let's see if I can define the parameters of my test.

Purpose

What do you want to accomplish with your test?

The purpose of my test is to determine the usability of one of the core flows of my product—the ability to find and book an event. I want to make sure users know how to find events and can book them, so I need to make sure the way I've structured that is intuitive for people.

I'd also like to probe a little into the value proposition of some of the features I haven't prototyped out. I intend to ask users how they feel about going on group tours, if they want to meet people during those tours, and if they'd be open to connecting with them after the tours. That will allow me to better design the "Friends" feature I intend to put into this product were I to release it.

Scope

What part(s) of the product will you be testing, and what are their flows?

The scope of my test is directly related to the purpose—the core flow of finding an event and booking it. I will not be testing other elements of this product (it's just as important to define what is not in scope).

In the future, I will need to test the usability of the Friends feature, but that's not in scope of this test.

Audience

Who will you be testing with?

I'd like to test with people like my persona, Jay—so people who like to travel, travel alone, and want to maximize their travel by experiencing things like a local, meeting people, and seeing the sights. To find this audience, I'll rely on my personal network and social networks to find participants.

Moderation

Will you be conducting the test, or will you use an external service to do the testing for you?

I'll be there. I don't want to use a service to do unmoderated testing, because part of the purpose of this test is to ask users what they would want in social features and whether or not that would be valuable.

Remote

Will you be present with the users, or will you connect virtually?

I'd like to do this testing remotely—I'll be able to select from a wider user pool, and I don't have a facility where I can conduct this testing more easily.

Software/Hardware

What technologies do you need to test with? Do users need to bring devices to test on?

To accomplish this, as of this writing, I'd use Figma. My designs and prototype are already there. I can create a share link that I give to users to test with. I'd need video conferencing software that lets me share my screen, like Zoom or Google Meet. I'd also ask that users connect with their laptops or computers, to test the prototype. It would be better to test on phones, but the reality of testing prototypes is that everyone has a different phone size and I'd need to make different prototypes for different phones, which is a little too much overhead for this project.

Finally, to help record the conversation a bit more easily, I would use Otter.ai to get transcripts of each conversation. It will be easier to capture quotes that way than by having to listen to each video, trying to find what users said. If I'm using Zoom, I may use their recording software instead.

AUTHOR'S NOTE
One time, I was testing prototypes with a user, and they connected with their phone instead of their laptop. The design was too small, and they couldn't see all the buttons I wanted them to interact with. I had to adjust the prototype on the fly to make sure the interactive elements were visible on their screen. I try to avoid that scenario as often as I can by testing the prototype ahead of time and requesting that users come with a specific device before the session, or providing that device myself.

Quantitative

What metrics will you track for quantitative results?

For the quantitative metrics that I'll track, I want to relate them to the purpose—can users get through the event booking flow? For that, I'll track:

- **Task completion**—What percentage of users were able to complete the task without assistance?

- **Error rate**—How many errors did a user make along the way toward completion?

- **Task satisfaction**—What number, on a scale from 1 to 5 (with 1 being the lowest), would users give this experience for their satisfaction with it?

- **Safety**—What number, on a scale from 1 to 5 (with 1 being the lowest), would users give this experience for their feeling of safety with it?

  For the safety question specifically, it would be nice to get some early signals about how confident and safe users would feel going to events with this product.

Qualitative

What metrics will you track for qualitative results?

For the quantitative metrics that I want to track, I'll relate them to the task flow in addition to the future of the product. I'll track the following aspects for this test:

- What did users like about this experience?

- What did users dislike about this experience?

- What would they want to add to this experience?

- For the Friends feature specifically, what would they want to see from that experience?

With the structure of the test in place, I feel confident that I can move on to recruiting for the test.

Usability Testing: Recruit and Conduct

For this exercise, you need to find users and test with them. To do so, you'll need to figure out what method you want to recruit with, then from there, conduct the testing.

Let's start by thinking about the script for my test. I'm going to go screen by screen through my prototype and write down the questions I want to ask about each screen. This will make sure that I'm prepared for the usability testing and that I know what I want users to do at each step in the process.

FIGURE A.6.1 is the homepage of the prototype and is designed to introduce the user to the product. I want to know what the user is thinking when they land here and what they think this product can do for them.

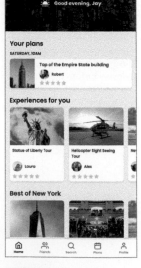

FIGURE A.6.1 The first screen in my prototype, the home page.

I'd ask the following questions:

- What are you seeing on this screen?

- What do you think this product can do for you?

- What would you want to interact with first?

I'd then direct them to the first step in the prototype, which is to search for events to look at. I hope they will interact with the search icon at the bottom, but before they click it, I'd ask:

- What would you expect to see on the next screen?

This question would expose a sense of expectations before they navigate to the next step.

The second screen in the prototype shows users what they can expect when starting a search. Given the number of activities in the product, they would need to narrow down by location before looking for activities. However, this may not be intuitive for users—they might start thinking about *what* they want to do rather than *where* they want to do them. I'd probe for that as users start to take in the search landing screen (**FIGURE A.6.2**).

I'd ask the following questions:

- What are you seeing on this screen?

- Does this match your expectations?

I'd then direct them to search for activities based in New York City and hope they interact with the first option that's present—the image that says New York City. Before they interact, I'd ask, again:

- What would you expect to see on the next screen?

On the third screen (**FIGURE A.6.3**), the user can access specific event categories.

I'd ask the following:

- What are you seeing now?

- Are these categories interesting to you?

- Do you feel that any categories are missing?

- Did you expect to search by city, then by category? Why or why not?

FIGURE A.6.2 The second screen of my prototype, the search landing page.

FIGURE A.6.3 The third screen in my prototype, which shows activities in a location.

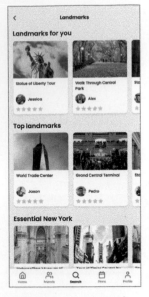

FIGURE A.6.4 The fourth screen of my prototype, which shows activities based on landmarks in New York City.

FIGURE A.6.5 The fifth screen in the prototype, which shows an activity detail page.

From there, I'd ask them to look for activities based on famous places in New York City. I'd avoid using the word "landmarks" (which is where I want them to go) because I don't want them to look for the specific word I say. Rather, I want them to find the concept I'm referring to.

Before they click anything, I'd ask:

- What would you expect to see on the next screen?

In general, this is a good question to ask before the user goes to the next screen, so that you can get a sense of what they expect and plan for it in your designs.

On the fourth screen (FIGURE A.6.4), the user can select a specific activity.

I'd ask the following questions:

- What are you seeing now?
- Does this match your expectations?

From there, I'd ask them to look at the Statue of Liberty tour, which would take them to the fifth screen in the prototype (FIGURE A.6.5). I'd ask, again:

- What would you expect to see on the next screen?

On this screen, I'd want to know the following:

- What are you seeing on this screen?
- Is this information interesting to you? Is it valuable?
- What would make you interested in booking this experience?
- What would make you feel safe booking this experience?

The safety question is an important one—I identified earlier in the persona work that safety is crucial for my persona, so additional verification might be needed here to make users feel safer.

Once I get the answers to my questions for this screen, I'd move to the next step—the booking flow (FIGURE A.6.6).

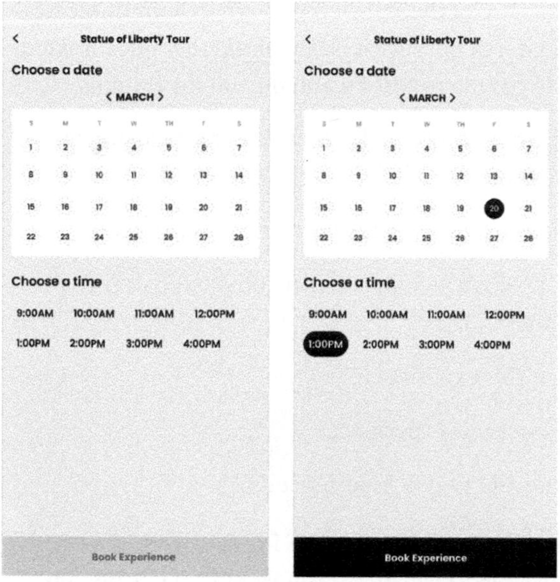

FIGURE A.6.6 The sixth and seventh screens in my prototype, the booking options screen before and after selections are made.

I'm bundling these two together questions-wise because they're very similar—they're the same screen, just different states of it. I need both screens for my prototype, but I can have the same question set for the two.

- What are you seeing on this screen?

- Are there any additional booking options you'd like to see?

- What would you expect after making all your selections here and moving on to the next step in the process?

These questions will allow me to better develop this screen in the future and help anticipate customer expectations once I make my product.

After the user finishes booking the experience, I have one last screen in the prototype (**FIGURE A.6.7**). Before clicking Book Experience, I'd ask, one last time:

- What would you expect to see on the next screen?

Here, I'd ask the user the following:

- What are you seeing now?

- What did you expect to see?

- Do you know if your event has been booked?

FIGURE A.6.7 The eighth screen in my prototype, the confirmation results.

I'm curious if the banner at the top of the screen is enough to communicate that the event has been booked. I'm not sure it is, so asking that question outright is important to know if I got the results I wanted from my designs.

Since this is the last screen in the prototype, I'd then ask some closing questions about the overall experience:

- On a scale from 1 to 5, how satisfied were you with this product?

- On a scale from 1 to 5, how safe would you feel going to an event booked using this product?

- What did you like about this experience?

- What did you dislike about this experience?

- What would you want to add to this experience?

- Imagine that you could interact with the other people from this tour and add them as friends. What would you want to see from that experience?

- Is there anything else you'd like to share?

These closing questions are important. They let me know how successful and meaningful the flow was for the user. They give me signals as to what they liked and didn't like so I can make adjustments. Finally, they let me know more about how I can define and evolve the Friends feature, which is a crucial component of this product.

I also offer an opportunity for the user to share anything they'd like to about the experience. Not all users share afterward, but some do, and they usually have really good insights.

Now that I have my test plan complete, to test my designs I would try to find people to test with. I would reuse the screener survey from Chapter 2 to find my test participants, aiming for six people to test with. I'd use various social media outlets and communities to share the survey, such as LinkedIn, Facebook, and Slack. From there, people would take my survey and identify whether they want to be a part of testing, and I'd follow up with the best candidates to test with. After that, I'd test my designs and look at the results!

Usability Testing: Analyze Results

After conducting usability testing with six participants, I made the stoplight chart shown in TABLE A.6.1.

TABLE A.6.1 Stoplight Chart for Usability Testing Results

	U1	U2	U3	U4	U5	U6	AVERAGE
Satisfaction	5	3	4	4	5	5	4.33
Safety	5	2	4	3	4	3	3.50
Completion Rate	100%	100%	100%	100%	100%	100%	100%
Errors	0	2	1	1	0	0	0.67
City then Activity	✔	/	✔	/	/	✔	/
Event Felt Safe	✔	✗	✔	/	✔	/	/
Satisfied by Booking	✔	/	✔	✔	✔	✔	✔
Saw Notification	✔	✗	✗	✗	✔	✔	/

I structured this table to best demonstrate the results of each part of the usability test. The columns represent each user, followed by an average of the overall sentiment or results of all users. The rows represent insights regarding the usability testing, such as satisfaction scores, errors, or individual aspects of the test that I wanted to track.

- **Satisfaction**—This represents the satisfaction score users provided for the prototype. Overall, most users were satisfied with the product, which is a great sign that this product could help them with their needs.

- **Safety**—This represents how safe they felt going to the actual event. This result was lower, in part because some users didn't feel like there were enough assurances or information to verify the tour guide or that they'd be in a safe environment. Some sort of verification process or signal might help here.

- **Completion Rates**—This represents completion rates. No one had issues completing the task, though there were a few snags represented later in the table.

- **Errors**—This tracks errors; in this case, there were a few errors where things could have been more clear or more visible to the user, such as the notification at the end of the flow or the process of choosing the city first when searching. There isn't much I can do about the latter (it's a limitation of the product's data) but for the former, I can improve the UI before launching the feature.

- **City then Activity**—This tracks whether users felt searching by city and then by event type was intuitive. This result was mixed—some users thought this was fine, but others would have preferred searching by activity first, as an activity would help determine where they wanted to travel.

- **Event Felt Safe**—This shows how many users thought the event would be safe to attend. Results were mixed here—the fact that this event was booked through a product helped improve user confidence, but there was no verification process and no reviews of the person taking people around. Additionally, there was no guarantee that the people who were also at the event would be safe, so there was some concern there as well. Additional verification methods—like a checkmark on the tour guide, seeing the profiles of who else was attending, or an onboarding to the app that caused the users to verify themselves—would make them feel more comfortable going to the event with others.

- **Satisfied by Booking**—This represents satisfaction with the booking options for the event. For the most part, people didn't feel like anything was missing there.

- **Saw Notification**—This shows who did or didn't see the notification. About half the users missed it (the notification somewhat blends into the background), so improving the animation and contrast of that notification will help others see it in the future.

Hopefully these results illustrate what you can work toward for your usability testing for your projects!

CHAPTER 7: IMPLEMENTING YOUR DESIGNS
User Stories

Let's take another look at my design solution in **FIGURE A.7.1**.

My solution is to allow solo travelers the ability to find events hosted by local tour guides and connect with that tour guide and other travelers to enhance the solo travel experience. To facilitate implementing this solution, I can write user stories that explain the tasks that solo travelers should be able to perform when using this product. Let's take another look at the formula in **FIGURE A.7.2**.

FIGURE A.7.1 High-fidelity wireframes for my traveler app.

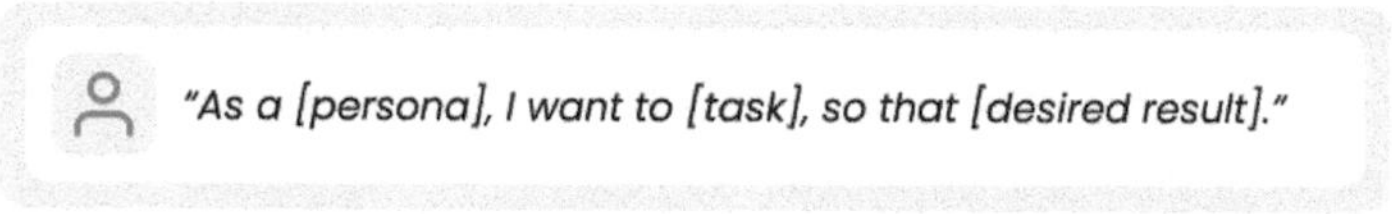

1. Home screen
2. Search for location
3. Search for event
4. Select an event
5. View event details
6. Schedule event
7. Select schedule details
8. Confirmation

FIGURE A.7.2 The formula for writing user stories.

"As a [persona], I want to [task], so that [desired result]."

To deliver the user stories needed for this solution, I'll have to think of all the tasks that solo travelers want to complete so that those tasks make their way into the product.

Let's start with events:

- *As a solo traveler, I want to find different types of events in the city I'm traveling to so that I can experience things like a local.*

- *As a solo traveler, I want to see an event's details, including reviews, a verified host, and the participants, so that I can feel comfortable going to this event.*

- *As a solo traveler, I want to leave feedback about an event so I can share my experiences with others and keep track of how much I liked an experience.*

These user stories feel like a good place to start. They cover the basics of event information—what events exist, what their perceived quality is, and how a user can provide feedback.

In writing these user stories, I've noticed that some of these stories include elements that aren't currently in the designs, like seeing other attendees on an event page, or the screens that represent what happens after an event is over. Sometimes, this happens—and that's OK. It's better to catch these now, rather than find out after you've committed a development team to the work (or worse, launched the product!). Part of the reason why you write user stories at some point during the project is to make sure you cover all these use cases so that the user experience is holistic and complete.

What about booking events and tracking the events solo travelers have participated in? Let's write some stories for those as well:

- *As a solo traveler, I want to be able to book an event (immediately or in advance) so that I can save my spot in an experience when I'm traveling.*

- *As a solo traveler, I want to see a schedule of my upcoming events so that I can plan my trip and confirm my attendance.*

- *As a solo traveler, I want to see a history of my past events so that I can be reminded of all my experiences.*

These user stories capture the event management experience—booking, scheduling, and history. This allows solo travelers to plan their trip, build a schedule, and reflect on their previous experiences.

What about a solo traveler's profile? How do solo travelers have a presence in the product, and how do they interact with one another? How can I be sure that the company can recall the information of the people that use the product to book events?

- *As a solo traveler, I want to be able create an account and log in to the product so that I can access my information.*

- *As a solo traveler, I want to have a public profile so that I can connect with the people I meet in an event before an event, during an event, and after the event is over.*

- *As a solo traveler, I want to keep track of the people I meet on events so that I can continue the conversation and develop deeper connections.*

These user stories cover the ability for users to establish accounts, manage profiles, and connect with other users outside of actual events. These speak to the need for users to have a presence in the product and use that presence to support making connections with others.

These are just a few of the user stories I could write for this project. They don't cover other essential elements required to make this solution work, such as the tour guide user experience (posting an event, having a tour guide profile, reading reviews about a tour guide's profile, and so on). There are other stories most likely required to make the traveler user experience function as well.

The truth is that there's a lot to making a brand-new product that goes outside of the core problem to solve—in this case, allowing solo travelers to maximize their travel experiences. While "creating a profile" isn't something that supports that problem, it's required for creating a functioning product. Making sure you write the user stories that enable a functioning product, in addition to addressing the problem to solve, is all a part of creating user stories.

User Flow

To make my user flow, I decided to start from my Chapter 5 task flow from the Appendix (**FIGURE A.7.3**).

Book an event

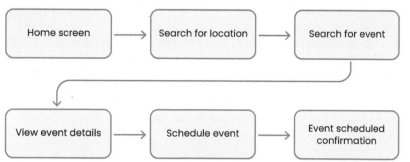

FIGURE A.7.3 A task flow for finding and booking an event.

This is a great baseline to start thinking about all the logic I want to capture in my user flow—the journey a user goes down when booking an event. I thought about additional elements, like the app surfacing results based on the user's location—whether or not there are any search results based on a location—and conflicts the user may have if they try to book two events at the same time. The user flow for this journey is in **FIGURE A.7.4**.

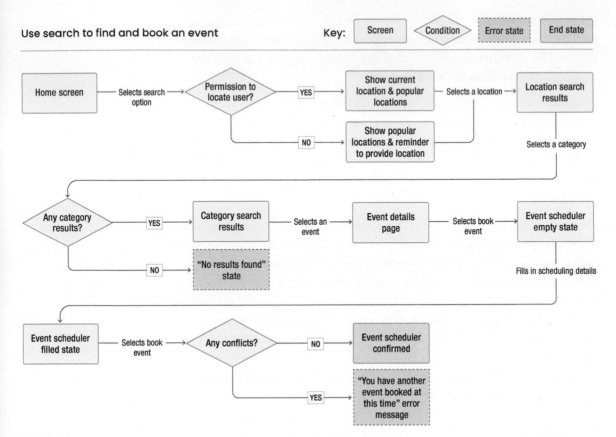

Use search to find and book an event

Key: Screen | Condition | Error state | End state

Home screen —Selects search option→ Permission to locate user? —YES→ Show current location & popular locations —Selects a location→ Location search results

Permission to locate user? —NO→ Show popular locations & reminder to provide location

Selects a category

Any category results? —YES→ Category search results —Selects an event→ Event details page —Selects book event→ Event scheduler empty state

Any category results? —NO→ "No results found" state

Fills in scheduling details

Event scheduler filled state —Selects book event→ Any conflicts? —NO→ Event scheduler confirmed

Any conflicts? —YES→ "You have another event booked at this time" error message

FIGURE A.7.4 A user flow for using the search function to find and book an event.

A lot has changed from the task flow! What was so easily represented at a high level became complicated once I got into the specifics and thought about all the edge cases that could come from it. I now have conditional logic (represented by diamonds) and error states (represented by red boxes) to help show additional possibilities that could happen to the user as they move through this flow.

To transition from task flow to user flow, I included a few new elements as well. Outside of the new shapes, the steps a user takes are on the arrows that link between screens and states. This helps separate what the user does versus what the system does and makes actions and destinations clearer to someone reading this flow. I've also included a key in the upper-right corner—contextually, I'd hope that each element of this user flow makes sense to the reader, but I went ahead and described each shape in the key in case it doesn't.

Style Guides

Working from my high-fidelity designs, I took the main themes from those screens and put them into a high-level overview of my visual-design decisions, as shown in FIGURE A.7.5.

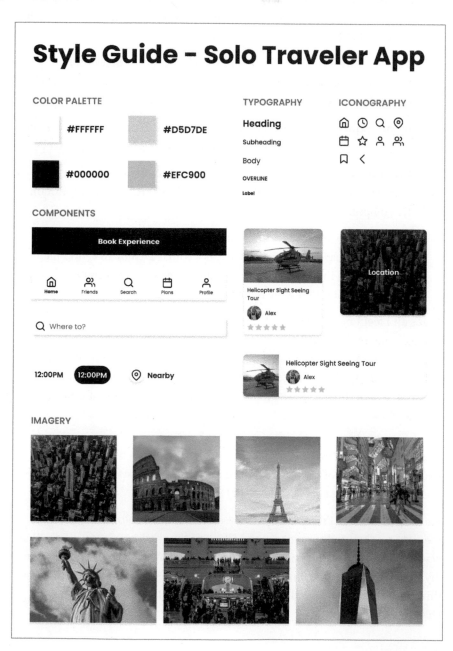

FIGURE A.7.5 A style guide for the solo traveler app.

In my style guide, I hit the core elements of my designs:

- **Color**—I use three main colors in my design: black, white, and gray. I do have some components that are yellow (the reviews on the cards), so I add that to the color styles as well. Note that I'm not counting the colors on images, since that's not a part of the UI system, but rather the content that the system surfaces to the user.

- **Typography**—I use one font family: Poppins. From that font family, I have a heading, a subheading, a body, an overline, and a label classification, all of which happen at different points in my designs.

- **Iconography**—I have one family of icons, from Feather Icons, and I use several in my designs. They all have a similar weight, style, and feel.

- **Components**—I include several types of components. I have my buttons, app bar, search field, and cards. These are the most common UI components in my designs.

- **Imagery**—I wanted to include some images, especially since this product so heavily relies on the places a solo traveler can visit. I include both location imagery (generally a square card in my designs) and event imagery (generally a wide rectangle in my designs).

That's all I feel I need for my style guide at this level. I show off the smaller visual elements (like color, typography, and iconography), how those elements combine into components (like buttons, text fields, and cards), and the stunning visual imagery I rely on for my product (the locations and the events). Combined, these should give people a good sense of how my product feels.

Design Systems

I put together a list of my most common repeated elements and created styles and components for each, as shown in **FIGURE A.7.6**.

Starting at the top, I've created atoms—styles for each color in my designs, the typography used throughout the app, and the shadows on my cards. That way, I'll always have the same style, no matter where the element appears in my solution. If I want to change my primary color, for example, I can choose this master component and change the value, and then everything else will change automatically.

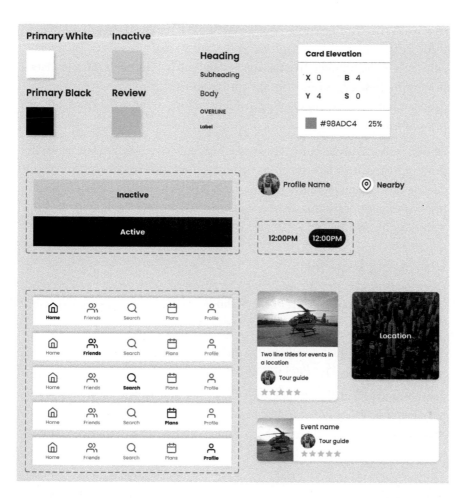

FIGURE A.7.6 The master components that power the design system for my solo traveler app.

Styles also help me design faster—instead of trying to remember which values I chose for my shadows on my cards, I can pull the style from here and apply it immediately.

Moving on to the next row of components, you can see things starting to get a little more complex, with molecules from my design system. Those colors from the styles start coming into play on the buttons. There is text combined with other design elements. You can see how the atoms are starting to combine into more complex elements.

If I were to update an atom used in these molecules, they'd update automatically as well and flow through the rest of my designs, keeping me consistent and helping me to design more quickly and at scale.

In the final row, you see organisms—even more complex components that incorporate atoms and molecules to make larger structures that are repeatedly used in the product, like the app bar and cards. Although the metadata in some of these organisms (like the cards) changes significantly across the product, the master components provide structure to those organisms so that I stay consistent.

Design systems can be quite robust and detailed, especially as your product grows and scales. In fact, there are designers dedicated to creating and maintaining the design systems of larger products so that they feel like a unified user experience. If you like this type of organization and thought applied to your designs, you may want to consider that as a career option in the future.

Delivering Designs

Working from the user stories I created from another exercise, I can visualize the screens required to deliver each of those stories. I'll demonstrate this for the user stories that come from the screens in my prototype.

> *As a solo traveler, I want to find different types of events in the city I'm traveling to so that I can experience things like a local.*

For a user to find an event, they need the ability to search for that event and see a list of search results. In **FIGURE A.7.7**, I show the screens needed to do that—from the home screen to the location search screen to the event search screen to a list of events in a location.

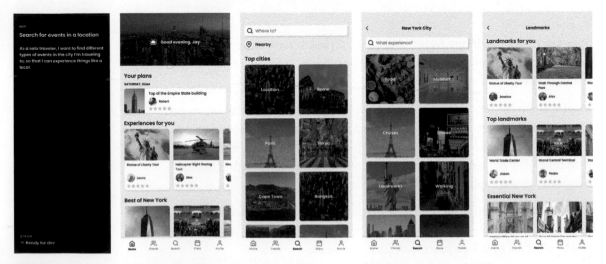

FIGURE A.7.7 The screens required to deliver the happy path for users looking for an event in a location.

A user could take other steps to find an event—they could just choose an event on the home screen, for example. There's also conditional logic to consider, like if there are no search results. To accomplish the happy path, however, and communicate my designs to the rest of the team, the path in Figure A.7.7 will suffice.

Let's try another user story.

> *As a solo traveler, I want to see an event's details, including reviews, a verified host, and the participants, so that I can feel comfortable going to this event.*

For this story, it's pretty simple—I need to show a list of events and then the information of a specific event. I'm able to do this in two screens, which makes this story easier to communicate (**FIGURE A.7.8**).

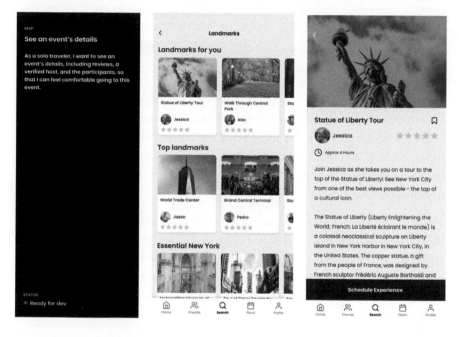

FIGURE A.7.8 The screens required to deliver the happy path for users who want to learn more about a specific event.

Let's try one last story.

> *As a solo traveler, I want to be able to book an event (immediately or in advance) so that I can save my spot in an experience when I'm traveling.*

For this story, it's also somewhat straightforward from my prototype—show the event, show the selection screens, then show the event being booked (FIGURE A.7.9).

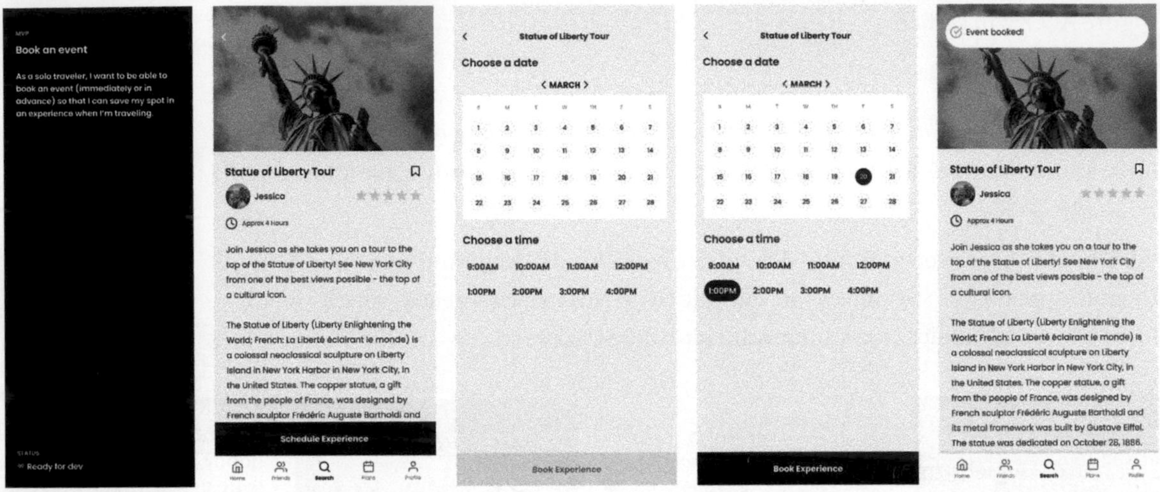

FIGURE A.7.9 The screens required to deliver the happy path for users to book an event.

However, I do want to say that this story has a little more to it that's not being captured here, mainly for the animations and state changes that go into making selections. Do buttons animate as the user taps them, like on the calendar or the time picker? How does the banner at the end of the flow appear and disappear on the screen?

These are nuances that can't be captured presenting the flow in this way and shows us that there may need to be supplemental forms of documentation when you deliver designs. Hopefully, in a real-world scenario you could reference motion guidelines or write separate documentation that outlines how systematic things enter and exit the screen, like presses of a button or notifications.

INDEX

brainstorming, 165–173
    best practices for, 170–171
    example of, 391–393
    explanation of, 166
    process overview for, 166–170
    situations for avoiding, 172
    tenets of good, 173
    themes based on, 169–170, 392–393
    time limits for, 168, 170–171
brand
    product perception related to, 37
    style guides portraying, 299
British Design Council, 10, 129
business goals, 39–40

C

Carbon, by IBM, 309
card sorting, 243
career development, 367–368
    See also jobs in UX design
Cars method, 195–197, 398–400
case studies, 322–333
    demonstrating expertise with, 332–333
    designing for non-readers, 328–331
    explanation and example of, 322–323
    images used in, 331–332
    showing your process in, 323–325
    storytelling framework for, 326–328
choices
    presenting too many, 60
    represented on flow charts, 285
Chrome browser, 35
clarifying questions, 344–345, 350
closed-response questions, 77–78, 80, 371
coded prototypes, 206, 207
coding, learning about, 353–354
cognitive load theory, 53–55
cognitive overload, 52–62
    cognitive load theory and, 53–55
    difficult-to-discover information and, 58–59
    explanation of, 52–53
    internal inconsistency and, 56–57
    overstimulation and, 60–61
    reducing for users, 55, 61–62
    too many choices and, 60
    unnecessary actions and, 57–58

collaboration
    Agile methodology and, 26
    prioritization based on, 195
    sketching process and, 175
color palette, 296–297
colors
    in stoplight charts, 264–265
    in style guides, 296–297, 426
    in UI design, 46
    in wireframes, 220, 224, 226, 228–229
combine theme, 187
communication
    developer involvement and, 352–353
    images in case studies for, 331–332
    sketching as form of, 175
comparator sources, 152, 156
competitive analysis, 71–72, 136, 149–155
    considering companies for, 152
    data collection for, 153
    defining the goal of, 151, 156
    explanation of, 149–151
    logistics gathering for, 152–153
    setting criteria for, 151–152
    summarizing results from, 154–155
    two styles of, 150–151
competitive research, 71–72, 136–156
    choosing the right technique for, 155
    competitive analysis for, 71–72, 136,
        149–155
    examples of, 387–391
    explanation of, 136–137
    external factors in, 140–143
    feature comparison for, 136–137
    internal factors in, 138–140
    lightning demos in, 143–149
    steps in process of, 137
    SWOT analysis for, 138, 142–143
completion rates, 267, 419
component library, 307
conceptual ideation, 161, 165–173
    brainstorming as, 165–173
    visual ideation and, 173
conducting usability tests, 245, 260–261,
    414–418
confidential information, 322
consistency in design process, 300–301
consultant mindset, 358
content design, 37

Discord groups, 77, 83, 98
discovery process, 11
divergent ideation, 181
documentation
    of project development, 23, 26
    of usability test results, 269, 274
do-it-yourself recruitment methods, 257–258
DoorDash, 42–43, 188
dot voting method, 192–193
Double Diamond process, 10–12, 129
double-barreled questions, 82
Dribbble design platform, 333–334
during-test questions, 259

E

ease of use, 34, 242
easy questions, 80
easy warmups, 178
efficiency of products, 242–243
Einstein, Albert, 130
eliminate theme, 190
empathizing, 63–108
    affinity mapping for, 103–107, 374–379
    in design thinking process, 12, 15–16, 63–64
    exercises and examples of, 370–379
    research types for, 64–75
    surveys used for, 70, 75–87, 370–371
    user interviews for, 66, 70, 87–103, 373–374
    writing problem statements and, 133–134
engineers, 352–355
    communicating with, 352–353
    delivering everything to, 354–355
    speaking the language of, 353–354
epics, 280–282
errors
    critical/non-critical, 253
    rates of usability, 242, 253, 267, 414, 419–420
evaluating usability, 243–244
evaluative research, 72–73
events, sequence of, 283
expectation setting, 349–350
experience
    empathy related to, 15
    questions about past, 92–93
experts, talking with, 16
exploratory questions, 345–346

external factors, 140–143
    opportunities, 140–141
    threats, 141–143
external recruitment methods, 257
eye tracking, 66

F

Facebook, 98, 418
facilitators
    for ideation session, 164
    for user interviews, 88
fast follow, 28
Feather icons, 227, 297
feature comparison, 136–137
feedback, 341–351
    asking questions with, 345–346, 350
    benefits of summarizing, 350–351
    context required for, 344–345, 348–349
    critiques offered as, 343–348
    example of structuring, 345
    giving to team members, 341–348
    personal response to, 351
    positive statements in, 346
    providing to designers, 342–343
    receiving from others, 348–351
    setting expectations for, 349–350
    summary of process for, 347–348
feelings/thoughts, journey map, 124–125, 384
fidelity levels, 201, 204–206
    coded or functional, 206, 217
    determining your use of, 231–233
    high fidelity, 206, 216, 225–233
    low fidelity, 204–205, 216–221, 231–232
    mid fidelity, 205, 216, 221–224, 232
    prototyping tools for, 207–208
Figma, 126, 167, 173, 206, 311–312
flow charts, 285–293
    choosing for projects, 292–293
    exercise on creating, 293
    explanation of, 285–286
    implementation facilitated with, 293
    task flows as, 286–287
    user flows as, 287–290, 423–424
    wireflows as, 291–292
flow-based processes
    for ideation, 181
    for organizing screens, 314–318

images
    in case studies, 331–332
    in personas, 113–114, 380
    in sketches, 177
    in style guides, 295, 426
    in UI design, 48–49
    in wireframes, 227
implementation, 275–320, 420–430
    art and science of, 275–276
    delivery of designs, 311–318, 428–430
    design systems for, 299–311, 313, 426–428
    in design thinking process, 10, 13, 19,
        275–277
    examples of working with, 420–430
    exercises related to, 284, 293, 299, 310–311
    flow charts for, 285–293, 423–424
    linear vs. iterative approaches to, 20–21
    style guides for, 294–299, 425–426
    user stories for, 278–284, 420–423
improvement tracking, 356
inconsistent designs, 300
indirect competitors, 152
industry roles. *See* jobs in UX design
information
    confidential, 322
    difficult-to-discover, 58–59
initiatives, 280–282
in-person testing, 250, 413
insights, journey map, 125–126, 385
inspiration
    in IDEO's human-centered design, 9–10
    lightning demos for, 143–146
interactivity
    color indicating, 46, 56, 229–230
    of prototypes, 202
internal factors, 138–140
    strengths, 139
    weaknesses, 139–140
internal inconsistency, 56–57
internal recruitment methods, 256–257
interviews. *See* user interviews

J

jobs in UX design, 360–367
    design systems designer, 365–366
    motion designer, 366–367
    product designer, 360–361

    UX designer, 362–363
    UX researcher, 364
    UX writer, 365
    visual or UI designer, 363–364
journey maps, 120–128
    actions on, 123–124, 383–384
    elements for creating, 122–126
    example of using, 382–384
    explanation of, 120–122
    illustrations of, 121, 124
    insights on, 125–126, 385
    order for working on, 127–128
    persona/background on, 122, 383
    phases created on, 123, 383
    reasons for using, 126–127
    templates for, 120, 126
    thoughts/feelings on, 124–125, 384

L

landscape matrix, 66–69
language
    of engineers/developers, 353–354
    establishing your visual, 306
lawyer mindset, 359
layouts in UI design, 50, 230–231
leadership, 357–360
    asking for opinion of, 359–360
    consultant mindset adopted with, 358
    relying on facts with, 359
leading questions, 81–82
learnability of products, 241
Lee, Geunbae, 120
legend for user flow, 290
libraries
    component, 307
    stock, 227
lightning demos, 143–149
    process for creating, 144–149
    strategies for successful, 149
lines in sketches, 176–177
Ling's Cars website, 52, 61
LinkedIn, 77, 83, 363–364, 418
logistics gathering, 152–153
Lonely Planet website, 390
long-term memory, 54–55
lorem ipsum text, 223
Louvre museum, 189

steps in creating, 202–203
task flows for, 208–215, 401–402
tools for making, 206–208
wireframing process for, 215–233, 402–411
pull quotes, 265–266
purpose of usability test, 247–248, 412
put to other use theme, 189

Q

qualitative metrics, 253, 267, 414
qualitative research, 67
quantitative metrics, 252–253, 413–414
quantitative research, 67
questions
    clarifying, 344–345, 350
    closed-response, 77–78, 80, 371
    double-barreled, 82
    "easy" and "neutral," 80
    exploratory, 345–346
    leading, 81–82
    open-response, 78–79, 92, 371
    past experience, 92–93
    safety, 414, 416
    unbiased, 92
    usability test, 258–259, 260–261, 415–418
    user interview, 90–93
quotes
    journey map, 125
    persona, 381
    usability test, 265–266

R

rearrange theme, 191
recording
    usability test sessions, 260
    user interviews, 100
recruiting participants
    for surveys, 82–83
    for usability testing, 245, 255–258, 261–262, 414
recruitment services, 83, 98, 102
relational ideation, 162–163, 182–191
    mind mapping for, 182–185
    SCAMPER technique for, 185–191
reliability of products, 8, 239

remote testing, 250–251, 413
research, 64–75
    behavioral vs. attitudinal, 65–66
    brainstorming based on, 170
    competitive, 136–156, 387–391
    evaluative, 72–73
    formative, 69–72
    landscape matrix for, 66–69
    ongoing process of, 75
    qualitative vs. quantitative, 67
    stages of design, 69–75
    summative, 73–75
    See also surveys; user interviews
Rohrer, Christian, 65, 66, 68
ROI research, 73

S

Safari browser, 35
safe space for ideation, 165
safety, feelings of, 378, 414, 416, 419, 420
satisfaction of users, 243, 414, 419, 420
scales, scoring, 263–264, 265, 267
SCAMPER technique, 185–191
    adapt theme, 188
    combine theme, 187
    eliminate theme, 190
    modify theme, 188–189
    put to other use theme, 189
    rearrange theme, 191
    substitute theme, 186–187
science and art, xi–xii
    of defining the problem, 110
    of implementation, 275–276
    of prototype creation, 199–200
scope of usability test, 248–249, 412
scoring scales, 263–265, 267
    See also metrics
screen organization, 314–318
screener surveys, 87, 97–98, 257, 262
scripts
    for usability testing, 258–259
    for user interviews, 88–89, 93–96, 372–374
search apps, 43–45, 178–179
sensory memory, 53, 55, 57
sequence of events, 283
shapes in wireframes, 220

elements of, 88
finding participants for, 97–99
follow-up actions for, 102
introductions to, 89
preparing for, 87–96
questions used in, 90–93
scripts for, 88–89, 93–96, 372–374
structuring, 93–95
tips for successful, 102–103
See also surveys
user needs
hierarchy of, 7–9, 238
UX triad and, 39
user stories, 278–284
creation of, 280–282
examples of, 420–423
exercise on writing, 284
explanation of, 278–280
implementation structure and, 284
prioritization of, 282–283
user testing
definition of, 243
See also usability testing
usercentric experience, 31–32
users
customers as synonymous with, 20
recruiting for usability tests, 255–258
surveying current, 83
thinking from perspective of, 1–2, 211
understanding goals of, 280–282
UserTesting.com service, 83, 98, 102, 257
UX. *See* user experience
UX designer role, 362–363
UX Folio platform, 335
UX researcher role, 364
UX writer role, 365

V

video conferencing software, 413
video demonstrations
of affinity mapping, 104
of brainstorming, 167
of Norman doors, 3
of prototyping, 205
of user interviews, 101
Vimeo website, 147
visual design platforms, 333–334
visual designer role, 363–364

visual ideation, 161–162, 173–182
conceptual ideation and, 173
sketching as, 173–182
visual language, 306

W

Walter, Aarron, 7–9, 238
warmups for sketching, 178–179
Waterfall methodology, 21–24
Agile blended with, 27–28
benefits and criticisms of, 23–24
general description of, 21–23
situations for choosing, 28–29
weaknesses, competitive research on, 139–140
Webflow platform, 207, 338
websites
bare-bones editors for, 335–336
creation of customized, 337–339
editor services for building, 336–337
portfolio PDFs vs., 339–341
weird or crazy ideas, 165, 171
Whimsical tool, 207, 224, 396, 405
whiteboarding tools, 144–145
wireflows, 286, 291–292
wireframes, 202, 215–233
exercises and examples of, 402–411
explanatory overview of, 215–216
fidelity-level decisions for, 231–233
high-fidelity, 216, 225–233, 407–411
low-fidelity, 216–221, 231–232, 402–404
mid-fidelity, 216, 221–224, 232, 405–407
prototypes vs., 217
tools for making, 224
Withlocals website, 389–390
working memory, 54–55, 61
writing
case studies, 322–333
problem statements, 133–134
user stories, 284

Y

Yahoo search, 44, 179

Z

Zoom video conferencing, 188, 413
Z-pattern reading behavior, 66

Pearson's Commitment to Diversity, Equity, and Inclusion

Pearson is dedicated to creating bias-free content that reflects the diversity of all learners. We embrace the many dimensions of diversity, including but not limited to race, ethnicity, gender, socioeconomic status, ability, age, sexual orientation, and religious or political beliefs.

Education is a powerful force for equity and change in our world. It has the potential to deliver opportunities that improve lives and enable economic mobility. As we work with authors to create content for every product and service, we acknowledge our responsibility to demonstrate inclusivity and incorporate diverse scholarship so that everyone can achieve their potential through learning. As the world's leading learning company, we have a duty to help drive change and live up to our purpose to help more people create a better life for themselves and to create a better world.

Our ambition is to purposefully contribute to a world where:

- Everyone has an equitable and lifelong opportunity to succeed through learning.

- Our educational products and services are inclusive and represent the rich diversity of learners.

- Our educational content accurately reflects the histories and experiences of the learners we serve.

- Our educational content prompts deeper discussions with learners and motivates them to expand their own learning (and worldview).

While we work hard to present unbiased content, we want to hear from you about any concerns or needs with this Pearson product so that we can investigate and address them.

Please contact us with concerns about any potential bias at https://www.pearson.com/report-bias.html.